BRAINWASH

BRAINWASH
The Cover-Up Society

GUY ARNOLD

First published in Great Britain in 1992 by
Virgin Books
an imprint of Virgin Publishing Ltd
338 Ladbroke Grove
London W10 5AH

Copyright © Guy Arnold 1992

The moral right of the author has been asserted

A catalogue record for this book is available from the British Library

ISBN 1 85227 425 5

Typeset by TW Typesetting, Plymouth, Devon
Printed and bound in Great Britain by Mackays of Chatham PLC, Chatham, Kent

Contents

Foreword

MANY YEARS AGO as a landed immigrant in Canada I was entertained to lunch in downtown Toronto and had for dessert that inevitable North American speciality: apple pie. My host drew my attention to the size of my piece of apple pie, each of whose three points extended over the edge of the plate. 'It is certainly a large piece,' I said, at which he smiled in a superior fashion and indicated the smallness of the plate upon which the apple pie reposed. 'They give you tiny plates here,' he said; 'it's all part of the consumer society, comes from the United States, of course; it is designed to make you think you are getting more than is the case.' Brainwashing! The Americans, indeed, say that everyone is brainwashed – and knows it – except for the British. And that was my starting point.

It is my contention that at many levels the British are superb brainwashers: they have brainwashed themselves about their uniqueness and, until recently, had managed to brainwash half the rest of the world as to their inherent superiority as a people, a task that was greatly aided by their possession of the world's largest empire. Now, however, bereft of their empire and unable on their own to maintain the standard of living to which it had long accustomed them, they fall back upon illusions – but the emperor has no clothes.

When I began work on this book and approached people for their views on the subject, often their responses ran along the following lines: 'That is very interesting, you mean the Nazis, Goebbels, the Russians, Korea, Big Brother, the United States (the admass society)' and they would mention almost anyone and any country except Britain. 'No, I am interested in British brainwashing.' 'What do you mean, British brainwashing!' Outrage or, if not outrage, incomprehension at the suggestion of British brainwashing was a common reaction. *They* do it, of course, but not *us*. And in a sense that is the essence of what brainwashing is about. During the Cold War which coloured everyone's lives for half a century many assumptions were taken for granted without either evidence or any attempt to check that a claim made sense. The term *communist* was almost always a term of abuse rather than a description of a political belief while the *free world* allies embraced any villainous regime as long as it claimed to be anti-communist. A crisis of such dimensions as that presented by the Cold War in its heyday made it easy to suspend judgement so that many people accepted what they knew to be a charade or untrue provided it was done by *our side* in order to combat the communist menace presented by the other side. It is a short step to extend such an attitude to cover every other kind of activity. We accept lying and doublespeak from our politicians or other leaders as long as they do not go beyond a certain prescribed norm of behaviour and the best brainwashers never do. Because of the excesses associated with it, the Cold War brought awareness of brainwashing to a public that formerly had taken such activities for granted. But the art of brainwashing is as old as settled societies and the most important question to ask about it is simply: when is it acceptable and when does it become manipulation designed to make people do what otherwise they would reject?

I have discussed the subject with a great variety of people who kindly gave me of their time: in jobs and experience they range from an ex-cabinet minister to a young policeman; in their answers they often reflect a society that finds the concept – that it is brainwashed – hard to accept. The young, on the whole, take it for granted that brainwashing is part of their lives; the middle aged and old are far more wary of a proposition that could make a nonsense of their lives. When I broached the subject to one classic establishment figure he began, aggressively, by insisting that he was not one of those people who are always ready to denigrate Britain and her achievements, which was both beside the point and yet very much to the point as well. 'Of course,' he went on judiciously, 'we do make mistakes sometimes, like any other people . . .' Another reaction was the advice not to use the term 'brainwash' since it would give offence! Two reactions to the idea of British brainwashing were especially interesting: the first was outrage – 'what do you mean, British brainwashing?' – as though such an activity was only ever carried out by foreigners, and preferably dictatorial foreigners to boot, although it was tacitly assumed that people like the Americans would also succumb to it. The second reaction was one of smugness: that British brainwashing is best, but with the unspoken assumption that we only brainwash *them*, never ourselves.

During the course of a long conversation with a Scotsman I noticed how he shied away every time I actually used the word 'brainwash' so that I found myself deliberately injecting the word into our talk to obtain his reaction and he became aware of what I was doing. Then, at the end of our session just as I took my departure, he said: 'I suppose all of us, people of my generation in Scotland, have been brainwashed by the time we are eight years old – with William Wallace and Jesus Christ!' He had gone to the nub of the problem. A difficulty, as I discovered, was that to put questions about brainwashing to highly articulate professional people who have risen in the British system is rather like asking them to deny their birthright. When I made an approach to one such person his first reaction was to demand, tartly, what made me think he knew anything about brainwashing. Perhaps nothing in this connection could be higher praise than the *Sun* comment of 7 June 1983 on Tony Benn that he was 'bent on the destruction of Britain as we know it'.

A quite different reaction which, curiously, I only came across towards the end of my investigations, was the claim 'that we are all brainwashed all the time' with the implication that, as a result, we can all proceed about our business without further ado. When I first met this reaction I was not sure whether to be pleased – that at last people were not only recognising the extent to which they are manipulated but were prepared to admit to it as well – or unhappy, and in the end I was not pleased at all. Such admissions, often made in blasé, world-weary fashion, suggested that a new orthodoxy had come to be accepted: if we all admit to being brainwashed all the time then none of us need do anything about it.

What I have attempted to do in this book is differentiate between those forms of brainwashing that can be seen as the necessary teaching processes upon which any society depends, and the more insidious and dangerous forms of brainwashing designed to manipulate us and force us into behaviour patterns that are solely for the benefit of the ruling élite, the 'establishment' or those I have described as the 'deciders'.

Acknowledgement

The author wishes to thank Constable & Co. Ltd for permission to reproduce the two poems which appear on pages 40 and 278, and which are taken from *170 Chinese Poems*, translated by Arthur Waley (1962 edition).

TEXT REFERENCES

For simplicity, text references throughout relate to the bibliography. The convention used for the references is as follows: author (omitted when apparent from the immediate context); work (indicated by year of publication); and page reference.

For example, (Brown, 1963:9) refers to page 9 of J. A. C. Brown's 1963 publication, *Techniques of Persuasion*.

Glossary of special terms

Accepted wisdom no need to ask questions.

Against the national interest against the interest of the ruling party, government, minister, department.

Use appropriate channels ask the Establishment to discipline itself.

Bias you are not supporting my line; you are airing an alternative viewpoint.

Consensus not rocking the boat.

Why are you always criticising your own country? we are wrong but keep quiet about it.

Debt credit.

Seek change in a democratic way do not go on 'left-wing' demonstrations.

Those who denigrate their own country those who deplore its abuses.

Established values what the hierarchy wishes to maintain.

Hearts and heads if you are a Tory before you are thirty you have no heart, if you are a Socialist after thirty you have no head – property destroys idealism.

Impartiality support for the official line.

Ivory towers those who shut themselves in ivory towers – those who will not sully their hands with convenient lying.

Left wing anyone who opposes the establishment view (There is no *right-wing* equivalent usage – i.e. those who would oppress the people).

Left-wing bias any view that does not bolster the orthodox establishment line.

No useful purpose will be served it is against the interests of the government to tell the truth.

Loyalty to party (or government or any other group) allow them to do what you know to be wrong.

Not in the public interest would embarrass those in power.

Glossary

Rationalisation   reduce the labour force by sackings.

Saves taxpayers' money   the government intends to be mean.

The real world   where power and greed prevail and principles do not apply.

We have to live in the real world   we must accept dishonesty.

Let's be realistic   something unpleasant is being contemplated.

Recovery   putting right what the government allowed to go wrong in the first place.

Running down your country   asking awkward questions about the way it is run.

Ruthless   becoming efficient by reducing the workforce.

A solemn and binding agreement   an admission of government defeat.

Subversive   a person who reveals what government prefers to keep concealed.

Witchhunt   when officials claim a probe is turning into a witchhunt they mean their own wrongdoings are in danger of being uncovered.

Part One
Introduction

1 The Cold War brings awareness

The more you talk about what most people don't
understand, the greater is their respect for you.
CONFUCIUS

ANIPULATING OTHER PEOPLE'S THOUGHT PROCESSES has a history
that goes back at least as far as the ancient Greeks and in
our modern world assaults upon other people's minds for
religious, political, business or social reasons have become
part of the fabric of our everyday existence. Most people have become
familiar with the concept of 'brainwashing' although what they mean
by the term varies according to circumstances. Techniques of interrogation that a brutal world has made commonplace have their roots in
an older science of thought reform which derives from the inquisitorial
activities of the medieval church. In our own time the Soviet purges
of the 1930s, the extraordinary success of the Nazis in converting a
nation into Hitler supporters in only twelve years, the Chinese
Communist thought-reform programmes each in their way taught a
similar lesson concerning the techniques and pressures that could be
brought to bear upon 'dissident' citizens by an authoritarian or
totalitarian state. Awareness of the extent to which a ruthless state
will attempt mind control has been brought home to people in the
West by means of the polarisations of the Cold War with the immediate
general result that a generation came to believe that such activities
belonged to 'them' – our ideological enemies in the Cold War – but
not to 'us'. As the Communist Manifesto conveniently lays down: 'But
Communism abolishes eternal truths, it abolishes all religion and all
morality, instead of constituting them on a new basis; it therefore acts
in contradiction to all past historical experience.' Brainwashing in its
many forms is concerned to replace past historical experience with
new concepts.

Real fears exist among people in modern societies that efforts from
above – by the 'decision-makers', whoever they may be – will be made
to manipulate them as opposed to merely influencing them, which is
the crucial difference. Brainwashing, however defined, is essentially

the deliberate manipulation of people's minds. H. J. Eysenck claims, after citing a number of examples in his *Sense and Nonsense in Psychology*, 'They all suggest that a knowledge of certain principles governing the relation between body and mind have been quite well understod from time immemorial' (1957:73). 'Attempts to change the opinions of others are older than recorded history' (Brown, 1963:9). The crucial question is, when do such attempts become more than acceptable persuasion and turn into manipulation?

In his series of popular books such as *The Status Seekers* and *The Hidden Persuaders*, Vance Packard revealed the enormous pressures to conformity that corporate business exerted in the USA during the 1950s and 1960s, contrasting earlier generations of what he called 'inner-directed' people with those about whom he was writing who were largely guided in their behaviour 'by the expectancy of the crowd with which they associate'. And he poses the question: 'But when you are manipulating, where do you stop? Who is to fix the point at which manipulative attempts become socially undesirable?' (1960a:196) Brainwashing, in fact, is the historic antidote to fear and its skilful use depends upon an understanding of man's inadequacies. It is this which makes the process dangerous and potentially stifling of mental vigour. Indeed, brainwashing is a form of intellectual 'squaring', making acceptable what the decision-makers want people to believe.

We live in an increasingly precarious world and though the Cold War posed the awful threat of nuclear destruction it also provided parameters within which people could live out their lives. The post-Cold War world will become more rather than less precarious, for the pressures of overpopulation and increasing demands upon dwindling resources will see ever more powerful states emerging to control what there is, while populations, lacking both faith and certainty, will become more and more subject to attempts at psycho-logical and other controls from above. Already in the 1950s C. Wright Mills could write in *The Power Elite* that 'Entire brackets of profes-sions and industries are in the "opinion business", impersonally manipulating the public for hire.' (1958:305) Since most people are suggestible and a majority like to follow the fashions of the time, they present generally easily manipulable material. As William Sargant claims in *Battle for the Mind*, 'Politicians, priests and psychiatrists often face the same problem: how to find the most rapid and permanent means of changing a man's belief.' (1957:13) Those in the business of manipulation use the varying human emotions as the basis for their persuasion techniques, playing upon anger, fear, hope, guilt, pride, ambition. Many of the people they would manipulate fall under the category of 'true believers' (Brown, 1963:290), those who seek authoritarian control of their lives and who in consequence require what has been called a 'self-seeking system' that automatically discounts evidence which bears adversely upon the doctrine they follow. Some degree of conformity is essential to any modern society; as always, the problem concerns the dividing line between the minimum necessary to make life bearable for large communities living under modern conditions and the temptation to which all ruling élites fall prey, to make people conform for the convenience of the rulers as opposed to the necessary happiness of the people themselves.

Any consideration of what we call brainwashing must ponder the question: when is the process acceptable or how much of it is ever acceptable? And when does it exceed any permissible bounds to become a threat to more important values? Broadly, brainwashing may be divided between necessary conditioning for survival – to make life bearable; and deliberate manipulation by groups for reasons of power. The dividing line between these two areas is often difficult to discern.

What to do about belief is a problem all dictators and all those who would manipulate the mass of the people have to face, for torture does not change people who have accepted a faith although it may create martyrs or encourage duplicity. As many writers and thinkers not necessarily sympathetic to religion have pointed out, it is a feature of our social lives that many find it impossible to do without. As Thomas Paine puts it: 'That many good men have believed this strange fable (Christianity), and lived very good lives under that belief (for credulity is not a crime), is what I have no doubt of. In the first place, they were educated to believe it, and they would have believed anything else in the same manner.' (1937:9) Educating people to believe something can take many forms. One of these is the concept of the élite: educating the intelligent and, to carry the process a step further, encouraging *them* to breed rather than the less intelligent. In *The Scientific Analysis of Personality*, Raymond B. Cattell writes: 'The unintelligent individual costs roughly twice as much to educate (because of special classes etc.), and even then achieves and contributes far less than a child of good average intelligence. He is more prone to become a delinquent and is politically a danger by being a ready prey to the sly slogans of demagogues.' (1965:39) Now it would be difficult to find a more loaded and one-sided statement than this: on the one hand he wants the so-called intelligent both to have the education and to breed more of themselves for the future; on the other he believes that even if the unintelligent are educated they will merely provide cannon fodder as it were for the demagogues (read manipulators). His is a depressing view based upon assumptions of élitist superiority but it may be true for all that. Two writers on education, Hutchinson and Young, whose book *Educating the Intelligent* made quite an impact at the beginning of the 1960s, fall into one of the traps that any consideration of brainwashing makes almost *de rigueur*. First they analyse Marxist success: 'Marxists have had considerable success in deliberately propagating Marxism through the Russian education system. Like the Nazis they have shown how generations of children can be effectively indoctrinated provided the entire resources of the state's schools are used for that purpose.' Then, from this, they go on to argue:

> The lesson of Marxist education, however, is not that we should ourselves devise a narrow system of ideas which should be taught in every school. It is rather that we should examine the philosophy upon which our education is based, a philosophy which is immensely richer than Marxist philosophy, and that we should then make sure that the education which we give to our children does in fact express our philosophy. (1962:56)

On analysis, despite verbal gymnastics, the authors are saying that we in the West should indoctrinate as do (or did) the Communists. What our Western societies have in fact produced are cultures of automatic expectations rather than of attainable rights; typical of such expectations is the assumption that people have a 'right' to go to university. It is a right, moreover, that is only partially modified by ability.

The dilemmas faced by those who enjoy the benefits of our immensely richer (Western) philosophy (referred to by Hutchinson and Young) were brought out starkly amidst much angry denunciation from his own church by Charles Davis, the lapsed Roman Catholic priest whose book, *A Question of Conscience*, was not welcomed by the Church. Explaining his decision to leave the priesthood and marry, Davis claimed: 'I found I could not get Roman Catholics to commit themselves to any definite belief or to any interpretation of authoritative statements clear enough to form the basis of a discussion about the Roman faith.' (1967:43) Davis said that many other Catholics agreed with his arguments but were not prepared to do anything about them and here he brings us to one of the principal advantages always enjoyed by brainwashers or manipulators: surrender makes life easier and most people are too lazy to do otherwise so they present facile material for brainwashing activities. The majority are never a problem; it is the odd man out who upsets the pattern and disrupts any easy process of manipulation. 'A man who wishes to make a profession of goodness in everything must necessarily come to grief among so many who are not good.' Thus said Machiavelli, but substitute intellectual integrity for goodness and what he says covers the problem which those who wish to oppose intellectual manipulation must face. Most people seek a role: either as a member of the crowd, the obedient mass who follow the leader, or as authority figures. Thus, socially, the doctor may be meek and uninspiring but in his white coat he becomes an authority figure.

The name of Pavlov is ineradicably associated with the idea of the conditioned reflex and the West came to assume that the worst aspects of Soviet torture and other techniques of brainwashing were directly derived from Pavlov's experiments even though this was never the case as far as Pavlov himself was concerned. He did, however, make a statement whose implications were chilling enough: 'Our objective investigations of the complex nervous phenomena of the higher animals fill us with a reasonable hope that the fundamental laws underlying the fearful complexity in which the internal world of man is manifested to us can be discovered by physiology, and in the not far-distant future.' (1928:114)

In recent memory, mass manipulation, the use of state power to control thought processes – in effect, state brainwashing – has been associated indelibly in the Western mind with Hitler's Germany, Stalin's Russia and the China of Mao Zedong. A difficulty in defining more precisely what we mean by brainwashing stems from the fact that many people half recognise brainwashing for what it is and then dismiss the subject from further attention. It has not – or so they would claim – actually impinged upon them.

Everyone knows that *Mein Kampf* was Hitler's blueprint for Germany; few had read the book and those who did read it at the time of Hitler's rise to power did not believe that he intended actually to do what he said he would do. The Hitler phenomenon will puzzle generations to come, for this extraordinary man mesmerised a highly advanced, sophisticated people into doing his will until they had wrought havoc and destruction upon all around them. Hitler claimed that Germany had been stabbed in the back in 1918, that is, the Germans were not to blame for their defeat. He proceeded to find scapegoats and devise techniques of control for a whole people that have possibly never been equalled. He understood, moreover, some of the basic problems of the human material with which he had to work. He knew who could be converted and who had to be destroyed: 'The *petit bourgeois* Social Democrat and the trade-union boss will never make a National Socialist, but the Communist always will.' His henchman Roehm claimed he could turn the reddest Communist into a Nazi within weeks.

Nazi techniques will be studied by anyone concerned with the business of control; the denunciation of parents by children is obvious as a tactic of control, but how does the state apparatus ensure that any such denunciation takes place? Hermann Rauschning said: 'Marching diverts men's thoughts. Marching kills thought. Marching makes an end of individuality.' (Brown, 1963:104) In his diaries Albert Speer describes how as a young man in 1931 he saw Hitler handle a stadium full of SA members. 'No speeches were made. Hitler had decided on another tack. Silently we stood, hour after hour.' Hitler did not speak but paced through the ranks drawn up to attention and only his footsteps and those of his entourage could be heard. When years later Speer told Hitler how he had inspected him personally as he stood in the ranks, Hitler replied: 'I know. I remember you exactly.' And no doubt he did. In 1938, after the Party Rally at Nuremberg, Hitler summoned Speer and went over the events of the previous day. He said: 'Several of the acts have now reached their definitive form.' Speer records, 'I had long thought that all these formations, processions, dedications were part of a clever propagandistic revue. Now I finally understood that for Hitler they were almost like rites of the founding of a church.' (Speer, 1976:85, 262) At his trial Speer claimed that 'Hitler's dictatorship differed in one fundamental point from all its predecessors in history. It was the first dictatorship in the present period of modern technical development, a dictatorship which made complete use of all technical means for the domination of its own country.' (Huxley, 1958:47)

Goebbels, however, is the name we have come to associate with modern propaganda: tell the big lie often enough and it will be believed. Hugh Trevor-Roper writes that it was Goebbels who worked out the style and technique of the Nazi Party's public ceremonies and created the myth of the Führer, giving him the halo of invincibility: 'Goebbels was an impresario of genius, the first man to realise the full potentialities of mass media for political purposes in a dynamic totalitarian state' and 'To the end, he could distinguish the objective truth from his own propaganda. To the end he combined fanaticism with detachment: a politically cultivated fanaticism with an intellectual detachment. That indeed is why his propaganda was so effective.' (1978:xvi, xvii) But during the course of World War II the Germans made two major mistakes: they antagonised the rest of the world by the brutality of their behaviour and 'allowed their own propaganda to be constantly on the defensive'. (Brown, 1963:96) They also intensified their anti-Semitic propaganda when the war was going badly in a classic move to blame a scapegoat. The success of German indoctrination was testified to in 1941 by Maisky, the Soviet Ambassador to London, who told D. N. Pritt that captured German soldiers, regardless of age or background, were so deeply imbued with Nazi propaganda that they accepted everything which they had been told as true. (1966a:30) One final reference to the effectiveness of Nazi techniques of indoctrination is worth mentioning. In his chilling documentary account of the Final Solution, the writer Gerald Fleming describes how Himmler uses the phrase 'it is the Führer's wish' when he persuades top-ranking army officers, reluctant to massacre Jewish women and children in cold blood, that though he understands their natural repugnance, none the less they must carry out the Führer's order. And they did. (1985:xxv and 53)

The Soviet Union used techniques as chilling as those of the Nazis. Lenin, when told that the end does not justify the means, replied: 'What else does?' A typical Soviet tactic when necessary was simple suppression of information including scientific research that was deemed anti-Marxist. Stalin's purges worked, according to Brown (1963:109), because faithful Communists he wished to destroy had nothing else to fall back on, so they confessed to sins against the party. A major feature of the Communist approach was a constant bombardment of boring propaganda which was impossible to escape: it became a part of everyone's life and as such was absorbed however resistant the recipients of it might have been originally. A great deal of Soviet broadcasting was cultural, without advertising, and with little effort at being what in the West would be called entertaining; rather, classical music or programmes aiming to 'improve the mind'. At the beginning of World War II radio sets were confiscated and replaced with ones that could receive only 'wired broadcasts' transmitted over telephone lines by the official Soviet stations. The USSR understood only too well that total control of the media was central to any broader control of the population as a whole.

Western fears of a monolithic Communist Bloc, stretching from the Elbe to the China Sea, which followed the triumph of the Chinese Communist Party under Mao Zedong in 1949, helped create rising paranoia during the early days of the Cold War and this was greatly reinforced when stories of Chinese 'brainwashing' techniques came to light during the Korean War. Much of the approach in Communist China in fact has been based upon the technique of making everyone, even the least important, feel themselves to be part of the whole, and Chinese thought-reform programmes were designed primarily for their own people to eradicate former capitalist ways of thought and behaviour. What in the West we came to call 'brainwashing' grew from indoctrination techniques developed in China after the 1949 revolution and these also drew upon Soviet experience. (Watson, 1978:289) The Chinese did not spread their Communist revolution only by appealing to the intellect. They also created anxiety and fear of external enemies. And yet an American woman after four years in a Chinese prison could claim: 'The main thing about a Communist prison is that it is a place of hope' (Sargant, 1957:144). The term 'brainwashing' first came into currency in 1951 (it was used by Edward Hunter in *Brain-washing in Red China*) and was a translation of the Chinese *hsi nao* (wash brain). Following the indoctrination treatment of Allied (UN) prisoners during the Korean War, the term came to have a wholly pejorative association in the West. The Chinese segregated prisoners in Korea according to race, nationality and rank while group meetings were banned and lower ranks were put in charge of higher ranks. Prisoners were subjected to extreme physical hardship and the regime imposed upon them was unpredictable. Pressures were applied to prisoners to collaborate and give up their existing loyalties, and the guards ensured the destruction of any group structure among the prisoners. In the very different climate of 1991 (July) the Chinese Communist Party opposed young people wearing T-shirts bearing such messages as 'I'm depressed, leave me alone' or 'There's no tomorrow, let's get drunk', suggesting instead such uplifting T-shirt slogans as 'Study hard' or 'Get better every day'.

The twentieth century has been a century of ideologies and this fact has lent itself to the need for and extensive use of propaganda and every other available technique of persuasion. The Communist threat to the Western way of life – real or imagined – from 1946 to 1989 concentrated the Western mind wonderfully upon aspects of manipulation. Too often, however, the outcome of such concentration was the conclusion that only *they* manipulated (which was easy enough to demonstrate) but that *we* never did anything similar. As Sargant says in *Battle for the Mind*, 'Great Britain and the USA therefore find themselves at last obliged to study seriously those specialized forms of neurophysiological research which have been cultivated with some intensity by the Russians since the Revolution, and have helped them to perfect the methods now popularly known as "brain-washing" or "thought control".' (1957:13) The Cold War, indeed, stimulated much Western thought about manipulative techniques. Thus Cattell argues: 'Indeed, the capacity of democracy to survive in competition with other systems will depend on a rich application of the findings of behavioural science, with the individual's consent and insight.' (1965:353) One cannot help wondering at his final clause: is it put in for effect, lip-service to Western individualism, or would the West act with or without the consent of individuals?

In his essay 'The Prevention of Literature', George Orwell sees techniques of control used in totalitarian societies as absolute and permanent: 'The organized lying practised by totalitarian states is not, as is sometimes claimed, a temporary expedient of the same nature as military deception. It is something integral to totalitarianism.' He goes on: 'Totalitarianism demands, in fact, the continuous alteration of the past, and in the long run probably demands a disbelief in the very existence of objective truth.' (1957:164) The Cold War witnessed endless and often very crude disinformation tactics by both sides. In *The Truth Twisters*, Richard Deacon (a former MI6 operative) says: 'The overwhelming evidence shows that the Soviet side practised really calculated evil, sowing seeds of doubt and hate all around the globe. The more bizarre forms of planting rumours by the Americans, for example the vampire scare in the Philippines, were at least linked to putting down guerrilla actions.' (1986:45) The trouble with those who engage in such activities is that in the end they believe their own propaganda. Far more subtle in his appraisal of the effects of state activities on both sides is J. A. C. Brown, whose *Techniques of Persuasion* is a classic source of reference. 'Yet (paradoxically, because the authoritarian's use of power is open and naked like that in the

Middle Ages) it may be that the citizen living under these circumstances feels less manipulated than the American or Englishman whose real fear is of the "hidden persuaders" who attempt to manipulate him unawares.' (1963:35)

The Cold War may have popularised the idea of brainwashing and led people in the West to regard it as an evil phenomenon emanating from the other side, but it was practised in our societies long before the present era. The subject is curiously beguiling and, too often, it beguiles the very people who claim to understand it best. Thus, in his book *The Biological Time Bomb* (1968), in which he examines genetic engineering, Rattray Taylor comes to a perverse conclusion for, although the majority of his examples are taken from Western experiments, he suggests none the less that actual genetic engineering is most likely to occur in an Eastern country such as China. Brown (1963) suggests that the West is not open to the techniques used in Communist countries. He was, of course, writing long before the events of 1989, at a time when the Cold War appeared set in a fixed mould; perhaps now, with the end of the Cold War and the crumbling of barriers, techniques of control will be used equally by governments facing a set of new though equally formidable problems. Brown was writing at the same time as Richard Hoggart and Raymond Williams, whose books, *The Uses of Literacy* and *Communications*, were then much in vogue, and their authors were seen as standard-bearers of the left. Brown attacked the left-wing nature of their views and, by implication, suggested that they were brainwashed while ordinary people escape the effects of such a process. His line appeared to be that intelligent people manipulate facts and ideas to prove what they want, but his argument rebounds on him. The political right which in broad terms wishes to maintain the status quo of which it is the main beneficiary eschews the concept of brainwashing which, by implication, would suggest that they (the right) are the manipulators.

In the course of the Korean War 7,000 US servicemen were captured and one in three collaborated with their Communist captors in some way (13 per cent of these were subsequently charged with offences); 2,730 (30 per cent) died and 21 elected to remain behind when the time came for repatriation. (Watson, 1978:290) Just how much these figures tell us of the success of Chinese 'brainwashing' or, on the other hand, the failure of American 'indoctrination' it is hard to say, but the figures certainly shocked the US. Following the Soviet invasion of Hungary in 1956 American broadcasts did more damage than good by inciting the people to revolt and hinting at American assistance which was never forthcoming. In Cold War terms it might be argued that at this stage the USA – in comparison with either the USSR or China – had simply not got its act together. This was also the period when great trust was placed in aid as a weapon to win friends and help people withstand Communist advances. In *A Nation of Sheep*, which examines many aspects of American behaviour at this time, the author, William Lederer, tells the story of how, in order to fool American investigators sent to inspect the impact of US aid in Thailand, the Thais took a complete village, evacuated its inhabitants and repeopled it with carefully selected middle-class Thais who had been instructed how to behave for the benefit of the visiting Americans; these, in consequence, were deeply impressed by the impact of their aid and went away happy. Whether or not such a deception comes under the heading of brainwashing is a moot point: certainly demonstrating to people what they want to see or hear is a fundamental technique of manipulation. (1961:36)

But if the Americans came a poor second to the Communists in some of these activities, they were second to none in the market-place, as the books of Vance Packard or William Whyte (*The Organization Man*) demonstrate. Packard's *The Status Seekers* is about manipulation that takes people's fears (of not making good in a thrusting society) and uses them to manipulate their behaviour as it also panders to their desires. In *The Organization Man* Whyte examines the behaviour of the American corporation man and makes the point that while company men belong to 'collectives' they cannot bring themselves to use the term. Imbued with ideas derived from the Protestant ethic, Whyte's 'organization man' believes in initiative, thrift and individual salvation through hard work. In fact, he is not too distinguishable from anyone else and therein lies his strength and his acceptability, for he is not seen as a threat.

At least at this time (1961) John Hannah, President of Michigan State University, did not mince his words: 'If we do not hesitate to indoctrinate our children with a love of truth, a love of home, and a love of God, then I see no justification for balking at teaching them love of country and love of what this country means.' (Cockburn and Blackburn, 1969:333) In 1968 occurred the '*Pueblo* incident', when the US spy ship of that name was seized off Korea and its crew of 82 were subjected to torture and severe psychological pressures with the result that many made 'confessions'. But, as the US authorities subsequently discovered, those who stood up well to such treatment did not necessarily adjust easily again to civilian life, for it is the 'maverick' or potential odd-man-out who is most able to resist such brainwashing assaults. Awareness of Communist 'brainwashing' activities forced Americans to consider counter-measures of their own. More important, even in a climate rendered poisonous by McCarthy, the Cold War also led American intellectuals to look at the manipulations which took place in their own society; many of these were unconnected with the Cold War.

Belief in one's own system is essential to its success and sometimes such belief is achieved only by an almost conscious effort at self-persuasion. As Mills argues in *The Power Elite* (1958), 'We simply must believe that the American rich are happy, else our confidence in the whole endeavour (the money making ethic) might be shaken.' But though they found themselves behind the Russians in the early stages of the Cold War, the Americans had long resorted to techniques of suppression that they so much deplored in their ideological rivals. As Bertrand Russell said of Americans purging school and other libraries: 'The *Index Expurgatorius* has become a recognised part of the policy of those who say that they fight for freedom. Apparently the authorities no longer have sufficient belief in the justice of their cause to think that it can survive the ordeal of free discussion.' (1956:209) Perhaps as a reflection of the loss of innocence that came with the Cold War, there appeared in the USA at the beginning of the 1990s a new cult to delay growing up, to keep teenagers innocent for as long as possible. That in itself represents a denial of reality.

The French, fighting grimly to hold on to empire and losing it, devised psychological techniques in Algeria to protect their own troops from the insurgents' propaganda and to re-educate captured rebels. But if Algeria brought out some of the worst aspects of French behaviour and demonstrated manipulation at its most unpleasant and brutal, an intellectual *tour de force* of brainwashing or perhaps myth-creation is Gaston Bonheur's elegant book *Qui a cassé le vase de Soissons?* (1963). In this charming book the author assembles a collection of stories and extracts from famous French authors to demonstrate what makes a Frenchman: history, the nostalgias of childhood, the heroisms of France's story, whose end result is to leave the reader with a lump in his throat saying: French is best. It is a superb example of the artless art of brainwashing.

The great majority of writing or commentary on brainwashing in all its forms during the period since 1945 has been dominated by the fears raised by the Cold War, with the result that impartiality has taken a back seat. In Britain an added problem of distortion has come from the right-wing nature of the many intellectual refugees who have fled to this country to escape Communism and subsequently played an important role in public affairs. At a personal level Sir Anthony Eden wrecked a distinguished career over Suez, at least in part because he had persuaded himself that Nasser was a dictator similar in kind to Hitler and Mussolini, and he had made his reputation in the 1930s by resigning and joining Churchill in the wilderness to oppose the dictators. The comparison was nonsense but self-delusion was part of the Suez story. In his definitive *Suez* Keith Kyle demonstrates just how the British manage to apply one law to themselves and a totally different one to other people:

> The whole French diplomatic performance in the Middle East was usually portrayed through Foreign Office eyes as a kind of utterly perverse intrigue. When it took on a more sinister shape it became 'collusion' and, in the circumstances of 1956 (Suez), French collusion meant, above all, collusion with Israel. Thus 'British collusion' conveyed the sense that Britain, contrary to her normal practice, had joined in that sort of game. (1991:318)

Selwyn Lloyd, writing in 1977, said with apparent sincerity: 'I suppose that at sometime I must say something about collusion – collusion implies something dishonourable and we were all honourable men.' (Thorpe, 1989:265)

In a famous opening paragraph of *The Acquisitive Society*, Tawney writes:

> It is a commonplace that the characteristic virtue of Englishmen is their power of sustained practical activity, and their characteristic vice a reluctance to test the quality of that activity by reference to principles. They are incurious as to theory, take fundamentals for granted, and are more interested in the state of the roads than in their place on the map. (1961:9)

That could be a definition of a people who almost as a matter of course will brainwash themselves. The shattering impact of World War II upon British power and her subsequent place in the world led to many conscious attempts to tell the story of Britain and her achievements to the world, and perhaps a majority of them fall into the brainwashing, myth-making category. Sir Arthur Bryant, with his elegant style and mastery of history, casts a spell upon his readers as he tells of stout yeomen rallying to their country's cause and paints an heroic picture of 'the island race'. He must rank as one of Britain's finest myth-makers. Lord Attlee makes his own curious contribution to mythology at the conclusion of his Chichele lectures delivered at Oxford in 1960. His subject was the Commonwealth and at the end of the final lecture he says: 'One further rather curious link in the Commonwealth must be mentioned, and that is the game of cricket' (1961:54). On the other side of this myth-making coin we have Wayland Young writing about the Profumo affair which almost toppled the Macmillan government: 'But our society as a whole is majestically hypocritical; the way it combines condemnation with indulgence is known all over the world.' (1963:94)

Anthony Sampson's *Anatomy of Britain* enjoyed great vogue when it appeared in the early 1960s and his affectionate appraisals of the British Establishment – military, civil service, church, public school, Oxbridge – convey the unmistakable impression that the British wish to remain ossified in a structure dominated by class, tradition and romantic interpretations of history, no matter what else changes. There is, indeed, a kind of naïvety that emerges repeatedly from the writings and comments of British observers: it is one of surprise, perhaps shock is not too strong a word, if it is suggested that we, the British, are capable of the kind of behaviour that we attribute readily enough to others. An immigrant to Britain, quoted in Jonathan Green's *Them*, says with great perspicacity: 'The English want the world to be as they expect, the way that is comfortable; they don't like the challenge, quite simply, they don't like the challenge.' (1990:114)

2 People as material

Men are so simple and so ready to obey present
necessities, that one who deceives will always find
those who allow themselves to be deceived.

MACHIAVELLI

CYNICS AND THOSE WITH A SENSE OF HUMOUR are more likely to
survive any sustained assault on the mind while religious
people would do less well; so argued Sargant in his *Battle
for the Mind*, and examining Communist techniques employed to break down someone's resistance – isolation, fatigue,
tension, uncertainty, the use of vicious language and seriousness (for
no humour is allowed) – he is probably right. The term 'to brainwash'
came into popular usage during the 1950s, following the revelations
of crude methods of indoctrination employed by the Chinese in Korea.
American prisoners were apparently more susceptible to these pressures than the British, while the Turks appeared to be unaffected by
them. According to Brown (1963:265) no real brainwashing took
place in Korea but only intensive political indoctrination. Broadly,
without entering into a sterile discussion about the precise meaning of
brainwashing, here it is taken to cover all forms of mind manipulation.
A major problem concerns personal attitudes and attachments. Most
people are committed to a religion, a political party, a way of life or
set of dogmas to which they cling and for each of which they claim a
superiority to rival beliefs. Many people will adhere to these personal
beliefs throughout their lives and any questioning of them is much
more likely to be treated as an assault than as a reasoned enquiry. Is
the man who claims to have voted Labour or Tory all his life (and
adds that nothing will make him change his view) brainwashed or, in
Thomas Paine's words, 'educated' to it, just as Paine claimed that
many are educated to Christianity, and is such educating brainwashing? Kant said that we cannot know things as they really are in
themselves but only as they appear to us.

Writing in the *Standard* about private education (in the early 1980s)
a woman first insisted that as a good 'liberal' she opposed fee-paying
schools as élitist but then went on to argue that because of special

circumstances in her particular situation she was going to send her children to fee-paying schools anyway. Everyone in fact has his or her own particular vested interest and as a rule that must be the starting point if the behaviour of an individual is to be understood fully. The psychologist Eysenck claims that politicians regard psychology with suspicion because it tends to substitute facts for stereotyped thinking and adhesion to dogma: 'Why debate an issue in terms of *opinion* when it can be debated in terms of *facts*?' (1953:309)

Referring to various methods of propaganda that he has discussed, Brown says, 'None of the practices described above are propaganda unless they are part of a *deliberate* scheme for indoctrination, as happens in totalitarian countries.' (1963:22) The clear implication of this statement is that it (indoctrination) happens *there* (in the Communist, totalitarian world) but not *here*. Brown, like so many Westerners over these Cold War years, managed to persuade himself that Western essays in propaganda, indoctrination or censorship were somehow run-of-the-mill everyday affairs which did not count, although the moment the other side did the same things they became sinister. Whenever an investigation touches upon an area of particular concern to an individual – religion, for example – he or she will 'switch off', unwilling to have a favourite dogma or shibboleth questioned. It is this very unwillingness to question a belief that is the greatest aid to indoctrination in all its forms, since most people find it hard to recant and admit that a lifelong adherence to a belief has been a mistake.

And yet people are rarely as gullible or suggestible as commentators believe. Thus, surveys of the British election of 1959 indicated that practically nothing influenced people's attitudes during the election campaign but rather it had been the long process of political communication and actual change between the elections that persuaded people. If true, that is certainly encouraging, but may also turn out to be very depressing when, during the mid-1990s, we begin to understand the aftermath of the events of 1989 which led to the collapse of the Soviet empire. After more than seventy years of Communism in Russia and forty in Eastern Europe, the people of those countries appeared only too ready and willing to throw off the yoke of a system that for the majority had so obviously been imposed. And yet already by late 1991 it was becoming clear that many people who had known no other way of life did not in fact want (or, perhaps, were by then unable) to embrace Western ways.

Lecturing at Harvard in 1898, A. V. Dicey said: 'Public opinion itself is, after all, a mere abstraction; it is not a power which has any independent existence; it is simply a general term for the beliefs held by a number of human beings.' This may be so but as Windlesham demonstrates in *Communication and Political Power*, both the Macmillan and Wilson governments 'were powerful forces in the creation of public opinion' over the issue of Britain and the Common Market (1966:154–5). On the other hand, the same author quotes an American, V. O. Key, as defining public opinion as 'those opinions held by private persons which governments find it prudent to heed'. Despite this, he finds that on the issue of entry to the Common Market (1961–3), 'The conclusion must be that public opinion had little directly attributable effect on what actually happened.'

Any technique of manipulation has as its object an end to inquiry and is operated to make people accept what the manipulators desire they should believe. In part, of course, all such manipulation of thought processes resolves itself into self-justification – of the individual or nation – and people will go to great lengths to convince themselves that what they have done is right. Tawney approaches this conclusion in *The Acquisitive Society* when he writes: 'For happiness is individual, and to make happiness the object of society is to resolve society itself into the ambitions of numberless individuals, each directed towards the attainment of some personal purpose.' (1961:32)

Most people have a limited capacity for objectivity which increases or decreases depending upon the degree of their personal commitment to the subject under examination. In a majority of cases a person who comes across something contrary to his own perceived opinions will either ignore it or change the rules rather than admit that, perhaps, his own opinion is grounded in false assumptions. The question of objectivity is intimately bound up with that of the use of the media and people's reactions to it. On the general subject of tolerance, for example, Richard Hoggart claims: 'Genuine tolerance is a product of vigour, belief, a sense of the difficulty of truth and a respect for others; the new tolerance is weak and unwilling, a fear and resentment of challenge.' (1957:177) Hoggart opposes the cult of the common man as an alternative to media management by press barons. He poses the uncomfortable question: why rely on the people? What have the people done to justify any such reliance upon them? All too often, sadly, the answer must be nothing at all. During the heady 1960s when so many old assumptions appeared to be under challenge, Colin Morris, a populist if ever there was one, said that 'Student action is the only truly international movement of our time'; although, briefly, that may have been the case, it was not to last long. (1969:35)

The unique quality of individual human beings has long been advanced as their special claim to superiority above all other animals. In *The Natural History of the Mind*, Taylor says: 'Human beings desire strongly to appear as unique, in the sense of being distinguishable from their fellows; they do not want to be ciphers. Modern society tends to make people into ciphers – the production line worker must die and another person step into his shoes and carry on. His contribution has no unique character.' He goes on to claim: 'Those who seek to order society constantly frail to grasp the need to give expression to this basic need.' (1979:115) In fact, one might question Taylor's conclusion here. Perhaps those who order society, while knowing full well this need for uniqueness, consciously bypass it. Too many unique people would make any society impossible to run. And, expressing a contrary view, Brown argues that mass movements draw their adherents from the same types (hardly an argument for uniqueness) and, moreover, claims that such movements are interchangeable. (1963:106) What people want, in fact, is to belong to the mass, so one kind of mass will do as well as another. And since one of the great problems facing our world is overpopulation, it is likely that total manipulation of people in masses will become both easier and the norm rather than otherwise.

'Conditioning, called brain-washing by the news agencies, is the production of reactions in the human organism through the use of associative reflexes.' (Condon, 1960:33) The crucial question for manipulators through the ages has been just how can beliefs be firmly implanted in the mind and the extent to which people can be switched to new beliefs which are contrary to those they formerly held. Much of the answer depends upon the physiological state of the subject whose beliefs are to be altered. Stress is a prerequisite for brainwashing and the more anxious the subject (for example Londoners during the Blitz) the greater the likelihood that they will be induced to believe what otherwise they would have dismissed as fancy or propaganda. Constantly, however, those who examine this subject return to the question of religion. Sargant, whose *Battle for the Mind* was a seminal book in its time, destroys many of his own arguments with his statement: 'Man cannot and should not try to exist without some form of religion.' (1957:214) Why ever not, one has to ask, and is not the success of religion – any religion – the result of endlessly applied brainwashing that has been elevated into a way of life?

Brown provides some excellent analysis of brainwashing techniques: 'Brainwashing first takes deliberate and active steps to strip the individual of his self-hood and then strives to build up something new on the foundations.' Thus, when a subject for brainwashing 'dies to the world', the second stage follows in which he is made to feel guilty – by accusation or under psychological stress, a state of mind that can produce both self-betrayal and betrayal of friends and colleagues – so that he renounces his old life and is ready to embrace the new – whatever is offered. This kind of manipulation, for example, produced the readiness – the compulsion – to confess that became a feature of those purged under Stalin. Most 'brainwashing' is hardly conducted at this clinical level but the object is much the same: a switch of allegiance and belief that will make the subject a pliable follower of the new. Brown claims that brainwashing can work in the sense of planting a new ideology 'when the new belief is a perfect substitute for the old ones', but interestingly he does not address himself to the question of how the old beliefs came to be adopted in the first place. (1963:293)

Aldous Huxley achieved fame with his novel *Brave New World* in which he painted the picture of a future society where everyone is made happy by soma drugs and other conditioning. A quarter of a century after the publication of *Brave New World* Huxley produced a non-fiction follow-up, *Brave New World Revisited*, in which he looked at actual developments that had taken place since the appearance of his novel. He discovered that a new technique which he had not envisaged, that of subliminal persuasion – flashing words or images on a cinema or television screen so fast that they cannot be seen although they are subconsciously absorbed – had been devised and one more way of mind manipulation was available. Taylor writes that one experiment – flashing the word 'ice-cream' on cinema screens – had two results: there was a slight increase in the demand for ice-cream and people complained that the cinema was cold! (1968:152) This kind of activity is as yet in its infancy but clearly the possibilities are wide-ranging. Huxley pioneered the idea of teaching during sleep (with taped information under the pillow, for example), and the possibility in a rigidly controlled situation of feeding people with information without their ever being conscious of the fact is clearly substantial.

Much more advanced has been the training of executives in

America: 'Like all well-designed indoctrination courses, the social life of the trainee is built into the programme: to get ahead one must get along, with one's peers and with one's superiors.' (Mills, 1958:144) According to Taylor, another experiment shows that if you smile at someone every time he uses a certain word he will begin to use it more often without being aware of the fact. (1979:87) These and other experiments at the very least demonstrate how suggestible are ordinary people. How much further they could be taken effectively is another question. More practical brainwashing comes from quite other approaches. Henry Fairlie, writing in *The Establishment*, said of the BBC: 'Here is the real danger of the B.B.C. It does not preach; it does not even try to persuade; it brainwashes, and it brainwashes with such a skill that no one notices. This is its value to the Establishment.' (Thomas, 1962:189) And Marshall McLuhan, whose examination of the media upset many accepted views of its worth, examined another phenomenon of the 1960s, the 'teach-in': 'We now experience simultaneously the dropout and the teach-in. The two forms are correlative. They belong together. The teach-in represents an attempt to shift education from instruction to discovery, from brain-washing students to brainwashing instructors.' (1967:101) But changing modes of behaviour is more difficult than it might appear and, as Tawney says correctly, 'Revolutions, as a long and bitter experience reveals, are apt to take their colour from the regime which they overthrew.' (1961:31) Alex, the hero of Anthony Burgess's *A Clockwork Orange*, is brainwashed at the end and what emerges is a good deal less human than the original character: 'But you, O my brothers, remember sometimes thy little Alex that was. Amen. And all that cal.' (1962:196)

Is brainwashing a myth? On 14 October 1988 the *Independent* reported that nine Canadians who had been used as guinea pigs in brainwashing experiments financed by the CIA during the 1950s came to an agreement with the US Government to receive compensation. In 1949 high-ranking CIA men were reputedly horrified by the blank face of Cardinal Mindszenty during his treason trial in Budapest and believed he had confessed after brainwashing. And so in 1951 it was decided to carry out experiments in sensory deprivation (to ensure that the West caught up with techniques that it believed the Communists were then using). Experiments were conducted under the Canadian psychiatrist, Dr Ewen Cameron. He gave patients drugs which induced sleep lasting ten days and then administered shock treatments (two a day) so that at the end of 30 days patients had been reduced to a dependent, childlike state in which they would be ready for 'brain-washing'. In another of his experiments Dr Cameron considered that poor mothering was a cause of mental illness and so first reduced his patients to a childlike state so that they could be 'remothered' in the hospital environment. Patients were exposed to tape-recorded mess-ages, repeated thousands of times (up to sixteen hours a day) using microphones under pillows. He described this as psychic driving. For the first ten days patients were given negative messages: 'You don't get along with people . . .' Then for a subsequent ten days they received positive messages: 'You want other people to like you . . .' Patients were kept docile during this 'repatterning' with injections of curare and beeswax so that they remained in a state of semi-paralysis. Although the experiments were carried out by a Canadian in Montreal the CIA was footing the bill. Typically, the US Government admitted no guilt in relation to the nine Canadians who claimed and received some $400,000 in compensation in 1988, but settled out of court rather than face litigation and publicity about CIA activities in the 1950s. It is an unsavoury story which shows the West behaving at least as ruthlessly as their ideological enemies in the Cold War.

Many people appear to want to be brainwashed; or, at least, cannot make the effort which resistance to the process requires. It is unwill-ingness to resist that plays into the hands of those who wish to induce conformity, of whatever kind. This readiness to surrender or, at any rate, not to resist is what makes the process so insidious and potentially dangerous. It is not possible to claim simply that 'we' – ordinary people – are brainwashed by 'them'. The deciders will attempt to do this anyway but they need willing or at least pliant victims and many people provide exceptionally malleable material for brainwashing. Indeed, the process of brainwashing or manipulation would prove very difficult without malleable or 'willing' victims but, as Sir Joshua Reynolds said, 'There is no expedient to which man will not resort to avoid the real labour of thinking' and the success of brainwashing or manipulation will depend to a large extent upon the fact that people seek a quiet life. 'The ordinary person senses the greatness of the odds against him even without thought or analysis, and he adapts his attitudes uncon-sciously. A huge passivity has settled on industrial society.' (McLuhan, 1951:21)

The temptation to do nothing about perceived manipulation – perhaps in the hope that somehow things will turn out all right in the end (a powerful and convenient human escape mechanism) – is usually far more prevalent than any effort to combat manipulation, since most people, although they talk of freedom, are far more concerned with security while, at the same time, they are animated by a compelling need to believe the best of themselves. This compulsion to assume the best gives free rein to complacency: people will believe that they are unaffected although others ('them') may be brainwashed. This complacent approach also assists the manipulators. A capacity to resist brainwashing or manipulation must depend in part upon intelligence but still more upon an existing drive to be free in the sense of deciding for oneself. Machiavelli believed that 'There are three different kinds of brains, the one understands things unassisted, the other understands things when shown by others, the third understands neither alone nor with the explanation of others.' (1940:86) The great majority of people fall into the second and third of these categories, but it is the second category – those who understand with assistance – who are most likely to provide the mass cannon fodder for manipulation, depending of course upon the source of the assistance.

Partisanship is a prevalent human characteristic; for example, people like their newspapers to be partisan and reflect their views rather than to be impartial and objective. It is relatively easy to categorise people, and a majority like to be seen as belonging to particular interest groups. 'In this usage, the public is composed of the unidentified and the non-partisan in a world of defined and partisan interests.' (Mills, 1958:305) And parallel with the need to belong to an interest group is the tendency of big organisations to level people down to a common denominator where it is harder to be an individual rather than just a member of the group. People want to be socialised, to belong, and as Eysenck argues, those who are difficult to condition will be relatively under-socialised while, comparatively, those who are easy to condition will be over-socialised. (1957:263) Discussing 'rising' in the corporate world of the United States, Mills says cynically although no doubt accurately: 'And never let your brains show.'

In 1956 (in the USA) Gallup came to the conclusion that 'The depth approach to politics seemed justified by the growing evidence that voters could not be depended upon to be rational. There seemed to be a strong illogical or non-logical element in their behaviour, both individually and in masses.' (Packard, 1960a:151) This finding, curiously, must be a source of hope that there is a 'maverick' element in human nature that cannot easily be manipulated. On the other hand, the British historian, Sir Lewis Namier, thought that the English 'perceive and accept facts without anxiously inquiring into their reasons and meaning.' If this judgement by a naturalised Pole is accurate, then the English, as he described them, provide excellent material for manipulation. In *The Hidden Persuaders* Packard asked: 'Is it healthy in a democracy that citizens desire a leader who will protect them?' During the 1980s British political commentators likened the country's authoritarian Prime Minister, Margaret Thatcher – the first woman in that role – to a 'nanny' and they had a point as far as the British were concerned.

All children are conditioned, in varying degrees, by their parents and family surroundings, and by the time they have grown up, many have come to accept their place in the class system to which their parents belong. Taylor suggests:

> In a slightly deeper sense, men never completely unlearn the assumptions and patterns acquired in youth, and progress depends upon their removal by death – a thing which has often been demonstrated in the history of science. It seems likely therefore that the rate at which society can change is keyed in some measure to the average life span. (1968:216)

Certainly it is true that a high proportion of people vote or act the way they do because their parents did, because it is expected of anyone belonging to their own class. In other words, they follow a pre-ordained pattern of behaviour, and understanding the pattern is the first prerequisite for those who would manipulate. If in addition the manipulators also understand how to work upon the two emotions of anxiety and guilt which operate so strongly in most people, then half the battle of manipulation has been won. Hypnotists, for example, often find that their best subjects are not neurotic but normal, socialised people, and the release which the hypnotist brings about is that of an existing pattern of behaviour or wish-fulfilment. (Brown, 1963:75) Despite the many claims that man is a rational animal the evidence points in other directions; it is, indeed, a mistake to assume that people want to be rational, for too often, in fact, they are happy to be fooled if the result of the fooling is also to make life easy for them. It is always easier to do as others do, while failure to conform is regularly punished by most societies. The majority of people find it much easier not to stand out as individuals for that makes life too difficult. While Freud pointed to the irrationality of the man in the street, Marx saw man as socially conditioned rather than operating according to autonomous reason. These facts of human behaviour are the starting point for those who would manipulate or brainwash.

Conditioning begins in childhood and, for most people, continues through life. It is the exception who breaks away and questions the broad concepts that have governed his or her life, and continue to govern most other people's lives. When the phrase 'accepted wisdom' is employed by the media or those in authority, they have, although they may not be aware of the fact, ceased to think about the topic under discussion and instead are simply propagating the line which the government, or society, or the establishment of the day, wishes everyone to take for granted.

Free will, the capacity to discern and choose, is what man claims distinguishes him from other animals, yet, too often, he is quite extraordinarily reluctant to exercise this quality. Or, to put the matter in a different way, most people seem only too ready to surrender their unique characteristics and accept instead norms imposed upon them by others. Human beings, through their various religions, have persuaded themselves of their unique qualities and like to think that they are superior to all other living things because of their intellect and powers of reasoning, but curiosity and inventiveness on the one hand are all too often offset on the other by the mental laziness that too readily accepts 'received wisdom' from above and ceases to question those who provide it. That, in essence, is why most processes of brainwashing work.

And in case such reasoning appears too remote from everyday affairs, it is worth looking at the way Brazilians reacted to the demographic census conducted in September 1991. In this mixed-race society of an estimated 153 million inhabitants, a majority, against all the evidence, claim to be white. In fact about 40 per cent of the population is believed to be black (although in the 1980 census only 5.6 per cent of the population was registered as black) while perhaps another 40 per cent are of mixed race. But the success of the dominant whites has persuaded generations of non-white Brazilians to deny their true colour or ethnic origins (a legacy of slavery) and aspire to be what they are not rather than admit to being what they are. Such behaviour is a demonstration of just how susceptible to brainwashing people can become.

3 Techniques of persuasion

Be easy, man!
The easy man lives to eat the best dinners.
T. S. ELIOT

ECHNIQUES OF PERSUASION ARE LEGION, ranging from the crudest torture to the subtlest suggestion. Propaganda, repetition, appeals to loyalty, positive techniques designed to build up the ego of the subject to be persuaded, negative techniques to break down opposition. For the first time in history mass communications make it possible to reach great numbers directly and peacefully: 'as electricity creates conditions of extreme interdependence on a global scale, we move swiftly again into an auditory world of simultaneous events and over-all awareness.' So argued Marshall McLuhan and he continued: 'Today we live on the frontier between five centuries of mechanism and the new electronics, between the homogeneous and the simultaneous.' (1962:141)

War has always been seen as providing special licence to manipulate the truth. In World War I, for example, the French exaggerated their casualties in order to get the British to take a greater part of the front, and the Germans underestimated theirs so as not to cause a loss of morale. (Deacon, 1986) A generation later, World War II and then the Cold War made us familiar with the concept of brainwashing: psychological warfare, political propaganda, state use of the media as a weapon of control. But everything has its day and fashion is both an ally and an enemy of brainwashing, for people simply become bored with a particular line or totem of the establishment. This appeared to have happened with the BBC by the late 1980s (quite apart from any assaults upon it by the Thatcher government). And, at the beginning of the 1990s, it had become almost *de rigueur* in certain circles to blame present ills upon the licence of the 1960s.

Techniques of persuasion are tried and tested: some work, others do not or at least not so well. Speaking of the 1979 Lusaka Commonwealth Conference and the eventual agreement to hold a

Lancaster House conference to resolve the Rhodesia question, Lord Carrington, Britain's Foreign Secretary at the time, said: 'Matters had, of course, been undoubtedly helped by the Queen's presence to open the conference, which conferred on it a particular dignity and sense of occasion.' (1988:296) Did Lord Carrington really believe that? Perhaps, coming from his own establishment background, he did! At a quite different level in British politics, when Labour holds power (especially in difficult circumstances) the right talks of the need for a national government, but when the Tories are in power national governments are not on the agenda. The implication, of course, is that the right are both the natural government and more to be trusted in a crisis than the left.

Governments are in a position to alter the rules to suit their objectives and on awkward issues such as using the civil courts (with no counsel or jury) in Ulster the British Government produced no evidence to substantiate its claim that the denial of a fundamental right was based on grounds of national security and, therefore, that the courts could not inquire further. (Thornton, 1989:13) Governments, indeed, have every advantage and when cornered can always resort to delaying tactics – calling for a report or setting up a Royal Commission – which in the end, as a rule, mean that nothing is done at all. In its widest sense brainwashing consists of a whole range of varying techniques: some techniques will be more effective than others, just as some people will be more resistant than others. And though, sadly, force or the threat of force to make people change their opinions is a constant of many societies, successful brainwashing is much more likely to be designed to appeal to what people want, while its pressures will be verbal and psychological.

From Ulster to Vietnam, Chile to China, torture and other brutalities have been practised upon prisoners and dissidents, and it is a sad fact of our world that too often force is the first rather than the last resort to change people's opinions. Writing in the *Independent* (25.2.1986) Andrew Rissik said of torture and torturers:

> Until recently, the greatest experts in anatomy were professional interrogators, not doctors. The desire to hurt was more practical and effective than the desire to heal. And, if the torturers themselves are perverts and sadists, we must remember that they are, in a sense, the elected representatives of the larger ideologies which produce them.

Torture may be the crudest method of manipulation – after all, it forced Galileo to change his mind and accept that the world was flat and not round as he had said – but it also leads on to more subtle relationships. Jean-Paul Sartre suggested that torture results in a strange contest of wills: 'The torturer pits himself against the tortured for his "manhood" and the duel is fought as if it were not possible for both sides to belong to the human race.' (Deeley, 1971:34)

The range of manipulative techniques in use is enormous. There is the crisis technique. Writing in the mid-1950s, Aldous Huxley said: 'Permanent crisis justifies permanent control of everybody and everything by the agencies of the central government.' (1958:17) There has been plenty of that kind of approach through the years of the Cold War, and successive British governments have come close to that philosophy in their handling of Ulster. Government propaganda is probably the best understood form of brainwashing and everyone is familiar with it. According to Watson, many people round the world believe only the BBC and the 'Voice of America' when their own countries are in turmoil and, as he argues, credibility takes time to build up but pays off. Watson was writing in the 1970s when the Cold War was still at its height; the assumption in this case was that the two principal Western systems responsible for overseas broadcasting had achieved a major propaganda victory by sticking to the truth. (1978:431) That conclusion is debatable but the implication is clear: that propaganda can be an instrument for good as well as harm, depending upon who the propagandists are! Deacon, in his book *The Truth Twisters* (again concerned with the Cold War), argues that there was no point in the USSR, for example, getting pro-Soviet propaganda into openly pro-Soviet media, for people would merely react to that by saying 'they would say that, wouldn't they'. Instead, the technique must be to infiltrate anti-Soviet media and attempt to play upon the appealing conceit that 'we' – the media in question – are impartial. During the second half of the 1980s when constant storms hit the BBC in particular but the media generally about the way they handled Ulster, they were told how important it was to project a 'positive image'. Roger Bolton, who lost his job over his television film *Death on the Rock*, quotes a British Army captain involved in psychological operations in Northern Ireland as saying: 'The important thing (in propaganda) is to get saturation coverage for your story as soon after the controversial event as possible. Even when the facts come out the original image is the one that sticks.' (1990:235)

Brainwash .

Modern propaganda, certainly since Goebbels, has always been associated with repetition and ever since Huxley's *Brave New World* and the sleep teaching which he later called Hypnopaedia, the idea of using endless repetition to implant an idea during sleep has hovered on the fringes of the manipulation world. Eysenck records an experiment on children in which they were played a record when asleep which endlessly repeated 'I must not bite my fingernails'; the incidence of nail-biting dropped as a result. (1953:216) But a far more sinister use of this technique was tried in the CIA-funded Canadian experiment during the early 1950s (see pp. 22–3). One of the more simply dishonest advertising techniques has often been used in notices of plays or books in which a line from a review is plucked out of context to give the impression that the play or book in question received far more favourable reviews than in fact was the case. But a majority of propaganda, especially perhaps political propaganda, is probably more important in reinforcing already held views than it is in changing people's minds. One of the most important techniques is affirmation: the evangelist, whether religious or political, does not argue but only repeats endlessly and encourages crowd contagion, often by inducing emotions of either guilt or fear.

A major part of all brainwashing is concerned with reinforcing the system which those in power in any given society control. As Carmichael and Hamilton observed in *Black Power*, 'Elaborate doctrines are developed to show the inevitability and rightness of the existing scheme of things.' (1968:8) And one of the most persuasive techniques trotted out to deal with would-be reformers is always the plea that they should join or remain in the party or church or organisation which they criticise, and work to reform it from within. Many do so and by accepting the system which they had set out to reform are lost, enmeshed within its beguiling structures. The British have made great play with the concept of free speech, which too often has been an escape outlet to ensure that critics of the system are sidetracked from action into words. Max Nicholson, an ex-mandarin, who had his book *The System* published in 1967 and was suitably ignored by the Establishment, commented upon free speech as follows: 'the peculiar tradition, so often commented on by foreign observers, that even the lowliest Englishman felt, and was accepted as being, quite at liberty to comment most candidly on the sovereign, the state of government and any other national issue, centuries before he possessed any voting power or other civic right to do so or could expect his views to be taken seriously'. (p. 29)

'Buying in' or patronage is the most successful of all weapons simply because most people want to belong anyway and many people will criticise the system in order to make a nuisance of themselves so as to be bought in. It is one of the oldest techniques for dealing with dissidents: 'work from within and help us to reform'. Once the dissident has swallowed this line he can be controlled and his criticisms smothered. In both Britain and the USA outsiders who may also be potential critics, such as academics, are bought in but then they are bound into the system as well, for example, by the use of the Official Secrets Act: 'It is always easier to discover the truth about contemporary power than to publish it; the difficulties are greatest for those who have been participants.' (Mackenzie, 1967:215) Raymond Williams, who spent a lifetime examining the structures of British society from an outsider position on the left, shows how the system works at the level of ordinary people who are hardly in the bracket of those aspiring to power or influence: 'We are invited to possess and consume at appropriate levels, as delivered by this or that set of leaders and celebrities; the ordinary enjoyment of some possessing and consuming locks us – or is intended to lock us – into this deep sense of the nature of society.' (1989:147) Few more successful campaigns at 'locking in' have ever been conducted than that of the British Tory Party with its appeal to become members of 'a property-owning democracy': own your own house and be locked into the system for life with mortgage payments.

Witold Starecki, a Polish immigrant, says, 'People in England don't challenge the system. They are told something and they accept it.' (Quoted in Green, 1990:125) And certainly in Britain people are subjected to an endless bombardment of assertions that what is must be right. In essence, of course, the system has to be benevolent: 'It is easy to fight obvious tyranny; it is not easy to fight benevolence, and few things are more calculated to rob the individual of his defences than the idea that his interests and those of society can be wholly compatible.' (Whyte, 1956:440) And on top of benevolence comes the well-worked theme pinpointed so amusingly by Anthony Sampson in his *Anatomy of Britain*, 'It may seem odd, but it *works*', which has been used to explain every kind of snobbery or anachronism that continues to stifle British society. (1962:49)

Loyalty is a key weapon in reinforcing the system and is a potent brainwashing tool. Calls to loyalty include party, union, church, class, neighbours, community, country; in fact, the list is as long as there are institutions or communities which can be singled out from the mass. The instinct of loyalty is not of itself bad; the uses to which that instinct have been put – 'my country right or wrong' – have often been appalling. Tracing loyalty back to its early beginnings, Desmond Morris claims that while co-operation in hunting was essential to survival, 'Loyalty on the hunt has become loyalty in fighting, and war is born.' (1967:175) And then loyalty to the tribe becomes loyalty to the leader and so dynasties are born, but, as D. N. Pritt observes, 'Loyalty always outlasts proof that it is no longer deserved.' (1966a:314) During the Vietnam War the White House and the Pentagon ran a sustained campaign against the Saigon press corps and attacks would be made upon anyone who questioned the official line, 'not just on reporters' accuracy but their manhood and their patriotism' (Mercer *et al.*, 1987:248). And Britain's Prime Minister, Margaret Thatcher, made the phrase 'one of us' notorious. Loyalty is made to override most other values, especially in politics: 'The rules of political life are fairly simple. Progress up the political ladder of ambition has to be firmly based on loyalty to the party.' (Ponting, 1986:32)

The system and loyalty are underpinned by references to common sense. Emphasis upon common sense all too often means an appeal to the lowest common denominator of the group and is reinforced by the cult of the common man which politicians use when they wish to base policies upon prejudices rather than reasoning. Most people like to insist that they are ordinary; they go on to force others to be ordinary – like them – as well. As Richard Hoggart put it, 'keeping down with the Atkinses'. At the same time certain characters – the would-be iconoclast or Gilbert Harding figure – is pushed forward as an example of freedom in a society that is increasingly unfree. (1957:186) Reliance upon common sense is a well-developed British political technique and, one might almost say, when in doubt refer to common sense. As Cockburn and Blackburn argue: 'The cult of common sense accurately indicates the role of linguistic philosophy in England. *It functions as chloroforming ideology, blotting out* the very memory of an alternative order of thought.' (1969:237)

The other side of the common-sense coin is the well-developed technique of dismissing the intelligent. Those who present a danger to the system by stepping outside the accepted limits of conformity have to be discredited and their influence destroyed. This is done by appeals to loyalty, by ignoring, smearing, casting doubts upon their arguments with faint praise. If you must be intelligent, then reassure the herd by demonstrating that you do not have superior intelligence and that so-called difficult things are easy: 'Dr Fink not only knows his stuff, he knows how to write . . . with humour, relaxed and easy.' (McLuhan, 1951:28) When, in defence of the white communities in Africa, the high Tory, Lord Salisbury, wished to damn the policies of the radical Tory Colonial Secretary, Iain Macleod, he did so not by any detailed reference to those policies but by the simple expedient of describing him as 'too clever by half'. When Charles Davis left the Roman Catholic priesthood and published his book *A Question of Conscience*, the Church first applied the loyalty pressure to him and said he should attempt reform from within; then it conceded that some things might be wrong – perhaps to demonstrate that it was open-minded; finally it ignored him and treated him as a non-person. Enoch Powell, whose logical exactitudes have often baffled the lesser minds around him, has been anathema to the left and an embarrassment to the right so it has been necessary to render him outside debate. The left has done this by using the smear tactic of describing him as a 'fascist', after which no more need be said. The right to whom he belongs has had a more difficult task, so has fallen back upon the expedient of damning him with faint praise: he is *too logical*, that is, he doesn't understand the common man.

In *The Organization Man* Whyte observes: 'It is now coming to be widely believed that *science has proved the group is superior to the individual.* Science has not, but that is another matter.' (1956:53) To state something as though it is an infallible truth or has been proven beyond dispute is a well-developed technique. The exploitation of authority at many different levels is used to reinforce the status quo: 'I read it in the papers' or 'I saw it on television' turns into 'it must be true'. The eyewitness account, 'I was there', has the double advantage of excluding or at least reducing to a secondary level those who were not there and daring those who would contest what is being claimed to accuse the person who was there of being a liar. There are, indeed, endless ways of making us accept propositions from authority about how our society is run.

Aldous Huxley had a good deal to say about the manipulation of mobs which is one of the cruder forms of brainwashing:

But crowd-delirium aroused by government agents, crowd-delirium in the name of orthodoxy, is an entirely different matter. In all cases where it can be made to serve the interests of the men controlling church and state, downward self-transcendence by means of herd intoxication is treated as something legitimate, and even highly desirable. (1961:366)

He goes on:

Assemble a mob of men and women previously conditioned by a daily *reading* of newspapers; treat them to amplified band music, bright lights, and the oratory of a demagogue who (as demagogues always are) is simultaneously the exploiter and the victim of herd-intoxication, and in next to no time you can reduce them to a state of almost mindless subhumanity. Never before have so few been in a position to make fools, maniacs or criminals of so many. (368)

In the age of Hitler who can gainsay Huxley?
Thomas Paine wrote:

But pure and simple Deism does not answer the purpose of despotic governments. They cannot lay hold of religion as an engine but by mixing it with human inventions and making their own authority a part; neither does it answer the avarice of priests, but by incorporating themselves and their functions with it and becoming, like the government, a party in the system. It is this that forms the otherwise mysterious connection of Church and State; the Church humane and the State tyrannic. (1937:144)

Techniques of mass religious conversion are very old and include the use of physiological weapons – drugs, fasting, mortification, confession, drumming, dancing, inducing fear, incense and ritual. Speaking of Russian ballet, Sir Nevile Henderson, British Ambassador to Hitler's Germany, said, 'but for grandiose beauty I have never seen any ballet to compare with the Nuremberg rally.' And Hermann Rauschning said: 'Hitler has a deep respect for the Catholic Church and the Jesuit order; not because of their Christian doctrine, but because of the "machinery" they have elaborated and controlled, their hierarchical system, their extremely clever tactics, their knowledge of human nature and their wise use of human weakness in ruling over believers.' (Huxley, 1958:65, 51) When Charles Davis said he no longer believed what was imposed on him by the authority of the Church he found that 'those I spoke with would not take this reason seriously; they did not see it as creating an impossible obstacle to my continued membership.' Thus, in effect, they argued: belong anyway, an argument that ignored any basis of faith and revealed those who counselled Davis to behave in such a fashion as so deeply brainwashed that membership of the Church had become more important to them than belief. (1967:43) By making the Pope 'infallible' the Roman Catholic Church ensured that he could scotch any questioning from within. One of the great triumphs of organised religions in British society – a habit that continues into an age of non-belief – is the social custom, reinforced by the laws against blasphemy, that forbids one to criticise another person's religion. We may attack the absurdities or hypocrisies or whatever of capitalism or Marxism or socialism or of any other 'ism', but not religion, although those other beliefs may be as important to the people who espouse them as are religions to those who hold them. We have allowed ourselves to be persuaded that beliefs in a religious sense should be treated with kid gloves; we do not extend the same courtesy to people's beliefs in political, economic or social affairs. There is no logical reason why we should not argue that to speak badly of Marxism is just as reprehensible as to speak ill of Islam – but we do not do so.

The British set great store by groups and group membership; the public-school system and old school tie have been used for a hundred years to create such groups, and to a very high degree social skills depend upon understanding group mechanisms: team work, group loyalty, group dynamics, group thinking. Entrance to a group is governed by demanding acts of membership, surrenders carrying out some deed that justifies acceptance. The terms used by business in Whyte's *Organization Man* each imply 'control' – adjustment, adaptation, social orientation, team work, group dynamics, group living and loyalty – and people are asked to sacrifice their own beliefs so they may belong. 'What is needed is an administrative élite, people trained to recognise that what man really wants most is group solidarity even if he does not realize it himself.' (1956:40) The process is designed to sublimate individuality to the group where 'No one . . . ever need face a problem alone' and so provide security. There is, in our modern society, always a group to espouse any cause and often, one suspects, it is the 'togetherness' of the group that is the attraction rather than the cause itself. One never needs to be alone and there is no need for a personal sense of guilt or responsibility, for the problem becomes a communal one. Possibly Japan has gone further than any other industrial society in creating corporations that look after their members from the cradle to the grave but, aware of the way frustrations can build up and undermine the best corporate plans, the Japanese have introduced the custom of making dummy images of the managers of big corporate organisations so that workers may go to a room set aside for the purpose and punch or beat the images of the bosses to let off frustrations. The custom appeared in Britain in 1983.

The techniques discussed here are the necessary buttresses for our ruling élites whose often highly artificial positions require constant reinforcement. Elites fascinate because of the power they wield and, still more perhaps, because of the privileges, real or imagined, which their members enjoy. The attraction of the élite and the desire to belong (despite egalitarian denials) make them potent forces in all societies. A powerful aspect of any élite is the belief that its members are superior to the people around them. One élite technique, used by public schools for example, is to insist that their members are not superior to non-members so that in the end they assume that they must be but ought not to show it. As a rule membership of an élite is marked by the possession of some quality – wealth or class – that is generally envied and valued. The political élite is perhaps the most immediately important since its members are the power holders of the body politic. Elitism, in fact, is profoundly anti-democratic and yet the British, who like to claim some special responsibility for the spread of democracy, love élites and are only too happy to join one or more as the summit of their social or other ambitions. 'The power of any minority is irresistible as against each single individual in the majority, who stands alone before the totality of the organised minority.' (Bottomore, 1966:9) And élites have at their disposal – to manipulate the masses – universal compulsory education and the media of mass communication. Brainwashing is a necessary instrument of élitism and its many practices are very much alive in contemporary Britain. The *Independent* of 8 November 1990 carried a photograph on its front page showing peers and peeresses arriving at the Palace of Westminster for the Queen's Speech in the House of Lords to mark the opening of the new session of Parliament. Assorted Boy Scouts were on duty to open the car doors of the arriving peers who are apparently incapable of this simple physical function themselves while, no doubt, the Boy Scouts had been told beforehand what an honour and privilege it was to do duty as subservient attendants to the upper Establishment on one of its public appearance days.

'When firmly-established facts oppose political dogma, the reaction of the politician almost invariably is to deny the fact, rather than to change the dogma.' (Eysenck, 1953:301) We live in an age of opinion polls, yet it is doubtful that they have much affect upon the opinion formers. Thus, politicians find out what is public opinion, not so as to do what the public wants but rather in order to find out what more has to be done to bring the people round to accepting what the politicians intend to do anyway. 'Public opinion' has long been used to justify actions often only remotely connected with the public's wishes. Opinion does not make the politicians behave as the people wish; rather, it is used by the politicians as a justification for their actions. The very recent practice in Britain of almost weekly polls to show the state of the political parties and the popularity of their respective leaders (using samples of approximately 1,000 at a time) is as much designed to give the impression of a public that is eagerly involved in the political process as it is to find out the answers to the questions which have been posed.

Smear tactics are another instrument of political brainwashing. Figures such as Tony Benn or Ken Livingstone of the left have been made into bogymen by a right-wing press; essentially, they have been turned into subversive fear figures threatening 'our way of life'. Their arguments are rarely addressed except very superficially. The social scientist W. J. M. Mackenzie, writing of the radicalism of such men as Paine and Mill, says: 'The doctrine's strength lay partly in this diffuseness, in the fact that it appealed (and still does) to the young and mass audiences rather than to grave intellectuals, and that when it was in its prime it offered practising politicians so much scope for easy rhetoric.' (1967:84) Here is a classic example of writing down and, hopefully, off altogether. Thus, radicalism appeals to the young (immature) and mass audiences (mobs) and allows easy rhetoric to practising politicians (place seekers?) as opposed to having an appeal for 'grave intellectuals' who in this context are clearly the Establishment. The fact that radicalism does not appeal to 'grave intellectuals' is surely the pity. The mention of age is a standard technique of denigration: to mention the age of young people is to suggest immaturity and so lack of understanding; while to use old age ('80-year-old Mr . . .') is to suggest that a critic may be an old fogey. And the creation of alternative, pejorative terms for the real ones is another technique of denigration: thus a Communist becomes a Red, a trade union leader becomes a union boss, a German becomes a Hun or Boche, a Jew becomes a Yid, and a Black becomes a Nigger. At the same time one bolsters one's own side or cause by inventing nice-sounding names for less attractive ones so that in the Cold War capitalism became 'free enterprise'. (Brown, 1963:27)

The story of the British Empire is full of brainwashing techniques and opponents of British rule were smeared often in unique ways: thus Mohamed Abdile Hassan, who successfully defied the British in Somaliland for a generation, was dubbed the 'Mad Mullah', though more commonly opponents would be described as degenerate or sinister, barbaric or full of guile (a term applied to Archbishop Makarios of Cyprus). And during the Cold War those who asked awkward questions or queried what was being done could, as a rule, be silenced by the simple expedient of suggesting they must be Communists. Once it had been suggested that someone might be a Communist the damage had been done to his career whether or not there was any truth in the suggestion. While in British political life since 1945 the term 'left wing' has generally been used as one of abuse. When in the late 1980s Britain was isolated in the councils of the Commonwealth on the issue of applying sanctions to South Africa, the Foreign and Commonwealth Office, and still more the Prime Minister used the technique of denigrating the policy they opposed since their own was clearly unacceptable to the majority. The British won, or at least did not lose, the sanctions argument because they had taken pains to produce papers and information handouts to flood the press who, lazy as a profession, will reproduce what they are given rather than write something from scratch, and the Prime Minister's Office under Bernard Ingham was very good at keeping the press supplied with ready-made material. More important, the British talked of not using *punitive* sanctions as though the object of the exercise was to hurt people rather than to influence policy. At Kuala Lumpur in 1989 the British statement claimed that the Commonwealth should concentrate on encouraging change rather than on further punishment (of South Africa), as though the rest of the Commonwealth had argued the opposite when in fact it had done nothing of the sort. The tactic had considerable success.

In the preface to an English edition of *L'Etranger* (*The Outsider*) Camus wrote: 'the hero of the book is condemned because he doesn't play the game.' Later he adds that the hero 'says what is true. He refuses to disguise his feelings and immediately society feels threatened.' (O'Brien, 1970:20) The urge to conform is one of the strongest forces motivating human behaviour. People's desire to be like their neighbours, to fit into the community, plays into the hands of those who would control them for whatever purposes. Most people appear as willing enough victims so that one may well ask whether manipulation and brainwashing is not only unavoidable but also acceptable? In many cases conformity has been made both more attractive and easier to impose because of mass education and adult literacy and, for example, Cecil King spoke from long experience when he said that only those who had worked in the popular press could know just how stupid was the British public. Conformist psychology can demean but is, none the less, one of the most powerful of all instruments for regimentation. Such conformity, moreover, is made all the easier since the group in any case will punish the outsider.

'Everyone is doing it' is the normal defence offered by those who decide to cheat: join the black economy and evade paying income tax. The claim to universality takes away the sense of guilt which cheating might otherwise induce; it also drags in others since no one wishes to be guilty on his own and, so powerful are the pressures of majority behaviour, often those who do pay their income tax in full keep quiet about it so as not to appear priggish or arrogant. Speaking of organised religion Rhadakrishnan has said: 'it is not God that is worshipped but the group or the authority that claims to speak in His name. Sin becomes disobedience to authority and not violation of integrity.' As Richard Hoggart argued in *The Uses of Literacy*, 'All classes require conformity to some degree; it needs to be stressed here because there is a tendency to stress upper- and middle-class conformity and to regard the working-classes as more free from it.' (1957:86) They are in fact no more free from it than anyone else. As Hoggart also claims, 'You need only believe what the rest believe.' Ten million people cannot be wrong. Fairlie, who lambasted the BBC in the essay he wrote for *The Establishment*, says that 'It [the BBC] fears, and when it does not fear it despises non-conformity; and if non-conformity must be allowed its say, it will gently rob it of all anger and all laughter, of all passion and all heartache, until it lacks both pith and point.' (1962:188) Herbert Marcuse speaks of modern society 'which, in order to sustain the profitable productivity on which its hierarchy depends, utilizes its vast resources for waste, destruction and an ever more methodical creation of conformist needs and satisfactions.' (1969:62)

But perhaps the last word on conformity should be left to Arthur Waley's translation of the seventh-century Chinese poet, Wang Chi's 'On Going to a Tavern' (1962:75):

These days, continually fuddled with drink,
I fail to satisfy the appetites of the soul.
But seeing men all behaving like drunkards,
How can I alone remain sober?

4 Endless ramifications

There is a host of intellectuals and others who believe that sacrifices of freedom are needed in the name of efficiency.

RAYMOND BLACKBURN

THE RAMIFICATIONS OF BRAINWASHING and where these ramifications lead give to the subject its extraordinary fascination. What does and does not constitute brainwashing cannot be defined with any precision. At one end of the scale come those techniques with which everyone is familiar: learning by rote, repetition, saluting the flag, the rituals of Church and State, advertising, propaganda, patriotism, learning deference to authority. These are followed by what might be described as learnt assumptions: foreigners are funny, British is Best, we are the most democratic society in the world, freedom is a British birthright, in fact all the stereotypes that custom, training, education and, above all, attitudes have brought people to accept without question. Then there are the less pleasant aspects of the subject: censorship, suppression of information, secrecy, each carried out in the name of a beneficent state – Big Brother knows best – and although people are uneasily aware that these things are done (and done constantly) they try to persuade themselves that such activities are necessary 'in a modern and complex society' and then, perhaps guiltily, they think of other things. The darker aspects of this kind of activity – torture, denial of liberties, genetic engineering – are assumed only to happen elsewhere: they (foreigners) do such things but we do not.

Religions have used brainwashing techniques since earliest times, and the alliance between Church and State, which has also been a feature of societies since they began to organise themselves, was always an alliance of necessity: each needed the other to brainwash the people they wished to control. So deep does such brainwashing go that it is possible for a Roman Catholic to complain of the overt brainwashing that is employed by the more extrovert evangelistic sects without also realising that he or she is the product of similar techniques which have been refined over the centuries. Dr Johnson may have said that patriotism is the last refuge of the scoundrel, but it is a refuge that is regularly trotted out by our politicians and media to devastating effect: it works both negatively and positively – we are best, they are funny or dangerous or not to be trusted.

We live in an age that is tailor-made for brainwashing: the state and the media have enormous power and most people are subjected to a constant barrage of advertising, propaganda and other pressures to accept, to conform, to do as do their neighbours, and to be a part of the community. Man's natural inclination towards conformity, indeed, is one of the most appropriate ready-made weapons for those who would brainwash; so advertisers go for the 'kids' and get them to badger their parents because they want the same things that all the other 'kids' have. At the other end of the manipulating scale comes genetic engineering. There are increasing signs now that scientists and others are preparing the ordinary public to accept, as in some areas we have already, that genetic engineering is a proper activity for a sensible society to pursue. Preparation or carefully doctored propaganda to familiarise people with a new concept is a necessary introduction to an acceptance of any brainwashing activity. Such activities are part of our modern society and most people are aware of brainwashing and that they are its targets: they accept the term in relation to advertising or television or political propaganda and, indeed, are relatively so familiar with such activities that after accepting that they take place they then dismiss them from their minds: to know is to *know*, so no more needs to be done. It is a dangerous trap. At the same time such people claim to be Christians or patriotic or tolerant without ever examining the basis of the claims they make, because they have been brought up to believe what they claim for themselves without question. And that too is the result of brainwashing.

The practice which grew up in Victorian times of caricaturing other European leaders as tyrants persuaded the British to think more highly of themselves in contrast, especially as they also saw foreigners generally as slightly absurd or sinister:

> The weakness of the Englishman's attitude towards foreigners was that he expected them to think and behave exactly like himself. When, true to their own alien natures, they failed to do so, he either laughed at their folly or – if their behaviour outraged his moral code, as it frequently did – became justly indignant. And as, being a free-born Briton, he scorned to conceal his laughter or disapproval, misunderstanding between

him and his Continental neighbours was bound to arise.
(Bryant, 1990:116)

National or patriotic brainwashing – the building-up of patriotism –
always has two sides to it. There is the image of the British themselves –
'a free-born Briton, he scorned to conceal his laughter or disapproval'
– on the one hand, but that has to be matched by the image of the
foreigner or enemy, the contrasted outsider who inevitably, by his
failings, boosts the self-image of the beholder. Likeness is a crucial
ingredient in this process and phrases such as 'one of us' (made famous
by Margaret Thatcher) or 'he speaks the same language' are at the
same time inclusive and exclusive terms which praise those who belong
and by implication denigrate those who do not. As Barbara Ward
said: 'Nothing so concentrates one's national feeling as being aware
of somebody else's.' (1959:19) Most national stereotypes are in the
form of the 'one of us' image and assume that 'we' are unchanging in
our values and behaviour while foreigners are funny. In a giveaway
remark that tells volumes about his attitudes, Selwyn Lloyd, explaining
his part in the Suez Affair, said 'I hated the efficacy of Radio Cairo –
as powerful as Goebbels.' (Kyle, 1991:321) The British certainly
resorted to broadcast propaganda at the time of Suez and on the whole
it came a poor second to that of Radio Cairo. Thus, the man who as
Foreign Secretary had overall responsibility for such propaganda
dismisses its failure by a curious smear tactic: he admits the efficacy
of Radio Cairo but then compares it to the work of the by then almost
mythical arch-fiend of propaganda, Goebbels. In his inimitable way
Arthur Koestler makes the right sort of comparison when he says:
'English is the only sensible language, because a knife, for instance, is
called by the French *couteau*, by the Germans *Messer*, and so on,
whereas we English call it a "knife", which is after all what a knife
really is' (1963:14).

The term 'brainwashing' has connotations about 'them' for many
Britons: we do not do it, they (foreigners and dictators and so on) do.
Foreign countries such as China, Czechoslovakia, the USSR, South
Africa have often complained about what they consider to be the
one-sided coverage by the BBC of human rights abuses in their
countries, although the British have always replied that they were being
impartial with the implication that they always are impartial and since
we have managed to persuade ourselves over a long period that this
is the case we tend to be outraged if such foreigners suggest that

impartiality is not a feature of our reporting when it comes to matters that closely affect us, such as Ulster. When Japan launched its full-scale attack upon China in 1937, Britain's Foreign Secretary Anthony Eden was outraged, not at the attack as such so much as the fact that it was made by an 'upstart' nation encroaching upon 'white race' preserves: we, the superior, white British, could be imperialists where and when we pleased, but not the Japanese. Concern for the Chinese did not appear to bother Eden. (Ponting, 1990:25) A generation later, in the context of British politics, Tony Benn records how he talked with members of some pressure groups for change: 'They were sort of tempted by what I was saying but they think of socialism very much in terms of race relations – somewhere else rather than at home.' (1989:50)

We define the groups around us, including ourselves, according to stereotypes and then try to fit everyone into the groups. As Walter Lippmann said: 'For the most part we do not see and then define, we define first and then see. In the great blooming buzzing confusion of the outer world we pick out what our culture has already defined for us and we tend to perceive that which we have picked out in the form stereotyped for us by our culture.' (Quoted in Eysenck, 1953:244) Further, we proceed to give to all members of a group the characteristics that in reality apply only to selected individuals, for it is never truly possible to describe a whole group according to stereotypes although we constantly try to do so. When a clever writer such as Orwell, in his essay 'England Your England', turns his skill to describing his countrymen he creates a picture that becomes part of the national stereotype. Thus, in one of his essays he picks out characteristics that go to make an Englishman: 'The gentleness, the hypocrisy, the thoughtlessness, the reverence for law and the hatred of uniforms will remain, along with the suet puddings and misty skies.' (1957:90) By the 1990s a majority of those characteristics might appear to have dropped away, yet the stereotype will be clung to for much longer. The British like to think they have a sense of humour while insisting that others, the Germans for example, do not. The psychologist Eysenck conducted a series of tests with British and American groups and discovered that the Americans' perception of the British was remarkably similar to the perception the British had of themselves, except that the Americans did not think the British had a sense of humour. Britons faced with such a finding did not ask whether, perhaps, the Americans were right and accept that they, the

British, did not have a sense of humour but, instead, denounced the findings to say that foreigners – in this case the Americans – did not know what they were talking about. For many years after World War II there was a British stereotype of America that was synonymous with violence and was set off by trigger words such as 'horror comics', 'Hollywood' or 'teenager', although the all-pervasive process of Americanisation of the Western world has now rendered such stereotypes obsolete. It is always easier to place people in stereotyped categories than to examine them as individuals and, apart from groups within their own society, the British have long applied this practice to all foreigners. Ever since World War II the British have denounced fascism, yet people who do so often hold views close to those that the term embraces: 'What they disapprove of,' says Eysenck, 'is the conventional stereotype of the Fascist; they have no objection against the essence of what constitutes Fascism.' (1953:249)

The stereotype is always acceptable because while, at its best, it mildly and humorously denigrates foreigners, it also uplifts the 'denigrators' even when poking fun at their own foibles. The peculiarities of foreigners are always slightly absurd; those of ourselves mere eccentricity. For their part – so successful have British projections of themselves been – many foreigners still imagine Britain to consist of people with Oxbridge accents, the royal family and the attributes of endless stately homes (upstairs and downstairs) – what we exported to the Empire. In the years during which the British have debated the issue of whether or not they belong to Europe, they have been obliged to give a good deal of attention to the Continental foreigners who live next door to them and they have often disliked what they have found. 'The foreigner is an infringer of taboos. He talks too much; he is serious when he should be light, light when he should be serious; he has wit, but no humour; he is intelligent, but he shows it; he mistakes modesty for lack of *esprit*.' (Mander, 1963:31) Although the British find all foreigners difficult they have reserved a special place in their pantheon of stereotypes for the Germans, partly as a result of fighting against them in two world wars and partly because they have perceived the Germans as the greatest threat to their own world-wide dominance. Arthur Bryant paints a classic British view of them: 'They were neurotic, they were voluble and they were vain. They were also intensely arrogant. They were so obsessed with their own point of view that they were constitutionally incapable of listening quietly to, let alone seeing, anyone else's.' (1990:236) A more skilful denigration of the Germans is achieved by Maynard Keynes in his memoir *Dr Melchior, a Defeated Enemy*, in which the author describes Germans, French and English – and Jews, although here his hero is a Jew. It is 1919; the Germans arrive at Versailles:

> Erzberger, fat and disgusting in a fur coat, walked down the platform to the Marshal's saloon. With him were a General and a Sea-Captain with an iron cross round his neck and an extraordinary resemblance of face and figure to the pig in *Alice in Wonderland*. They satisfied wonderfully, as a group, the popular conception of Huns. The personal appearance of that race is really extraordinarily against them. (1949:19)

These and other stereotypes are derived from attitudes which have often become so deeply ingrained that they make up part of the national psyche. Selwyn Lloyd, who was an undistinguished but enduring politician of the post-war years, was at heart a little Englander who boasted of the fact that he had never set foot outside the country (except in the war). In 1952, however, he visited South Korea when the war between the two halves of that country was still in progress and delivered himself of the following remarkable sentiment: 'The Koreans were much more likeable than I expected – they are obviously a turbulent and quarrelsome people . . . it is a tragedy that they cannot be a British protectorate for 25 years.' (Thorpe, 1989:165) Such a thought delivered at that time in the world's history demonstrates a mind quite astonishingly closed to any possibilities except those suggested to it by a lifetime of brainwashing about the supposed benefits conferred upon lesser peoples by the British Empire. Exactly thirty years later another war-horse of British politics, James Callaghan, wrote comparing the Korean and Falklands wars: 'There was a thirty-year gap between Korea and the Falklands. The battles were fought by different generations but the fighting spirit had endured.' (1987:102) Here a different kind of message is being conveyed by a respected political figure, a message essentially of patriotism and comfort: nothing about the British changes. The wars and the situations might be different but the old bulldog spirit is there, the same as ever.

A very different technique and attitude is described by Tony Benn in his diaries. He was invited to speak at a *Financial Times* lunch for bankers. Charles Villiers (Chairman of Guinness Mahon) was in the chair and introduced Tony Benn, who gave a speech which he says had nothing radical in it yet it frightened the bankers because they realised he was serious. When he sat down, 'Charles Villiers then stood up and said, "A very important speech and I can assure you that Tony Benn loves his country as much as you or I do" implying that after such a speech they would assume that I was a traitor. It was a most significant comment to make.' (1989:43) It is also a classic example of patronising denigration, the assumption that anyone who thought differently to the in-group – in this case the bankers – was wrong and to be dismissed as dangerous. Only occasionally are the British able to stand back and look at themselves objectively as Cyril Connolly does in the following passage:

> And the mixture of complacent philistinism, smug superiority, and latent cruelty in the English character. Land of the cat and the hangman, of military punishments, badger-baiting and homosexual hounding, of savage prosecutions of banned books, land of co-respondent and bottled sauces, of sinister officiousness. (Koestler, 1963:190)

Needless to say, when a British writer or commentator lets himself go to that extent, he is at once branded as un-English and it is asked why the British are always so ready to demean their own achievements. They are not; that too is a myth.

Attitudes change – or have to be changed – according to needs. Thus, at the time of the Falklands War there was a televised picture of the hold of a great ship acting as a troop carrier full of tough young men, many stripped to the waist, bawling out bawdy songs and making rude signs at the cameras; they were patriots going to bash the 'Argies'. Very similar young men causing trouble at football matches are described as 'worse than animals'. Now, a society which, in the space of a few years, can first exalt and then condemn the same characteristics of behaviour in the same group of its young male citizens stands to answer for a great deal. Much is said and written about hooliganism. The (apparent) rise in violence is blamed on permissiveness, the arrival of Commonwealth immigrants, the relaxation of parental control and a lowering of respect for those in authority. There was once a time when the British police were described as 'wonderful' and as far as we knew did not carry guns, but that perception of the police has disappeared in proportion, which is especially noteworthy, as the incidence of crime has risen. Whenever particular outbursts of violence occur, such as the 1981 Brixton riots, these are followed by reference to the 'good old days' when there was not so much nasty violence or it was better contained. This is a reflex action rather than bearing much relevance to the real past. At the 1978 Tory Party Conference there were calls for the birch and flogging for soccer hooligans, as though such measures would stem the growth of violence. Twenty years earlier at the 1958 Tory Party Conference there were similar calls for flogging and the birch. Indeed, such calls are as much a part of the adrenalin-inducing ritual that keeps Tory Conferences lively as they are a seriously intended solution to the problem, although those who call for such measures would certainly like to see them applied. Geoffrey Pearson's book *Hooligan*, which appeared in 1983, analyses society's approach to crime through the ages; he demonstrates that contrary to current demonology there was just as much violence in past times as today and that claims which insist that the rate of crime is rising faster than ever before have to be seen in the light of how statistics are treated and still more, perhaps, how the politicians at any given time treat the problem and wish to have it treated. He quotes, for example, the following passage from *The Times* of 2 January 1863: 'The dangerous classes seem to be getting the better of society – Under the influence of philanthropic sentiments and a hopeful policy, we have deprived the law of its terrors and justice of its arms.' (1983:119) In spite of claims made during the 1980s that violence had become worse, in fact identical claims were made a hundred years earlier. And as crime increases, so race and youth are blamed. Writing in the *Sunday Telegraph* on 29 November 1981 Peregrine Worsthorne said: 'Brixton is the iceberg tip of a crisis of ethnic criminality which is not Britain's fault – except in the sense that her rulers quite unnecessarily imported it.' This little passage says it all: crime is un-British, done by imported foreigners (Blacks) and would not have happened except that the politicians stupidly allowed them in! Similarly, over the years, the young have been blamed for a state of affairs which disturbs the Establishment. As Pearson argues, anger at such phenomena as 'Teddy Boys' or 'Mods and Rockers' is often less that they are youthful and sometimes violent and destructive and a threat to law and order, than that they represent a new mode and therefore a threat to the existing status quo. (1983:19)

When 1984 came and went there were a good many references to Orwell's famous book and a tendency to smug comment to the effect that he had got it wrong but, looking at the violent eruptions by young people in 1991 at such places as the Blackbird Leys estate on the outskirts of Oxford, Lord Scarman (the author of the report on the Brixton riots of 1981) pinpointed sheer boredom among young men as a principal cause of the troubles. Referring to the young joyriders or troublemakers at the Blackbird Leys estate Lord Scarman said: 'They are bored. They look at the world they have been born into, and they can't see anything but an endless period of grey tedium. They see the natural span of life extending to 80 rather than three score years and ten, and that only extends the tedium.' He went on to suggest that the challenge to society is to make life look much more attractive than it is. (*Independent*, 11.9.91) What Lord Scarman was describing was a bleak world of the kind portrayed in Orwell's *Nineteen Eighty-Four*; what governments are most likely to prescribe as a solution is some form of 'soma' drug of the Huxley variety.

The attitude of the British authorities, the Establishment, is nearly always 'freedom so long as you choose to agree with us, freedom so long as we do not find it inconvenient.' (Blackburn, 1964:26) Too often, in Britain, people are regarded as potential troublemakers for the state or as 'causing trouble for the police', and it is forgotten that both the state and the police are supposedly there for the good of the people and not the other way round. In this regard paternalists of the Establishment are often furious when the system which they control is attacked as not being ideal; they respond with hurt anger by saying such things as 'I have given my life for this system' as though that fact necessarily makes the system a good one. (Williams, 1989:24) C. P. Snow, who in his writings created the vivid imagery of the 'corridors of power', said in 1968: 'The forces which hold our advanced society together are very strong. Only people whose vision of the future is limited to about a week underestimate those forces.' (215) He was writing about Britain's place in a world where, demonstrably, her power was rapidly declining, and inherent in all he said was a regret for the passing of a time when Britain was more influential than she had then become. He went on: 'It has never been more important to be tough-minded. There are a lot of gestures, protests, sacrificial actions, which aim at good things, which are in spirit progressive – and which in the result, objectively, end up by being the opposite of progressive.' (216) It is an interesting passage from a man who spent his life in public affairs and was an acute observer of them. In the end, perhaps, no one is able to escape his past. Snow wanted to continue with the broad stream of approaches that had carried the Britain he knew all his lifetime, and 1968 was the time when the permissive decade of the 1960s had reached its height in terms of the influence of new ideas. Snow here is setting himself against the changes he saw coming and speaking as an Establishment figure who had, despite all his capacities, brainwashed himself into an acceptance of a view of things that was already outdated. He was also writing at a time when the world appeared to be fixed in its Cold War parameters, and almost by definition any ideological confrontation of that nature is accompanied by and requires brainwashing or everything falls apart.

No subject lends itself more obviously to techniques of brainwashing than patriotism, and the British, who can sometimes be quite nauseous about it, have managed also to create one of their myths: that patriotism is embarrassing and that they simply take it for granted – unlike other nations – so that it surfaces automatically when required. As Arthur Bryant describes it:

> For though in Britain the State had long disinterested itself in the private citizen's patriotism or capacity for war, the British with their long history retained a stronger national consciousness and underlying unity than probably any other people in the world. They took their love of country and their willingness to die for her for granted. (1990:239)

This is splendid stuff but ought not to be analysed too closely. One wonders when he speaks of a 'stronger national consciousness and underlying unity than probably any other people in the world' whether he gave even a passing thought to the Japanese or Chinese? One suspects not. Such roseate assumptions about British patriotism break down under stress and, for example, when Hugh Gaitskell, in his capacity as Leader of the Opposition, queried the government's actions at the time of Suez – what were highly dishonourable and disreputable transactions – he was dubbed a 'traitor' by hysterical partisans of Eden's policy. (Kyle, 1991:434)

In 1991 at the time of the Gulf War, in which about 20,000 British servicemen took part, the tabloid press went in for an excess of vulgar flag-waving. The *Sun* offered five million free Union Jack stickers: 'Attention! It's Sun Flag Day, folks, so today's the day to show your colours for Our Heroes in the Gulf.' And Professor Norman Stone wrote an article for the same paper, whose jingoism could only be described as excessive as well as vulgar, in which he produced such witchhunting passages as the following: 'I have even confronted a gaggle of young Left-wing teachers at Ruskin College, Oxford, who told me that ours was a divided and racist society. People like them are all around – in the social services, in town halls. Anti-patriotism is their creed.' (7.2.91) Had the war gone on for any length of time, possibly Professor Stone would have headed McCarthyite witchhunts for the unpatriotic!

Once the Gulf War was over there were arguments about whether there should be a victory celebration, and another British newspaper, the *Standard*, tackled the subject of patriotism in a somewhat different fashion from the *Sun* by praising the British at the expense of the Americans, which is always a popular approach. The opening of a leading article on 10 April 1991 ran as follows: 'The soldiers, sailors and airmen who fought so gallantly and so successfully to liberate Kuwait deserve the highest praise. The British forces, in particular, handled themselves with a quiet, steady professionalism which might, perhaps, be emulated by the brasher Americans.'

The 1980s, the Thatcher decade, certainly produced their share of brainwashing, not least about the 'iron lady' herself. Under her leadership class polarisation, often in the form of a gulf between the 'haves' and 'have-nots', became an all too frequent feature of British life and one of the curious by-products of her strong leadership was admiration for strength as opposed to achievement: 'It was evident that she was indeed a singular politician and many now began to admire her merely for her resolution – no matter what she was being resolute about.' (K. Harris, 1988:118) By the time of the 1987 election, so apparently strong had her grip upon the country become, it was possible for Ken Livingstone to argue in all seriousness that, had Labour won, there would have followed: 'Resistance . . . by the Civil Service and mendacious judges, and obstruction by Reagan and the Common Market. And the Press would go berserk.' (Coleman, 1987:108) Whether those results would have followed an electoral defeat for Thatcher is beside the point; the fact is that her success in office had persuaded many people that such would be the case and, at one level, that is what brainwashing is all about.

Another area that merits particular attention is that of genetic engineering with its many ramifications, for here we are far closer to the Huxleyan and Orwellian worlds of fiction, while some of the implications for the future are truly frightening. At its most simple, elementary-level genetic engineering begins with birth control, and it is notable that in almost all discussions of world programmes of birth control it is always the Third World that must do the controlling so that there are less of *them* to threaten *us*! We have already entered the age of test-tube babies and heart transplants, and in theory almost anything else can be transplanted, so that at last Frankenstein is becoming a potential reality. In *The Biological Time Bomb* Gordon Taylor examines the possibility of body spare parts. He cites a *Times* report (back in the 1960s) of thugs in Syria killing travellers for spare parts. And gruesome as that may sound, by 1990 a scandal broke in Britain with the story of Turkish peasants being lured to London by promises of money to donate one of their kidneys to Harley Street clinics. Taylor also considers the possibility of people who have been injured beyond repair none the less being kept alive on life-support machines until one of their vital organs – a kidney for example – is required, when it would be taken for a client-patient and the damaged subject would then be allowed to die. (1968:72) In May 1966 a unanimous decision of the French National Academy of Medicine stated that a man whose heart was still beating could be ruled to be dead. The consequences of such a decision are far-reaching. In any case, in an age when hospital and medical care have become an ever greater call upon national resources, whole categories of people are liable to be excluded from resuscitation treatment (the old, the insane, the mentally or physically handicapped, for example), and although at first this may be done solely for reasons of limited resources it may well develop into real genetic engineering, for the very act of choosing which groups are to be passed over is an act of engineering and can be seen as the beginning of the planned survival only of the fittest. As another would-be genetic engineer has argued: 'Society has needs at all levels of ability, and all are equally worthy, but in a progressive society the birth-rate obviously needs to be encouraged in a way to produce adjustment rather than dislocation between occupations and the necessary talents for occupations.' (Cattell, 1965:41) The chilling use of the word 'progressive' in this passage is more than just suggestive of what scientists might soon get up to. A science-fiction story by John Gunn, *The Immortals*, has as its theme the old and the rich keeping themselves alive indefinitely by renewing body parts from the young and healthy, who are hunted for this purpose and deemed expendable. The story was published in 1962; its theme is hardly fantastic any more.

In *The Biological Time Bomb* Taylor raises the political issue of such genetic engineering when he poses the question as to which nation would be most likely seriously to embark upon such practices.

> But, as with many other biological developments . . . the decision may not lie with the west. If an oriental despot should decide that he could produce more rugged soldiers, more brilliant scientists, more skilful workmen or more fertile women by such techniques, he might pour the necessary resources into making them practicable, and then impose them. The problem which would face the western civilizations would then be whether to compete or perhaps face extinction – culturally if not militarily. (1968:26)

The above passage is a splendid example of loaded language (oriental despots), they do it, we don't, and presenting the West with a one-way choice – to compete or face extinction. Interestingly, to date, most breakthroughs in genetic engineering, beginning with experiments in Hitler's Germany, have been achieved in Western nations rather than under oriental despots.

The logic of genetic engineering is the creation of a super race, as Hitler and his scientists accepted automatically. After a discussion of how to weed out weak varieties of wheat, Gordon Taylor continues:

> In the case of men, of course, one cannot afford to throw away the unsuccessful variants. And methods of identifying specific defects, such as those already discussed, cannot be applied to the kind of sensual characteristics, such as intelligence or even disease resistance, which manifest only in the adult organism: but it is precisely these which most interest us in the human case. (165)

The author does not tell us why such weeding out cannot be applied to human beings, and the number of times those who discuss genetic engineering insist that of course it will not be applied to human beings must make anyone with moderately critical faculties become intensely suspicious. Why are scientists interested in the subject except in terms of how they can alter human beings? The denials, along with the increasing volume of information and experiments, are simply part of the process which is required to prepare us for eventual manipulation. The validity of such suspicions was borne out in 1991 when it was announced that safeguards on medical experiments involving human volunteers were to be strengthened. Under new requirements, ethics committees will have to publish annual reports and explanations for rejecting research applications, although these are not legally enforceable. At least the government recognised that there is a growing problem to be faced. (*Independent*, 20.8.91) The announcement in May 1991 that mice embryos can now be made to change sex merely went to reinforce the advances that are constantly being made in genetic engineering: after mice, men?

A quite different aspect of the subject concerns the use of DNA profiles by the police. In 1989 it was suggested that the Home Office might create a national register of the DNA profiles of convicted criminals to be operated along similar lines to fingerprint archives, and this raised a whole new series of possibilities; any such 'bank' of DNA samples collected by the police would, according to *Liberty*, ignore legal safeguards and pose a threat to civil liberties. In a letter to Kenneth Baker, the Home Secretary, John Wadham, *Liberty*'s legal officer, claimed that:

> Home Office discussions with the police on the establishment of a national DNA index were taking place without public or parliamentary debate; DNA data was already being collected by police without people's knowledge or consent; there were no safeguards or statutory controls and no details were being given to the public on how the information from DNA profiles would be used. (*Independent*, 18.8.91)

It sounded all too familiar: the state once more amassing information about its citizens for its use without their consent. Shortly after these revelations it became known that the Home Office was planning to identify children as young as five or six as potential criminals: the object was to identify children whose genetic background made it likely they would drift into crime. The implications go far beyond that limited aim. (*Independent*, 16.9.91) However (and as usual the cynics would argue) the government did not wish to allow the positive use of DNA where immigrants are concerned: thus, where DNA tests are a sure way of proving a family relationship and could therefore be used to allow relatives of immigrants already in Britain to come and join them, the government opposed using the test as a clinching argument. (*Independent*, 28.1.89) Advances in genetic engineering are now so rapid that they place a range of new weapons in the hands of government and there is an overwhelming need to regulate scientists and still more, perhaps, responsible government departments. The need to take decisions in these matters is far more likely to be transferred or fudged, so that no one will actually assume responsibility for regulating the scientists or the Home Office or anyone else until we find that genetic engineering has made such strides that it is difficult if not impossible any longer to control it. The British have always been good at what might be termed the art of transference: somehow no one is to blame and therefore nothing can be done. There exists the very real danger that a complaisant government will allow such practices to take hold until they have become one more aspect of control in what already is a highly manipulated society.

Part Two
Where Manipulation Takes Place

5 Institutions

However, the Establishment in England has a knack
of looking after its own.

C. P. SNOW

A LL OUR MAIN INSTITUTIONS use brainwashing as a matter of course:
the Church with repetition, the army with drill and regimental
loyalty, the law with ceremonial mysticism, the BBC with its
careful use of accents, the press with its insistence upon
'freedom'. Necessary brainwashing may be seen as those processes of
manipulation and training attached to the main institutions of our
national life and extending to politics and the Civil Service. The impact
of brainwashing often long outlasts belief in the original institution.
Thus, many who claim to be Christians would not wish to examine
too closely the basis of their faith for fear they would discover how
meaningless it is. What they want is a faith undisturbed by doubts to
provide a cloak of comfort through life. We need to distinguish
between functional brainwashing, which is concerned with the acceptance of society's institutions, as opposed to brainwashing designed to
manipulate individuals or groups so as to make them the instruments
of others – if, in fact, such a distinction is ever possible. The process
will not be easy. As Lord Radcliffe said in the 1950s, at a time when
authority was less questioned than it would be later: 'The British have
formed the habit of praising their institutions which are sometimes
inept, and of ignoring the character of their race, which is often superb.
In the end they will be in danger of losing their character and being
left with their institutions: a result disastrous indeed.' (1952)

Of course, attitudes to institutions change. There was a time, for
example, when the BBC was simply there, one of those institutions
like the monarchy which were expected to go on for ever. Its
pre-eminence after World War II, when it pursued its magisterial way
as an arbiter of national standards, should have alerted its hierarchy
to the likelihood of challenge. Questioning of institutions does take
place periodically, even if challenges to one set of institutions which
result in changes normally lead only to their replacement with another

set of institutions so that the process begins all over again. Willie Hamilton writes: 'Already by the 1960s there was evidence, especially among the young, of an intensified questioning of existing institutions. The Church was becoming an irrelevance. The House of Lords was something to be laughed at: a political geriatric unit. Parliamentary democracy at large has come to be regarded with a good deal of scepticism and cynicism.' (1975:9) Hamilton was not alone in seeing institutions in trouble at this time. Another observer claimed: 'Great institutions are usually either broken up and reshaped by revolutionary force or they survive as curious, empty shells on the shore of time.' (Davis, 1967:190) A constant of British public life is the obeisance paid to democracy and freedom, yet it is instructive that in matters of justice and law and order the police are answerable to the law of the land, the military to the Crown, military intelligence to the MOD, MI5 to the Home Secretary and MI6 to the Foreign and Commonwealth Office. In other words, none is directly answerable to a democratic institution. (Bunyan, 1976:3)

As the political parties held their 1991 annual conferences in the last series before a general election there were real signs that Britain might face major constitutional changes during the decade. 'British institutions, however much they try to adapt, carry the imprint, seemingly forever, of the genetic code from the era in which they were conceived. It is part of the glory of being a settled, stable society.' (*Independent*, 11.3.91) Leaving aside 'the glory of being a settled, stable society', there were growing questions about the role and future of the monarchy and still more about the constitution and parliamentary system, so that it was just possible Britain faced one of those periodic times of upheaval that have altered her political and social priorities and direction. Certainly the old left/right antagonisms embodied in the concept of capital versus labour seemed dead. The question is: what would replace them?

A conundrum for any society is the question: how much does achievement in any sphere depend upon access to the principal institutions and how much are individuals able to progress on the outside? As Mills writes: 'Celebrity is not inherent in any personality. To be celebrated, to be wealthy, to have power requires access to major institutions, for the institutional positions men occupy determine in larger part their chances to have and to hold these valued experiences.' (1958:11)

Ritual is the necessary companion of institutions and we seem to require ritual in our lives as we do food. The BBC in its heyday created an astonishing paraphernalia of ritual for the solemn celebration of public occasions: 'a monarch has a birthday, the national anthem is played before the news; one monarch dies, the loudspeakers go silent; another monarch dies, solemn music.' (Thomas, 1962:175) This kind of overt public obeisance to royalty which was in place after 1945 has now passed but, as Tony Benn points out, 'State occasions are always interesting because it is then that Britain presents itself in the way that the establishment thinks is proper. Discipline, authority and order are all part of the ritual.' (1990:529) And the importance of ritual may best be illustrated when it does change. Leo Abse describes how a country vicar complains of modern death services: 'For pervading the service was a relentless forced cheerfulness. They even wore white stoles instead of the customary purple or black ... To pretend there is no sadness and sorrow – to behave in fact as if there is no death – is to abuse the psychology of the funeral service which exists to bear our grief.' (1989:78) And yet, the more that things change so the more they remain the same, and under ten years of Thatcher Britain experienced a curious reversal, with Labour defending such institutions as the Crown and Thatcher attacking them. Some institutions have become so embedded in our public life that only major institutional reform which alters the framework rather then merely tinkering will be needed if the deadening effect of their outworn practices is to be removed from public life, and yet the problem remains: will the new simply – and at speed – create its own rituals and resume brainwashing the public into acceptance where the old left off?

As the British public edges towards a fairer electoral system – some form of proportional representation – and a Bill of Rights, so growing scrutiny of the parliamentary system shows just how much of a sham parts of it have become. Writing nearly a quarter of a century ago Humphry Berkeley said: 'Parliament, which knows much less than the meanest member of the Cabinet, becomes a backwater, incapable of creating anything more than a brief eddy.' And continuing his examination of Parliament he tackles the myth that the House of Lords has become more progressive: 'The second [myth] is that the institution of life peerages has transformed what would otherwise be a reactionary and even bloodthirsty chamber of hereditary backwoodsmen into an enlightened and progressive chamber.' (1968:62, 109)

Control of institutions by the Establishment (or new establishments which arise as new institutions are created) is an abiding theme of

British public life. In *The System* Max Nicholson goes back to the new Civil Service created in Victorian times by Trevelyan, which found no university candidate able to qualify. 'This lack however was soon made good, and before long the system was proving as useful a "fresh avenue of employment" to the right products of the right schools and universities as it previously had been to the right protégés of the right noble patrons.' And so we entered the new era of Oxbridge men without professional qualifications but steeped in classical learning and the concept of the good all-rounder so beloved of the Civil Service was born. Nicholson continues: 'This archaic non-profession, constituted on mistaken lines to fulfil a role which has long since ceased to exist, needs to be promptly and completely replaced by something reasonably related to the world in which Britain now has to function, and to the kind of people that the British are.' (1967:58, 205) Nothing of the kind has happened. In 1965 the Secretary of the National Whitley Council Staff Side of the Civil Service reported, unsurprisingly for the representative of such a body under pressure for change: 'We should do roughly what we are doing today but we must be ready to take people from elsewhere and create opportunities for advancement in the Service. Broadly, however, we are not far off the mark at the present stage.' Such smugness is hard to beat. The fact is that no system willingly embarks upon a series of major changes, for these almost always spell the end of the comfortable existence which its members enjoy. Changes have to be forced from outside. Returning to Humphry Berkeley: 'Written questions are an even less satisfactory method of eliciting information from Ministers, when it is borne in mind that the answers are prepared by Civil Servants who have a vested interest in protecting their Minister or concealing their own mistakes and failures.' (1968:93)

Civil servants on civil servants and their system provide an amusing if, in the end, depressing picture of how the system is always manipulated for the advantage of the status quo. Antony Part, in *The Making of a Mandarin*, writes:

> In the 1930s the administrative class, 2,000 strong, was regarded as a profession and was held in high esteem as a challenging and worthwhile career, particularly at Oxford and Cambridge, which in those days supplied most of the new entrants. This was an unfortunate narrowing of opportunity which has now been largely remedied. (1990:20)

Part continues his assessment of the Civil Service with what might be a definitive description of all that is wrong with it:

But I think it fundamentally important that the Civil Service should remain a 'service'. It is the consciousness of this that binds the whole show together, necessarily not quite to the same extent as in the armed services, but in very much the same way. (190)

A very different civil servant, Clive Ponting, whom the system sacked, writes in another vein altogether (after 'Oilgate' – the revelations about how BP and Shell supplied the illegal Smith regime in Rhodesia with oil through the UDI years): 'Government is not about truth and it is in very short supply in Whitehall. By stretching words as far as they can go and putting great importance on every nuance, the Civil Service is able to "draft round" a political problem for Ministers.' (1986:27) The Civil Service, Ponting tells us, obeys rules of behaviour as though in a club, and the Code of Conduct of the Civil Service states: 'although the rules of conduct for the Civil Service are largely unwritten they are nevertheless well known.' And many of these impartial mandarins go on in retirement to top jobs in industry where their accumulated knowledge in government can be of further service. Following the case in which Ponting came to national prominence (for passing on information to Labour MP Tam Dalyell about the cover-up concerning the sinking of the *Belgrano*) and lost his job, the Head of the Civil Service, Sir Robert Armstrong, issued guidance for civil servants if they found themselves asked to do things they thought to be wrong. They should talk to their Permanent Secretaries and 'transfer the burden of conscience' – or in other words be loyal to the Minister at all times and say nothing. Such advice must call to mind the colourless civil-servant figure of Adolf Eichmann.

As Tony Benn claims: 'The civil servants want to move slowly along the escalator towards their knighthood and retirement and they have no interest whatsoever in trying to develop new lines of activity.' (1988:209) Benn complained how a minister is really not in charge and how 'the department would much prefer to work without me altogether.' At least Michael Heseltine has a more refreshing approach to the Civil Service than its assorted mandarins: 'I believe that our aim must be to seek wherever possible to make the culture of the Civil Service less easily distinguishable from that of private industry and commerce. Whitehall should become a world where promotion rests entirely on merit and not on seniority; where the ablest travel fastest; where the failures are retired.' (1987:54–5)

The myth that civil servants are impartial is just that: a myth. They are conservative – with a small 'c' but often a capital 'C' as well. Antony Part, who was Benn's Permanent Secretary at Trade and Industry during the second Wilson administration (1974–6), attempts to explain in his book *The Making of a Mandarin* what most observers would suggest was his far from impartial behaviour in that position. Having made the point that Benn was isolated in Wilson's Cabinet he says: 'But he did not resign, and the Prime Minister did not ask him to do so. In such a situation a Permanent Secretary is liable to be faced with a dilemma. To whom does his loyalty lie – his Secretary of State or the Prime Minister?' This is typical Civil Service disingenuousness; since his Secretary of State was still *in situ* and the Prime Minister had not asked him to resign, there could be only one possible answer to his self-questioning. Having added that it seemed important to him not to 'sneak' to colleagues outside the department (about confidences from Benn) – his colleagues, he tells us, 'were helpfully understanding about this' – he concludes this poisonous section of self-exculpation as follows: 'Mr Benn . . . has said publicly on one occasion I rang the editor of a national newspaper to be disloyal to him, but he never produced evidence to support his hostile assertion. Wherever the truth lies, my relationship with him was brought to an end . . .' It takes no genius to read between those lines and accept that what Mr Benn had said must have been the truth. (1990:173, 175)

A Fabian Society pamphlet entitled *Labour and Whitehall*, published in September 1991, suggests that a Labour government could counter Whitewall obstruction by removing security of tenure from top civil servants (something that should have been done a long time ago). The pamphlet advances a number of suggestions for Whitehall reforms to counter the difficulty that Labour governments have always complained about – of getting their policy changes through the system. Professor Christopher Hood, one of the contributors, argues: 'If one really wants to make progress in changing the social, ethnic and gender mix among the "top chaps", lateral entry [to the Civil Service] may be the only way to do it.'

As Peter Hennessy points out (*Independent*, 6.1.91) the system of Civil Service recruitment today is essentially the same as that introduced by Trevelyan more than a century ago. 'Whitehall continues to pick its top people 30 years ahead. Unless the practice changes, the Cabinet Secretary and the Permanent Secretary to the Treasury of the 2020s are already in the hierarchy today. This is crazy.' (1991) Only during the emergency of World War II did the Civil Service bring outsiders into its ranks and, as a consequence, performed as never before or since. It is time it returned to that wartime practice.

Bland assumptions of superiority are as much a part of the system as more concrete manifestations of activity. Sir William Hayter, who was a top Foreign Office mandarin and ambassador, had his elegant little book *The Diplomacy of the Great Powers* published in 1960; in this he makes comparisons primarily between Britain, France, the USA and the USSR. It is an engaging exercise indulged in at a time when British power was obviously in steep decline and even if it was written with tongue in cheek (which seems not to have been the case) its assumptions about British superiority sit ill against a performance that did not match the claims. Of the USA he says: 'The American's distrust of foreigners is compounded of a suspicion that they are inevitably after his dollar and a fear that they may be smart enough to get it.' (14) His compliments are backhanded, as when he discusses the greater importance the French attach to cultural matters than the British: 'The French sense of proportion is here, unusually perhaps, sounder than the British. Countries without great economic power but with a great cultural wealth should regard the projection of their culture as a political operation of the first order and should entrust it to high-powered and competent persons. France does.' (40) After more analysis along these lines Sir William reaches his inevitable conclusion, having first paid a few pages of attention to the diplomatic perfor-mance of lesser powers: 'However, all I am claiming for British diplomacy is that it is better than American, Soviet or French.' (42) It is certainly a bravura performance.

If one reads the autobiographies of politicians or other public figures, there is a monotonous regularity about their backgrounds: Eton and the Guards, Harrow and Cambridge and pseudo-deprecatory references to the formative influence such institutions had upon their characters. It is at least refreshing that the last three Conservative Prime Ministers came from no such background, although Lord Whitelaw is reputed to have referred to John Major as the sort of chap who would comb his hair in public. Speaking of this Oxbridge kind of background Antony Part with unconscious irony remarks of his time at Cambridge: 'Books which have given the impression that the communist element was large in Cambridge and Trinity do not paint a true picture.' (1990:15)

One of the most biting comments upon the Establishment comes from Max Nicholson, who says that the system which they control 'is held together and driven by a triple fear – fear of facing new facts, fear of facing the people and fear of facing the future.' (1967:494) This may be true, but the British Establishment has also long been expert in accepting and absorbing criticism and protest, perhaps especially in the form of lampoons upon itself. When at the beginning of the 1960s *The Establishment* featured as a night-club act, the leading members of the hierarchy at once patronised it to laugh at themselves. A readiness to acknowledge what is happening is a sound way of ensuring that it continues to happen. But readiness to accept criticism appears to have been matched by a growing carapace of indifference so that unawareness of being brainwashed by their own cleverness has bcome possibly the terminal flaw of the present members of this élite. The Establishment – the 'great and the good' – will go to almost any length to keep itself in power. In a BBC-organised debate at Warwick University, Richard Crossman said: 'My main central belief is that the Establishment when tested will be found wanting – that on any issue where the Establishment says "I know", I instinctively wonder if they do, and nearly always I'm right.' (Howard, 1990:284–5)

But as C. P. Snow remarked, 'the Establishment in England has a knack of looking after its own' (he was describing how Tizard – out of a job in 1942 because of his rivalry with Churchill's mentor Lindemann – was elected to the presidency of Magdalen College, Oxford) and he put his finger on a key aspect of the Establishment which, essentially, is a system organised to ensure jobs for the right people. (1960:51) However, it is the unctuous rituals of the Establishment that have become such an ingrained cement of British public life. As Benn describes the memorial service for Tony Crossland at Westminster Abbey: 'It was the establishment recognizing and at the same time burying the idea of social democracy. First of all we had the Dean saying a few words about Tony's incisive and lively mind, about his passion for a just and equal society, his unfaltering desire to raise up the under-privileged and to care for the less fortunate. Then we had the national anthem . . .' But as Benn also points out, in relation to another Establishment service, this time at St Paul's for the 1977 Jubilee celebrations: 'We haven't removed the grip of this crowd from British society, far from it, but on the other hand the public accepts it all and the press plays it up to divert people from unemployment and the cost of living and the EEC and so on. It is a very important ingredient in British life and it has to be thought about.' (1990:57, 161) Willing victims!

The Establishment of the day, however constituted, works to preserve the status quo from which it benefits, and so by definition is against change or progress, and the more successful it is the more retrogressive it must become. Few Establishment stories have been more disgraceful than the prolonged cover-up on behalf of the traitor Sir Anthony Blunt, the fourth man in the Burgess and MacLean affair: 'The Establishment was desperate that the truth about Blunt should never be known: it showed that they were prepared to protect one of their own. All those who should have known were aware of Blunt's treachery but they allowed him to continue as a prestigious art historian and Surveyor of the Queen's Pictures solely because he was "one of us".' (*Evening Standard*, 26.4.91) The Establishment, indeed, will go to great lengths to prevent itself being shown up in a bad light.

One of the worst results of Establishment arrogance about its place in British society comes out in the way top people award themselves huge salary increases at times when the country at large is being told to tighten its belt and work harder. This became so insistent a part of British public life during the Thatcher years as to indicate an almost total contempt on the part of those possessing power and position in relation to everyone else. It was as though they could not see what impact their actions had or, if they did see, felt it did not matter, so secure were they in their sense of untouchability. The insensitivity of the Governor of the Bank of England, Robin Leigh-Pemberton, who in any case is a very rich man, in accepting a 17 per cent pay increase in May 1991, at a time when he was preaching that pay settlements should not exceed the rate of inflation, demonstrated just how arrogant and self-assured in their apartness such people believe themselves to be. Hopefully, however, such bland indifference to the feelings of those who do not belong to the magic circle in which the Governor and others like him move, presages an early downfall of such a system, although such a hope is almost certainly a pipe dream.

Such an Establishment, of course, requires some form of opposition, since attacks upon it can be used to rally a quiescent majority into supporting the system which otherwise is at risk. Much modern protest, often apparently mindless, is in part an inarticulate reaction to manipulation by the Establishment. Margaret Thatcher, abrasive and uncaring though she may have been, was in her way a radical, especially where the Establishment was concerned, which is why she was so hated in its circles. Although there were other causes, the massive 'no' vote by the Oxford dons (738 to 319) against giving the Prime Minister an honorary degree in 1984 was in part an Establishment revenge upon a woman so contemptuous of its ways. She had, after all, treated with suspicion if not worse the Church of England, the universities, the BBC, the Civil Service. As Antony Part says: 'The definition of private enterprise coupled with denigration – or an approval of denigration – of the Civil Service has had the effect of making it more acceptable for civil servants, not only in mid-career but on retirement, to move out into the private sector.' (1990:183) Which is one way of excusing civil servants from following their supposed role as impartial public servants and allowing that they should be place seekers like everyone else. And, Part added, 'She [Thatcher] was determined that anyone who filled a top post should be "one of us".' Thus one kind of Establishment figure has to be replaced by another. The Thatcher assault upon bastions of the Establishment included reducing the Civil Service to its smallest numbers since World War II.

As Clive Ponting has remarked (see page 63), truth is in short supply in Whitehall. In the most celebrated British scandal since 1945, 'Jack' Profumo, the Minister for War in the Macmillan government, admitted lying to the House of Commons over the Christine Keeler affair and so brought his political career to an end. On the other hand, Selwyn Lloyd, the Foreign Secretary at the time of Suez, lied to the House about collusion with Israel but was subsequently elected Speaker of the House of Commons. (Kyle, 1991) One can only suppose that – to paraphrase the late Professor C. E. M. Joad – it all depends who is lying and upon what topic.

Patronage and honours are vital weapons in the Establishment's armoury. The Labour Party, which periodically fulminates against the privilege or other class anomalies of the House of Lords, would not be without it for worlds, for where and how on earth would the party otherwise reward its faithful hacks? Honours are a principal weapon of both the Prime Minister of the day and more generally the Establishment as a whole, and although Harold Wilson briefly did away with honours they soon came back, for British society would be lost without them. Anthony Sampson, in his analysis of honours, *The Anatomy of Britain*, pointed to the absurdity of endless letters after the names of British representatives abroad and said however much people pretended to laugh at the system, almost everyone accepted honours when these were offered. One of the few impressive honours, he suggested, was the Order of Merit or OM, 'though in 1961 the fondness of the octogenarian OMs Lord Russell and the late Augustus John for demonstrating in Trafalgar Square caused some pain to the others.' (1962:292–3) Civil Service mandarins take the honours system seriously, as twice a year their members who have reached a certain stage in their careers receive their appointed rewards. There is, or there ought to be, something ludicrous in the thought of the main Honours Committee, which is chaired by the Secretary to the Cabinet and has in attendance the Prime Minister's Private Secretary and the Private Secretary to the Queen. Much of the present honours system, ironically, originated in the heyday of Empire, in which reward was not financial but an honour, and the Order of the British Empire which was inaugurated in World War I was still going strong in 1991. By 1918 a Byzantine system of honours, mainly concerned with positions and achievements in the imperial hierarchy, had been developed, with knighthoods for governors and various other lesser honours down the line. Thus the Order of St Michael and St George (which had originally been created in 1818 to reward Maltese and Greeks who had helped the British in the Napoleonic Wars) became the 'gong' for Africa. (Lewis and Foy, 1971:141) But as Ronald Segal asked in *The Race War*, why was Sir Cyril Osborne MP knighted in 1961 at the height of the race-immigration debate that he had done so much to stir up? (1966:284) The gradations of the system are pure class snobbery. Thus colonels become Ordinary Commanders (Military Division) of the Order of the British Empire (CBE), lieutenant-colonels are awarded the OBE, while the British Empire Medal (BEM) is reserved for ordinary members of the public (no rank) or 'other ranks' in the services. An examination of the *London Gazette* or the display of the honours list as it appears twice yearly in the quality newspapers provides the hierarchical structure of awards so that one knows what kind of people in what sort of jobs will appear under each division – KBE, CBE or simple BEM and so on. Yet, absurd though the system undoubtedly is, twice a year a large number of people wait in trepidation to see whether they have achieved the reward suitable to their time and position in life, a reward which binds them to the system. The farcical nature of awarding an honour to anyone who passes a certain career point has long been commented upon but comments, even ribaldry, have not brought the custom to an end.

Honours grow in numbers and absurdity as the system they serve declines. 'The need to impress the natives with stars, uniforms and ribbons, it has been noted, rose just as the natives had begun to lose their astonishment at British technology.' (Lewis and Foy, 1971:141) Much was made of Harold Wilson's resignation honours list (as also of Margaret Thatcher's), yet there was a sort of rough justice in both lists: if you are going to maintain an absurd practice then do so in an absurd fashion.

> In his resignation honours list, allegedly drawn up in purple ink by Marcia Falkender (who was herself created a Peeress in the same list), he included names like Joseph Kagan, a rich Jewish industrialist of Lithuanian origin, who was given a Peerage and later a prison sentence for fraud; and Sir Eric Miller, who shortly afterwards on the Jewish Day of Atonement was found shot dead in the garden of his Hampstead mansion under highly suspicious circumstances. (Sutherland, 1988:229)

The author of this passage refers to Wilson's 'notorious' honours list, but apart from the overt racism of his remarks about the Jewish recipients of honours, surely what was 'notorious' about the list was the fact that its recipients did not come from recognised Establishment circles. Roger Bolton, in *Death on the Rock* (1990:115), makes the point that endless honours flow from the government to media personalities presumably to keep them on the right side, while Hugo Young recounts that when a minister told Thatcher how 'pro' the press were she was unsurprised: 'That's because I've been so kind to them.' She had given knighthoods to the editors of the *Sun*, *Sunday Express* and *Daily Mail*. (1989:510) Perhaps Lloyd George had the right idea after all when he sold honours; by 1919 the going rate for a peerage was £100,000. Alternatively, those who are punished by not receiving the honour that as a rule would be automatic to their service or position – Julian Critchley was an obvious omission as a notable Tory backbencher during the Thatcher years – should be elected to a special anti-honours division of their own, for they must have done something worthwhile to merit being passed over in such a fashion. At least there was a refreshing flavour to the story that John Major had determined not to award honours to some two dozen heads of privatised companies while he is in office because of the excessive pay increases they had awarded themselves.

There was a time, now in the distant past, when public figures who committed a crime (whether criminal or social) were, to use the words of the late Marquess of Salisbury, 'hounded from public life forever'. But alas, not any more, and nowadays there is not even a pretence that such things matter: not, at least, if you have money and power. With photographs in the press of the freshly released (from prison) Gerald Ronson shaking hands with the Queen Mother, all pretence that a crime had disgrace or that an honour had honour attached to it passed from the Establishment scene, it would seem, for ever.

6 Monarchy, Army, Church

All evidence goes to show that there can be no
new Protestant Revival while the policy continues of
appealing mainly to adult intelligence and reason
and until Church leaders consent to take more
advantage of the normal person's emotional
mechanism for disrupting old behaviour patterns
and implanting new.

WILLIAM SARGANT

I N EDWARDIAN DAYS and, indeed, until much later in the century, a
glimpse of the monarch was enough for most people and more in
any case than the great majority could expect – an occasion to be
treasured. By 1983, however, the Queen threatened to sue the *Sun*,
for by then a mixture of familiarity and vulgarity had brought the
monarchy and the people much closer to each other, destroying a great
deal of the magic and mystique in the process. And it is magic and
mystique which have formed such important ingredients of the royal
show that Stafford Cripps described as 'all bunk and bunting'.
Remoteness can be an excellent tool but it is not possible in the
television age. Willie Hamilton, the engaging Labour MP whose
republican instincts have made him a persistent critic of the entire
paraphernalia of the monarchy once addressed an open letter to the
Queen in which he said:

> You must surely agree that, by birth and upbringing, by the
> surroundings in which you live and the company you keep, you
> cannot possibly understand the feelings and the way of life of
> the millions of ordinary people it is claimed that you keep united
> in one big happy family. It is a claim you have never contra-
> dicted, but in your heart of hearts, deep inside yourself, you
> must know how absurd it is. (1975:1)

In fact, today, none of the media dare leave the royals alone, and if
the tabloids indulge in sleaze the 'heavies' use this as an excuse to
pontificate and then, when the heavies pontificate, the tabloids say
they are just looking at the human-interest story, building another
myth that the royal family are both 'royal' and 'just like us'. We seem

to have lost our sense of humour over the royal family, possibly because of those awful tabloid fellows crawling through bushes in pursuit of photographs.

As Hamilton also says after suggesting that clowns might do just as well: 'The difference is that the British people must also soak up a lifelong brainwashing about the value of the Monarchy – in schools, in the rapidly emptying churches, in a press which is largely and sycophantically pro-monarchist. If we are a conformist, conservative society, it is because life is easier that way.' (16) Richard Crossman said of the monarchy in 1963: 'What gives the British monarchy its unique strength is the fact that the court, the aristocracy and the church – not to mention the middle classes – are just as credulous worshippers of it as the masses.' (Arnold, 1989:133) Most commentators refer to the element of showmanship in the monarchy. As Sampson said: 'In its blend of showmanship, religion, diplomacy and occasional public hysteria, the monarchy remains an important part of the national character.' He pointed out that only in Britain is there still a monarchy on the grand scale 'supported by religious processions, courtiers, and a titled aristocracy.' (1962:33, 220) But the monarchy also has its diplomatic uses and it is not just the British who are brainwashed about it: 'After the Anglo-American alliance had been cracked by Suez in 1956 it was not long before leaders on both sides of the Atlantic saw that a Royal visit to America was needed, so that Royalty could heal the breaches which politicians had made.' (Clark, 1957:57) It is often claimed of the monarchy, as of other British institutions, that it is an anachronism that works; it is assisted unashamedly by the snobberies which surround it. This process is helped by the *bon mots* of Queen Elizabeth the Queen Mother. Following a meeting with ex-President Carter of the USA, she is credited with the remark: 'He is the only man since my dear husband died to have the effrontery to kiss me on the lips.' Over the years the palace PR machinery has become efficient and smooth; its principal task is to ensure that the royal family is portrayed only as it wishes to be portrayed. The Queen's visit to the United States in May 1991, following the Gulf War, was a carefully calculated appeal to the American love of royalty so as to emphasise the 'special relationship'.

The story of the near-bungled royal visit to Nepal in 1961 makes absurd reading, yet the lesson of that story revealed under the 30-year rule is that little seems to change. Preparations for royal visits take place many months in advance and on this occasion we have Nepal's ambassador in London warning the Foreign Office that 'Tuesdays are inauspicious days for travel' (the Queen wished to depart from Nepal on a Tuesday), and a Foreign Office note warning that 'clearly, the mass of the Nepalese public are superstitious and unsophisticated'. Gradually the Foreign Offices of the two powers sorted out the protocol: the Queen would not travel in King Mahendra's plane, which was a Russian Ilyushin 14, and the royal party would not arrive in top hats and tails; a tiger shoot was included on the agenda and so special royal toilets had to be laid on. Then came the problem of writing the Queen's speech well in advance . . .

But although royalists might like to think in terms of divine right or at least behave as though the monarchy will survive for ever – it has a better chance of doing so in Britain than it would have in most other countries – in fact the monarchy with its numerous advisers has to work hard at maintaining its grip on public affection, and it needs public relations experts to ensure, if possible, that only the acceptable face of monarchy is exposed to public view. This is far from easy in an intrusive, television-dominated age, and revelations of the less savoury behaviour of the numerous younger royals is meat and drink to the media and possibly helps to keep the show on the road. The Queen alone would be dreadfully dull. But as Thomas Paine wrote two centuries ago: 'As in my political works, my motive and object have been to give man an elevated sense of his own character, and free him from the slavish and superstitious absurdity of monarchy and hereditary government.' (1936:ix) Clearly Paine wrote in vain.

The pretence is maintained that the Queen is the real ruler of Britain. The forms persist: the state opening of Parliament, the Queen's speech, state occasions, deference – not least by the so-called political left – which combine to perpetuate the myth. The annual *Official Handbook* gives us the official line: 'Elizabeth the Second, by the Grace of God of the United Kingdom of Great Britain and Northern Ireland and of Her other Realms and Territories Queen, Head of the Commonwealth, Defender of the Faith.' As the same handbook tells us, the ceremony of the coronation has remained essentially the same for over a thousand years and 'Ceremonial has always been associated with British kings and queens, and, in spite of the change in the outlook of both the Sovereign and the people, many traditional customs and ceremonies are retained.' (COI, 1988:31, 33–4)

An article which appeared in the *Observer* on 7 January 1990 examined what it called the myths and taboos of the monarchy and, while pointing out the absurdities, none the less in the end came down on the side of survival for the institution, and this, indeed, is a well-used technique employed by the responsible press: impartial critical analysis that, somehow, always ends by saying 'yes'. The article was curiously ambivalent and, for example, pointed out: 'The prerogative of the Crown; the enthronement of "The Crown in Parliament", is the special and particular symbol of our status as subjects instead of citizens. It is a rubbing-in of the fact that we have no rights, properly understood, but rather traditions . . .' Sections of the British Establishment, for example, resent the Queen's concern with the New Commonwealth or Prince Charles constantly worrying in public about such subjects as the ecology, the inner cities or the problems of youth. And it points out the extent to which the monarchy buttresses the British class system: 'Our class system – another source of constant fascination for foreign visitors – is also based rather on the hereditary principle. And, while monarchy is not directly responsible for this delicious if disreputable fact, it is hard to imagine the social pyramid enduring as long as it has without a crown at the apex.' It is indeed, for the whole system of honours and patronage would 'look tawdry and corrupt if it were not sanctified by the mystery of the Crown', which of course is why the Establishment maintains the monarchy. In a form of peroration this article concludes: 'It [the monarchy] is an obstacle to the objective public discussion of our own history. It tribalises politics. It entrenches the absurdity of the hereditary principle.' And then, after pointing out that the kind of degrading and abnegating propaganda applied to the monarchy would arouse contempt if displayed in Zaire or Romania, it concludes, 'It is, in short, neither dignified nor efficient.' One would have thought after such a tirade that there was only one possible conclusion to be reached: to demand an end to the monarchy altogether, but no such suggestion is forthcoming. As usual the real conclusion – unstated – must have been, 'It's odd but it works – to keep the British people in their place.'

The stilted approach to the monarchy continues unabated. Tony Benn records how in 1977, on the occasion of the Queen's Jubilee, the Callaghan government presented her with a coffee-pot: 'The Queen, who can't say good morning without a script, referred to a bit of paper and said, "Prime Minister, thank you very much indeed. I feel sure the coffee-pot will be more useful than a picture".' (1990:185)

The monarchy, in fact, is about wealth and privilege, which is why it is so sedulously cultivated despite its irrelevance to the modern age in which it finds itself. The monarchy and its court following perpetuate some of the worst snobberies and class distinctions of British society, but those with a vested interest in its perpetuation form a major part of the old Establishment where royal patronage and the honours system are interdependent. Times, of course, change and while the mild criticisms of the kind offered in the 1950s by Malcolm Muggeridge or Lord Altrincham met with outrage, and Harold Wilson, the socialist, became Harold Wilson, the royal sycophant ('It's a pitiful story of retreat from red-hot republicanism to unalloyed sycophancy' [Hamilton, 1975:7]) today it is possible for the press to lambast the royal family because to do so falls in with the public mood, or at least a substantial part of it. As a *Standard* editorial pointed out on 1 March 1991:

> There are many obvious reasons for the Royal Family's current unpopularity: the brash behaviour of the Duchess of York, the crankiness of Prince Charles, the embarrassing talentlessness of Prince Edward, and so forth. But in trying to explain why republicanism is sweeping through the land, we must also take into account the excruciating sycophancy of those who defend the Royal Family in print.

What will be interesting is to see how the Establishment copes with current attacks upon the royal family and ensures the survival of the anachronism; their most likely ally, for entirely mundane reasons of survival, will probably be the tourist industry.

It did seem in 1991 that at last the royal family might be made to declare its wealth and pay income tax, for there is no obvious reason why the Queen, the richest woman in the world, should enjoy tax immunity when she is also supported by the Civil List payments voted by Parliament. Arguments and pressures to reveal the royal wealth, and disgruntlement that Prince Edward, for example, should have an annual allowance of £100,000 (Willie Hamilton described him as 'a bloody parasite') at least demonstrated one of those temporary changes of public mood in relation to the monarchy. A solution to the problem of the Queen paying income tax was advanced by the *Independent* and represented a typical Establishment ruse to allow the royal family the best of all worlds. The editorial suggested that a Royal Fund, topped up each year by payments equivalent to the tax bill that would be appropriate, should be established. 'The fund could expect to disburse approaching £40m a year. With such sums at their disposal the administrators would have a significant impact on education, the arts, social policy and scientific and medical research, and in doing so add lustre to the House of Windsor.' (28.6.91) The suggestion amounts to classic fudging so as to perpetuate the system, for why should taxes from the monarchy be given back to the monarchy to dispense as though it is providing largescale charity for the British people, with £40 million a year to hand out in order 'to add lustre to the House of Windsor'? Paying taxes is not a question of adding lustre to anyone's name but, no doubt, that is the kind of solution which may well be adopted. As it happened, the main parties were unmoved by the ten-minute rule Bill of the Liberal Democrat MP, Simon Hughes, in July 1991 to abolish the Queen's exemption from paying taxes.

Prince Charles, the heir to the throne, has caused problems for the system principally because he has failed to fit into a pattern that the public requires of its royals and that the Establishment would prefer. His interest in ideas earned him the astonishing back-handed compliment of the *Sun* in August 1987 when it advised: 'Stop that thinking!' It went on to suggest that the best modern rulers have been dim and, by implication, should remain so (a wish relating to their royalty that could be forthcoming only in Britain). Such strictures illustrate better than almost anything else what should be fed to the British people to keep them happy. Not since Victoria's consort Prince Albert have we had a thinking royal, and Albert, of course, was extremely unpopular. When, during 1991, Prince Charles entered into the educational debate, predictably he provoked widespread reactions including a short letter to the *Independent* from a Mr Poole: 'Perhaps if the Royal family paid income tax and showed sufficient interest in the maintained sector to send its children to state schools, there would be resources available and positive motivation for hard-pressed teachers to instil in their pupils Prince Charles's English?' Mr Poole put his finger on the key to royal pronouncements of that kind: remoteness. (April 1991) And that remoteness from reality was amply demonstrated in May 1991 when Prince Charles visited Prague in Czechoslovakia, where he lectured the Czechs about the danger of losing their souls in a headlong rush into capitalism, had his armoured Bentley driven 800 miles for his use (after condemning cars as polluters) and slept in a separate suite from his wife on the curious grounds that they needed separate bathrooms.

The fact which can only be to the good is that the 1990s opened with some healthy criticism of the royal family – more than it had had to put up with in many years – as the absurdities of all its princelings and their doings, the anguishings of the heir to the throne, and the boring nature of the Queen herself became constants of public or media attention. Royalists were at least able to seize upon the occasion of Queen Elizabeth the Queen Mother's ninetieth birthday as an opportunity for hype (and pretended non-hype) about 'this wonderful woman'. The real question for the 1990s, as far as the monarchy is concerned, will be how the Establishment can rehabilitate the royal family in the affections of the nation so that the system can continue. A rescue operation will certainly be needed, for the brainwashing efforts of generations appear to be wearing thin.

The Army rather than either the Royal Navy (the senior service) or the Royal Air Force is the pre-eminent service in relation to the workings of the Establishment and it was very much in the news during 1991 when the biggest cuts in its size and budget for many years were announced. For the upper crust, the announcement that the Life Guards and the Blues and Royals who make up the Household Cavalry are to merge into a single regiment caused shock in those wealthy circles whose sons habitually join one or other of them. Outrage was to turn into intensive lobbying to save regiments, some fourteen of which were to merge or disappear altogether under the King reforms.

There are two kinds of brainwashing that may be associated with the army. Institutional brainwashing or training associated with drill and duty to Queen and Country, whose most terrible end result in recent British history was the unchallenged acceptance of the slaughter in the trenches during World War I. The other form of brainwashing, part of our present age, concerns capture in war: either, how to break down a captured enemy who has also been indoctrinated; or how soldiers should be trained to resist brainwashing once captured. As Watson pointed out in *War on the Mind*: 'Since the Korean conflict, the military have, however, taken the liberal arts and the social sciences a lot more seriously – or at least have devoted more time to them in training their men.' (1978:299) A great deal of attention has been devoted to psychological operations (Psyops) since 1945 and the idea, prevalent in struggles against people who have been mobilised for guerrilla warfare, of winning the hearts and minds of the population. A more fantastic idea is the possibility of a direct link between the brain and a computer so that it would be possible to think 'fire' or 'a bit left' and such thoughts would be transmitted to a missile. Here is a form of mind control that would make war even more devastating than it is already, but the fact that it is a possibility or at least that it is considered possible demonstrates how those who run armies have always tended to regard soldiers as little more than robots to be controlled and manipulated in battle.

Over the ten years from 1982 to 1991 the British Army (and other services) took part in two small – or not so small – wars: in the Falklands (1982) and the Gulf (1991). They acquitted themselves well on both occasions, but it is ironical that in the first case the Falklands crisis came just in time to prevent the implementation of cuts which otherwise would have made it impossible for the British war fleet actually to have operated in the South Atlantic, while in the second case swingeing cuts in the army were announced shortly afterwards on the grounds that the end of the Cold War made possible a radical reduction of Britain's armed forces. It is also instructive that though these two wars required the rapid dispatch of troops to far corners of the world and no use of nuclear weapons, the cuts, none the less, are to be of the mobile forces rather than the country's nuclear arsenal or means of delivery. While the Minister of Defence, Mr Tom King, is seen as its enemy by the army and anti-traditional in his onslaught on the regiments, he also represents a new tradition which has grown up since 1945: that Britain should remain a nuclear power at all costs so that she keeps her place at what we have been pleased to call the 'top table'.

There is a certain irony in the way *The Sunday Times*, on 29 May 1991, greeted the news that NATO is to have a new Rapid Reaction Corps, led by Britain, which will contribute two of its five divisions (at a time when Britain remained deeply divided about her future role in Europe): 'The proud traditions of the British Forces, in which service to the Crown is an honourable tradition followed by many families of officers and men from generation to generation, now finds expression in a crucial geostrategic structure which will keep the peace in Europe and the West into the next millenium.' The justification for Britain's large military expenditure since 1945 has been the Cold War, but since that has been brought to an end by Gorbachev, what is the continuing justification for one of the largest military expenditures (on a per capita basis) in the world? Critics of the 1991 defence cuts claimed they were 'Treasury led', that is, saving money regardless of military needs, but the services have always represented a powerful vested interest and were set to fight hard to retain as much influence and as large a share of the budget as possible. Long after the disappearance of her world-wide role, with no Empire to defend, Britain still spends 4 per cent of GDP on defence (as opposed to 3.5 per cent for France and 2.9 per cent for Germany, which are both wealthier countries). What is it that Britain has to defend over and above these two European neighbours? The British Navy remains the fourth largest in the world and there is a clear reluctance to cut the services down to a size commensurate with Britain's wealth and real responsibilities. A deep part of the reluctance stems from a lingering desire still to see ourselves as a major power, the special ally of the United States, a role which in real terms disappeared a quarter of a century ago.

The biggest outcry raised by the King cuts came from the army, fourteen of whose regiments are to disappear or merge with others. In fact the regimental system is outmoded and hardly fits with the requirements of modern warfare, but is clung to by the army as though the fighting ability of Britain depends upon it. Neither the Royal Navy nor the Royal Air Force have such a system, nor is it deemed necessary by other major military powers, although the British argue that it is essential to *esprit de corps*. If all regiments were scrapped and a more unified system used instead, Britain would be brought more in line with the Europe to which she still so reluctantly belongs. Instead, fierce arguments to maintain an outmoded system will continue to get in the way of more important arguments about future effective structures. Loyalty is a vital ingredient for any army but there is absolutely no reason why it should not be given to the division or some other larger recipient of it rather than the old regiment. Indeed, through all the British services it is only in a part of the army – the infantry and cavalry (now armoured) regiments – that the system of regiments is seen as essential to military performance. It is tradition that is at stake rather than military efficiency. Despite endless moaning from the traditionalists, Britain is proposing cuts that are less than those being adopted either by the USA or her European allies, most notably France and Germany. As the *Independent* observed of the bitter reactions to the cuts: 'This is atavistic Britain at its worst.' (25.7.91) A cynic might almost think that the British military establishment is sorry to see the end of the Cold War.

A major campaign to persuade the government to rethink the army cuts gathered momentum during September 1991 with senior retired officers coming to the defence of the old system. Campaigners fighting to save famous regiments fell back on the dubious tactic of trying to persuade leading companies to postpone making donations to Tory Party funds as a means of exerting pressure upon the government. In Scotland, where nine regiments are to be reduced to six, campaigners targeted 200 companies; in many cases retired army officers sit on their boards. And, unsurprisingly, the royal family, whose leading members supply so many regimental colonels-in-chief, entered the fray on behalf of one of its most loyal support groups. The Queen, the Prince of Wales and the Duke of York each expressed disapproval of the cuts. Few other subjects, including those of far greater national importance, can muster so many irate petitioners and lobbyists as a bastion of tradition when its very foundations are threatened.

Cuts in the Household Cavalry or the Brigade of Guards threaten something more important than defence: the tourist industry. Although the changing of the guard at Buckingham Palace may be a vital tourist spectacle – tourists bring an estimated £5bn a year to London – it has nothing whatever to do with an efficient fighting army. None the less, as Tom Webb of the London Tourist Board told the *Standard* (16.10.91), at least 20 per cent of 'long haul' tourists visit London for the pageantry: 'The ceremonies in London are unique and people come here specifically to see them.' Major John Savelle, the adjutant quartermaster of the Royal Military School of Music, said: 'It is widely accepted that Britain's military bands are the best in the world. They are Britain's bread and butter. We are very good at putting on a nice uniform and playing an instrument.' That comment, sadly, would seem to represent more of the Establishment view and the apparent need of the British to reassure themselves about their history and ceremonial than arguments about an effective fighting force and what the country can really afford.

As Charles Davis writes in *A Question of Conscience*, 'The modern rebellion against the Church is the determination of men to be themselves.' (1967:197) This may be seen as special pleading, since Davis began as a priest in the Catholic Church but revolted when he wished to marry, yet there is a revolt or perhaps a simple drifting away from an institution which seems less and less relevant to so many people. There is, however, a wide gap between indifference and true intellectual rejection. Thomas Paine was the target of furious invective and hatred from the establishment of his day because he questioned the truth of the Church in a way that those who opposed him found difficult to answer logically.

He [Satan] is then introduced into the Garden of Eden, in the shape of a snake or serpent, and in that shape he enters into familiar conversation with Eve, who is no ways surprised to hear a snake talk; and the issue of this tête-à-tête is that he persuades her to eat an apple – and the eating of that apple damns all mankind. (1937:8)

The Church today seems largely an affair of unbelievers adhering to a form, as opposed to believing a doctrine, and they are loath to admit the inadequacy of the form since it has become a part of their institutional lives. The French philosopher Teilhard de Chardin tries very hard against the evidence. Having first claimed that Christianity has an extraordinary power to attract, he goes on: 'But the fact remains that for some obscure reason something has gone wrong between Man and God *as in these days He is represented to Man.*' (1964:260) Many clerics, desperate to restore a belief, that has probably passed away for ever, come up with statements comparable to de Chardin's, hoping for a return to the comfortable days of belief, or at least routine public acceptance, which many of them took to be the same thing. Bertrand Russell, who was an old-fashioned atheist to the end of his long life, saw the Christian faith as responsible for widespread intolerance, and pinpointed one of the church's principal techniques as its encouragement of fear: 'But I should scorn to shiver with terror at the thought of annihilation. Happiness is none the less true happiness because it must come to an end, nor do thought and love lose their value because they are not everlasting.' (1957:43)

William Temple, Archbishop of York, writing during World War II, put his finger upon both a dilemma of the Church and an outside perception of it when he said: 'It is commonly assumed that Religion is one department of life, like Art or Science, and that it is playing the part of a busybody when it lays down principles for the guidance of other departments, whether Art and Science or Business and Politics.' (1942:7) If people are truly Christian (or any other religion) then of course their faith will be a part of all they do, and the fact that the Archbishop could say that at the height of a grim war signified that the bulk of the people were not Christian believers but only nominal Christians as a result of habit. Since 1945 Britain has become a largely agnostic or at any rate non-religious society but the forms struggle on, although how much this is the result of centuries of brainwashing and how much because people often seem to have an urgent need to believe in something is difficult to determine. In general, however, there is lack of belief. In medieval times people flocked to the churches; today the position has been reversed and the Church has to seek a congregation and in many cases attract people by gimmicks. And ironically, lack of belief – since belief is usually the result of brainwashing anyway – makes manipulation easier, because people have nothing to which they can turn with any certainty. According to Brown (1963:14), 'For centuries of European history "truth" was Catholic truth,' but probably no other church has ever been as successful as the Catholic Church in its techniques of manipulation and brainwashing. Desmond Morris, one assumes with tongue in cheek, tries to explain man's need for religion in biological terms: 'At first sight, it is surprising that religion has been so successful but its extreme potency is simply a measure of the strength of our fundamental biological tendency, inherited directly from our monkey and ape ancestors, to submit ourselves to an all-powerful, dominant member of the group.' (1967:180) One last intellectual stricture upon religion from Bertrand Russell is uncompromising: 'My own view on religion is that of Lucretius. I regard it as a disease born of fear and as a source of untold misery to the human race.' (1957:18)

Between 1979 and 1989 Roman Catholic churches lost 14 per cent of their congregations, Anglican churches lost 9 per cent, the Methodist and Reformed churches lost 11 per cent and 18 per cent respectively. The figures appeared in the English Church Census to which the Archbishop of Canterbury elect, Dr George Carey, wrote a foreword in which he said, 'we are not holding our youngsters in the faith'. The churches have embarked upon a decade of evangelism although it is unlikely to do them much good. According to the research organisation Marc Europe, of 3.7 million adults who went to church (only one in ten of the population of a supposedly Christian country) 1.3 million were Catholic and 1.14 million Anglican. Interestingly, for a Church that has remained or tried to maintain more traditional standards than the Anglicans, Nicholas Coote, assistant secretary of the Bishops Conference of England and Wales, said there was 'not enough flexibility' in Catholic services, which were failing to attract young people. Most churches in England appear to be in long-term decline and, as the new Archbishop of Canterbury inelegantly puts it, they have fewer 'bums on seats', although few clergy appear ready to face the most likely logical explanation for this: that no one any more believes their message. (*Independent*, 5.3.91) In one of those pompous editorials newspapers periodically indulge in when the question of Christianity is discussed, the *Standard* accused the new Archbishop (Dr Carey) of tinkering with the teachings of Christianity and then asked rhetorically: 'Why is the Church of England no longer true to the doctrines, the history, the traditions and the beliefs of Christianity? And why does it stand against the history, the traditions and the beliefs of England herself?' (19.4.91) The answers to the *Standard*'s questions could perhaps be taken in two stages: first, the present generation has simply ceased to believe; and second, arising from the phrasing of the question, this collapse of belief is largely because the indoctrinations of the Church inherent in such phraseology about the traditions and beliefs of England herself imply a process of brainwashing that no longer works. Periodically, as the bulk of the population becomes increasingly indifferent to religion, there are attempts to 'put God back into the schools' as a recent report suggested (*Standard*, 14.6.91) at a time when it has been found that 57 per cent of 18- to 24-year-olds do not know what happens on Good Friday.

A major deception long connived at by Church and State has been the claim that the two are separated and that it is not the business of the Church to involve itself in awkward politics. That is what Archbishop Temple (see page 82) was saying uncomfortably in wartime and what so infuriated Mrs Thatcher and her ministers about Dr Runcie in his day, when he suggested from time to time that the Church should be concerned with the economic and therefore the political state of the British people. As the *Official Handbook* says blandly:

> The Church of England's relationship with the state is one of mutual obligation – privileges accorded to the Church balanced by certain duties which it must fulfill. The Sovereign must always be a member of the Church, and promises to uphold it; Church of England archbishops, bishops and deans are appointed by the Sovereign on the advice of the Prime Minister; all clergy take an oath of allegiance to the Crown. (COI, 1988:205)

This kind of Church–State relationship, of course, becomes most apparent in wartime when, as Mills observes, 'Religious institutions provide chaplains to the armed forces where they are used as a means of increasing the effectiveness of its morale to kill.' (1958:6) And when the government finds itself facing a moral dilemma, as it did in the heyday of the campaign against the bomb, it called in the bishops to its assistance – and they came. Tony Benn describes how he went to Keele to see his son receive his BA: 'We were asked to join in the most revolting prayers: praying to Almighty God to see that a suitable supply of qualified manpower was there to run society.' (1989:52)

Colin Morris, writing towards the end of the 1960s, when much had changed, at least superficially, said how the Church as then constituted was beloved of the Establishment for keeping things as they were. (1969:143) It is in this role, certainly in recent history, that the Church has been seen as a bastion of the status quo: as a pillar of official society the Church may be criticised in the abstract but in concrete terms it usually comes up to scratch on behalf of the State. Thus in May 1940 the Church Assembly held two sessions to discuss the war. 'The first concludes with a declaration that "War is contrary to the mind and spirit of Christ": but at the second meeting the same Churchmen "rejected the pacifist contention that participation in war was necessarily contrary to the will of God".' Just so has the Church behaved through the ages. (Callander, 1961:35) And as an American chaplain described his war service: 'In the Navy I learned it was important to conduct services to emphasize the areas where there was theological agreement and not bring up the theological point anyone could take exception to.' That, perhaps, could be seen as the perfect example of how the Church works for the State in maintaining the status quo. (Whyte, 1956:406) And after generations of such behaviour, no wonder Britain's Prime Minister, Margaret Thatcher, was angry with Archbishop Runcie when, on the occasion of the Falklands thanksgiving service, he said: 'War is a sign of human failure and everything we say and do in this service must be in that context.' It was meant to be a service of triumphalism but it was notable that, with a discretion which did their sense of popular survival credit, no members of the royal family were present.

Institutions have self-perpetuating lives that ignore the signs of decay long after these have become apparent to outsiders. Instead of clerics asking themselves the most obvious question of all – why it is that the faith they teach appears to be treated as redundant by the majority of the population? – they excuse falling attendance in their churches by suggesting instead that they are failing to get the message across properly, with the general implication that if only they could overcome this extraordinary difficulty (which was not a difficulty in past ages) then all would be well. They are, of course, helped in this because the Establishment needs the Church to continue, since it is one of the system's props even if, perhaps, no longer a major one. Unable to find many believers in the years since 1945, the Church has become involved in fashionable causes. Orthodox Christians tend to sneer at the image of a 'swinging church' that came in with so many other changes to a staid Establishment-dominated society during the 1960s, but those who sneer might pause to reflect that if the Church does not swing it might go out of business altogether. The Church has become an irrelevance to the great majority. In his book about Cold War activities, *The Truth Twisters*, Richard Deacon, whose overall standpoint would appear to be on the extreme right, says: 'Christianity has in recent years been repeatedly distorted into a kind of "front organization" for international communism by ministers of various churches in Britain.' (1986:68) That is to stretch rather too many points, though what the Church, or parts of it, certainly did do was speak out about oppression (such as apartheid in South Africa) and that was not regarded with any pleasure by the orthodox Establishment. The sad thing about such speaking out was that the Church was probably less motivated by an automatic sense that it had to denounce evil than by its search for a stand that would appeal to people who otherwise did not take any notice of it.

William Sargant, who is quoted at the head of this chapter, wrote an important book about brainwashing and other techniques for control of the mind, and yet he himself would appear to be peculiarly mesmerised by earlier brainwashing about the Church so that, for example, he comes up with statements that somehow assume that Christianity is different from all other religions. Thus, in one of his more naïve passages, he states: 'The truths of Christianity have nothing to do with the beliefs inspired by the rites of pagan religions or devil-worshippers.' (1957:79) Why ever not, one is tempted to ask. It is time, in fact, to accept that 'We are a secular state, and by pretending otherwise, we are living a lie.' (Wilson, 1991)

John Gummer, Minister of Agriculture and a member of the General Synod of the Church, belongs to its orthodox wing. In January 1991 he welcomed Dr Carey's statement of faith issued the previous December and in a thinly veiled attack upon the outgoing Archbishop of Canterbury, Dr Runcie, said: 'We who uphold the orthodox faith must see to it that 1991 is the year we stopped being picked off one by one by those whose liberal views have so dominated the 80s.' His views would be highly popular with a dwindling segment of the Church. He spoke of the new Archbishop, Dr Carey, as possessing

'conviction religion', presumably in opposition to religion derived
from logic. (*Independent*, 4.1.91)

Few occasions in British life call out more public hypocrisy than
the great festivals of the Church – Easter and Christmas – when the
media produce their sanctimonious editorials about faith and speak
of Britain as a 'Christian' society. It is not and has not been so for a
long time. In an editorial of March 1989 the *Independent* took Dr
Jenkins, the Bishop of Durham, to task and reminded readers that the
Bishop had spoken of the Resurrection as 'a conjuring trick with
bones'. The overall effect of the editorial was that the Bishop was
correct but that such things ought not to be said. (27.3.91) And the
BBC continues to produce endless religious programmes and *Thought
for the Day*, despite the fact that a majority of the population are
agnostic and that probably the most seriously religious people in
Britain are now Muslim.

People may need something to satisfy their spiritual cravings but
not, it would seem, what the old orthodox churches offer. By 1991,
with arguments raging in the Anglican Church about the ordination
of women, tolerance for homosexuals or whether or not baptism
should be denied to children whose parents are not committed
churchgoers, it was plain that the Church had lost its way. Interestingly, the *Standard*, which on the whole is more likely to come to the
assistance of the institutions of Britain than not, had a splendid piece
of anti-Church and anti-royal-family invective published on 15 July,
at the time of the General Synod. The author, Geoffrey Wheatcroft,
attacked those clerics who wanted to exclude from Church services
non-Christians – in this particular case baptism for the children of
non-churchgoers – 'To exclude 97 per cent of the country from the
traditional rites of passage is a form of arrogance.' The phrase 'the
traditional rites of passage' of course is a giveaway. To exclude the
97 per cent is, in fact, exactly what a church that had faith in itself
would do, but since for generations 97 per cent of the country or
thereabouts has not attended church regularly, to do so would be to
wind up the Church. None the less, the author destroys his own case;
or rather, he simply emphasises that we are a nation of non-believers
so what does it matter anyway? As he concludes:

> If the narrow-minded, politically bigoted clergy and bishops
> have their way, the Church of England will fall apart sooner
> than they know. It is time for the rest of us to remind them that

the Church is more than just a dogmatic sect. It belongs to all of us. Given a few more years of the Prince of Wales's politico-metaphysical ruminations, or of Princess Michael's 'books', or of Her Royal Fergieness just being herself, and this country will be a republic. Given a few more years of the Synod and the present bench of bishops, and violent anti-clericalism will sweep the land.

What the author clearly wants is a return to the institutions of a staid Church that does not ask of itself awkward questions, and a well-behaved monarchy without a human face – in fact, the old staples of the Establishment which ensured the survival of the system for such a long time.

Both the great institutions of Monarchy and Church are dangerously close to total irrelevance after being impressed upon the British people for centuries as though they represented absolute values. It is clear they do not do so any more. Once one begins to examine the absurdities of institutions that should only ever be regarded through the rituals of mystical acceptance, then such institutions are in trouble. Perhaps Bertrand Russell may be quoted here, though in fact he was speaking of human beings: 'Nevertheless, even after making allowances . . . I cannot but think that Omnipotence operating through all eternity might have produced something better.' (1957:24)

7 Myths

'What do you think of Western civilization?' asked the
interviewer. 'I didn't know they had any!' replied
Mahatma Gandhi.

ALI MAZRUI

NATIONAL FIXATION POINTS like the two eyes of Harold and Nelson
have great value: at Hastings Harold (gallant but a loser) lost
his eye, his life and the battle for the throne of England; at
the Battle of Copenhagen Nelson 'clapped his glass to his
sightless eye' and did not see the Admiral's signal to fly. He was a
winner. How the British have loved those two eyes over the centuries.
The picture of wicked King John biting his lips in fury at Runnymede
as his barons supposedly deprived him of power in order to provide
ordinary Englishmen with liberties is the basis for more myths than
all the clauses of Magna Carta. George Orwell invoked a different sort
of England to the heroic one of Harold and Nelson: suet puddings
and red pill-boxes, beer and endless foul language (the worst in
Europe), love of flowers and ingenuity in hobbies, while an even more
recent commentator, Tony Marlow MP, said 'Cricket, cathedrals,
"Land of Hope and Glory", an enduring distrust of foreigners ...
classically define the best of England.' (Green, 1990:1)

The post-war period which has seen the decline of Britain as a great
power has been a rich period for myth-making. Thus books such as
Charles Allen's *Raj, A Scrapbook of British India 1877–1947* (1977)
are fun, indulging as they do in a special kind of retrospective nostalgia
– 'we were absurd, perhaps, but it worked! Good old us!' Myths are
facts or half-facts that have been twisted to suit the temper of the times.
How the British have loved to believe that their war effort (1939–45)
was greater than that of any other combatant (it might have been more
sensible had it been less), while the concept of the *Pax Britannica*
created one of the longest-lasting myths of all.

The British have a horror of cleverness and both Churchill and
Macmillan, who had first-class minds, went to great lengths to disguise
the fact under a cloak of mannerisms in order to survive politically.
Anti-intellectual and indifferent to culture, the mix which goes to make

up the British is extraordinary and the ramifications which the pursuit of what makes an Englishman open up to us are legion. Writing in 1991, the Tory MP Bruce Anderson described the Tory Party of John Bull nationalists and economic liberals and went on to say: 'Because of this, English nationalism cannot be exploited by radicals or reactionaries. It is harnessed to conservatism, to buttressing the establishment and the institutions of the state. No one need feel threatened by English nationalism.' (20) In opposition, the Labour Party has constantly threatened to abolish the Lords; in power it has other things to do. Moreover, the Lords are important as a justifying myth, a necessary bogyman for the people's party to rail against.

The British are excellent myth-makers and since the 'permissive' sixties have increasingly persuaded themselves that class is a thing of the past and that deference disappeared as the mid-Atlantic Newspeak replaced the Oxbridge accent. We are, perhaps, especially good at political myths but these, too often, remain myths precisely because we are even better at manipulating. Thus, the idea that 'the will of the people must prevail' is reduced to the simpler proposition that 'the force of the majority of the people must prevail, because if it were challenged, it would prevail.' (Barker, 1958:35) In fact, it is rarely challenged because our political manipulators ensure that endless lip-service to freedom sidetracks more potent challenges to the real possessors of power.

British claims to superiority at psychological warfare, founded upon genuine achievements during World War II, were too readily assumed to be of top quality when the practice had fallen away so that, during the Suez crisis of 1956, for example, the British came a poor second in propaganda to the despised Egyptians. (Kyle, 1991:454) The myth-making business is always intriguing and sometimes unpredictable. Drew Middleton's book *The British* (1957), written by an American Anglophile, might have been made to order and was highly acceptable in the grim year of new political realities which followed Suez. We are tolerant and civilised, we like to think, and yet we reacted to the Ayatollah Khomeini in Iran much as our forbears did to the Turk. Tony Benn, who no doubt will be accused of political trimming, has said: 'I was always against the Common Market but the reality of our isolation is being borne in on me all the time. This country is so decrepit and hidebound that only activities in a wider sphere can help us escape from the myths that surround our politics.' (1987:204)

World War II provided us with a rich treasury of new myths: Dunkirk, standing alone, taking the Blitz with stiff upper lips. Yet in the Channel Islands which the Germans occupied there was little resistance and a great deal of collaboration, with Jersey and Guernsey passing anti-semitic laws voluntarily. After the war nothing was said about the collaborators and only in 1991 did detectives from Scotland Yard's new war crimes unit begin to investigate atrocities committed during the Nazi occupation, including the death camp on Alderney and the betrayal and deportation of Jews to Auschwitz. Reports compiled after the liberation have gone missing and there is clear evidence of a cover-up. (*Observer*, 30.6.91) Even the glorious 'few' of 1940 need not have been. The shortage of pilots during the Battle of Britain was in part due to the class system, since administrative desk jobs were reserved for officers (pilots) and the hidebound system would not release them to fly if it had to replace them with other ranks. And many of the figures for Germans shot down were exaggerated, while the most successful RAF squadron, No. 303, was Polish. Similarly, the myth of all working together in the war does not bear close examination. Class divisions remained and large numbers of the middle and upper classes were desperate to flee Britain, while the War Cabinet refused to ban private evacuation: 'Most of the children returned after 1942, once the danger of invasion and defeat had disappeared.' And although we make much of the Blitz, Britain lost a mere 40,000 dead by bombing as opposed to 590,000 in Germany. Despite talk of stiff upper lips there was much resentment of the King and Queen or Churchill coming to the East End to view bomb damage. (Ponting, 1990:131, 136, 147–8) After the war the myths were perpetuated at the expense of truth, while Britain struggled to maintain her great power status against steadily declining power. The Battle of Britain was boosted as a great victory – Britain's morale desperately needed a boost – but although it was a victory it was a very close thing: the figures were exaggerated and the picture painted by Churchill of pilots 'undaunted by odds, unwearied in their constant challenge and mortal danger' was an exaggeration to say the least. As Charles Frizell (a friend of the pilot Richard Hillary) said: 'The Battle of Britain ideal of the noble fighter pilot is as much nonsense as Rousseau's ideal of the noble savage.' As Derek Robinson argued in the *Standard* (22.1.91), 'For any myth to persist as long as this one has, there must be a public appetite for it. The concept of the fighter pilot as superman has huge appeal.'

Dunkirk, possibly the greatest defeat in British military history as well as a betrayal of our French allies, was turned with great skill into a glorious British action, an extrication against impossible odds, defeat into victory. While the Royal Navy evacuated 130,000 British troops from the beaches, it took off only 15,000 Frenchmen and the stories persist of the British clubbing the French back into the sea. When Churchill flew to Paris during the evacuation, Weygand, Commander-in-Chief of the army, complained that the French were being left behind at Dunkirk, and although Churchill promised that they would leave Dunkirk arm in arm with the British, it did not happen. But the British took off their able-bodied men and left the wounded, while abandoned field-guns amounted to twice the total remaining in England. (Coleman, 1990b) When the British began the retreat to Dunkirk they left their Belgian allies stranded on their flank and sustained a mere 500 casualties in eleven days of retreat, for they were not fighting a rearguard action. After the failed offensive at Arras, General Gort was concerned only with evacuation and withdrew from Arras without consulting the French, while his Chief of Staff, General Pownall, when asked about the evacuation of the Belgians, replied: 'We don't care a bugger what happens to the Belgians.' And although much was made of the little ships they in fact took off only 26,000 men, or 8 per cent of the total. And even if such a stunning defeat can be turned into a sort of miracle victory – at least the men were rescued to fight again later – they were demoralised: officers deserted the men to get to the ships first; discipline on the ships was only maintained by armed sailors; back in England some men threw away their arms and telephoned their wives to bring them civilian clothes so that they could abandon their uniforms; while the press were told to blame the French for not fighting while saying the British Expeditionary Force was undefeated. (Ponting, 1990:90, 92)

The British turned the defeat of Dunkirk into a victory by emphasising the stubborn heroic qualities of the British character – the fleet of little ships that went to the rescue – while playing down the fact that the BEF had not so much been chased out of France as been run out with ignominy. Sir Arthur Bryant, the supreme myth-maker, says of Dunkirk: 'After the traditional fashion of their race in the hour of crisis, the waiting men showed no sign of panic or despair, nor – it would seem – of any visible emotion at all. They merely waited, with a kind of dogged faith. And presently their faith was justified.' And later, in a passage whose near lyricism matches its doubtful veracity, he goes on to describe how in the lovely summer of 1940 'in forge and factory, field and mine her people, with a fierce, unresting, yet quiet intensity, worked as they had never worked before in her whole history.' (1990:271, 272)

War is never a clear-cut affair and accounts vary, not least depending upon the viewpoint of those telling the story. At Calais, for example, Clive Ponting recounts how British stevedores refused to work under German shelling and had to be dragged from hiding by the troops. (1990:89) On the other hand, it is claimed that the defence of Calais for vital days in May (22–26 1940) prevented the Germans from cutting off the BEF, and six in ten of the men were killed or wounded while the rest were captured and only 30 out of 3,000 were taken off in the end by the navy. The war diary of the German 10th Panzer Division records: 'The enemy fights with a hitherto unheard of obstinacy. They are English, extremely brave and tenacious.' (Coleman, 1990a)

Characteristically, perhaps, Winston Churchill, who up to 1940 had been one of the most hated and reviled figures in British politics, was turned into a national icon as a result of his war leadership, to such an extent, indeed, that in the post-war era it became as difficult to criticise him – once he had been raised above politics – as it was to say anything disrespectful of the monarch – 'who cannot answer back'. But in 1940 Churchill did not succeed Chamberlain by popular choice but rather because Halifax resolutely refused to take the premiership although virtually everyone who mattered preferred him to Churchill. And the much vaunted war speeches in fact had a curiously chequered history and when the BBC asked him to repeat his famous speech of 4 June 1940 ('We shall fight on the beaches'), which was originally delivered to the House of Commons, he refused and so an actor, Norman Shelley, actually imitated his voice over the radio. R. A. Butler, who in any case could not stand Churchill, described his speeches as 'beyond words vulgar' and after he became Prime Minister in 1940 claimed that 'the good clean tradition of English politics . . . had been sold to the greatest adventurer in modern political history . . . . a half-breed American.' (Ponting, 1990:81) Interestingly, the image of Churchill the dunce at Harrow – one that long appealed to the anti-intellectual British – was far from the case and only recently has his biographer, Martin Gilbert, discovered early Harrow reports that showed Churchill to win history prizes and excel in Latin and Greek while his masters wanted him to try for Oxford or Cambridge. (*Observer*, 24.3.91) The fact is, of course, that after 1945 the British needed an icon in proportion as their power declined, and Churchill fitted the bill.

Other wartime myths such as heroism in the face of the Blitz turn out to be very different when examined closely. The story of the Blitz as revealed through Tom Harrisson's *Living Through the Blitz* (1976) shows, inevitably, that the reality was very different from the myth: there was panic and selfishness, incompetence and cowardice, while stoicism was often, in truth, no more than resigned fatalism. Harrisson's book raises a fundamental question about myth-making: in wartime it may be justifiable to cover up the truth in order to present to the world a picture of heroism in the face of a brutal enemy – all part of necessary propaganda – but for how long afterwards is it permissible or desirable to perpetuate such myths?

If there is a consensus about such things, then British war propaganda has often been lauded as the best of all the belligerents in World War II, a view sedulously cultivated by Britain, but such views too easily turn into myths and Churchill was certainly responsible for a good deal of myth-making in terms of Britain's relations with the United States and his own relations with Roosevelt. Thus, the day before he gave his 'We shall fight on the beaches' speech, he told the Prime Minister of Canada, Mackenzie King: 'We must be careful not to let Americans view too complacently the prospect of a British collapse, out of which they would get the British fleet and the guardianship of the British empire, minus Great Britain . . . Although the president is our best friend, no practical help has been forthcoming from the United States as yet.' The much-vaunted Churchill offer of joint Anglo-French citizenship in June 1940 in fact had a brief and inglorious history: the original idea was Monnet's rather than Churchill's and although the head of the French War Cabinet, Reynaud, welcomed the idea, the other ministers saw no merit in it and regarded it as a way to make France a British dominion. (Coleman, 1990c)

But the year of 'their finest hour' was also a year in which a number of secret peace feelers were put out by the Germans and the Cabinet discussed the possibility of surrendering those later bastions of defiance, Malta and Gibraltar, as well as parts of Africa if their surrender could purchase a peace. Later, however, these considerations of peace were covered up. British scorn for the French Vichy Government does not quite match with what Churchill said to his Private Secretary on 1 November 1940: 'De Gaulle is definitely an embarrassment to us now in our dealings with Vichy.' (Ponting, 1990:187) And although Churchill makes much in his war memoirs of his relations with President Roosevelt, during 1940 he was to write 23 times to Roosevelt but received only six replies. (Coleman, 1990d) So with no prospect of a peace Britain stood defiant and alone! In fact, that too was rhetoric, for Britain never stood alone but had Canada, Australia, New Zealand and even South Africa standing with her, although for purposes of myth-making they were conveniently forgotten. In any case, as D. N. Pritt, admittedly speaking from a left-wing viewpoint, tartly observes: 'But it is a black mark for our ruling class that, in a world in which most nations hated Fascism and wanted an end of it, they had so conducted the affairs of their country that for the moment no state in the world was prepared to stand with them!' (1965:241)

Arthur Bryant was a myth-maker extraordinary and his last book, *The Search for Justice*, which was published posthumously, is a masterpiece of its kind, painting a picture of Britain that makes even the grim parts seem heroic. Phrases such as 'in more regimented lands' are used to contrast British freedoms with repression elsewhere, while his general theme of the *sensible* quality of British workers is used to suggest that, unlike more hot-headed Continentals, they are not revolutionary and in the end will always return to their duty. His description of farm workers in the 1830s (or any other group) almost always conjures up a more rosy picture than reality would suggest was the truth: 'They took pride in their mastery of oven and vat, in their skill in keeping a garden, in raising poultry and bees. Above all, they valued the Christian virtues of decent living and good neighbour-hood – honesty, truth, and purity of work and life.' (1990:74) Bryant's use of language is constantly designed to gild his story – 'Britain would be honourably installed in Egypt' (for example, of her take-over in the 1880s on behalf of the moneylenders) or the statement, 'Because Englishmen wished to exercise power not for its own sake but to further moral causes' – and to help create the myth that the British were somehow special and different from their Continental neighbours. Speaking of Britain's performance in World War I, Bryant first lays claim to the non-military character of the British people: 'Never a military nation, when it came to testing the martial virtues, Britain had outlasted all others. That was why she won.' Having made this claim he continues, with skilful denigration, to write off the other main combatants as follows: 'Though the exhausted French, the broken Russians and the still mainly untried legions of the United States all contributed to victory, the dominating force in the world on November

11th 1918, were the five million fighting men' of the Empire. (251) Now flattering as such pictures are – 'men who rode straight to hounds' (the gentry of England) – in the end they distort reality.

In 1988 a row developed over the exhibition at the National Maritime Museum on the 400th anniversary of the Spanish Armada, with sections of the press outraged because the museum decided to look at the event dispassionately. (*Independent*, 7.7.88) *The Times*, in a leading article of the preceding year, said: 'Historical pageants, national anniversary festivities should properly be concerned with projecting myths not recording facts', while in the *Daily Mail* A. N. Wilson called for more pride in national achievements. Does more pride, one has to ask, mean being economical with the truth? And if there can be outrage at a true portrayal of an event that is four hundred years old, how much reliance may be put upon the depiction of more recent historical events whose impartial examination might show Britain in a less favourable light than that portrayed by the accepted myth?

One of the most sedulously developed of all myths is the peace-loving nature of the British people. The fourteenth-century chronicler Froissart wrote: 'The English will never love or honour their king, unless he be victorious and a lover of arms and war against their neighbours ... They take delight and solace in battles.' And, as Thomas Callander, a modern chronicler of the British Empire, claims: 'More than two centuries of almost incessant fighting with Portugal and Spain, Holland and France, were needed to found and protect it.' (1961:27) While, at the time of the Falklands conflict of 1982, the Argentine Foreign Minister Costa Mendez told the US Secretary of State, General Haig, 'I think no one can challenge Great Britain on her title of world champion on the use of force in the conquest of her territories.' (Freedman *et al.*, 1990:205)

The many myths surrounding Britain's claim to be a parliamentary democracy look as though they may come under serious challenge during the 1990s. As Humphry Berkeley claimed in the 1960s, parliamentary democracy had already collapsed at Westminster, although since Gladstone 'the theory that Parliament controls not only the Cabinet but the Prime Minister as well has been preserved to this day, like the many myths of party politics, as part of the "British way of life!" ' (1968:44) As he also claimed, correctly it seems,

> Parliament is not in practice sovereign. The Prime Minister is not, and has not been for a very long time, *primus inter pares*.

We do not have Cabinet Government. The ancient parliamentary rivalry between the Lords and the Commons has for years been irrelevant. For the issue is not whether the House of Lords should for a few fleeting months defy the elected Chamber, but whether Parliament as a whole can ever act as a curb on the Government. (23)

Yet the British still tend to behave as though their parliamentary system is the cynosure of all eyes and the envy of foreigners.

With more hope than political reality, R. H. Tawney defined democracy as a type of society which involved 'the resolute elimination of all forms of privilege which favour some groups and depress others' and 'the conversion of economic power, now often an irresponsible tyrant, into the servant of society'. (Andrews and Jacobs, 1990:293) His hope has never remotely been realised. The basic concept of democracy is that ordinary people should enjoy control of their affairs and not be manipulated. But this is far from the truth. Capitalism rather than democracy is what the West is about. Churchill, in 1945, ordered captured German arms to be stacked ready to be reissued to the Germans should the Russians continue their advance across Europe. Pritt was of the opinion that the idea that the Cold War only began after the end of World War II and was solely the fault of the Russians does not stand up against the overt hostility of the West to the USSR which had long antedated 1945. (1965:282) This view stands despite the fact that Pritt was of the extreme left wing by British standards, and it is necessary to say this or else the view is likely to be dismissed by the old expedient of saying, 'He would say that, wouldn't he.' Speaking of Russian intentions in Eastern Europe at the end of the war, Denis Healey says: 'There is no doubt that the Russians never intended to keep this promise (to establish democracies in Eastern Europe). Indeed there is some evidence to suggest that they did not fully realize that the Western powers were sincere in demanding free elections.' The second sentence represents Mr Healey at his most subtle or most naïve. Does he really imagine the West did not know that the Russians would not hold democratic elections? (1990:36)

A constant refrain of British politics since 1945 has been to make Britain *Great* again, to return to the 'top table'. The sense that she is no longer a great power has had a traumatic impact upon politicians, leading them again and again to follow policies that were beyond the country's strength. Britain might not be able any longer to apply the

Pax Britannica round the world but that has not prevented her from acting as though she still had the ability to do so. Arthur Bryant claims, 'For this pragmatic race, hatred of power was an obsession.' (1990:2) The contrary would appear to have been the case and, most especially, when Britain was so clearly losing it. At some time between 1870 and 1914, Britain, the first industrial society and richest people on earth, began to lose momentum and, as David Marquand argues, 'Increasingly, the Church, the public schools and the universities disseminated an ethos of gentlemanly economic conservatism, which slowly undermined the industrial spirit of earlier days.' (1988:166) Indeed, if anyone is responsible for British loss of power it is the gentlemanly élite at the top who, ironically, miss it so much. The result of this economic and power decline has been the creation of a new myth, not sustained by any notable evidence, that the quality of life in Britain is commensurately better than it is in those countries like Germany and Japan which have so manifestly surpassed us in economic performance.

Richard Crossman wrote of the 'Yangtse Incident', subsequently mythologised in a 'stiff upper lip' film: 'British warships are as out of place on the Yangtse as Chinese warships would be on the Thames.' In the climate of 1949 such a view was not welcome. (Howard, 1990:151) At least, as the last decade of the century opened, some British people appeared ready both to question and laugh at British attitudes. Thus, the *Standard* on the subject of men's tears: 'Question: Why were Diego Maradona's tears contemptible while those of Paul Gascoigne were touching? Answer: Because Mr Maradona is not British. He is a Latin. When they cry, they make a song and dance of it. When we cry, it is a manly thing – a restrained sob or two which we struggle to control.' (9.7.90) The fact is, as a Mr Graham Binns pointed out in a letter to the *Independent* of 16 August 1991, the British have regarded half the countries of the world (he names them) as hate objects at one time or another and the remainder, including Europe, the USA and the old Commonwealth, with disdain. The British, in fact, are imbued with endless assumptions of superiority and, as Lionel Gelber wrote in the mid-1960s: 'The British, however, began to lose their touch when they assumed pre-eminence had been foreordained. And they must uproot remnants of that fallacy before they again make their way.' (1966:94) A lot of uprooting still requires to be done.

8 Empire

For Britain is the only major country in the West
whose status has rested on overseas props.

LIONEL GELBER

MPIRE IS CREATED for the benefit of the imperialists; other
'humanitarian' justifications come later. Lord Carnarvon,
Colonial Secretary under Disraeli, said there were two kinds
of imperialism: the first was Caesarism or despotism; the
second, the British kind. This, he suggested, consisted of 'a world-wide
trust, keeping the peace, elevating the savage, relieving the hungry, and
uniting in loyalty all the British peoples overseas. Imperialism certainly
entailed expansion, but it was not bullying expansion, it was merely
the extension of British institutions and wholesome influences, if
necessary by force.' (Morris, 1973:388) The Victorians, or at least
some of them, persuaded themselves that British imperialism really did
amount to this astonishingly idealistic extension of British power – 'if
necessary by force' – and subsequent generations have allowed the
idea of a benign British imperialism to colour their view of themselves
and the rest of the world. On the whole it has been a disastrous
heritage.

As Lionel Gelber suggests, many British institutions were conditioned by empire, and subsequently, when empire had gone, the
institutions remained to continue artificial, inflated lives no longer
buttressed by the imperial forces which originally justified them.
(1966:84) Lord Carnarvon's concept of British imperial expansion is
idealistic to the point of parody. Callander's very different view suggests
that the building of the British Empire 'was a process that was destined,
as Lord Acton observed, to render her annals the most sanguinary of
all Christian nations and nothing can be more instructive than a
searching investigation of its real pattern and principles.' (1961:19)
Today, we live in a cynical age in which empire is out of fashion, yet
even in its heyday at the turn of the century such critics as Hobson
were clear as to what empire was really about: 'There is first the habit
of economic parasitism, by which the ruling State has used its provinces,

99

colonies and dependencies in order to enrich its ruling class and to bribe its lower classes into acquiescence.' (1902:194)

An article that appeared in *Fortune* magazine in 1935 claimed that since 1776 the USA had filched more territory than any country except Britain: 'And as between Great Britain and the U.S. it has been a close race, Britain having conquered something over 3,500,000 square miles since that date, and the U.S. (if one includes wresting the Louisiana Purchase from the Indians) something over 3,100,000. The English-speaking people have done themselves proud in this regard.' (Mills, 1958:177) The illusion of power is often as effective as actual power and the Empire survived in part because of its sheer world-wide extent: at the beginning of World War II, during Britain's darkest hour, the Americans still assumed that the Empire gave to Britain resources of power which in fact did not exist. Empire was a bloody business and 'it was observable that whenever Christianity comes, there comes with it a sword, a gun, powder and ball.' (Lewis and Foy, 1971:9) The Church in fact became a partner in imperialism and when imperialism went the Church largely went with it.

By 1934, when the world was becoming steadily more threatening as far as Britain was concerned, the First Sea Lord, Admiral Chatfield, could say to Warren Fisher at the Treasury: 'We have got most of the world already, or the best parts of it, and we only want to keep what we have got and prevent others taking it away from us.' (Ponting, 1990:19) The Admiral was speaking only sixty years after Lord Carnarvon had laid down loftier principles of empire, but it was the hard-headed principles of 'having and holding' that prevailed while the loftier ones became the window-dressing. The fact is that Britain got so used to possessing the largest empire in the world that she also became accustomed to believing that it carried with it special privileges, and the belief in the privileges long outlasted the empire itself. And, as James Morris wrote in *Farewell the Trumpets*, once the British quit Palestine, 'Churchill, in opposition, foresaw "a steady and remorseless process of divesting ourselves of what has been gained by so many generations of toil, administration and sacrifice".' (1978:515) It is, indeed, remarkable that when Britain had to divest herself of empire there were far more regrets at losing our hard-won gains than congratulations that we had achieved our lofty aims in preparing our subjects for independence, although there was a good deal of self-congratulation on that score too.

And although, always, the claim was that Britain ruled with

impartiality and justice, the seamier side of empire emerged brutally
from time to time to belie the picture Britain wished to present to the
world. The British certainly employed torture in Kenya during the
Mau Mau uprising and when a Captain Law gave evidence of the
beating of Kikuyu prisoners, 'Twelve days after Captain Law had
smuggled a letter out of prison to the then Colonial Secretary, Alan
Lennox-Boyd, detailing the ill-treatment, he was summarily flown
home.' Similarly, 'In May 1953, a British barrister, Mr Peter Evans,
said that two Kikuyus had been taken into the bush and shot dead
when they refused to admit to membership of the Mau Mau. Three
days later Mr Evans was declared a prohibited immigrant and ordered
to leave Kenya: a government statement said the move was "purely
coincidental" with Mr Evans' allegations.' (Deeley, 1971:46, 47) The
real story of empire was about power and the use of ruthless methods
to maintain that power; the mythology was about a mission to carry
civilisation to the dark corners of the earth. Empire was also about
'providing jobs for thousands of Britons otherwise difficult to employ
in the officer-like circumstances to which they had become accustomed'. (Morris, 1978:504)

Imperial language is full of euphemisms such as 'the mandate of
civilisation', while humanitarians nearly always found themselves in
impossible moral dilemmas although, somehow in the end, they came
down on the side of empire:

> But the very humanitarians who applauded his [Gladstone's]
> dislike of imperialism could not refrain from using the national
> might to suppress wrong-doing and cruelty. They hated force.
> But when it came to the point they hated slavery more. They
> did the hating and the soldiers they deplored did the fighting.
> And the end of it was a still larger empire than before. (Bryant,
> 1990:201)

It was, of course, when articulate natives began to demand the
freedoms that Britain supposedly believed in that the system ran into
trouble. And so it became necessary to find pliant instruments of
imperial policy in the form of moderates who would not demand too
much (in the way of freedom) too soon. The term 'protectorate' had
splendid implications of the strong looking after the weak but, as D.
N. Pritt suggested, it was a hypocritical name which allowed the
imperial power to profess to protect from outside threats while

securing the advantages of a colony without the need for conquest. (1971b:83) When Mussolini invaded Abyssinia Lord Ponsonby exposed British cant about empire when he said: 'The fool! Can he not understand that, if there had been any prospect of profit in taking that country, the British would have done so long ago?'

The left has possibly done even more than the right in British politics to perpetuate myths about Britain's overseas mission. In his memoirs James Callaghan writes in measured tones about empire to give the impression that, although we might have been a little bit selfish here and there, it was not really more than that: 'And so the Empire grew. But its direction slowly changed and after the First World War concern began to grow that the balance had tipped too far against the interests of the native peoples and too much in favour of Britain's commercial interest in exploiting the natural resources of the colonial peoples.' (1987:119) And one of the best imperial proconsuls of the post-war era, Hugh Foot (later Lord Caradon), really does make it seem as though we were there (in the colonies) solely for the good of our subject people, and the very title of his book of memoirs – A Start in Freedom (1964) – ignores the fact that the British deprived their colonial peoples of their freedom in the first place.

The period 1945 to 1980 witnessed the disappearance of the British Empire, with Rhodesia finally becoming Zimbabwe in the latter year, and during this time a great deal of whitewashing and *post facto* justification was matched by increasing revelations about the seamier side of the process so that the end result, for the British, has been a complex mix of nostalgia, retroactive guilt and justification combined – 'even if we did some bad things the Empire as a whole was a good thing, look at them now' – while (and perhaps this is the most important legacy of all) the British have yet to accommodate themselves to the reduced standard of living that loss of empire so manifestly entails. Of course, if possible, allow your imperial subjects to do the justifying for you, and when the Prime Minister of the new state of Nigeria, Sir Abubakar Tafawa Balewa, paid tribute to the Colonial Service on Independence Day, 1 October 1960, he supported perfectly the myth Britain wished to perpetuate: 'We are grateful to the British officers whom we have known, first as masters and then as leaders and, finally, as partners but always as friends'. (Arnold, 1989:9)

The myths about empire as trust were exposed, for example, in relation to Uganda. During the year that preceded its independence, when its affairs ought to have been of great concern to the imperial parliament, there was only one adjournment debate of thirty minutes on the subject, eight oral and 21 written questions, and sixteen of these 29 questions came from the same person; as Andrew Hill and Anthony Whichelow, the authors of this investigation, point out, 'the awareness amongst colonial people that their affairs need to reach a crisis before they are discussed in the imperial parliament can hardly be reassuring'. (1964:35) All too often, in fact, the British wanted the glory of empire without any bother or expense. It was not all neglect, but crisis was the operative word and, as D. N. Pritt says of the Kenyatta case: 'There were many strange features in the case, and the prosecution evidence was of the poorest quality. It aroused great interest in England, causing a resurgence of genuine liberal sentiment, and even some public feeling of responsibility for British colonial activities.' (1966b:71)

' "Great is the rectitude of the English, greater is the power of a lie" is a proverbial saying throughout India.' (Hobson, 1902:296) Most peoples are 'racist' in the general sense of believing themselves to be unique and therefore superior to outsiders, but few people had so many opportunities as the Empire provided to the British to see themselves as superior (although not just in that general, localised sense) to everyone everywhere. There was, for example, fury in British India at the Ilbert Bill of 1883 that would have made British residents subject to Indian magistrates and the bill had to be withdrawn since it outraged 'the cherished conviction which was shared by every Englishman in India . . . that he belongs to a race whom God has destined to govern and subdue'. (Cross, 1968:52) Cecil Rhodes, a prime advocate of imperialism, when challenged about uncontrolled expansionism had what, for him and his supporters, was an unanswerable reply: 'We happen to be the best people in the world, with the highest ideals of decency and justice and liberty and peace, and the more of the world we inhabit, the better it is for humanity.' (Callander, 1961:15) Now a politician or propagandist may, because of the nature of his calling, be excused for making so extravagant a claim, but when the claim is believed by the person who makes it then brainwashing of a most insidious kind has succeeded beyond any reasonable expectation.

Such attitudes persisted, one way or another, down to the present time. Harold Macmillan, whose 'wind of change' speech has been seen over the years as a radical departure from older attitudes, was none the less imbued with ideas of white superiority and, for example, in relation to the Korean War said: 'I am sure that a moral defeat would mean the end of the white man's position in the East and that the moral collapse might easily spread to the West.' (Horne, 1988:325) As Conor Cruise O'Brien points out in an introduction to Camus' *The Plague*, 'Most European criticism, ethnocentric to the point of imagining itself universal, slides easily into colonial assumptions and perspectives and only notices the appearance of "politics" when these assumptions and perspectives are contested.' (1970:49) The persistent antagonism towards the New Commonwealth demonstrated in the ruling circles of Britain as well as the media has as much to do with the fact that after two hundred years of Empire the British were at last obliged to meet their former subject peoples on equal terms than because of any differences of policy in Commonwealth councils. Shreela Flatter, a recent immigrant to Britain, says of the Empire: 'The empire was fantastic in its day, and they [the British] have always managed to defeat everyone else in Europe. Whether the attitude was positively dinned into them, or whether it was just one of the assumptions that came with empire I don't know. But it certainly was one of the most racist empires, no doubt about it.' (Green, 1990:143) Despite her comment about racism Shreela Flatter would also appear to have been brainwashed about British superiority!

What might be termed the positive language of empire spoke of civilising missions, the burden of empire, law and order, a sacred trust, and each of these phrases implied an impartial and superior fount of order and civilisation that worked for 'their' good. The negative language of empire was usually racist and warned of the yellow peril, tribalism, miscegenation, and can be traced through to the sudden European fears being expressed in the 1990s about huge immigrant hordes threatening to swamp the north. This kind of language was balanced with frequent references to white civilisation. A sort of apotheosis was achieved by Lord Rosebery in 1910 when he delivered the Rectoral address at Glasgow University and described the Empire in the following, almost spiritual, terms:

Human and yet not wholly human, for the most heedless and the most cynical must see the finger of the Divine. Growing as trees grow, while others slept; fed by the faults of others; reaching with the ripple of a resistless tide over tracts and islands and continents, until our little Britain woke up to find herself the foster-mother of nations and the source of united empires. (Buitenhuis, 1987:2)

A touchstone of imperial awareness concerns attitudes to education from either side, as it were, of the imperial divide. On the subject of the Commonwealth, Attlee took an entirely Anglocentric view: 'Common culture? There is something in that as well. One finds it easy to discuss literature with educated Indians and Africans because they have absorbed a great deal of British culture.' (1961:53) His reaction made sense in the light of education for the élite in India and elsewhere in the Empire where private boys' schools were run like British public schools: 'They were assiduous and highly successful brainwashers' which fostered in the boys 'an active sense of their duty as loyal subjects.' (Morris, 1968:141) In British Guyana, set in the midst of Latin America, the schools taught neither Spanish nor the history of the continent; all education was Anglocentric and the same applied throughout the British West Indies. As George Jackson wrote in *Soledad Brother*: 'I know now that the most damaging thing a people in a colonial situation can do is to allow their children to attend any educational facility organised by the dominant enemy culture.' (1971:30)

The sense of British patriotism which emerged strongly in the eighteenth century has played a crucial part in forming attitudes to outsiders, whether imperial subjects or not, and much of this patriotism has been fostered by song and poetry: 'From James Thomson's *Rule Britannia* (1740) to Elgar–Benson's *Land of Hope and Glory*, from Shakespeare to Kipling, stretches an anthology of patriotic song and poetry unmatched elsewhere in the world.' (Callander, 1961:26) And, curiously perhaps, this patriotism and belief in British superiority brought with it – at least in the Empire – the problems of 'face' and the losing of it. In the imperial story the British made great play with 'face saving' but it should be axiomatic that the more people attribute a quality to others, the more in fact the quality belongs to themselves and in the East, particularly, constant British concern with loss of face became an excuse for racial apartness from the people amongst whom they lived, while they excused their conduct by talking of the necessity to save the face of the people they ruled. In fact, the Chinese especially but also, for example, the Vietnamese, are prepared to make public confessions of their shortcomings. It was far more the British, often operating in an alien culture they only partly understood, who felt the need to save face, and the creation of 'face' in the first place became part of the panoply of imperial tricks whereby the British set themselves apart from those they ruled. As Sir Charles Johnson, Governor of Aden in the 1960s, argued: 'It is the British and not the Orientals who

care most about these things, and for whom they must be maintained
... As a race we ourselves possess most of the characteristics which
we ascribe to the peoples of the East.' (Cross, 1968:144)

Following World War II, which has been described as Britain's last
– and greatest – imperial war (to save the Empire), British weakness
and a series of irresistible international forces combined to bring an
end to the European-controlled empires, and once the process got
underway it proved unstoppable. The 'die-hards' fought tooth and nail
to prevent decolonisation; the more realistic, who saw that the time for
end of empire had come, argued that independence was what we had
created the Empire for in the first place. And so the justifications began:

> Thus we see, on the one hand, that Soviet Russia required for
> the control of an oppressed nation, Hungary, an army of
> occupation greater than the whole strength of the British Army;
> while, on the other hand, British colonial statesmen in all parts
> of the world – in the West Indies, in Nigeria, in the Rhodesias,
> in Borneo – are feverishly working to create the machinery for
> administering new national groups. (Carrington, 1961:24)

Such claims warrant careful examination. If the British were working
'feverishly' to prepare their colonies for independence one is bound to
ask what they had been doing for the preceding couple of generations.
And in the Rhodesias violence, racism and the willingness in Whitehall
to pander to a ruthless white minority hardly merit the claim that
anyone was working feverishly to create the machinery for a new state.
A more balanced view of the imperial legacy than that just quoted
comes from Barbara Ward:

> If you believe – as I do – that the most valuable and yet most
> precarious human good is freedom, the British imperialists must
> be allowed their part in bringing this great ferment to the East.
> Concepts of self-government and individual human rights were
> no part of the Asian tradition ... In retrospect the British may
> be proud of having helped to create in India the attitudes of
> mind, the temper and the philosophy which were among the
> forces which ultimately drove them out. (1959:98)

Thus, even when we deprived people of their freedom, it was in order
to teach them a better understanding of it!

It is possible to find endless justifications for empire, most especially in the years since 1945, as it disappeared, and they come from both left and right in the British political spectrum. Much of the reputation of Iain Macleod, who has become a myth in his own right as the 'progressive Tory Prime Minister the British never had', rested upon his period as Macmillan's Colonial Secretary at the beginning of the 1960s, yet his views, in fact, are quite remarkably unradical, indeed almost imperial: 'If we fail in Central Africa to devise something like a workable multi-racial state, then Kenya will go too, and Africa may become no longer a source of pride or profit to the Europeans who have developed it, but a maelstrom of trouble into which all of us will be sucked.' (Home, 1989:183) Rhodesia did become a maelstrom of trouble but one resulting from white selfishness and the determination not to live up to the lofty ideals of Lord Carnarvon (quoted at the beginning of this chapter) but rather to attempt the entirely selfish philosophy of Ian Smith, enshrined in his famous phrase about black majority rule – 'not in my lifetime'.

The greatest intellectual sleight of hand of all was two centuries in which Britain proclaimed liberties and freedoms while she brought a quarter of the globe under her imperial control. As W. S. Blunt confided to his diary: 'the British Empire is the great engine of evil for the weak races now existing in the world' and 'The gangrene of colonial rowdyism is infecting us, and the habit of repressing liberty in weak nations is endangering our own.' (Callander, 1961:48) And one of the greatest ironies of all in the imperial story, no matter what claims were advanced about preparing people to rule themselves, was that the longer the British remained in a colony the more they convinced themselves that they should continue there if law and order were not to collapse. And although Macmillan received much praise over the years for his 'wind of change' speech, he had no intention of following through the logic of what he had said. He refused to condemn the Sharpeville massacre, saying that the racist policy in South Africa was 'their responsibility, not ours', and opposed any pressures to force South Africa to leave the Commonwealth, as it was obliged to do in 1961, principally through fear that its strong economy would be lost to the sterling area. Winston Churchill, then in retirement, did not want Macmillan to make his 'wind of change' speech at all: 'Why go and pick a quarrel with those chaps?' he asked. (*Independent*, 2.9.91)

Britain relinquished her empire because she had no choice rather than for any other reason. She then expended a great deal of energy trying to persuade herself and everybody else that that had always been the intention although, as Raymond Blackburn argued: 'Nor have we convinced anybody but ourselves that our motives in liquidating the Empire were anything but practical and selfish.' (1964:146)

An outpouring of books about the Empire continued for many years from the independence of India in 1947 and many, while paying lip-service to the political fashion of the times that denounced empire, were in fact nostalgic justifications for British rule. The trilogy of books about the Empire by James Morris – *Pax Britannica, Heaven's Command* and *Farewell the Trumpets* – capture brilliantly the spirit, the nostalgia, the pomp and the sheer self-deluding nonsense of Empire so that the author contrives to make his readers feel just how unique we were and does so, moreover, when poking most fun and demonstrating the absurd nature of our imperial pretensions. On the death of Winston Churchill Morris says:

> Churchill died and it [the Empire] died with him. It had lasted too long anyway: the subject peoples had outgrown its tutelage, and would progress much faster without it. For the British it was more of a wrench than they knew, for though by now the imperial idea seemed as antiquated as steam trains or anti-macassars, the existence of Empire had impregnated all their lives. (1978:551)

9 Immigration and race

... that cannibals were at least as civilised and
pleasant as old Harrovians ...

TOM HARRISSON

T HE BRITISH HAVE NEVER SUGGESTED that they were not able to rule
themselves but have frequently 'discovered' that others lack this
capacity and especially, of course, those that at one time or
another we managed to bring under our political control. The
emergence of virulent forms of racism in Britain has paralleled the end
of empire, particularly when former subject peoples, some with
genuine naïvety believing in the moral superiority of Britain, have come
to its shores as immigrants. They have been cruelly disabused about
its role as the 'mother' country, a phrase that was once used in all
innocence, for example, by West Indians. Brainwashing is essential to
racism, indeed it is a point of departure, for it is always 'they', the
outsiders, who have to prove themselves, never 'us'. Endless jokes or
terms of abuse levelled at 'Pakis' or 'thick Paddies' are, of course, part
of the general stock in trade of racial abuse, but at higher levels,
assumptions of superiority operate quite differently.

> When Britain announced recently that it was withdrawing
> troops from East of Suez, the American Secretary of State
> remarked that something would have to be done to fill the
> 'power vacuum'. This involved Saudi Arabia, India, Pakistan,
> Ceylon and Malaysia. The white world in their own way were
> saying that all these blacks amounted to nothing, for power was
> white and when white power is withdrawn, a vacuum is created,
> which could only be filled by another white power. (Rodney,
> 1969:18)

Power, indeed, is what confers prestige and acceptance. When the
negotiations for the Covenant of the League of Nations were underway
following World War I, the Japanese proposed that the Covenant
should include a declaration on racial equality (at that time Japan had

been a British ally). The proposal, however, was firmly resisted by the Australian Prime Minister W. M. Hughes, no doubt horrified at the prospect of a yellow peril now sanctified by League equality, and he was supported in his opposition to the Japanese proposal by Britain. Unsurprisingly, therefore, Britain found herself opposed by Japan in World War II and although, up to that time, there had been a 'disinclination to believe that any Asiatic troops could be a match for the white man. Indeed the existence of the British Empire was inexplicable save on such an assumption' (Cross, 1968:229), in fact, the British were to learn otherwise, and with the fall of Singapore in 1942 Japan had her revenge. That event, possibly more than any other, marked the end of white superiority in the East.

Slowly, in the years since 1945, the British have been obliged to come to terms with a world in which white superiority is no longer taken for granted. Unfortunately, too many Britons have found this difficult if not impossible to do, and all too few have achieved the transition in relations with grace. At one level racial antagonisms, the determination to look down upon members of another group, fulfil the need to focus upon a scapegoat which most people appear unable to forgo. It is an aspect of human behaviour which is very powerful and difficult to eradicate. This attitude of looking down upon funny foreigners was brought out clearly by Eden in his memoirs on the subject of the Abadan oil crisis and the personality of Persia's prime minister: 'The British people did not suffer directly and had difficulty in taking Musaddiq seriously. He was the first real bit of meat to come the way of the cartoonists since the war. "Old Mossy" with his pyjamas and iron bedstead, became a familiar figure.' (Eden, 1960:198)

Throughout the period of empire the British were entirely in favour of emigration by themselves to whichever parts of the Empire they wished to settle or work in; only when the process was reversed after 1945 and former imperial subjects thought to come in their turn to Britain did the British abandon the principle, for such people had to be stopped. The British, indeed, simply did not believe that others could come to their island – which suddenly became very small and over-crowded – and settle in it as they themselves had done in so many parts of the world. Thus when the *Empire Windrush* arrived unannounced at Tilbury in 1948 with four hundred West Indian immigrants on board, it caused something of a panic in the government leading to the creation of a Cabinet Committee on Colonial Immigration. In 1951 the

Home Secretary, Chuter Ede, came close to recommending controls.
(Hennessy and Seldon, 1987:51)

By 1962 immigration had become a major political issue and it did
not take much to strip away the mask of tolerance to which the British
had laid claim for so long. At Smethwick, which was to become
notorious for the attitudes to immigration that were expressed there
by politicians, Patrick Gordon Walker, a former Labour Cabinet
Minister and Commonwealth Secretary, lost both his nerve and
whatever racial tolerance he might once have laid claim to when, in
his attempts to counter the overtly anti-immigrant Tory candidate,
Peter Griffiths, he made statements such as that of 31 August 1962:
'This is a British country with British standards of behaviour. The
British must come first.' In the run-up to the general election of 1964,
when he lost the seat to Peter Griffiths, Gordon Walker's supporters
also issued the following statement: '*Urgent Stop Press be Fair*
Immigrants only arrived in Smethwick in large numbers during the
past ten years – while the Tory Government was in power. You can't
blame Labour or Gordon Walker for that.' (Foot, 1965:58, 58–9)
Parallel to this growing racist attitude towards immigrants was one
of deepening frustration against what came to be known as Third
World countries – former colonies or semi-dependent territories – that
we no longer controlled. The Suez crisis of 1956 really brought this
attitude to the fore when Britain failed and failed ignominiously to
control Nasser. 'But she had, humiliatingly, lost the power, and the
realization led to a deep racial embitterment among many Britons.'
(Segal, 1966:276) A few years later, in 1961, the word 'Congo' became
synonymous with disaster in Africa, and that troubled land formed
the backdrop for the activities of some of the worst white mercenaries
to operate in Africa; they were known by local whites in the Congo
as 'les affreux', the terrible ones, and yet they could be described in
the *Sunday Telegraph* of 26 November 1961 as 'unlikely unshaven
Galahads [who] alone in this tortured continent are ready to shed their
blood in the cause of non-racialism'. They shed plenty of blood but
ensured that little of it was their own.

As Barbara Ward argued: 'We took with us in our colonial dealings
an ignorant and almost irremovable racial prejudice.' (1961:67)
Unfortunately, the position in which the British overseas found
themselves simply served to strengthen these prejudices. It was a
racialist empire and as Lord Rosebery had once asked, 'what was
Empire but the predominance of race?' The racialism endemic in empire

became even worse because it was built on to the British class structure. 'By moving to the colonies, an artisan or clerk became an aristocrat – by virtue of his race alone, the unquestioned superior of coloured wealth and culture.' (Segal, 1966:275) The end of empire not only brought these possibilities to an end; it also reversed the process of migration and thereafter, as the aid age got underway, British aid was more likely to go to those countries and governments that played up to British sensitivities (Kenya, for example) rather than to those that asked awkward questions about her past role (Nyerere in Tanzania), while the almost inevitable troubles that bedevilled the newly independent countries of the Third World gave endless ammunition to British racists.

The relentless application of further immigration controls by Britain during the 1960s (1962, 1965, 1968, followed by the Immigration Act of 1971 and further rules of 1973) 'shattered the tradition of free entry.' (Holmes, 1988:309) Thereafter Britain became more overtly racist in her attitudes towards would-be or actual incomers from the New Commonwealth and it is as though the growth of this attitude was a revenge for the emergence of the New Commonwealth in place of the old Empire over the same period. Following Enoch Powell's speech of 20 April 1968 in Birmingham (the River Tiber foaming with much blood) and the general racial hysteria of that year, the International Commission of Jurists said: 'There is no doubt that the United Kingdom's reputation as a bastion of civil liberties has been seriously shaken.' (Arnold, 1989:55) Later that year Powell gave another similar speech at Eastbourne while Edward Heath, the leader of the Tory Party, moved steadily to the right on the race issue. Both the Powell approach and later that of Sir Keith (later Lord) Joseph, who used statistics to demonstrate the dangers of breeding by the lower orders, reflected a growing racist trend in Britain. The point, of course, is not so much that the British were racist but that for so long before these pressures were brought home to them in their own country they had claimed a superior tolerance as opposed to other, less enlightened peoples.

Few occasions allow more hypocrisy than the House of Commons debating and then passing increasingly repressive legislation while its members protest how much it hurts them to do so. Labour MPs have often made appeals to the Commonwealth ideal when there was no question of votes being involved, yet 'Only after large-scale Commonwealth immigration started did the "ideal" mean something in terms of votes. And then the mere possibility of losing votes because of the "glorious Commonwealth ideal" was enough to make most former Commonwealth enthusiasts forget all about it.' (Foot, 1965:191) And as another commentator, Trevor Smith, points out: 'In 1968 the Labour Government rushed a bill through all its stages within the space of a week which deprived East Africa Asians of their rights as citizens of the United Kingdom to enter this country.' (1972:83) And so the wretched process of rapid reversal went on. During the 1968 debate in the House of Commons on the Immigrants Bill, Sir Dingle Foot said: 'It may not be racialist in intention, but it will certainly be racialist in effect ... the effect of this legislation, inevitably, will be that the great majority of Europeans who have not elected for Kenya citizenship will be able to come here. The overwhelming majority of Asians will not.' (Steel, 1969:179) As Ruth Glass pointed out succinctly in a letter to *The Times*, 'if you are white your British passport is valid; if you are brown, it is not'. Labour was in power and responsible for passing this act; they did so with the overwhelming support of the Tory opposition. Iain Macleod, still regarded at that time as a radical, none the less went along with the majority. 'I detest the necessity for it', he said but he approved the bill anyway. Later, also in a letter to *The Times*, he expressed his contempt for discrimination but then excused his support for the measure: 'I have always held it a mistake to believe that legislation has any significant part to play in a field where there is so much ignorance and prejudice.' One can only presume that he meant to give way to the ignorance and prejudice. (Fisher, 1973:297) Those who claim to be anti-racist 'detest the necessity' but do it anyway; the racists merely do it. In his memoirs, which appeared twenty years after the event, James Callaghan (who had been Home Secretary at the time and piloted the legislation through the House of Commons) excused his own illiberal haste as follows: 'The immigration of large numbers of coloured people arouses particular passion and every Home Secretary since Rab Butler has been scorched by the flame. It was he, no less, despite his childhood in India, who decided with great reluctance in 1961 that he must bring forward the first Act in our history to control immigration from the Commonwealth.' (1987:263) There is nothing like drawing in your political opponents and ensuring that both sides are tarred with the same brush. Callaghan went on to say that 'None of my junior Ministers liked it any better than the Cabinet or I did.'

Labour has always been better on this subject in opposition than when in office and in 1991 with what looked like a 'no-holds-barred' election in the offing the subject of immigration once more raised its head. Roy Hattersley, the deputy leader of the Labour Party, warned of the prospects of a 'squalid appeal to racism' as he spoke of the Major government's proposed crackdown on refugees. In fact, and unsurprisingly, by 1991 Britain had one of the lowest levels of refugee admission in the West and the toughest immigration laws.

British aversion to foreigners has been equalled only by the readiness of her subjects to settle in other people's lands but to resent other people coming to settle in theirs. In 1949 the Royal Commission on Population stated that immigrants would be welcomed 'without reserve' only if 'the migrants were of good human stock and were not prevented by their religion or race from intermarrying with the host population and becoming merged into it.' (Holmes, 1988:210) That allows for considered discrimination and it is notable that in all the arguments about immigration during the 1960s the Irish remained by far the largest component of immigrants and they were excepted from the limiting legislation, although many of them had no better, and often worse, qualifications than those held by New Commonwealth immigrants. The 1962 Commonwealth Immigration Act made a special exception of the Irish, many of whom were unskilled. If all the statements by British politicians condemning racism are added together they come to a far greater total than those advocating controls and the wonder is how those who favour controls have always managed to win the political battles! Speaking in 1978, the year before she became Prime Minister, Margaret Thatcher managed both to extol the British character and its principled achievements round the world while also supporting a clamp-down on immigration: 'And you know, the British character has done so much for democracy, for law, and so much throughout the world, that if there is a fear that it might be swamped, people are going to react and be rather hostile to those coming in.' (Green, 1990:1)

When Margaret Thatcher did become Prime Minister one of the first tasks she faced was that of finding a solution to UDI in Rhodesia. Part of the problem arose from the fact that although Britain had used force to control uprisings in most parts of her empire before independence, she had 'discovered' that this was not possible in relation to Ian Smith and the white minority in Rhodesia. Denis Healey, who was a senior minister in Wilson's Cabinet when UDI was declared, subsequently justified non-intervention in Rhodesia by the curious argument that not only were Smith and his white supporters traitors but that, apparently, the British forces might turn into traitors as well: 'When British governments, under Macmillan as well as Wilson, considered the possibility of military intervention, they could not assume that the morale of Britain's forces would stand the strain.' (1989:223) Coming from the man who was to hold the post of Minister of Defence for longer than anyone else since 1945, that tells volumes about the attitudes of those who run Britain. As Stephen Dorril and Robin Ramsay suggest, government attitudes to white traitors in Rhodesia are symptomatic of all that is wrong with British society (1991:97).

In 1979 Britain's Prime Minister, Margaret Thatcher, and her Foreign Secretary, Lord Carrington, went to the Commonwealth Heads of Government Meeting in Lusaka, Zambia, to face united Commonwealth pressures to deal with Smith and his UDI; subsequently Mrs Thatcher executed her first U-turn and agreed to the Lancaster House Conference that led to the emergence of an independent Zimbabwe. In his memoirs Lord Carrington, who at the time was wrongly credited with persuading Mrs Thatcher to change her mind, 'the liberal mentor of the hard prime minister' makes a number of claims which between them show how his entire approach to the problem began from the viewpoint of the whites who had committed the treason rather than in terms of ensuring justice for the majority who had been deprived of it. He remarks that 'the Carter administration for domestic reasons was anxious to woo Black African goodwill', with the implication that this helped force his hand, while he speaks of the white minority, most of whom had willingly backed Smith in his treason, as though they were at a point of crisis rather than to blame for what had happened. He says: 'We were dealing with the lives and fortunes of people, many of them in origin British people, at a critical point in their history, and contrary to some impressions we were deeply aware of it and deeply cared.' By 1979 the war in Rhodesia had exhausted the whites and the South Africans wished to withdraw from their involvement. In his first speech to the House of Lords in 1979 Lord Carrington said of the so-called internal settlement in Rhodesia: 'There has been a fundamental change inside Rhodesia. There has been an election in which every adult man and woman has been enabled to cast a vote ... there is now an African majority in Parliament.' He asked Lord Harlech to visit various foreign countries to ascertain which governments would recognise the Salisbury regime's 'internal settlement' if Britain did. He found that no black state, nor the EEC, would do so while it would receive an adverse vote in the United Nations and break up the Commonwealth, and he goes on to admit: 'This assessment of the "internal settlement" and of the situation was by no means unexpected by me, but it was awkward.' Tut tut! one is tempted to say, the Noble Lord would have to go a little further along the road to real equality. On the subject of UDI Lord Carrington said, 'Smith's declaration of independence had been an unconstitutional act and his regime in consequence illegal – and thus difficult for the British Crown to recognise, even if sanitised so to speak, by an appearance of democracy. The international community perceived the difficulty very clearly.' This really is the most extraordinary statement to come from a British Foreign Secretary. Did he not perceive the difficulty clearly (as had the international community), and was that why over many years previous British governments had tried so hard to find a way of recognising Smith and his regime? (1988:287, 290) There was more in the same vein but what comes across from all the years of the Rhodesia story is the desire, if at all possible, on the part of almost all British politicians of both major parties to rescue the whites from the consequences of their revolt rather than to see justice done to the majority of the people who, overwhelmingly of course, were black.

A good way to understand the British is to view them through the eyes of foreigners and especially, perhaps, of newly settled immigrants. Jonathan Green's book *Them*, published in 1990, does just this. Its title alone makes a major point about British attitudes. What is interesting is what would-be immigrants thought before they came to Britain and what they found when they arrived. Racism has been described as a 'safe hatred', and although many Britons would not dream of indulging it they do indulge something else. As Gertrud Hartwig, one of the newcomers interviewed in the book, says of the English: 'They are more broadminded towards other races, other religions and so on. So long, that is, as they know their place and do not attempt to move too far into English society.' (1990:128) That is certainly a more friendly judgement than many.

A study carried out in the 1960s gives many examples of straightforward racism such as 'We're lucky here, we've managed to keep the buses white.' (Daniel, 1968:95) Since that time, however, the legislation controlling new immigration has become more severe, airport harassment has become more unpleasant, overt right-wing extremism is on the increase so that, by the beginning of the 1990s, it was no longer possible to argue that Britain's former reputation for safeguarding civil liberties had not been badly tarnished in relation to the immigrants who had actually settled in the country. The Jews were targets long before any significant coloured immigration occurred and, as Paul Foot says of Britain's refusing entry to Jews from Nazi Germany: 'If anyone seriously believed in the right of political asylum in Britain before 1933, the Government's immigration policy after that date must surely have disabused them.' (1965:111) And yet, one of the most remarkable examples of racism is to be found in the writing of Leo Abse, a Labour MP and Jew, who clearly thought he was being the opposite. Comparing racial attacks upon Jews and Blacks he says of Blacks:

> They have not the lineage of the people belonging to the Book (Jews); their research into their genealogy comes to a full stop with a bill of sale. The most rabid anti-semitism is more forgivable than attacks on the blacks: understanding may make it possible to forgive irrational attacks on the strong; but such charity must never, never, be extended to attacks, however unselfconscious, on the weak. (1989:168)

At the deepest level it would be hard to find a more truly racist passage than that and it illustrates how difficult the problem will always be.

During the two decades of the 1970s and 1980s successive governments made it increasingly difficult for new immigrants from Commonwealth countries (except the old white Dominions) to settle in Britain, and introduced the requirement for visas for visitors from such Commonwealth countries as India and Nigeria. By the beginning of the 1990s new attitudes and problems were moving centre-stage. Thus, an increasing number of visitors from the Caribbean were being turned back at the airports because immigration officials were not satisfied that they intended to leave at the end of their permitted stay. The report of the Joint Council for the Welfare of Immigrants revealed that for every visitor from Canada refused entry, 130 Jamaicans are refused entry, even though in the case of Jamaica there are still no visa requirements. (*Observer*, 1.3.90)

The issue of choice of schools had also reared its head, as it had much earlier in the United States, with the government decreeing that white parents should be free to take children out of schools with large numbers of Black or Asian pupils. Race relations experts described the ruling by the Secretary of State for Education and Science, Mr John MacGregor, that a parent's 'right to choose' overrides the race relations law as 'the first step to educational apartheid'. The question of choice was highlighted in April 1990 when a Mrs Carney of Middlesbrough removed her child from a school because her daughter was placed in a class of 24, only four of whom were white, and came home reciting 'songs in Hindu and drawing Pakistani vegetables'. (*Independent*, 24.4.90) Another, quite different issue concerned the decision of the Home Secretary to abolish legal aid in immigration cases; this is to render the most vulnerable even more so and represented the latest in a series of harsh measures designed to put pressure upon immigrants. It was not, by any stretch of the imagination, in the tradition of civil liberties that Britain has long claimed to espouse but appears progressively determined to abandon. (*Observer*, 18.8.91)

Racism is not a British disease, it is to be found almost everywhere; but the British have certainly added more than their quota to the universal prejudices and the sadness is that empire – the astonishing opportunities to understand people from every quarter of the globe that British predominance for two centuries ought to have produced – did nothing of the kind. Instead of opening windows to the narrow British it merely persuaded them of how unique they were. There are increasing signs, following the end of the Cold War, that Europe as a whole is about to turn in on itself and become racially extreme as much of it did during the Nazi era. Alarmist articles suggesting endless Third World hordes swamping Europe have not made for balance in approaching this most difficult of subjects, and as a bewildered Eastern Europe comes to terms with the end of the Communist era there are too many indications that it will become increasingly right wing and reactionary instead, and treat would-be immigrants from the rest of the world as though they are a modern version of the Mongol hordes who swept down upon Europe in 1240. It is unfortunate that in such a developing climate Britain has become more absolutely insular over the question of immigration than at any previous time in its history.

10 Education and class

So far as I know, there are extremely few school
stories in foreign languages. The reason, obviously,
is that in England education is mainly a matter of
status.

GEORGE ORWELL

SINCE 1945 THE EXPANSION OF EDUCATION, the explosion of the media
(television in every home), and the growth of literacy mean
both that everyone can be better informed and also that they
can the more easily be manipulated. And although Raymond
Williams could write at the beginning of the 1960s, 'For the first time
ever in Britain we are beginning to get a real range of good cheap
books' (1962:114) his hope was soon to be defeated by economic
forces, and by the 1990s it seemed that the continual take-over of
publishers by mega groups ruled by accountants had become one of
the greatest threats to culture. In Britain, culture has always been used
as a mark of class, and deep-seated middle-class antagonism to the
admass culture is not so much because it is seen as awful, but because
everyone can now share what was formerly exclusive. This class
emphasis can be seen in the way the media are divided between the
serious or 'heavy' newspapers and the tabloids, the rating of BBC radio
programmes, and the assumptions that this sort of person will read
or listen to one kind of programme and that sort of person to another.
In *The System*, which was published in 1967, Max Nicholson points
out the sharp class divisions between the ruling élite and the masses
as shown through their reading habits: 'the readers, nowadays, of *The
Times* and *Daily Telegraph* on the one hand (the élite) and the *Sun*
and *News of the World* on the other. These masses (who read the
latter papers) are psychologically in a state much as if they were under
alien administration.' (28) A general question needs to be posed about
education here: how much can a better system of education elevate
standards – for choice of what the media provide – and how much do
people want these standards to be elevated anyway and if they do not,
why not? Aldous Huxley took an entirely cynical view of mass
education and its uses: 'And finally there is that greatest of our social
inventions, free, compulsory education. Everyone now knows how to

read and everyone consequently is at the mercy of the propagandists, governmental or commercial, who own the pulp factories, the linoytpe machines and the rotary presses.' (1961:368) The technology may have changed since Huxley wrote those words but the argument stands.

People's perceptions and views are taken more than they know or would care to admit from the written word or the visual image. For many years the phrase 'I saw it in *The Times*' was a way of claiming that it must be true, although in the 1980s and 1990s the equivalent phrase is more likely to be 'I saw it on the television'. Lenin, whose name will always be associated with the class struggle, said: 'People always have been and they always will be the stupid victims of deceit and self-deception in politics, until they learn to look behind every kind of moral, religious, political, social phrase, declaration and promise to seek out the interests of this or that class or classes.' An examination of British literature and public life brings one repeatedly into contact with the class nature of our society. Bryant's particular gift was to suggest that class did not really matter because everyone was prepared to accept his pre-ordained place – a view that was of inestimable worth to the Establishment: 'By being jolly and having a good time when the occasion offered, the English poor reminded themselves and the rich men they served that Jack was as good as his master and that freedom was his birthright.' (1990:183) This statement does not bear close examination, although skilful use of language suggests a sense of equality despite the fact that 'Jack' is personal and 'the master' is not. Harold Nicolson, who in wartime conditions found himself eating, cafeteria-style, in the London University Senate House, records: 'It is absolutely foul . . . It is run on the cafeteria system and we have got to queue up with trays with the messenger boys.' (Ponting, 1990:141)

It is little wonder that foreigners have been perpetually astonished and mesmerised by the British class system. Other countries have class distinctions too but they do not go on about them endlessly. In Britain, in memoir after memoir, book after book on Britain or British politics, class is examined, dissected, denigrated, defended; we are told that it is in decline, that it no longer matters, that we are a classless society now. If in fact this were true the subject would drop from sight but it never does. As a perceptive American has said of the British attitude to class: 'And yet only in Britain could even the classless be regarded as a class.' (Gelber, 1966:97) Too often, quality has been associated with class since in such a class-conscious society standards are always assumed to be set by those at the top and passed down, while the divisions in the educational system which the comprehensive schools were designed to eliminate are now creeping back again – if they ever really disappeared.

Both George Orwell, in such essays as 'Boys' Weeklies', and Richard Hoggart, in *The Uses of Literacy*, demonstrated how literature and language are used to make class distinctions and how we even reserve different words for different kinds of people. Thus Arthur Scargill, the militant miners' leader, is dubbed a troublemaker but Lord Hanson, the take-over artist, is not. During the 1950s and 1960s the acceptable Establishment accent was Oxbridge which had also long been the norm for the BBC, although Harold Wilson made the regional accent acceptable after he became Prime Minister in 1964 and we entered the age of the classless, mid-Atlantic accent. Edward Heath, who came from a *petit bourgeois* background, emphasised, with his plummy Oxbridge accent, the British determination to rise – which means taking on the coloration of the ruling group.

Children present perfect, malleable material and every would-be manipulator through the ages – Jesuits, Nazis, Communists, or those who simply wish to perpetuate a forelock-tugging society – have known how important it is to get at them while still young. Only occasionally is a truly contrary view advanced, such as that of the nineteenth-century educationist Herbert Spencer, who, 'In contrast to the *authority* of teacher or author', write Hutchinson and Young in *Educating the Intelligent*, 'suggested that it was the *judgement* of the pupil which was the true aim of education.' (1962:65) And yet, too often, those who appear enlightened about education are possessed of curious blocks which show how much their views have been coloured by the society and upbringing to which they themselves have been subjected. Thus, Hutchinson and Young say first: 'Between the ages of eleven and thirteen or fourteen children should be taught the Christian religion and as much about the Christian ethical and moral system as they can then understand.' Here the authors assume that a religion (as opposed to an ethical or other system) should be taught in schools. They go on to say: 'It is a thoroughly mistaken view to suppose that young children are capable of approaching agnosticism. Neither mentally nor emotionally are they ready for such a view of life.' (73) Now this view, expressed here with *ex cathedra* authority, seems to be a nonsense – the product of the authors' own blinkered approach, the result of brainwashing in a 'Christian' society – and, moreover, a nonsense on two counts. Firstly, if children can be taught one set of principles at such an age they can be taught others, and during the present century children in that age group have been taught to be good (or not so good) Nazis, Communists and Christians, so why should they not also be taught 'about' agnosticism? Secondly, the claim that children are incapable of approaching agnosticism suggests that the subject is a mature subject (unlike Christianity or Communism) capable of being understood only by adults. And the logic of such a supposition in this case is that you do not teach children subjects that lead to questioning the accepted wisdom (Christianity) until they have already been moulded in a pattern of acceptance. This approach is the absolute contrary to Herbert Spencer's opinion that the judgement of the pupil should be the true aim of education, which these same authors quoted with apparent approval, and gives rise to the suspicion that, while wishing to give the appearance of balance – considering whether or not agnosticism can also be taught at the same age that Christianity is taught – they in fact do not wish an alternative to Christianity to be considered.

Education ought to be about choice and judgement but too often it is turned into indoctrination. Just as knowledge is the key to progress so also is its possession political and, as McLuhan asks of it: 'And education in this world [of the industrial-consumer society]? Is it education for use? Of course. But whose use? And for how long?' (1951:128) Much of our education as well as our literature is concerned to keep us in our places: it may be a question of class but just as likely it is a matter of functional position as one of Whyte's 'organization men'. A great deal of education, it would seem, is part of a 'buying-in' process to make sure that those who have such an education conform to particular norms rather than an attempt to equip students intellectually. And how much, to reverse the question, are students made into the drones of the system they serve? They must have brains and capacity but they must not question the system.

The 1990s opened with a major debate about British education and, although it had many nuances, in essence the debate was about the poor quality of what was on offer. Writing thirty years earlier Jackson and Marsden argued: 'The hard evidence suggests that if we could open education as freely to working-class children as we have done to middle-class ones, we would double – and double again – our highly talented and highly educated groups.' (1962:16) Given the fact that in the 1990s those who have the money will almost invariably take their children out of the state system on the grounds that it is not good enough, there would seem to have been few improvements since the 1960s, although much attention was given to education at that time. The British have always been mean about education. It is an élitist position and reflects the fact that far too high a proportion of the 'deciders' in our society come from wealthy backgrounds of private education and so assume that their like will rule. As a result they do not bother too much about the rest, who are regarded as the natural hewers of wood and drawers of water.

Elites always oppose the democratisation of luxuries, and if it is true that education is seen as a mark of culture, then its possessors will also see themselves as set apart by it and will not want to spread first-class education to everyone else. 'The majority, goes the idea, should be taught lesser skills; rather then tantalize themselves with aspirations, they should adjust to the fact of a fairly fixed social system.' (Whyte, 1956:45) C. P. Snow believed that élitist attitudes lay at the root of many British ills and, for example, he quotes the Chief Education Officer for the West Riding, Sir Alec Clegg: 'He tells us that there is no chance of human harmony in England until we pay whatever price we must (not only in money) to avoid the rancour of the educationally uneducated.' (1971:90) The marked and continuing reluctance of the British to extend education to all classes as much as possible reflects an élitist approach that is never far below the surface of public life; as Snow also remarked: 'The old pattern of training a small *élite* has never been broken, though it has been slightly bent.' (1961:36)

The public schools have become one of the boring perennials of discussion whenever British society is put under the microscope and, despite all arguments to the contrary, they are about élitism. No other country goes on so much as does Britain about the schools that were attended by its politicians and other leaders so that an analysis of the kind provided in *Ruling Performance*, which states that 73 per cent of Conservative MPs elected in 1959 has been to public schools, of whom 16 per cent had been at Eton, while 48 per cent of the Cabinet had been at Eton, appears a normal form of comment upon the background of our rulers. (Hennessy and Seldon, 1987:170) These schools continued to breed outmoded attitudes and perpetuate class barriers long after Britain laid claim to being an egalitarian society, while an endless stream of books about British public schools have for a century inculcated an element of snobbery and class into everyone's vision of British education: you went (to a public school); you didn't go; you wanted to go; you rejected the idea. (Quigley, 1982) Envy, perhaps especially on the part of the aspiring middle classes, has been nourished by the question of education – where they and their children were educated and where they would have liked to go to school. One of the most amusing quotes about those who go to public schools comes from an American woman married to an Old Etonian: 'Though one thing is true, if you take away the insecurities which is what really lies at the bottom of their problem, they are actually probably very very nice people and very worthwhile people.' (Green, 1990:147) On the subject of public schools Lionel Gelber, who demonstrated perceptive insights into the British, ended up by brainwashing himself: 'But for Britain to abolish public schools entirely might be to do more harm than good. On the debit side they have fostered class divisions; on the credit side the best have provided the intellectual substratum for those élite standards that Oxford and Cambridge have upheld, but which extended far beyond them. Prestige and power are not unrelated and the contribution that élite standards can still make to British prestige should never be minimized.' (1966:103) The fact that in 1991 the Education Secretary, Kenneth Clarke, could attack as hypocrites wealthy socialists who send their children to comprehensives and could go on to say that all parents yearned, often secretly, to be able to pay for their children to go to expensive private schools, stands as an appalling indictment of the British educational system from the man politically responsible for it. (*Standard*, October 1991) By 1991 it was reported that the number of parents sending their children to private schools had risen for the eighth successive year despite deep recession, and had reached 473,062 (members of the Independent Schools Information Service which represents 80 per cent of the private sector). One little gleam of hope surfaced in October 1991 when it was announced that the oldest Lord's fixture – the annual Eton–Harrow cricket match – was no longer to be held at that August venue (in part it seemed because the boys no longer behaved like gentlemen but chanted racist slogans); instead the matches will be held at the schools where the masters can keep better control. (*Standard*, 23.10.1991)

All education is a form of social engineering so the question as to who is responsible for it assumes enormous importance. Herbert Spencer said that 'The established systems of education, whatever their matter may be, are fundamentally vicious in their manner. They encourage *submissive receptivity* instead of *independent activity*.' (Hoggart, 1957:298) A system of education which encourages conformity may be valuable to the ruling élite but it is destructive of those it would educate. The process has been encouraged by segregating children into different schools according to ability, and although the comprehensive experiment was an attempt to get away from this pattern, it would appear that in the 1990s it is in danger of being abandoned. Of higher education it has been claimed that techniques of higher learning – lectures, exams, tutorials – may have little relevance to the subsequent career but a great deal to the system of which the student is now a part. (Cockburn and Blackburn, 1969:10)

As John Vaizey claims, 'It is the *un*importance of education which is the most striking characteristic of English social history.' (Koestler, 1963:223) It always appears as though every advance in education, particularly for the masses, has to be the subject of a debilitating political battle instead of being put in place automatically as a matter of sensible policy. Writing in 1962 Hutchinson and Young said: 'We are a rich nation and we want to become richer. We are an influential nation and we want to continue exercising our influence in the world. We need to use our greatest capital asset, our men and women, to the fullest possible extent. We must therefore offer them first-rate education. Nothing else will do.' (17) Thirty years later Britain was not providing the bulk of its children with first-rate education. The persistent way in which the British have failed to extend education upwards so that it is the norm rather than the exception for students to stay at school until eighteen and then continue to higher education has been noted again and again by social observers since 1945, so that one is forced to the conclusion that policy-makers in this regard are happy for the situation to continue. As Michael Heseltine could write in 1989: 'Only in Britain do a majority of sixteen-year-olds head immediately for the job market.' (140) And comparisons which are periodically made between Britain and other major economies are almost always to Britain's detriment. Thus, in 1991 the number of West German employees securing apprentice level certificates in mechanical engineering was five times that in Britain and two and a half time that in France while the flow of electricians was four times higher in both Germany and France than in Britain. (*Independent*, 3.6.91) Comparable figures in field after field tend to show that other industrial countries give greater attention to training than does Britain, which seems content to have so large a part of its population ill-educated and only semi-trained.

If education is the neglected child of an élitist society, snobbery is its sister. Bertrand Russell describes how in World War I he was addressing a pacifist meeting when rowdies came to break it up and the police stood by doing nothing. Then:

> one of the ladies among us went up to the police and suggested that they should defend me. The police, however, merely shrugged their shoulders. 'But he is an eminent philosopher,' said the lady, and the police still shrugged. 'But he is famous all over the world as a man of learning,' she continued. The police remained unmoved. 'But he is the brother of an earl,' she finally cried. At this the police rushed to my assistance. (1956:32)

The story may be funny, the implications are less so. When Churchill left the Admiralty in 1940 to become Prime Minister, the admirals reverted to pre-1913 arrangements to restrict lower-deck promotions to no more than 7.5 per cent of officer entry after the war (Churchill had increased the percentage target). (Ponting, 1990:143) Too often those who break out of the system appear as exceptions. As Tony Benn acidly comments upon the typists and secretaries used in Downing Street: 'These girls are from "good" families, having been to Roedean and other girls' public schools, because class is seen as the ultimate safeguard of national security.' (1990:73)

But although class remains a potent factor in Britain there is real class mobility, for the point of any class behaviour patterns is not exclusiveness alone, for that must lead to collapse but, rather, retraining for the new arrivals so as to make them fit in better as they move upwards. Class rising is about 'buying' your way into the next stage, and many who rise wish to forget the group from which they have emerged. In a class society 'the ruling class secures its position with the aid of education and the institution of the family, by making its ideologies the ruling ideologies of all members of the society.' (Brown, 1961:101)

D. N. Pritt, an eminent lawyer of the right class and background who, in his own words, progressed 'from right to left', saw the law as an instrument of class, and many recent cases – or, rather, the way people from different backgrounds are handled by the law – bear him out. Lester Piggot was convicted of tax fraud for £3.5 million and sentenced to three years in prison and his OBE was taken from him. Anthony Blunt betrayed his country and yet every attorney-general from 1964 to 1979 gave him immunity and he kept his honours, and he was to be disgraced only when the Establishment could no longer cover up for him. It is unthinkable that Blunt would have received such immunity over fifteen years had he come from the lower ranks of society. The three principals in the Guinness trial – Ernest Saunders, Anthony Parnes and Gerald Ronson – were given light sentences considering the scale of their corruption, while all too often working-class thieves get proportionately far heavier sentences. It is all part of the snobbery – encapsulated in the sort of remark by judges that 'given your place in society you have already suffered a great deal' – which is bound to continue as long as the judiciary are appointed only from the upper classes. In 1991 the London School of Economics (once seen as a bastion of socialism) suspended a professor on full pay after he had admitted fraudulently misappropriating £24,000 of research funds while it sacked outright a woman who worked in the canteen for not paying for one left-over hamburger worth 35 pence. (*Observer*, 12.5.91)

And just as we bring class into the law, so also do we bring it into pay and behaviour in the workplace. Why is it, for example, that only the workers are exhorted and threatened not to ask for pay in excess of the rate of inflation while management habitually awards itself rises far in excess of what it tells its workers they should settle at for the good of the country? The articulate middle classes are always arguing that they should have more to maintain their standards while workers must relate their wages to national productivity. Similarly, few things help perpetuate the class system more than segregation in the work-place – separate facilities for blue- and white-collar workers.

When the succession struggle to follow Margaret Thatcher as leader of the Tory Party was on, the three contenders, Michael Heseltine, Douglas Hurd and John Major, each in his different way, played the class card. Hurd felt obliged to play down his Eton background, Major played up his classlessness and Heseltine appeared in his green country Wellingtons. And although we make fun of class and pretend it does not matter, it clearly matters a great deal. As Colin Broughton pointed out in a letter to the *Standard* (21.12.90): 'Lord Whitelaw said that he was "constantly surprised and delighted" by John Major, as if the fellow were a performing monkey. Lord Blake remarked that he "uses a spoon the same as everyone else", as if decent behaviour were something to be worked at in a grammar school boy.'

The post-war years in Britain have witnessed endless reports on education and efforts to change it, yet as Britain entered the 1990s education was in a generally parlous state and admitted to be so on both sides of the political spectrum. Why? There was the argument about teaching history and that is especially concerned with brain-washing. On the one hand, there are those who feel it should be about British history, our past, shared experiences which supposedly help to make us the sort of people we are. On the other hand, another school of thought which, superficially, appears not to be brainwashed, wishes to make history into a study of 'United Nations history, in which past wrongs, oppressions and inequalities are redressed in the history books, and all knowledge is politicised.' (*Independent*, 1.3.88) In fact both kinds of history are a form of brainwashing: the 'pageant of the British people' of the kind at which Sir Arthur Bryant excelled; or the history of the modern world in which the bad behaviour of the old colonial powers such as Britain is highlighted. The second kind of history needs to be told, of course, but it must be told in perspective. Yes, the British have behaved badly, but then who has ever behaved well? And while the debate about teaching history raged – and was given much media coverage – Mr John MacGregor, the Education Secretary, announced that 'competition for undergraduate places in engineering has fallen in recent years' and this passed almost un-noticed. And now that a real debate about education had got underway it began to be noticed once more that British education was about élitism: 'The fundamental flaw in the British education system is that it is designed to produce a well-educated élite and an under-educated majority. It is not by accident that 65 per cent of our young people cease full-time education at 16. That is precisely the result the system is designed to produce.' (*Independent*, 8.9.90) The sad thing is that although there are plenty of people capable of making such an analysis, it is unlikely to make any difference. Neither political party shows any real intention of breaking the mould, of saying no matter what the cost we want all our young people to receive higher education and we intend to achieve this quickly, regardless of cost, simply because not to do it would be far more costly to our society in the long run. Since, as a society, we now treat our teachers with little short of contempt it is idle to imagine that education is going to be treated any better. Public confidence in state schooling is lower in Britain than anywhere else in Europe, and while only one-third of Britons claim to have faith in the education system the proportion is twice as high through the rest of Europe. (*Independent*, 3.6.91) Such findings make gloomy reading and bear out our general thesis that education is – and long has been – low-rated in Britain, not least because too high a proportion of our ruling élite has never been through the state system while too many of those who have been through it appear to think that they have risen beyond it and, therefore, that it does not matter any more. The entire educational philosophy needs to be turned on its head: it should be about what the students need, 'the judgement of the pupil' as the true aim of education and not the encouragement of 'submissive receptivity', which is what the system always seeks to ensure.

11 Advertising

Mazawatee Tea
Mazawatee Tea
Mazawatee Tea
Mazawatee Tea
Mazawatee Tea

THE PRINCIPLE OF REPETITION has always been at the heart of advertising. And although in a simpler age it was possible to see in a small railway station up to ten or twelve tin signs painted over with their message – Mazawatee Tea – stacked on the wall, one above the other, to make sure the traveller first had his attention drawn to them and then remembered just what he was being offered, modern practices, if more sophisticated, still rely upon repetition above all other factors. Thus, travellers on the London Underground can see the same advertisement on every fourth or fifth panel as they ascend or descend the escalators: if they saw it only once in passing they would forget it; having been bombarded with it twenty times they just might remember it for a short while. And although television now offers scope for sophisticated action pictures, a repeat performance in half-a-dozen slots at best viewing times of an evening is still seen as the surest way to capture attention. If advertisers were forced to choose between a highly sophisticated, one-off presentation and endless repetition they would go, almost certainly, for the repetition every time.

The best advertising has always been ingenious and fun, almost an art form, which has given it added attraction and impact: 'They come as a boon and a blessing to men, The Pickwick, the Owl and the Waverley pen.' The combination of a simple, arresting caption and an equally arresting picture – the upended glass and the words 'Down with Guinness' – have amused with their cleverness and so brought added lustre to the product being sold. A somewhat different technique was employed for years by the *News of the World*: huge posters showed four obviously lower-class, working women gossiping, the expressions on their faces indicating subject matter of a less than elevating kind, while the caption read: 'All human life is there', and so off the punter went to obtain his weekend's read of salacious stories.

We have long taken advertising for granted and expect those with products to 'sell', including, for example, political parties or other organisations seeking support, to bombard us with advertisements. How much notice people take of the advertisements in reality is another matter.

During 1991 protests forced the firm Benetton to remove large advertisements on hoardings which simply showed a new-born baby, umbilical cord still attached, wet and red with blood. The protests generally were at the unseemly and, to some, shocking nature of the picture. No message accompanied the baby, although the name of the company was displayed at the bottom of the advertisement. In this particular case the tactic, which had clearly been designed to attract maximum attention, backfired, but the assumption behind the advertisement was that what Benetton sells is so well known that there was no need to add any information about the actual products – for example, that this new-born child can depend upon Benetton until it dies – but that everybody scrutinising the advertisement would at once understand what was on offer.

The chief function of advertising is to deceive would-be buyers about the worth of what is being sold: either by suggesting that the product is actually better, more enduring, essential or unique when none of these conditions really applies; or by insisting that the lifestyle of the would-be buyer will be made complete only by its possession, because it is fashionable, special to his or her peer group, a sign of the rising executive or ideal virile male or chic woman-about-town, or the essential adjunct to every 'home' and so on. Advertising is seen as crucial in the admass consumer society and although it is found in all societies, including the poorest, it is in the wealthy societies of surplus capacity where it is really important. Most people are suggestible, and most people like to keep up with their peers, and 'In very few instances do people really know what they want, even when they say they do.' (Packard, 1960a:17) The fact that they do not know is a godsend to advertisers and an invitation to set upon them. Any publicity is worth having and only when no notice is taken do salesmen begin to worry. As Marshall McLuhan (1964) argued, critics of advertising as false and misleading are welcome to advertisers since they acclaim and accelerate attention to what has to be advertised (and provide the opportunity for some free publicity as well).

Advertising appeals to certain well-defined instincts: material greed, emulation, the desire for health and good looks, the need to be appreciated by others, the attraction of belonging – to the in-group, or those who are perceived by society to be leaders, the trend-setters, the fashionable. The list of adjectives and phrases is long and part of the advertiser's business is to think up new words and phrases which possess cachet and appeal, whose application to a product suggests that its possession is essential: 'young', 'executive', 'laid-back', 'svelte', 'new', 'different' – the list is endless and changes according to fashions but the word 'new' is consistently the most used, appealing to an insatiable demand for variety in what for most people is a drab world.

The primary aim of advertising is to make people buy what otherwise they would not buy or not buy in such quantities. It operates at several levels. In relation to essential products, soap for example, advertising techniques are employed at an elementary level, part of the cut-throat competition of a consumer society: 'washes whiter' implies but does not claim that it is better than other soaps in the hope that the particular product will outsell its rivals. At a second level of advertising the object is to persuade people to buy more than they actually need, whether it is extra clothes in which to be smart, a second 'family' car or useless knick-knacks that are supposed to denote that the possessors are 'in the swing', whatever particular 'swing' might then be fashionable. A third, top level of advertising concentrates upon snobbery: the desire of people to be different and have what others do not or cannot afford to have, with the Rolls-Royce at the top end of the scale. The obverse of this process is the need to make money, and the sheer volume of advertising bears testimony to its value: a newspaper or magazine that cannot sell enough advertising space does not last long. An issue of the *Independent Magazine* for December 1991, for example, devoted just over half of its 96 pages (50 in all) to advertisements, and such weekend magazines are primarily about advertising rather than editorial content. As the late Raymond Williams, a dour intellectual of the left, commented upon the widespread dependence of the media upon advertising revenue:

> From this it becomes one of the major purposes of communication to sell a particular paper or programme. All the basic purposes of communication – the sharing of human experience – can become subordinated to this drive to sell. ... The organisation of communications is then not for use, but for profit, and we seem to have passed the stage in which there has to be any pretence that things are otherwise. (1962:24)

Much selling depends upon gimmicks rather than quality, and advertising persuades people less on the grounds that a particular product is the best of its kind (although when a product can reasonably make such a claim this is by far the best line for advertisers to adopt) than that it is different (new again), that all teenagers or executives or members of some other peer group have one or use it or that some well-known national figure 'swears by it'. Thus, innovation, special features, impulse and the peer group are the tools of the advertisers' trade. Poor quality, cheap or useless goods can be sold by persistence as the jewellers Ratners have demonstrated. An extraordinary row developed in April 1991 when Gerald Ratner, the chairman and managing director of Ratners, addressed the annual convention of the Institute of Directors and said: 'Ratners has got very little to do with quality. People say "how can you sell for such low prices?" I say "because it's total crap". There is no point in beating about the bush. We even sell a pair of gold ear-rings for under £1 which is cheaper than a prawn sandwich from Marks & Spencer.' Later, Mr Ratner partly retracted what he had said, claiming that his remarks were 'tongue-in-cheek', but the fact is his company had been enormously successful. In his speech he also referred to the company's sales techniques: 'Some people say they can't even see the jewellery for all the posters and banners in the window. But it is interesting that these shops that everyone has a good laugh about take more money per square foot than any retailer in Europe.' At the time Ratners had fallen foul of the trading standards officers' prices review committee, whose chairman, Roy Hill, said he believed the public was being misled by stores like Ratners which offered huge discounts: 'Discounts are attractive to the consumer. But they have to rely on information supplied by the shops. In the past people thought they were buying reasonable quality goods at a high discount. But they are actually buying cheap goods at no discount.' (*Independent*, 25.4.91) Mr Hill is no doubt correct but people who could say 'no' continue to buy such goods, which is sufficient testimony to the power of one particular kind of high-pressure sales and advertising technique.

At a more 'sophisticated' level than Ratners there is an endless stream of advertising in the 'quality' weekend magazines for goods of dubious quality and little or no value, aimed essentially at those who might be described as rising 'executives' (now one of the most over-used words in the English language, much beloved by advertisers) to persuade them to buy such things as 'limited' editions of hand-painted china plates, or Picasso in print or signed reproductions by other artists. The fact that there are so many customers for Ratners' jewellery or 'exclusive' limited editions – itself a contradiction in terms – testifies either to the extraordinary potency of advertising or to the low general level of education which has failed to teach any kind of discrimination or sense of values – or to both.

Advertisers have long separated their would-be customers into groups, for the group trades upon that most seductive of human needs, the desire to belong. To begin with there are general groups – babies, children, teenagers, husbands, women (once-upon-a-time housewives but not in these days of women's liberation), grandparents, senior citizens. But then come the endless sub-divisions: professions of course, followed by the ubiquitous executive, although the term has now come to mean anyone who wants to feel he or she is above the general and on the make. They will make out better if they buy an executive watch or briefcase to persuade them that they are moving up the competitive ladder.

Children are the starting point. Advertisers have clearly taken a leaf out of the Jesuits' book: 'give me a child before he is seven and he belongs to the Church for life'. Children are fiercely competitive, so that appeals to their snobbish and peer instincts ensure that at an early age they begin to harass their parents into buying whatever may be the latest childish fashion.

> The advertisers begin by luring children. Since, because of parents' apprehension, most children no longer go out to play in the streets and in the immediate neighbourhood, and since the television, not the hearth, is now the centre of the living-room, the admen have a captive audience; the appetite of the child is inflamed by beaming an unremitting display of the latest mechanical and electronic toys. (Abse, 1989:52–3)

From children the advertisers pass to perhaps the most vulnerable and suggestible group of all, the adolescents or teenagers who are aspiring to adult status and are ruthlessly bombarded with adult tastes long before they have an adult purse to match. Here sex is a major weapon in the advertisers' armoury: fashions of course – male, female and unisex; and 'sexual excitation and titillation. The cigarette, the bath soap, the branded drinks, the motor cars, the perfumes, the package tours, all are eroticised by overt salacity or innuendo'. (Abse, 1989:53)

Back in 1951 the following passage appeared in an article in *Fortune Magazine*: 'We control a man's environment in business and we lose it entirely when he crosses the threshold of his home. Management therefore has a challenge and an obligation deliberately to plan and create a favourable, constructive attitude on the part of the wife that will liberate her husband's total energies for the job.' (Packard, 1960a:175) That was about management rather than advertising and belongs to an age when the role of the woman was seen as either housewife or adjunct to her male partner's career. Advertising then and for many years to come treated women in this light, aiming at them advertisements about minding the children, running the home, making themselves more glamorous for their men; only recently and only in part have attitudes changed as a result of women's liberation and the fact that more and more women are now holding real executive positions and have become advertising targets on a par with real executive men. None the less, many complaints received by the Advertising Standards Authority (ASA) are of sexist advertising: either using women's bodies – naked or part naked – to attract male buyers (the assumption still being that the man has the big money for spending); or depicting them still in the domestic role or as helpless sex objects to be cossetted or flattered – with expensive products. An ASA study, *Herself Reappraised*, published in 1990, showed that 56 per cent of women and 43 per cent of men agreed that 'the use of naked or semi-naked models in advertising is harmful' and similar percentages also agreed that 'advertisements always show women as sex objects'. (*Independent*, 28.2.90) The fact that people complain of the use of nudity in advertising is unlikely to prevent it continuing as long as advertisers believe it sells products: they will find ways round regulations until an outright ban is placed upon the practice – if ever.

The great problem with the Western economic system – the consumer society – is that it demands ever higher consumption as a means of survival, so that planned obsolescence is built into both production and advertising methods. Not very often does one come across an advertisement which suggests that a product will last a lifetime, which is why fashion is so important. If a product has been sold as the best of its kind it is not possible two years later to suggest that it must have worn out. The alternative is to suggest that everybody is now doing something quite different, so that the wonderful old product becomes a museum piece. Techniques vary all the time but most of them are concerned with deceit and flattery. As McLuhan writes, 'Effective flattery gains its ends partly by distracting the attention of the reader from its presuppositions and by its quiet fusion with other levels of experience. And in this respect it is the supreme form of cynical demagogic flattery.' Stress on exclusiveness and fashion is what makes people ditch the old and go for the new, although the converse of this, perhaps, is emphasis upon failure: 'To be without at least some of the new models marks a man as an economic failure.' (1951:82, 112) Both flattery and fear of failure are assisted by a range of appeal words such as 'exclusive' or 'top people', or by the technique – already referred to in the Benetton case (see page 131) – of assuming that the exclusive name is so well known that it becomes unnecessary to mention any product attached to it.

The Thatcher decade with its emphasis upon wealth and the rise of the 'yuppie' gave enormous impetus to advertising, with great emphasis upon suave, svelte, sophisticated products which would be shown off in settings that were a world away from the lifestyles of most of the people being targeted: homes had glamorous Hollywood-style interiors and drinks were served on tropical beaches while major advertising companies such as Saatchi and Saatchi became powers in the land. Leo Abse, the Labour psychologist/psychiatrist MP, made an important point about the advertising industry during Thatcher's period of power and influence: 'Thatcher's one other major ally in creating the fetishist society is the advertising industry both in its size and in its capacity to debauch. Political parties are now in danger of becoming subsidiaries of the industry.' And speaking of yuppies Abse said: 'The mask is worn by more and more yuppie parents. They are seduced by commercial advertising into the illusion that only by taking on larger houses and mortgages can happiness be achieved; the houses are stuffed with consumer goods and empty of love.' (1989:52, 54) Given the crisis of mortgage failures and repossessions that took place at the end of 1991, when the Major government was obliged to implement rescue measures to assist many of those who had been persuaded to buy beyond their means or long-term expectations, the advertising industry had a good deal to answer for.

Yuppies are only one kind of rising snob; an earlier generation had been appealed to by such slogans as 'Top People Take *The Times*'. Typical of the frivolity and nonsense to which snob appeal advertising lends itself was the Diners Club offer of gold walnuts for 'Executive stress relief': 'Two genuine walnuts, encapsulated in 22-carat gold, they fit comfortingly in the palm of one hand to relieve tension at those difficult times of day.' The walnuts could be ordered by telephone or fax 24 hours a day and would come in a suede pouch, delivered by freepost. The mind boggles at a generation of yuppie executive Captain Queegs (the paranoid Captain of Herman Wouk's novel *The Caine Mutiny*) wandering about London masturbating gold walnuts in their hands – until, of course, too many of them meet one another and realise that their toys are no longer exclusive. People who will fall for that will fall for anything.

The creation of fads, preferably by the rich and the famous, is vital to the advertising business. The extraordinary fetish about 'designer' clothes which became the rage of the 1980s was a classic example of advertisers misusing language. A designer is one who makes an artistic design or plan for the manufacturer and this, of course, will cover the designer of any mass-produced article, yet clever advertising and 'hype' suggested that such clothes were unique even though everybody who was anybody sought to wear them – and did so provided they could find the price. A high proportion of the most successful advertising is about glamour or perceived glamour, which is not necessarily the real thing at all, and creating aspirations in often foolish people so that they spend money on ephemeral objects which they cannot afford. It certainly works and many people display the latest glamour object only to discard it within a year as the advertisers persuade them that the rage of 1990 is old hat in 1991. A more down-to-earth form of advertising is the T-shirt or sports bag with a logo on it; here the customer becomes, quite literally, a walking advertisement for the company whose logo he wears or bears, and he ought, in sensible business terms, to charge the company for every public appearance he makes. Advertising has long been a multibillion pound industry although British performance and expenditure is dwarfed by that of the United States where, in 1989, Philip Morris became the first company to spend more than $2 billion on advertising in a year.

Television is now the most potent vehicle for advertising: the hoarding can be ignored and the newspaper advertisement can be skipped but the TV ad in the middle of a programme has to be endured, and even if its appearance provides a break to make sandwiches or get a beer from the refrigerator, one is still conscious of it. As early as the 1950s it was suggested that some mediocre programmes were so by design so as to highlight the impact of commercials, and although

that suggestion is clearly debatable the constant commercials hammer-
ing and beaming at the peace of viewers have become as much a part
of the television world as its programmes and, since television is by
far the premier form of entertainment with the majority of people
spending many hours every week in front of their sets, television
commercials must be absorbed even by those people who insist that
they ignore them or do something else when they appear.

The importance of all advertising – and the power of advertisers –
was emphasised in 1990 when the BBC was forced to shelve a major
documentary series on the history of British television commercials
because some of the advertisers objected. Advertisers did not want
products which had failed or been criticised to be aired again; they
did not want people to be reminded of old brands when they had
spent millions altering and improving them. In some cases companies
tried to insist that the BBC should show their current advertisements
along with the old ones. (Brooke, 1990) The dispute was all the more
pointed since the BBC itself is not permitted to advertise, although
suggestions that it should fund itself at least in part by advertising
have been advanced for 1996 when its Charter has to be renewed.

The 1988 Broadcasting White Paper made major concessions to
advertisers, breaking the ITV monopoly and offering companies new
channels for their commercials as well as making ITV more responsive
to advertisers' demands. Thus, a new Channel 5 was allowed to carry
advertisements, Channel 4 could sell its commercial air time independently of ITV, and a new ITV franchise was created to provide
programmes and sell advertisements through the night, as well as
advertising-funded local and satellite television. The White Paper
heralded a far more commercial-oriented television approach and did
not say much about how such advertising was to be controlled. The
new Independent Television Commission (replacing the IBA) would
be responsible for a code covering advertising and sponsorship. It was
clear that the 1990s would see a new television era of more advertising
and less control. The most important innovation of the 1990 Broadcasting Act was to open the door to television sponsorship, forty years
after it was banned when the Tories originally introduced commercial
television into Britain in 1954. Companies can now sponsor programmes and show their own products or advertising material at the
beginning and end of programmes. Meanwhile, increasing discussion
of the position of the BBC, as well as growing pressures from a less
than friendly government, indicate that by the end of the 1990s it, too,

is likely, at least in some measure, to rely upon advertising for its revenues.

From time to time the promoters of advertising find themselves in embarrassing positions when the demands of selling conflict with other principles. The issue of smoking is an obvious example of this although others include the double standards which are applied to advertising in Britain and advertising by the same companies in the Third World, where both lack of regulations as well as an inability to make them stick allow companies to use advertising (sales) techniques that would not be permitted at home. Evidence of the harmful effects upon health of smoking is now widely accepted, yet cigarette-manufacturing companies do all in their considerable powers to increase smoking while the government satisfies what it sees as its moral responsibility towards the British people by insisting upon a health warning on cigarette packets, which has little effect, because the government does not wish to take stronger action that might really cut down cigarette consumption since this would also cut down the government's tax take from this source. The usual hypocrisies are at work. This government hypocrisy was highlighted in November 1991 when the Health Education Authority launched its seventeen-volume report on smoking. The government wanted the authority to avoid any mention of advertising. The report's opening paragraph begins: 'We estimate that 110,000 people die before their time from smoking-attributable diseases. And yet cigarettes are still heavily advertised, cleverly promoted and widely sold in shops and supermarkets.' The huge costs of smoking – an estimated £400 million a year bill for the NHS – merely highlight what has long been known and argued by the medical profession, and yet the government opposes banning advertising and has opposed the EC proposal to ban advertising despite insistent calls for this to be done by the health profession. The question arising out of this government attitude is simply: how much is it reluctant to take stronger action because of pressures from the tobacco industry which it feels itself unable to resist; and how much, even if it had the nerve to stand up to the industry, is it determined not to do so in order to continue taking the easy revenues that come from taxes on all tobacco products? The answer, almost certainly, is a mixture of the two, but whatever it may be the fact that the government cannot bring itself to ban advertising represents an enormous victory for the power of that particular lobby.

The Americans pioneered many aspects of what we have come to call the depth approach to advertising: searching for people's self-images, their secret distresses or hidden needs, in fact any aspects of their characters which are not at once apparent but which may be exploited by the clever advertiser. Sex, snobbery, class, caste, wish-fulfilment, upward mobility, neurosis, health and many more aspirations have long been on the advertisers' hit list; their problem is finding the best way to activate these human desires and weaknesses and translate them into a wish to buy a product that supposedly will answer a deep and unmet need. They have certainly worked hard enough at the problem and back in the 1950s experimented with subliminal techniques, although these have been banned. As the British Institute of Practitioners of Advertising said of this technique in 1958: 'The free choice by the public to accept or reject is an integral part of all forms of professionally accepted advertising and does not appear to be available to recipients of subliminal communication.' (Brown, 1963:184) In December 1991, while Europe's political leaders met at Maastricht in the Netherlands to hammer out the future of the EC, a furious row developed between the Europen Commission and media owners determined to prevent further legislation designed to restrict advertising. The European Commission, with its growing tentacles, which is moving increasingly to control every aspect of the Community's life, will face a battle second only to that of its members' competing nationalisms if it tries to regulate advertising in any way likely to upset profits.

Advertising is now one of the half-dozen most important control factors in our lives. It is about profit, and in order to maximise this the advertisers have moved into every aspect of our lives, not just as salesmen, which is how they started out, but as social arbiters. The power of organised advertising is enormous and increasing, and those who would regulate it, except at the margin, face an uphill task in view of the vested interests it represents. Their chances are slim.

12 The media

This is a democratic country, so we are supposed
to have some idea of what is going on. For this we
depend on wireless and newspaper presentation of
news. But can we believe what we read and hear?

MASS OBSERVATION

SINCE TOM HARRISSON AND CHARLES MADGE pioneered Mass Observation just before World War II, the media dimension has been
broadened by its third arm – television – but the question, 'can
we believe what we read and hear?', is as relevant today as it
was then, although it requires the addition of 'and see' to round it off.
In his biography, Lord Reith wrote that 'Broadcasting has for long
been recognised as an estate of the realm.' Today television is the 'estate
of the realm' but whereas the radio, which in Lord Reith's day meant
the BBC alone, was generally regarded as serving the interests of the
Establishment, television is seen as potentially far more dangerous to
the politicians since its all-pervasive nature (present and turned on in
so many homes for so much of the time) means that if it is critical of
those in power the immediate impact of such criticism is likely to
outweigh any subsequent denials or attempts at a compensating
balance. Hence the constant threatening and bullying of the broadcasters that has become, if not new, certainly a heightened feature of
recent public life.

In the days of the BBC's monopoly of broadcasting the assumption
underlying its attitudes to authority was that it *ought* to be on the side
of authority. 'The BBC remains today as deferential to those in
authority and as predisposed in their favour as ever Reith could have
wished that it be. It allows fair play only when the two front benches
are agreed about a policy, and then only to the front-bench point of
view.' (Thomas, 1962:178, 183) The turning point which shaped the
modern media came in the mid-1950s when the commercial television
lobby won its battle to break the BBC monopoly. At that time a certain
amount of extra attention had to be paid to the masses, since the
profitability of commercial television would depend upon the size of
the audiences which could be attracted. Cecil King then said that either
you give the public what it wants or go out of business, while Norman

Collins (who had become one of the new television moguls) said loftily: 'If one gave the public exactly what it wanted it would be a perfectly appalling service,' although he and most others proceeded to give it 90 per cent of what it wanted. The views of these two men with their wide experience of the media demonstrated a major (if justified) contempt for the public they claimed to serve. A more detached but rarefied approach was that of Brown, who argued that 'the mass media are there to be made use of, and what use is made of them depends upon the individual himself.' (1963:161) This represents the intelligent man's view but assumes a capacity to choose which, too often, is belied by the sheer weight of bombardment that the mass media offers. If the intelligent public is likely to find difficulty in using a media which is primarily concerned with the mass audience, then other minorities, especially those of the left, will face as much difficulty. 'To be sure, the method of persuasion is still open to the minority, but it is fatally reduced by the fact that the leftist minority does not possess the large funds required for equal access to the mass media which speak day and night for the dominant interests.' (Marcuse, 1969:65)

By the early 1960s politicians had come to see just how important to their performance television was likely to be and so began to realise that a poor television manner could be a crippling disadvantage. At the same time, to use a phrase of McLuhan's, the 'electric media' came to mean that everyone was increasingly involved in what was going on: the sort of detachment that had been possible when news and views were distilled only by newspapers had disappeared. Unfortunately, the media are less concerned to animate the discussions of mass audiences and democracy than to transform the public into 'a set of media markets in mass-like society'. (Mills, 1958:34) Now this sort of media can work as long as the public is trustful, but if it is detected in telling too many lies it defeats its own purpose. Control of the media is axiomatic in dictatorships of whatever kind. But in democracies, if the control is not overt it is none the less there, and too often it is exercised blatantly as well.

What is certain today is the extent to which the media in all its forms pervades our lives, and the power wielded by those who control it. British culture is a mixture of Christian and Hellenistic influences yet 'Both [traditions] are now challenged by the barbarism of an unadulterated technology.' (Hutchinson and Young, 1962:31) This concern with the technology of the mass media is very important in an age when technology in so many forms is taken for granted: it is no longer a miracle or new but automatically accepted, and the result is that what the technology provides – on the television screen, for example – is automatically accepted as well. Marshall McLuhan, it could be argued, was obsessed with the electronic media, and yet he was right to be so.

> All media work us over completely. They are so persuasive in their personal, political, economic, aesthetic, psychological, moral, ethical, and social consequences that they leave no part of us untouched, unaffected, unaltered. The medium is the message. Any understanding of social and cultural change is impossible without a knowledge of the way media work as environments. (1967:26)

And he went on:

> an aspect of the new mass culture we are moving into – a world of total involvement in which everybody is so profoundly involved with everybody else and in which nobody can really imagine what private guilt can be anymore. (61)

McLuhan wrote those words in the 1960s; since then the involvement has increased.

The actual process of communicating information can be used to ensure that a particular view prevails; this can be achieved in many ways: by emphasis, omission, slanting, providing pictures of striking miners using force and restrained policemen standing by and so on. The media can also be used to stop people thinking, or at least to prevent their thinking with any profundity, and one of the most insidious developments that television has fostered is the extension of opinion as though it is news: the constant appearance of experts discussing a crisis as though their contributions, however profound, are a substitute for hard news which allows the viewer to make his own judgement. Indeed, on important issues, it is as though the media are determined that the audience should never have to be bothered with the awkward business of making a judgement for themselves, since the programme will provide endless judgements for them. Another factor in the electronic age is the encouragement of information exchange for its own sake, unrelated to events. And the visual requirements of television – an exciting picture or image – encourage distortion, since an alternative story of just as much importance tends to be ignored if it is unsupported by strong visual images: 'The nature of the medium [TV] inevitably encourages visually strong incidents and discourages explorations of undercurrents which, by definition, cannot be seen.' (Mercer *et al.*, 1987:11) There must be a constant struggle to have or to keep an open information system while commercial and political pressures between them aim to close the system in their favour. Television is concerned with effect upon the viewer rather than meaning, and one result of that approach became apparent in the demand of ITN in 1991 that the next British election should be covered according to news events rather than, as in the past, by the 'stopwatch approach' in which each party is allotted equal time in the news bulletins or other programmes concerned with the election. The ITN argument is beguiling but the end result could be even more insane political playing to the gallery than is the case at present. Thus, if Mr Kinnock, or his successor, manages in one day to make five dramatic public appearances to Mr Major's three, then he could get more coverage in the ratio of five to three. The prospect has intriguing possibilities. (*Independent*, 26.8.91)

Modern technology has ensured that the media exercise a pervasive influence over almost every aspect of society, so that whoever controls the media also exercises a substantial control over our lives. The myth, long perpetuated by British governments, that the BBC was independent was never believed in foreign countries, and quite rightly. Ultimately control of the BBC lay with the government which financed it through the licence system, and in a sense the BBC acknowledged the debt, in the days when it held a monopoly, by generally avoiding 'difficult subjects'. (Inglis, 1965:240) Only when commercial television broke the monopoly did the BBC have to compete, and to do so it became more – although not too much more – controversial. The controllers of information are extremely powerful. Tony Benn writes: 'They are in effect the new bosses of modern society. It confirmed my endorsement of the Chinese theory that private ownership of knowledge is what really seems to be determining our society.' (1988:403) And when direct control (by government) is not possible, then endless pressures, often extremely difficult to withstand, are exerted to silence those who might otherwise reveal what governments would prefer to conceal. Raymond Williams saw the dilemma posed by an extending democracy and a contracting control of communications: 'First, it is clear that the extension of communications has been part of the extension of democracy. Yet, in this century, while the public has extended, ownership and control of the means of communication have narrowed.' (1962:25) Maximum freedom of the media needs to be guaranteed; it should not be left under the control of minority interest groups whether these are commercial or government.

Television and radio were a BBC monopoly until 1954 and it was the possibility of enormous profits from managing television which led powerful pressure groups to insist upon breaking the monopoly. When Raymond Williams wrote in 1962 that 'The organization of communications is then not for use, but for profit, and we seem to have passed the stage in which there has to be any pretence that things are otherwise', he was already expressing what was an utopian view. (24) The real issue is the extent to which governments and public demand combined can ensure that those who run the media for profit can also be made to behave responsibly, and by the time that the auction for independent television licences took place in 1991 the omens were not good. As an *Independent* editorial of 26 August 1991 suggested in the wake of the auction, 'imports will rise, and quality will fall'. And it continued: 'The explanation of this sorry state of affairs is simple. Between 1979 and 1990, the Government – meaning the prime minister of the day and her attendant clique of ideologues and opportunists – saw new technology as an opportunity to bring the television industry to heel, where most of the newspaper industry already was.' Strong stuff, perhaps, yet the basic fear comes from the government: that it has to control television in order to prevent it from usurping the government's ability to persuade. The criteria of the highest bidder – subject to quality – in fact produced a scramble for the lucrative licences, and while some genuine concern for quality was written into the auction system, the successful companies will be tempted increasingly to produce only popular programmes rather than difficult or provoking ones so as to keep their share of the market, especially as 1994 will see the end of the take-over moratorium. It is absurd to pretend that the scramble for licences and the tears of those who lost were about quality programmes. It was about money. Two losers in the scramble were Thames TV, whose creative output had included *Death on the Rock*, and TV-am 'the darling of the former Prime Minister. But theirs was the kind of TV that Prime Ministers tend to like. It pacifies the multitude without trying to participate in the flow of events.' (*Observer*, 20.10.91) Thus, when take-overs become part of the television scene, companies are bound to aim more and more for the big audiences while quality generally is likely to deteriorate. If the 'profit' scramble among independent television companies takes the form that most commentators think is likely – lower standards and fewer intellectual or investigative programmes – then the role of the BBC (if it is left intact) will become more important than ever, although whether jealous governments would allow it to survive if it alone became the source of in-depth investigative programmes (at a cost to the taxpayer) is increasingly doubtful, at least in terms of current attitudes towards 'independent', that is, non-partisan, broadcasting which queries what the government of the day would prefer not to have queried.

The power of the media is testified to by the concern and attention constantly paid to it by governments, and although there is media freedom the pressures exerted upon it by governments are sometimes close to intolerable. In the long years of the Ulster crisis the government has consistently opposed any programmes that did not clearly support the government view, and those which failed to do so were dubbed defeatist or worse. (Bolton, 1990:22–3) The government has also 'managed' the media over issues of importance to it, such as the 1984–5 coal-miners' strike, by setting the parameters of discussion within which journalists could operate. But it is not only governments that exert pressures on the media. On environmental issues the nuclear industry, the motor industry, fishing and farming lobbies and other groups each have their own vested interests in controlling what is said. However, as Paddy Ashdown insisted in 1989, the government was 'blatantly trying to create a submissive and deferential broadcasting industry'. (Cockerell, 1988:34) As the media becomes more powerful and more pervasive, as it undoubtedly will, the pressures from governments are likely to become stronger and the idea of a 'hands-off' approach will increasingly recede into what in any case has always been a semi-mythical past. No government has ever been happy with a truly free media, and during the Thatcher years her press secretary, Bernard Ingham, became one of the most powerful figures in the government although technically he was only a press officer. His job was manipulation of the media on behalf of the prime minister.

Writing of the BBC in 1968, Tony Benn described its power as follows: 'With the exception of Government itself, there is scarcely any other body in Britain enjoying as much power as the BBC. And since the Government, quite properly, keeps at arms length from the BBC and makes no effort whatsoever to make it account for what it does,

it stands in a position of almost unique and unchallenged influence.'
(1988:109–10) Mr Benn would be unlikely to write in that vein in
1991, at a time when the BBC was much less powerful and much more
open to government pressure. In any case his 1968 view of the BBC
seems an impossibly idealistic one, for whenever the interests of the
government are at stake it has been prepared to exert enormous
pressures upon the BBC. Back in 1926, at the time of the General
Strike and the BBC's infancy, Lord Reith said of the government
decision not to take over the BBC: 'The Cabinet decision is really a
negative one. They want to be able to say that they did not comman-
deer us, but they know they can trust us not to be really impartial.'
(Miller, 1990:35) After the war the Tory Party's first-ever Head of
Broadcasting, John Profumo, said how he 'wanted to keep an eye on
left-wing bias at the BBC', and it is clear that from then onwards the
major political parties paid ever closer attention to what the BBC said
and did. By the 1980s threats about the renewal of its licence were
being made over BBC Ulster programmes as, for example, with
relentless government pressure to prevent programmes in which
members of the Republican movement were interviewed. (Bolton,
1990:50, 38) Indeed, the BBC was in trouble with the government
through most of the Thatcher years, and as Alan Protheroe describes
it, the sacking of the Director-General, Alasdair Milne, was more
brutal than anything in the Kremlin, while in the House of Commons
a Tory MP asked the Prime Minister to support the candidacy of
someone 'who could curb the treasonable tendencies of the BBC and
with the Herculean qualities to clean up its Augean stables'. (Cockerell,
1988:316) Such behaviour and such pressures from the centre of
government made nonsense of any British claims that the BBC was,
even by intention, independent of government.

But although the battle between government and a BBC which
refused just to mouth that government's views became overt and very
public during the 1980s, the struggle was not a new one. During the
Suez crisis of 1956 Anthony Eden brought great pressures to bear
upon the BBC not, for example, to interview the Egyptian, Major Saleh
Salem; he wrote to protest while other ministers wanted to bring the
BBC to heel, and the Colonial Secretary, Alan Lennox-Boyd, thought
it 'an outrage that a body widely believed to be in part at least
associated with the British Government should broadcast at such a
moment a speech by a notorious enemy'. At least Lennox-Boyd
exploded the myth which was still much cultivated at the time that the

BBC was independent (he clearly did not think so), while Anthony Nutting explained that the government was determined that the BBC should put its case across 'without having contrary views also carried to the confusion of peoples in certain parts of the world who did not understand our political system'. (Kyle, 1991:191, 337) That statement demonstrates the ambivalence of politicians who, in less fraught times, would make much of BBC impartiality and the fact that government did not control it. And finally, from reactions to the Suez crisis, Sir Ivone Kirkpatrick at the Foreign Office complained of the BBC fetish of attaching 'too much importance to impartiality'.

The competition of independent television certainly altered the parameters of broadcasting for the BBC, forcing it to re-examine its markets. Ian Trethowan claimed that the programme *That Was the Week that Was* 'swept through British broadcasting as a cleansing agent, scouring away the last of the bland and the banal' (Cockerell, 1988:86), but if the BBC became less bland it also went downmarket in order to compete and, as Anthony Hartley said in 1963, 'Even the BBC can stoop to putting on a thoroughly objectionable programme like *This Is Your Life* which draws its audience by a nauseating display of its victims' inner emotions.' (175) In his diaries Tony Benn complains of right-wing bias in the BBC, interviews that begin with loaded opening statements, so-called balance in which he was matched with three right wingers; for example, he describes Ford car workers complaining of a pay offer in which 'The BBC television coverage deliberately created the impression that motor-car workers are dangerous and violent, while the BBC is the voice of reason.' (1990:385) Now with Tony Benn complaining of the right-wing bias of the BBC and the Tory Party of its left-wing bias, it is just possible that sometimes the BBC was actually getting things right and what in reality the politicians were complaining of was the fact that the BBC did not support the particular views they wished to see advanced. Certainly, during the 1970s, which were an especially difficult time for Britain, the BBC often appeared to take a right-wing view which upset the Labour government in power, while during the 1980s it appeared to take a left-wing view which upset an especially authoritarian Tory government so that an impartial observer might be pardoned for coming to the conclusion that governments want the BBC – and presumably other media as well – only to take stands compatible with their policies. That, indeed, is what much of the public argument is and has always been about, and the media has to fight a constant battle to maintain its right to differ from the government of the day. When its presentation rouses the ire of the government of the day it is probably, on balance, doing a sound job.

Partly, no doubt, in response to government pressures and complaints, the BBC held a seminar on impartiality in 1988 as a prelude to issuing new guidelines on the subject; underpinning the seminar was the assumption 'that the BBC is an independent institution, answerable to the public rather than the state'. (*Independent*, 28.11.88) That would appear to be a very dangerous assumption to make. Thus, Lord Annan, who chaired a government-appointed committee on broadcasting for Labour in the 1970s, argued that 'broadcasters owe special duties to the state' with the suggestion that it should be careful about investigating the security and intelligence services, while Colin Morris, the BBC controller in Northern Ireland, argued at the same time that the ban (imposed by Home Secretary Douglas Hurd) on interviews with members or supporters of the IRA and Ulster Defence Association meant that 'impartiality is illegal' in Ulster. The fact is that the government – any British government – has the power to control the BBC although, as a rule, it exercises such control when it really wants to by covert and overt pressures and the additional background threat that it will take greater powers if the BBC defies it on an issue it deems of major importance. Government attempts to impose impartiality will either result in anodyne blandness or prove unworkable. Too often, however, for impartiality one should read support for the government line.

Wars are always an excuse for governments to take draconian powers and during the Falklands War in 1982 the BBC came under attack for its attempts to present an even-handed picture of events. The Conservative MP Robert Ardley claimed that the BBC was becoming 'General Galtieri's fifth column in Britain' while a Downing Street adviser to Margaret Thatcher said of the *Newsnight* coverage of the Falklands campaign, 'Of course you report the war, but you have regard to the fact of the society in which you live, and which pays your licence fee' (the sting was in the tail) (Bolton, 1990:130), while Norman Tebbit, complaining of Peter Snow's *Newsnight* presentation, said: 'Those words from an organization that is called the *British* Broadcasting Corporation will cut a scar for ever.' (Cockerell, 1988:270)

The Thatcher government waged a ruthless war against the BBC which it appeared to regard as a political enemy rather than a broadcasting organisation. Over the famous raid upon the BBC Glasgow premises in 1987 (over the banned Zircon programme), '... the police purpose was not fundamentally or technically a lawful one. Although their ostensible objective was to find evidence about the banned "Zircon" programme made by the BBC in Scotland, it was clear even at that early stage that their instructions were to teach the corporation a lesson.' The raid was a Downing Street responsibility which Roy Jenkins, then SDP MP for the Hillhead division of Glasgow, described as the work 'of a second-rate police state'. (Dalyell, 1987: 94, 108)

As commercial television appeared set in the 1990s to go down-market as a result of the financial burdens of the franchise system and competition from satellite television, the BBC faced a doubtful future in which it could either move towards greater commercialisation by being forced to accept sponsored programmes and advertising in order to survive, or become ever less important as a public service broadcasting organisation with little power or influence. If it is not to do one of these two things it requires a far more robust attitude on the part of government – less threats about controls and greater readiness to face real criticisms without constantly threatening to intervene. The prospects in 1991 did not appear encouraging. The argument about the National Health Service and the story of John Major, the British Prime Minister, angrily confronting the BBC's deputy director, John Birt, at a party during the Tory Party Conference in Blackpool had an all too familiar bullying flavour, which was all the more surprising coming from Thatcher's successor, who had appeared so much more relaxed and reasonable than she had ever tried to be. By then indeed the government and the Tory Party appeared to have become paranoid about the BBC, and their constant breathing down its neck was a far greater threat to liberty than any bias of which the corporation might reasonably be accused.

Television has made our culture image- rather than word-centred: 'Television has a unique ability to show the events and the people of the day. It has an unrivalled immediacy and impact. But the medium also has its weaknesses and among these are a limited ability to put events in context.' (Mercer *et al.*, 1987:13) Thus the viewer cannot discriminate between what he sees as he could between accounts in two different newspapers such as the *Sun* and the *Financial Times*. And there is no time for narrative form, only sound bites and immediate images. The average length of a shot is 3.5 seconds, so that there is always movement, something new appearing constantly on the screen which does not encourage reflection, with pictures emphasised at the expense of words. The result, too often, is that stories without good pictures are either omitted or over-simplified. Furthermore, in a highly competitive world, fear of channel hopping increases the pressures for brevity and simplification. As Neil Postman comments in *Amusing Ourselves to Death*, 'serious television' is a contradiction in terms; rather, television is transforming our culture into one vast arena for show business. Increasingly, moreover, television is our culture. 'Television does not ban books, it simply displaces them.' (1985:81, 144)

By the early 1960s television was present in most homes and had become the principal national leisure pursuit. In June 1963 BBC Listener Research estimated viewing hours per week stood at 11 for the upper middle classes and 13 for the working classes, while TV was seen to exercise a stronger hold on the under-sixties. The following year the British television audience was reckoned at 25 million while since then it has gone on to greater and greater strengths. Television remains far and away the major leisure pursuit among all classes principally because it is so easy and undemanding. It is defended on the grounds that it is educational, a comfort for old, single or lonely people, and keeps the family together – each of these reasons being descriptive terms for a 'soma' drug, for by and large it is less of a political influence than a soporific. The greatest objection to television is an intellectual one: that it trivialises and reduces serious matters to vignettes which all can digest and which acts as a drug of the sort envisaged in *Brave New World*. And as Neil Postman argues, 'But what I am claiming here is not that television is entertaining but that it has made entertainment itself the natural format for the representation of all experience.' (89) Everything and everybody is reduced on television to adjuncts of show business and the medium has become the principal means by which we learn of what is happening in our world. 'Because the electrical connexions in our TV sets are not actually in our brains there is no reason for being less alarmed at what a perverted science might do for "persuasion" on political, social, and commercial matters.' (Cattell, 1965:287)

Considerable claims have been made for television as a medium for use in education but arguably its greatest impact in this field is to equate education with a form of entertainment and, as a caption to a *New Yorker* cartoon put it: 'When you consider television's awesome power to educate, aren't you thankful it doesn't?' (McLuhan, 1967:128) The effects of television on children have long been debated, and arguments about violence and whether its presentation influences children or leaves them unharmed have become an important ingredient in a wider discussion about television's impact. As early as 1958 a Nuffield Foundation study of the effects of TV on children expressed 'deep concern', but by 1991 an article in the *Standard* lamented the fall in the standards of children's television because formerly such programmes acted as babysitters but now they no longer achieved this desirable aim!

In 1990 the Broadcasting Standards Council issued a first report on the effects of media violence on violence in society, and despite a large body of other evidence to the contrary, the report found that only 17 per cent of viewers link TV with rising violence. The report was basically reassuring but left the impression that perhaps no one wishes to disturb so lucrative and so powerful a body as those who run and profit by television. It is addictive, as Richard Ingrams suggests: 'I have always believed that television is a form of "high". It is certainly addictive, if figures suggesting that the average person watches at least four hours per day are anything to go by.' (*Observer*, 10.7.88)

Television creates a kind of pseudo-reality which reduces everything to one long, trivialised, sentimentalised stream of entertainment while values, whether political, religious or academic, are reduced to superficiality. When for example, do we see people pause on television to say 'let me think'? Rather, the answers always come pat while those who cannot give pat answers are visibly embarrassed. Then there is the need to have acceptable and glamorous faces on television (it used only to be voices) and these concerns first and foremost are those of the entertainment world rather than anything more serious, a point that is emphasised by the habit of ending the news with something amusing or light so that viewers can turn off their sets thinking that all is right with the world. Further, the interruption of any programme with advertising by definition trivialises it. Slickness, advertising, entertainment, lightness are the hallmarks of television and as long as this remains the case it will act more as a soporific or 'soma' drug than anything more serious, and that, no doubt, is what our rulers want.

The politicians dare not and will not leave television alone, for the living-room has become, in a sense, a polling booth and all the main political developments of the day – with comments – are paraded on our television sets. This is a comparatively recent but immensely important development. Michael Cockerell, in *Live from Number 10*, records some prime-ministerial attitudes to the medium. ' "Winston Churchill never looked at television, and he was not going to be televised himself if he could possibly help it." ' (1988:1) His successor, Eden, agreed to be televised giving a speech and the story is told that Lady Davidson, sitting on the platform behind him, began to fan herself because of the heat from the TV lights, and this distracted attention from Eden so a note was sent telling her to stop. 'A medium that could defeat the Lady Davidsons of this world could defeat anything; I realized then that the TV era had arrived.' (42) It was Harold Macmillan, however, who first saw the political value of television and consciously sought to acquire television skills. 'Through television, he had ensured that the public gaze had been more concentrated on him than on any other prime minister in history. He was the major political beneficiary when people felt they had never had it so good, but when things began to fall apart Macmillan was to become public scapegoat number one.' (75) But in his heyday he mastered the technique (of being televised) sufficiently well to earn from the *Spectator* the compliment that he was 'every inch the favourite fireside politician'. (Horne, 1989:149) Harold Wilson, whose political model was Macmillan, saw television as a necessary adjunct to political power and it is recorded that Wilson and Marcia Williams (later Lady Falkender) after a visit to the USA studied Kennedy's TV appearances and Wilson then began to adopt the Kennedy practice of using specific catch-phrases and paragraphs designed to be picked up and used by television. The long reluctance of the House of Commons to be televised showed a justifiable fear on the part of MPs that they would not be shown to best advantage and when in 1989 a six-month experiment in televising House of Commons procedures began, one of the Select Committee rules stated that 'On occasions of grave disorder the director should focus on the occupant of the Chair for as long as proceedings continue, or until order has been restored.' (In fairness MPs should have passed a comparable order at the time of the 1984 miners' strike that on occasions of grave disorder the cameras ought to have focused on the face of the most senior policeman present!) Eden, Wilson, Heath, Thatcher: each threatened television at different times because it did not behave in a way the government felt it should (that is, supporting the government line) and during the Thatcher years Norman Tebbit periodically took it upon himself to

threaten television, and especially the BBC, for its bias. Such threats
have become a constant of relations between Downing Street and the
medium and almost by definition politicians – in power – are
anti-television, although they also use it whenever the opportunity
arises.

Mrs Thatcher did not like television but was aware of its power
and its uses and allowed her advisers to groom her so that she was
projected in a softer, more caring light. She claimed that 'The picture
that comes into your living room is the most powerful form of
communication known on this planet.' (Cockerell, 1988:353) She also
said in 1986 that 'In today's world selective seeing is believing and in
today's world, television comes over as truth.' She, like many other
politicians, was only too anxious to control what 'comes over as truth'.
And yet little is new and when Norman Tebbit announced in mid-1986
that he was setting up a special unit to monitor all news and
current-affairs programmes on television for anti-Conservative bias,
he was only doing what Profumo had done forty years earlier. It
could hardly have come as a comfort to Margaret Thatcher or
Norman Tebbit that the controversial documentary *Death on the
Rock* came within one vote (in 1989) of winning the top British award
for television journalism (runner-up in the annual Royal Television
Society's (RTS) award). That programme especially, but others as well,
demonstrate some of the greatest strengths of television, and such
investigative journalism is loathed by governments.

It is the question of profitability which brings us to the core of both
the culture and the control debate. Profit is more likely to be derived
from programmes which aim at the lowest common denominator, the
admass market, than from those which educate and, judging by the
licence scramble of 1991, there is little indication that government will
exercise serious control over television (in the sense of insisting upon
high-quality programmes as opposed to appeals to the admass market)
or wants to do so. Serious programmes which are not governed solely
by profitability are far more likely to threaten the vested interests of
the Establishment (as well as its pocket) than programmes aimed at
the lower end of the market: 'soma' programmes, to use Huxley's
invented word. What the deciders in our society most fear is television
that stirs people up – and it has that capacity – instead of television
which keeps them happy or at least quiescent with a dull content –
and it has that capacity too.

13 The press and censorship

The popular Press, for all its purported
'progressiveness' and 'independence', is one of the
greatest conserving forces in public life today: its
nature requires it to promote both conservatism
and conformity.

RICHARD HOGGART

FREEDOM OF THE PRESS IS, of course, a guarantee of our liberties,
yet it is one of the great ironies of our time that whenever the
press actually exercises that freedom to expose the behaviour
of those in power all hell breaks loose. Moreover, those who
own the press have invariably used it to support causes or political
parties whose aims have often been antithetical to real freedom. In a
reminiscent article in the *Independent* (15.5.89) about his press-baron
contemporaries, Lord Cudlipp, who was editor of the *Sunday Pictorial*
just before World War II (1937 to 1940) and subsequently chairman
of the International Publishing Corporation (1968 to 1973), claims
that 'There is now no closed season in the national sport of castigating
the more odious of the present-day tabloids, but the follies of the higher
echelon newspapers of the Thirties were vastly more iniquitous.' He
proceeds to look at the pre-war record of such papers as *The Times*,
Observer, *Daily Mail* and *Daily Express*. *The Times*, under Geoffrey
Dawson, was the arch-appeaser of Hitler's Germany, and Dawson
suppressed his own correspondents' cables from Germany about
Hitler's plans. After discovering that there was criticism of *The Times*
among top Nazis, Dawson wrote to his correspondent in Berlin: 'It
would interest me greatly to know precisely what it is in *The Times*
that has produced this antagonism in Germany. I did my utmost, night
after night, to keep out of the paper anything that might hurt their
susceptibilities.' Under Dawson, Cudlipp continued, ' "The Thun-
derer" became "The Trembler". He was in and out of No 10 Downing
Street and the Foreign Office with the regularity of a clock-winder
from the Ministry of Works.' Of the *Observer* editor, J. L. Garvin,
Lord Cudlipp is equally scathing, portraying him as a man who
opposed any commitments in Europe 'that might make Hitler hesitate
in bringing all German-speaking peoples into the Reich'. Beaverbrook
of the *Daily Express* fares no better; he, too, was an appeaser, assuring

his public that there would be no war. Lord Cudlipp describes the first Viscount Rothermere, owner of the *Daily Mail*, not only as an appeaser but as someone who appeased because he approved of the dictatorships, while of German persecution of the Jews he wrote: 'The German nation was rapidly falling under the control of its alien elements . . . It is from such abuses that Hitler has freed Germany.' Rothermere, as Cudlipp reminds us, gave blanket endorsement to fascism in Italy, Nazism in Germany, and to Sir Oswald Mosley's fascists in Britain.

Now Lord Cudlipp, writing these reminiscences in old age, is concerned to make a point of his own: that while the quality newspapers before the war were both pusillanimous in face of the dictators and urged courses of action which were to Britain's subsequent detriment, his own *Daily Mirror* and *Sunday Pictorial* had taken a robust line against Hitler and called for Churchill's reinstatement in the government. He was also, in effect, defending the tabloids despite their general addiction to 'sleaze' on the implied grounds that on big issues they get it right while the quality papers may be snootily upmarket on matters of sexual and other mores but on the big issues often get it wrong.

There is, however, a special dimension to this argument. Because *The Times* and the *Observer* were appeasers before the war does not mean they did not have the right to argue for appeasement, for freedom of the press must always include the right to back any argument, no matter how unpopular it might be (and plenty of people were in any case strong supporters of appeasement). But although Dawson had the right to follow an appeasement line he was surely wrong to suppress news that went contrary to his arguments or wishes. If, as Cudlipp says, Dawson was in and out of 10 Downing Street and the Foreign Office then he ceased in practical terms to be a free agent and, instead, became a mouthpiece for government views. That kind of behaviour is the best argument against the lobby system which operates today and is designed to muzzle genuine investigation of government activities while feeding the press with doctored news.

Thus, freedom of the press at once brings us to the subject of who owns the press and how free any press will be in reality when its freedom is offset against the interests of its owners. Here we have to face another paradox about freedom. Those who own newspapers use them primarily as a means of earning money: they may also want them for prestige and employ them to back particular causes including, sometimes, freedom, but that last is not why wealthy men purchase newspapers, and all too often newspaper editors become concerned with freedom only when their own activities, for whatever reasons, are under attack. In dictatorships, even if the press is free in the sense of not being owned by the state, it is controlled as to what it says and prints. In Britain anyone can own and publish a newspaper provided he has the means to do so and in practice this means that the great majority of newspapers have always been owned by rich tycoons who by definition will be capitalist and therefore politically right wing. Thus the political right has always enjoyed an immense built-in advantage over the political left, whose constant complaint has been that it cannot get a fair press and whose constant search has been for a newspaper or newspapers that would support its cause.

During the 1980s and into the 1990s various leading members of the Tory Party, and most notably Mr Norman Tebbit, concerned themselves with the apparent anti-Tory bias of television and especially of the BBC. Their concern, however, has clearly not been about any abuse of freedom but about partisanship or the lack of it. Had such critics of television really been concerned with freedom they would also, surely, have attacked the major British newspapers – the *Sun*, *Daily Telegraph*, *The Times*, *Daily Mail* and *Express* – for their persistent right-wing bias and failure to give equal weight to left-wing views. They have done no such thing. On the other side, moreover, as Tony Benn points out, the language of the press is quite different depending upon whom and what it describes. Thus, he says, when Shirley Williams (a right-wing political figure) was beaten at the polls her defeat was described as 'a tragedy' but when he himself (a left-wing figure) was defeated at the polls the descriptive terminology was markedly different – 'Benn beaten back by polls' – rather as though the polls were lots of little units fighting for freedom against the Benn menace. (1990:494)

On the subject of controversy, Richard Hoggart says, 'The popular Press – though it makes a speciality of safe or pseudo-controversy – hates genuine controversy, since that alienates, divides, and separates the mass-audience, the buyers.' (1957:177) Now that view is perhaps over-simplistic and, for example, the idea of impartiality applying to the tabloid press need only be advanced for people to realise just how absurd such a suggestion is, for the tabloid press thrives on partiality. Controversy, as a rule, is acceptable only when it falls in with what is perceived to be the public mood. Thus, in 1991 the press (not just the tabloids) examined the royal family and the concept of monarchy with a more critical eye than in most people's memory, but they did so safe in the knowledge that, at least for the time being, the royal family had largely lost its attraction and popularity and that a great debate about the monarchy was already in progress. What the press rarely if ever does is initiate such a debate out of the blue, for that would be too dangerous and would be likely to offend too many customers. The popular press in fact is conservative, usually with a capital 'C' but always with a small 'c'. New ideas or genuine radicalism are dangerous – to selling newspapers – for most people want their newspapers to reinforce their prejudices, not disturb their consciences.

Occasionally, of course, the media forgets itself and freedom is misused. In his memoirs, Lord Carrington refers to the television programme *Death of a Princess*, which infuriated the Saudi Arabians with its portrayal of a public execution – they asked the British Ambassador to quit Riyadh. As Lord Carrington loftily writes: 'The incident demonstrated the sad irresponsibility of some entertainment media in a free society, with programmes made regardless of their impact on British interests.' (1988:339) Now, although this particular reflection of Lord Carrington is about television rather than the press, it merits a place in this discussion. It is a classic example of doublethink: having paid lip-service to freedom and that only by denigration – 'the sad irresponsibility of some entertainment media in a free society' – he then advances the real Establishment view which castigates programmes 'made regardless of their impact on British interests'. British interests are not, supposedly, what the media is about. Later in the 1980s, and still on the subject of Saudi Arabia, the government tried frantically to prevent the *Observer* from publishing the valedictory (Foreign Office) dispatch of Sir James Craig, who had described in unflattering terms Saudi competence, modesty and morality. After extracts from his dispatch had been broadcast on Israeli radio, had been sent world-wide over the wires by Reuters, had appeared verbatim in the *Glasgow Herald* while further juicy bits had been blazoned on the front page of the *Daily Mirror*, the government still attempted to prevent further public access to the information. Its justification was in terms of lost contracts (and therefore British jobs) and other awkward international consequences. In his efforts to prevent the *Observer* publishing any more the Treasury Solicitor, John Bailey (whose job it was to prevent publication), both threatened and cajoled and then let slip the remarkable sentiment: 'After all you [the *Observer*] and *The Times* run the show, you're not a silly paper – not the tabloid press.' An appeal couched in such terms has all the hallmarks of the incestuous, backscratching snobbery that is such an integral part of the British Establishment. These rather ridiculous manoeuvres, as usual, were represented to be in order to prevent publication of information 'injurious to the nation'. (*Observer*, 12.10.86) It is, indeed, remarkable how anything that upsets or embarrasses the government of the day can so quickly be represented as 'injurious to the nation' with accompanying pressures and threats to force the press not to publish.

The reverse side of this process can be seen when the right-wing press leap to the defence of a dubious government action, as it did in the case of the television show *Death on the Rock*, which so infuriated Margaret Thatcher, precisely because its allegations appeared difficult to rebut. The tabloid press mounted vicious attacks upon the key Gibraltar witness, Carmen Proetta, in efforts to smear her as a whore and brothel-keeper and, of course, as being violently anti-British. (Bolton, 1990:4) In this case the press showed itself no more concerned with freedom than governments which are so ready to exert pressures upon the press when its investigations or revelations prove embarrassing.

The press loves a scandal in high places because that sells newspapers. Demands for the truth made in such circumstances have little to do with ensuring that – at all times, it might be added – the public is told the unvarnished truth, but everything to do with obtaining a good story. Thus, when the press clamours for an inquiry into some public affair on moral grounds one can be fairly certain that it is titillation rather than fact that is the principal object of the exercise. Commenting on the Profumo affair, John Sparrow said: 'The Prime Minister is running a government, not a monastery; the thunderous campaign being mounted to make one Minister's misbehaviour the occasion for a moral condemnation of Mr Macmillan and the whole of his administration is the kind of organized hypocrisy which a healthy modern society can do better without.' (1966:22) It is rare, however, for our modern but not necessarily healthy society to make any effort to do without such titillation. One headline during the affair – 'Prince Philip and the Profumo Scandal' – was a classic example of the untruthfulness of the press; it was designed to couple two interests at the same time – the royal family and the Profumo scandal – and then, once the headline had sold the story, the paper went on to demonstrate that Prince Philip was not involved.

The power of the capitalist press was challenged in 1983 by Ken Livingstone when the GLC which he controlled withheld advertising from the *Standard* because of the political stances which it adopted. Here the normal position between the press and the political left was reversed and a major public body with large funds at its disposal (and at the time under the control of political left-wingers) used its position to put pressure upon a section of the right-wing press. That, however, was an exception, although no doubt it led to one more black mark being added to the anti-Livingstone score being totted up by the Thatcher government. Usually the left is only too anxious to court the press since it obtains so much less than its fair share of friendly coverage. What used to be said as a confirmation or justification for a fact or view that was being advanced – 'Oh, but it was in the papers' – is said far less frequently today, at least in belief, partly (in the case of the tabloids) because they have become more concerned with pure entertainment and increasingly leave to television the role of dispensing news and information.

The tabloids, indeed, have a good deal to answer for: they are less interested in news than in human-interest stories, while their opinions, which are too often strident in their prejudices, are concerned to whip up spurious moral indignation. The invasion of privacy, the hounding of both individuals and minority groups and the distortion of what people say are part of their stock in trade. None of this has much to do with either truth or liberty although the right to pursue a story, no matter what damage is done in the process, is always defended in the name of the people's right to know. It is tempting to go on about the behaviour of the tabloids, yet ultimately their bad behaviour has to be offset against possible alternatives. In the debate over bad press conduct and the desirability or otherwise of legislation to control newspaper behaviour, a Mr Borzello wrote as follows to the *Independent*: 'But if I had to choose between the *Sun* at its worst and government control of the Press, I'd take my chances with the *Sun* every time. The *Sun*'s power is finite; the Government's infinite. The *Sun* in the end will bow to public opinion; Government, especially this government, time and time again ignores it.' (8.12.89) The page-three phenomenon ('tit and bum') and the awful headlines – 'Gotcha!' for the sinking of the *Belgrano* – are concerned with selling and meeting a need that a large admass audience is clearly willing to pay for as opposed to the more staid, upmarket papers although, in recent years, these too have moved steadily downmarket.

Secrecy has long been an obsession of British governments and Britain has earned itself a dubious reputation as one of the world's most secretive societies, so it is not surprising that government and press find themselves in frequent conflict over what the latter may or may not publish. Such conflicts were a recurring theme of the Thatcher years and were highlighted by the *Spycatcher* affair. In 1986 the government tied itself in knots in its attempts to prevent Peter Wright, a former British agent, from publishing his memoirs in Australia. It failed but not before issuing numerous injunctions, for example, to prevent various British papers from carrying extracts or stories based upon his memoirs. Both the *Observer* and the *Guardian* published articles revealing how Wright's book contained evidence of criminal activities committed by MI5 between ten and thirty years earlier; as a result the High Court placed injunctions upon them which were so restrictive that neither was allowed even to say what it had already said three weeks earlier even though other newspapers round the world were able to do so; nor were they permitted to report what had happened in open court in Australia (as part of the case brought by the British Government against Peter Wright). As the *Observer* argued in its editorial of 13 July 1986: 'The Crown is using the law of confidence (it has not invoked the Official Secrets Act) in an unprecedented way to restrict freedom of the Press, even when the Press is seeking to expose serious wrongdoing by servants of the State. What the Crown is seeking to establish is that national security is paramount instead of recognising – as the European Convention on Human Rights does – that freedom of speech is itself a national interest and should be restricted only in rare and pressing cases.' British governments which throughout the years of the Cold War have been strong on the rhetoric of freedom, especially when addressing themselves to other (non-British) governments and their doings, have been only too ready to restrict freedom of speech in the British press on grounds of national security although, too often, such restrictions in fact have been to cover up their own breaches of the law.

The readiness of the Thatcher government to act as censors, particularly over the affairs of Northern Ireland and the publication of *Spycatcher*, did much damage to Britain's international reputation. In essence, the politicians of this era persuaded themselves that the national interest and the state and the government which they controlled were one and the same thing. Such a belief is profoundly anti-democratic and yet the behaviour of successive governments

towards the media over many years has demonstrated a growing belief
in Whitehall that this is the case. If freedom of the press is to be upheld
a constant battle has to be waged by the press against the determined
efforts of governments to control and suppress information. They do
this when such news is likely to damage their image (producing
arguments about the national interest as justifications for their actions)
but they have grown so much into the habit that they tend also to
suppress news even when no case for the national interest can be
advanced. It is an iniquitous and growing habit. Freedom of information ought not to be a gift of governments; it is and must be a right
that may be restricted only in the rarest and gravest of circumstances,
but such a state of affairs, if ever it was the case, ceased to be so during
the Thatcher years.

Demands for a Protection of Privacy Bill (one was presented as a
Private Member's Bill in the House of Commons by John Browne in
1989) were fuelled towards the end of the 1980s by growing public
anger at the excesses of the tabloid press. Thus, with both a Protection
of Privacy Bill and a Right of Reply Bill before the House of Commons
at the same time, the press found itself under greater pressure to reform
itself, in the sense of taking into account public susceptibilities, than
for many years. Calls for the press to put its house in order were made
as an alternative to government controls while the Press Council, which
is a voluntary organisation without power of coercion, carries little
weight with editors or publishers (it was replaced in 1990 after 37
years by a new Press Complaints Commission). As a result there was
growing demand for an enforceable privacy law. What was interesting
about these demands for curbs on the press was the manner in which
the press itself reacted to them: it is one thing to demand the right –
for the sake of free speech – to expose the activities of governments,
interest groups or individuals, but something rather different when the
press was under attack for infringing basic rights. The press reacted
with accusations of yet more restrictions on press freedom and raised
the question: how can statutory controls of the press be contemplated
in a country where there is no statutory protection of the press? The
difficulty about press control is that the tabloids 'know their real
commercial interests lie in giving the public what it wants and deep
down they resent having to restrain what Northcliffe called the
"demons of sensationalism", just to appease the moral minority.'
(*Observer*, 24.6.90) The press does not want any regulation but is
obliged periodically to demonstrate its readiness to behave better when

the sensationalism of some of its members causes too much public anger or disquiet. This is what happened at the end of the 1980s largely, as most of the rest of the press argued, because of the activities of Mr Rupert Murdoch's tabloids, the *Sun* and the *News of the World*. The result – in November 1989 – was the publication by the press of a Declaration and Code of Practice which included respect for privacy, race and colour, the opportunity for reply and prompt corrections, and also provided guidelines for the conduct of journalists. (It was signed by the editors of the twenty leading papers.) Once the furore of public concern over press misconduct gives way to other concerns the extent to which the press in fact insists upon its own code of practice is likely to depend upon the determination of those with complaints to pursue them publicly and with vigour. Like most other institutions or groups the press is ready enough to call for the need to control others but deploy batteries of arguments why it should be exempt from any form of control. The press, once described as an estate of the realm, has duties commensurate with such a status.

There has always been censorship, whether directly imposed by governments or more subtly imposed by pressure groups the press would prefer not to offend. 'The relevant question at any stage of human history is not "Does censorship exist?" but rather, "Under what sort of censorship do we now live?" The technology of the later twentieth century offers the means of silencing men – without the danger of making them martyrs – by the most effective method of all, by ignoring them.' (Thomas, 1969:318) The British have been told so consistently by their rulers that they live in a free society and are not subject to the restrictions and oppressions of other less fortunate or more totalitarian societies that it is important for them sometimes to see themselves through the eyes of outsiders. As Ali Mazrui points out: 'All Western protestations of freedom of speech are contradicted daily by censorship (official and unofficial) on Western mass media. . . . To a certain extent censorship in the industrialized world has moved from the printed word to the electronic media.' (1990:89) Mazrui's point about the electronic media merely emphasises the comparative importance of television in relation to the printed word, and the censors always move with the times.

Free speech is a splendid concept – in the abstract – but most societies are only too wary of it in practice. Selective suppression of views – achieved by highlighting their opposites while playing down what is unacceptable to the Establishment of the day – is a technique that is much used by the press. Great attention is paid to moral censorship of the kind pursued by self-appointed public censors like Mary Whitehouse or Lord Rees-Mogg, and their attacks upon soft pornography, public nudity or simulated sex on the stage, for example, are generally welcomed by the Establishment since they act as a diversion from more important censorship of views. This kind of censorship concern is not dissimilar to the government approach to cigarettes: a warning on the packets that deters no one and is not meant to do so.

In Britain it is probably true as an axiom that governments will censor when they can get away with it. The law of sedition is very wide and 'nothing but moderation on the part of Government and public feeling in favour of liberty prevents charges of sedition being freely used to check the expression of views hostile to the Government'. (Mackenzie, 1967:15) Of post-war British prime ministers probably Macmillan had the most open approach to censorship, derived perhaps from his other interests as a publisher. Prior to World War II, Macmillan published a book by Arthur Bryant in favour of Munich and, as they explained: 'We are publishers, not policemen. Everybody should be free to say what they like.' (Horne, 1988:114) Such an approach, regrettably, is far too rare.

However, the electronic media have made censorship much harder to apply since information can be simultaneously published in half a dozen places round the world, as the Thatcher government discovered during the *Spycatcher* affair. 'Censorship is being undermined by the revolution in communications technology which is making it increasingly easier for journalists to publish information and correspondingly more difficult for the authorities to stop them.' (Mercer *et al.*, 1987:349) Article 19, the international centre on censorship, uses as its *raison d'être* Article 19 of the United Nations Universal Declaration of Human Rights: 'Everyone has the right to freedom of opinion and expression; this right includes freedom to hold opinions without interference and to seek, receive and impart information and ideas through any media and regardless of frontiers.' The task of censoring news carried by the electronic media poses increasingly difficult problems for governments and only occasionally are they presented with such unique conditions for censorship as existed during the Falklands War of 1982. Then, for example, the ITN task-force reporter was told by an MOD press officer on HMS *Hermes*: 'You must have been told when you left you couldn't report bad news. You knew

when you came you were expected to do a 1940 propaganda job.'
(Cockerell, 1988:270) Those sort of conditions – the navy controlled
all communications – are not going to occur very often. Censorship is
more likely to be applied in more brutal terms – at least by government
– as, for example, when Thatcher admitted to the House of Commons
under pressure that her government had prevented the showing of the
Zircon film in the *Secret Society* series by Duncan Campbell on the
usual grounds of 'security'.

Government censorship has been a major factor in British public
life ever since 1940 (and much earlier too) when the exigencies of war
gave Whitehall the excuse to clamp down on awkward views in the
name of patriotism. The Cabinet in 1940, as Clive Ponting records,
was furious when mild criticism was aimed at it by the papers.
(1990:154) Subsequent governments have been far more touchy about
their dignities than concerned to ensure freedom of speech, yet no
government in modern times has been as ready to fetter and muzzle the
media or prevent people with knowledge from speaking out as that of
Margaret Thatcher during the 1980s. In 1986, for example, her Lord
Chancellor, Lord Hailsham, prevented Lord Justice Browne-Wilkinson,
who was president of the Bar's senate, from taking part in a Radio 4
programme (*Pillars of Society*) investigating the Bar, on the ground that
judges should not comment on matters of public controversy (a year
earlier he had prevented the same judge from chairing a public debate
on official secrets). In 1987 a government injunction banned the BBC
from broadcasting any programme containing interviews with past or
present members of the security and intelligence services or including
information obtained from them. On 19 October 1988 the Home
Secretary, Douglas Hurd, issued notices to the BBC and IBA under
clause 14 (4) of the BBC Licence and Agreement and section 29 (3) of
the Broadcasting Act 1981 (legislation designed for use in wartime)
whose effect was to prevent broadcasting of words spoken by representatives of eleven organisations or words spoken in support of those
organisations: Sinn Fein, Republican Sinn Fein and Ulster Defence
Association plus the IRA, INLA, Cumann na mBan, Fianna Eireann,
Red Hand Commandos, Saor Eire, the Ulster Freedom Fighters and the
Ulster Volunteer Force. This ban was implemented without notice and
was aimed especially at Sinn Fein, which then had 56 elected councillors
and one MP. (Thornton, 1989:11) As a Belfast barrister, Anthony
Jennings, said of these and other bans, 'The British are being acclima-
tised to breach of their civil liberties by watching the systematic erosion

of civil liberties in the Northern Ireland context.' And Mr Jennings asked whether it was just coincidence that following the killing of 35 people by the security forces between November 1982 and February 1985 (23 in undercover operations) the incidence of police shootings on the mainland has risen. (Jennings, 1988) As Kevin Boyle, director of Article 19, said of this ban: 'Although the situation in South Africa is vastly different from the situation in Northern Ireland, the means now being used by the British Government to stifle debate – political censorship – is the same as the means used in South Africa.' (*Independent*, 20.10.88) Predictably, South Africa's President, P. W. Botha, reacted with delight and commented that Mrs Thatcher 'does not hesitate to put terrorists in their place'.

In examining reactions to these government restrictions the *Independent* argued:

> It has to be admitted that when freedom of expression is considered under English law it is brought home to one how fragile this right is and how much depends on self-restraint on the part of the Government. In England the right to freedom of expression is residual and exists only so far as it has not been restricted by statute or common law. The same applies to the public's right to know. (12.1.89)

That, indeed, goes to the heart of any discussion of our much-vaunted freedom of speech. In April 1991 the House of Lords (Law Lords) unanimously upheld a ruling that all media organisations can be silenced by an injunction against just one newspaper regardless of considerations of public interest. This was in connection with the long-lasting *Spycatcher* saga following the publication of an extract from *Spycatcher* by *The Sunday Times*. The ruling related to an injunction against the *Guardian* and *Observer* of 1986. By the end of the Thatcher era injunctions against the media had become a commonplace of government–media relations.

In 1988 the government stopped the December issue of *Harper's* magazine because it contained extracts from a book, *Inside Intelligence*, by Anthony Cavendish, a former MI6 officer. As the publisher of *Harper's* said: 'This is not about top secret information. It is about government control of information. It is about government tyranny and authoritarianism.' (Thornton, 1989:14) Although it is an oft-quoted truism that truth is the first casualty of war, the government through the 1980s gave the impression, with its constant censorship and bans, that it was determined to throttle truth all the time. And government attitudes were reinforced by those of the self-appointed public censors of whom Britain is never short. Thus, in 1988 the chairman of the new Broadcasting Standards Council, Lord Rees-Mogg, sent a letter to assorted public and other figures asking for their help in 'drawing up . . . a code of practice on the portrayal of sex and violence and standards of taste and decency'. As Harold Macmillan remarked in another context, people should go to their bishops for such things. In 1989 the BBC refused to show the *Cabinet* programme of the *Secret Society* series in order not to embarrass the government (the programme alleges that the Conservatives tried to use civil servants and MI5 to combat the CND in the early 1980s and employed the machinery of government to do so). Nothing, perhaps, so aptly illustrates the extent to which censorship has become part of our way of life as the revelation of October 1991 that the report into the collapse of the Bank of Credit and Commerce International made available to the Commons Treasury Select Committee had been censored with some 540 items blacked out in a 44-page report. Angry members of the Committee accused the Treasury and the Bank of England of treating Parliament with contempt (*Independent*, 22.10.91), but Parliament, by then, had long been privy to such behaviour in relation to the people it supposedly serves. Its members should not have been surprised to be treated with equal contempt by government bodies since it is as likely to traduce as to uphold such liberties when these apply to the people at large.

14 Literature and the use of language

The best lack all conviction while the worst
Are full of passionate intensity.
                    WILLIAM BUTLER YEATS

ECOGNITION OF THE EXTENT AND PRACTICE of brainwashing activities can be found throughout literature, whether in accounts
of state oppression, social engineering or man's endless efforts
at self-delusion. Books that treat the subject (whether novels
like Huxley's *Brave New World* or non-fiction examinations of
brainwashing activities, many of which have already been referred to
in this book) are sufficiently numerous that as a result many people
have come to believe that they can spot brainwashing when it occurs
and so are equipped to avoid it. They then dismiss the subject from
their minds. When sophisticated people talk enough about a problem
they are able to persuade themselves that airing it and understanding
it is sufficient safeguard against succumbing to its pressures. At the
popular level, where brainwashing is removed into the future, there is
an enormous output of science fiction in which brainwashing is an
accepted part of the genre. Future societies in which thought control,
the use of drugs or some form of 'soma' to keep people happy are
seen as a normal aspect of our own world projected forward – but
not too far forward. A recurring theme in science fiction is the machine
taking over and man's dependence upon technology until he loses his
own inventiveness and becomes its servant. E. M. Forster is not
generally associated with science fiction yet he produced a short story
just prior to World War I, *The Machine Stops*, which is a minor classic.
It tells of a world that has accepted total dependence upon the machine
and is brainwashed into assuming that any alternative is both wrong
and dangerous. The story is really about the surrender of intelligence
and consequent dependence upon being told what to do. 'Then they
re-establish religion – the Machine.' (1947:138) The best science fiction
can be used as a means of warning the present generation of the likely
end results of existing authoritarian trends. Science fiction of this kind
is a form of escapism in which writers project into the future a state

of affairs that is sometimes perilously close to the world in which we now live; the genre allows authors to comment in fantasy form upon trends that are becoming all too real in the here and now.

In our present century World War I is an excellent starting point for examining techniques of brainwashing used in literature, and many of the best known literary figures of that time, including William Archer, Arnold Bennett, A. C. Benson, G. K. Chesterton, Sir Arthur Conan Doyle, John Galsworthy, Gilbert Murray, Sir Henry Newbolt and others, were drawn into government propaganda operations. John Buchan, one of the most popular British writers of the first half of the century, turned his undoubted talents and fluency with words to propaganda purposes and, for example, when writing of allied troops, always speaks in terms of 'splendid troops . . . shed their blood for the liberty of the world'. *Our* troops are always 'bronzed', 'quick to kindle to a fight' and so on. In his official account of the *Battle of the Somme* Buchan manages to elevate by words the planning which resulted in such a holocaust: 'The strength of our plan lay in its deliberateness, and the mathematical sequence of its stages.' But this deliberateness he extols, in fact, was precisely its weakness and led to the terrible slaughter. (Buitenhuis, 1987:95)

Aldous Huxley's *Brave New World* (the title, taken from Shakespeare's *The Tempest*, has become part of the language), which was published in 1932, presents a picture of a genetically engineered society which at the time of writing appeared little more than a fantasy, the creation of a clever writer, about a remote future world, with its test-tube babies and 'feelies', but is today far closer to growing realities. Control in Huxley's world is not exercised by fear of punishment; rather, it is achieved by 'systematic reinforcement of desirable behaviour' – that is, behaviour which those who run society deem to be desirable – non-violent manipulation and genetic standardisation. In 1958 Huxley published *Brave New World Revisited*, a non-fiction examination of what had happened in the real world between 1932 and 1957 – a mere 25 years. In particular he examined techniques of propaganda, and his principal point was that new techniques could be used to soften up and manipulate society without society realising what was being done. He claimed that dictatorship by drugs was no longer just a fantasy. He argued that the propaganda of the dictators relies on 'repetition of catchwords which they wish to be accepted as true, the suppression of facts which they wish to be ignored, the arousal and rationalisation of passions which may be used in the interests of the Party or the State.' (46) And although, writing as he was in the USA, Huxley transposes his criticisms to dictatorships and his Western readers would then have seen them applying principally to the Communist dictatorships, in fact such activities are to be found in most societies, including many that claim to be thoroughly democratic. In his satire *Ape and Essence* Huxley elevates the machine into a god and creates a society dedicated to perfection which defers to the fool-proof, talent-proof, inspiration-proof machine where human desire, the enemy of Reason and Order, must be held in check. In his last novel, *Island*, Huxley creates an utopia which the outer world destroys.

Huxley's contemporary, George Orwell, is probably better remembered principally, perhaps, because he focused upon the tyranny of a dictatorship that everyone could at once relate to Communism and the Cold War. Yet he, too, warned as much about the dangers in our democratic society as in dictatorships. *Animal Farm*, published in 1945, is a classic of betrayal – how the promise of revolution leads back, inevitably, to control by a power élite, but although set in a totalitarian (communist) society, the conclusion is stark enough: do not trust any politicians or wielders of power. 'No question, now, what had happened to the faces of the pigs. The creatures outside looked from pig to man, and from man to pig, and from pig to man again; but already it was impossible to say which was which.' (120)

Orwell's essay on 'Boys' Weeklies' highlighted the misuses of literature in the interests of class and raised the issue of the sheer volume of magazines aimed at the admass market and designed to perpetuate divisions. In this case he singles out the *Gem* and the *Magnet* with their stories of public schools designed to create envy and also admiration amongst their readers of what they could not themselves experience, so keeping people in their places in the system. Orwell, his critics would argue, was obsessed with the class system from which he had benefited, and yet few things this century have done more to perpetuate class divisions than the public schools. As the Canadian Buitenhuis, writing of propaganda in World War I, says of public-school stories: 'These stories promulgate the code of the public-school devotion to games and the spirit of sportsmanship (which was somehow shared by the other ranks, who had never been to public school). It was axiomatic that God was on the side of the good sportsman.' (1987:22) Class constantly rears its head in British literature and a follow-up to the public school is the 'chap' at university. In his Appleby detective stories Michael Innes (J. I. M. Stewart, the Christ Church, Oxford, don) usually has his detective moving in upper-crust society but, bowing to the spirit of the times, he allows to the young man who is the hero of *Appleby Plays Chicken* (1956) a little mild revolt against the Establishment – really to show that he has spirit – before he (inevitably) toes the line to become a sound member of the ruling élite. Arnold Wesker does much the same thing in his play *Chips with Everything*.

The date and title of Orwell's book *Nineteen Eighty-Four* entered the language as a term denoting brainwashing and state control, and the idea that 'Big Brother Is Watching You' came at the psychological moment of the developing Cold War. Many of Orwell's *Nineteen Eighty-Four* inventions and slogans – Newspeak, 'War is Peace', 'Freedom is Slavery', 'Ignorance is Strength' or thought crime, double-think, doublespeak or his hero Winston's job of bringing the past up to date – are too real to be seen as mere fiction. Governments of the future may well decide to have two-minute 'hate sessions' and the idea of the enemy in *Nineteen Eighty-Four*, Goldstein, first appearing on the television screen talking until his voice turns into a sheep's bleat is close enough to some present-day appearances on television no longer to be thought of as simply fiction. When good news is announced – a victory over the enemy – it is followed by bad news – a cut in the chocolate ration. When the wretched Parsons is arrested and imprisoned with Winston Smith: ' "Are you guilty?" asked Winston. "Of course I'm guilty!" cried Parsons with a servile glance at the telescreen. "You don't think the Party would arrest an innocent man, do you?" ' (1954:187) As Orwell also says: 'Who controls the past controls the future: who controls the present controls the past' (199), a thought worth pondering as we rewrite our history curricula.

The assumption factor in literature which treats some form of brainwashing as a natural aspect of the novel's world is very strong and reveals an awareness, at least among writers, of both the present extent and likely future threat of brainwashing in our society. Novels about brainwashing (*The Manchurian Candidate* by Richard Condon or *The Clockwork Orange* by Anthony Burgess) perhaps, inevitably, in our present era focus on brainwashing in essentially Communist or dictatorial societies with the implication that such activities could not happen here. It is an implication that becomes steadily harder to sustain although the methods used may be different. The Roman Catholic Index Librorum Prohibitorum, which bans to ordinary

Catholics books thought to be pernicious to the Catholic faith, is, in essence, a straight instrument of thought control and no different in intention to any other technique of brainwashing: allow the faithful to read only what reinforces or at least does not lead to a questioning of their faith.

Language can be used to reveal or to conceal and, as T. D. Weldon argues in *The Vocabulary of Politics*, to know the meaning of words is to know how to use them correctly. Words, he says, do not necessarily have meanings at all; they have a use. Thus, Justice and Freedom are used for purposes outside the intrinsic meaning of either. (1953:19) The misuse of words has, perhaps, become a speciality of the present age. In *The Church and the Bomb*, in which the Church of England wrestled with its soul and the position it ought to adopt about nuclear weapons, the problem of words was addressed as follows: 'The one side is the political and ideological struggle describes itself as the "peace camp", the other as the "free world". Peace and freedom have, in this context, acquired meanings that are only distantly related to the dictionary definition of these words.' (Salisbury *et al.*, 1982:67) Neil Postman claims that 'speech, of course, is the primal and indispensable medium' but goes on to argue that, while a message is a statement about something, the media rarely conveys messages; instead, it avoids doing so, preferring to imply things. As he says, 'Whenever language is the principal medium of communication – especially language controlled by the rigours of print – an idea, a fact, a claim is the inevitable result.' (1985:10, 51) Implication by the use of language rather than precisely stated fact has become a major part of the political doublespeak of our time. In *Hooligan*, which was published in 1983, Geoffrey Pearson analyses law and order over several centuries to show that, contrary to popular belief, crimes such as mugging and street violence are no greater now than at any other time. Few would believe this in terms of current statements by the police, MPs, the law-and-order lobby or the media, yet if Pearson is right this is a perfect example of how the misuse of language can distort an issue for political or other ends.

The language of politics is often the most revealing of all; as Marcuse claims, 'The established vocabulary discriminates a priori against the opposition – it protects the Establishment', and such phrases as 'typical criminal communist violence', 'launch sneak attack', 'evade a death trap' or 'in the dead of night' are part of the carefully scripted texts applied to one's political enemies. (1969:77, 75) In

Politics and the English Language, Orwell examines what might be called 'trigger' words: 'fascism' is applied to the undesirable while such words as 'democracy', 'socialism', 'freedom', 'patriotic', 'realistic' or 'justice' have several meanings depending upon the stance of the user. 'Democracy' is constantly used by tyrants who never allow any form of democracy to operate, because the concept is almost universally accepted as desirable. Other political words that lend themselves to misuse are 'class', 'totalitarian', 'science', 'progressive', 'reactionary', 'bourgeois', 'equality'. (1957:149)

Towards the end of World War II the 'peace-loving' countries which until then had remained neutral declared war on the Axis powers in order to affirm in the eyes of the world their peace-loving nature. Certain political terms – 'the state', 'authority', 'rights', 'the rule of law', 'freedom' – are regularly on the lips of the world's authoritarian rulers. Other, possibly vaguer, terms become the accepted bromides of political persuasion. 'Established values', for example, means what the state hierarchy wishes to preserve, 'against the national interest' (except perhaps in time of war) almost invariably means against the political interests of the ruling élite or party in power. Other phrases which have more general political connotations include the formerly much used 'Top People' slogan that originated with *The Times*, a 'Third Programme type' or 'the average reader of the *Daily Mirror*' or the mythical 'man on the top of the Clapham omnibus'. Such classifications have great value for those who wish to order society.

The key phrase of the 1960s was 'the permissive society', which covered an era when many new freedoms – often of an estimable kind – became common practice for the first time. In the 1980s the term 'permissive society' was constantly on the lips of Conservatives who wished to blame Britain's ills upon a particular generation. It is interesting, however, that those who invent such phrases have not, as might have been expected, talked of a 'repressive society', which, presumably, would cover what went before the 1960s or what came after it. In the field of labour relations there are in our élite-controlled society many phrases suggesting a dangerous working class but few that suggest an equally or more dangerous ruling class. A chief justice speaks of the danger of workers obtaining a 'stranglehold on the community' but judges seldom say anything about the stranglehold on society of the ruling class to which judges are more closely connected. (Pritt, 1970:95) In most reporting of industrial relations, management 'offers' while trade unions 'demand', management 'pleads' while trade unions 'threaten', and most industrial confrontations are reduced to a battle, with the almost invariable implication that one side has to win and the other to lose. It took that most balanced of 'wet' Tories, James Prior, to put an all too rare moderate view: 'Generally speaking, I believe that the terms "win" and "lose" should never be used in relation to an industrial dispute.' (1986:256)

Much modern usage is lax, the result in part of instant reporting for the electronic media, and words are often in danger of losing their meaning so that such absurdities are reported as 'heavy fighting in a demilitarised zone' or 'violence on a non-violent demonstration'. And always there is the different use of words applied to opposite sides: *we* have a victory, *they* are responsible for a massacre, *we* are freedom fighters, *they* are terrorists. This is the language of propaganda and the British have prided themselves on their propaganda successes in two world wars. In *The Great War of Words* Peter Buitenhuis examines British propaganda in World War I and shows how writers were mobilised to produce high-class propaganda: 'Private publishing houses were used for the publication of books and pamphlets to make it seem that British propaganda was solely the creation of private citizens' with the neutral United States as the prime target of British propaganda. Buitenhuis points out how the Bryce Report of 1915 which purported to expose German atrocities in Belgium was in fact a fabrication, although Bryce (a former ambassador in Washington) had impeccable Establishment credentials and would naturally be believed in the United States. While the propagandists were whipping up anti-German frenzy Bertrand Russell, in a plea to intellectuals not to allow themselves to be used for propaganda, wrote: 'No great principle is at stake, no great human purpose is involved on either side. The supposed ideal ends for which it is being fought are merely part of the myth.' (Buitenhuis, 1987:xvii, 50) He was largely ignored. Perhaps only the Germans have rivalled the British as propagandists. Goebbels knew that people liked to be bamboozled and periodically would interject in his speeches, 'Of course, this is all propaganda.' (Brown, 1963:112) But German propaganda, as Hugh Trevor-Roper writes, was never dull or predictable: 'Though crude and violent in form, utterly unscrupulous in substance and quite indifferent to truth, it was managed with an agility and a sophistication which extorted a reluctant admiration even from its enemies and victims.' (1978:xvi) Now this description is interesting not least because it implies – simply in the way it is written – that Britain would not stoop to similar crudities. In fact Britain did a great deal of so-called black propaganda, masterminded by Sefton Delmer, which among other flights of fancy described the Nazis as 'Bolshevik scum'. (Brown, 1963:100) Arguably Britain's most successful propaganda during World War II was the BBC telling the truth (although not necessarily the whole truth); and avoiding selection of news or increasing and decreasing the significance of events. But as D. N. Pritt argued: 'It is not possible nowadays to condition a whole people for aggressive war without not merely intensive propaganda on the general public but also the destruction of the freedom of opponents of such a war and such a propaganda to conduct any counter campaign.' (1966a:280) One of the major lessons of wartime propaganda was selection: not to mention, or to skirt over, facts and incidents harmful to your side or cause. It is a technique which has been used by the media ever since. But although selection is a vital aspect of propaganda it must also be positive. Negative propaganda is counter-productive. Rather it must adopt a systematically one-sided attitude towards every problem and never admit to error. Opponents are not to be argued with but shouted down.

Propaganda is most likely to succeed when it reinforces existing trends in public opinion rather than trying to oppose the general trend. Thus: 'Propaganda is limited by prevailing interests, social trends, and prejudices; it is encouraged by ignorance of the facts and is more likely to succeed when it flows with the social current than when it flows against it.' (Brown, 1963:77) More than forty years of the Cold War have accustomed us to live in a propaganda-dominated age and although we constantly speak of freedom of choice this in fact demands as a prerequisite an appreciation of what is on offer. Propaganda, on the other hand, is antithetical to free choice which it tries to limit either by avoiding argument and merely insisting upon the merits of one side only or by endless repetition of the faults, real or imagined, of the other side. Thus propagandists do not argue but constantly assert. This is the forte of the tabloid press, which wants only one side of a question to be presented.

There are a great number of what Richard Hoggart described as virtue or vice words. Virtue words include: 'new', 'different', 'unorthodox', 'frank', 'cheeky', 'outspoken', 'wide awake', 'live', 'vigorous', 'zestful', 'vivid', 'enterprising', 'ebullient', 'crusading', 'candid', 'audacious', 'youthful', 'sincere'; while vice words are 'pharisaical', 'timid', 'dull', 'equivocal', 'snobbish', 'canting', 'mealy-mouthed', 'conventional', 'hypocritical', 'pompous', 'humbug', 'official' and 'boring'. 'Simple' is an overworked virtue word and, for example, the 'decencies' (whatever they might be) are always described as 'simple'. Thus, at the time of the Profumo scandal the Bishop of Southwark spoke about 'the smell of corruption in high places, of evil practices and of a repudiation of the simple decencies'.

Trigger words are especially important to political parties, and for a long time the Tory Party almost defined itself with its constant reference to 'law and order', God, the Queen, patriotism, as though they had a monopoly of concern for these ideas. Mrs Thatcher constantly used the word 'freedom' which, on closer investigation, often meant lack of control over those who would manipulate others (and deprive them of some of their freedoms) and, according to Kay Andrews and John Jacobs, the authors of *Punishing the Poor*:

> Tenants have been told they will be 'freed' from council oppression as they are sold off into the private sector, parents 'freed' from the dogmatic rule of the schools, employees 'freed' from the domination of the trade unions as their employment rights are removed, and more recently from the oppression of laws which prevent them working all night when aged sixteen, and of course claimants are to be 'freed' from dependency upon the DHSS.

They continue this interesting catalogue as follows:

> When language is stretched beyond its common shared meanings and values, political exchange breaks down. The poll tax is sold to people, who *know* that it is fundamentally unfair, as increasing their 'personal control'. Means tests are justified as driving out 'dependency' when personal experience dictates that cutting insurance benefits, housing subsidies, or even student grants, makes it more difficult for families to free themselves. (1990:291)

The different ways in which the tabloid press deals with the two main political parties depends perhaps more upon the deployment rather than the misuse of words, although the latter is also a factor. Thus: 'In Tory tabloids, cows go mad, the French cheat and Labour is chaotic; whereas families are sacred, police officers are heroes and the

Tories are resolute. Those political paradigms matter most when the Conservatives risk defeat.' (*Independent*, 22.6.90) Richard Deacon, author of *The Truth Twisters*, who appears to be obsessed with the Communist threat, distorts the other way as, for example, in the following passage about Lebanon:

> Perhaps much more serious has been the almost total silence throughout Christendom concerning the fate of the besieged Christians of the Lebanon facing extermination from Soviet-provided tanks and guns of the Syrian army. Only the Israelis lend them any aid, while the Christian churches have allowed the idea to gain credence that these people are Christian in name alone and in fact are corrupt fascists. (1986:69)

In such a passage the clever use of words ('Christendom' which in our modern age is almost archaic but has a nice sound and is a good propaganda word – Christendom against dark forces; 'besieged Christians' facing extermination) paint a picture far removed from the actuality of what was and remains a brutal two-way power struggle. One could reverse the passage quoted above and substitute 'Palestinians' for 'Christians' facing extermination and the effect would be equally outrageous to the other side in the political argument. Later in the same book the author says, 'Racism is a word which is twisted to mean almost anything that aids the cause of world revolution and the downfall of non-communist regimes.' Deacon is a writer who misuses language, though principally by grossly over-stating his case.

One of the most over-used euphemisms for ruthless or selfish conduct which has to be disguised is the term 'the real world', which as a rule is brought into play when principles are about to be abandoned or ignored in favour of more selfish policies. Then we are told that in 'the real world' – as opposed to any weaker, more utopian world in which something else might be contemplated – power and money rather than other values are bound to triumph. Similarly, when politicians talk of realism they mean that something unpleasant is being contemplated; thus, over the years 1962–5 when both parties abandoned the British traditions of free entry for Commonwealth citizens, politicians of both parties spoke of realism. (Foot, 1965:234)

Towards the end of his long life, Bertrand Russell said, 'Freedom has come to be thought weakness, and tolerance has been compelled to wear the garb of treachery. Old ideas are judged irrelevant, and no doctrine free from harshness commands respect.' He was, no doubt, thinking back to an age less dominated by the relentless pressures of a world in which propaganda of one kind or another dominates so much of our lives. His views, unfortunately, would be seen as old-fashioned to an increasing number of people today, and perhaps the present generation would relate more closely to that modern icon, Arnold Schwarzenneger, who in an interview in the *Observer* magazine (10.11.91) said, 'My relationship to power and authority is that I'm all for it. Ninety-five per cent of the people in the world need to be told what to do and how to behave.' If he is right then the future for brainwashing is indeed bright.

15 Justice and civil liberties

You wanted justice, didn't you? There isn't any.
There's the world . . .

ARCHIBALD MACLEISH

BRITISH JUSTICE has long been upheld as something special, one
of the pillars of our unique way of life, the embodiment of all
that is fine about Britain. The notion of British justice includes
the jury system – 'twelve good men and true' – and the belief
that in the end justice will be done and be seen to be done. Such beliefs,
if ever they were really held by those who come up against the law, as
opposed to romantics idealising a Britain that has never really existed,
must have been rudely upset by the growing and apparently unstoppable catalogue of miscarriages of justice which became an all too
familiar part of the political scene during the 1980s and 1990s: the
Guildford Four, the Birmingham Six, Ulster, restraints on the media
and free speech and an apparently ever-increasing accumulation of
power in the hands of the state at the expense of the ordinary citizen.

There are many myths about the law, which are enhanced by its
attendant paraphernalia: the wigs and gowns; the ponderous language; the middle-class Oxbridge accents; the exalted position of
judges and the deference accorded them. In 1958 the Conservative
MP Nigel Fisher claimed that Britain was 'the very cradle of liberty
and tolerance' and at that time it was, perhaps, just possible for the
unthinking to believe such a claim and brush aside the occasional
revelation about intolerant or unjust behaviour as being just that –
occasional. The attitudes of commentators upon British justice or the
behaviour of the police have changed markedly over the years. Thus,
writing in 1957, William Sargant could say: 'Even in Great Britain
today false confessions are sometimes elicited quite unknowingly
despite the acknowledged integrity of the British police, specially
when evidence is being collected by them which may result in a
suspect's prosecution, trial for murder and his subsequent hanging.'
(180) A dozen years later Peter Deeley said: 'The British have long
prided themselves that as a nation they act towards the law-breaker

– whether his motives are criminal or political – in a humane manner: no bullying, no torture, no "bright lights" or outrageous psychological persuasion; that interrogations are conducted in a civilized manner which allows the suspect to retain some of his personal dignity.' (1971:40) Yet in 1976 Tony Bunyan's book *The Political Police in Britain* would administer a nasty jolt to anyone reared in the comfortable notion that activities of a political police are associated only with dictatorships.

Student and other unrest affected much of the Western world in 1968 and there was cause for congratulation in Britain at the way the London police handled the huge anti-Vietnam demonstration of that year. The Home Secretary, James Callaghan, had been advised to cancel the demonstration but allowed it to go ahead and it ended with the last of the demonstrators and the police linking hands in Grosvenor Square outside the American Embassy to sing 'Auld Lang Syne'. As congratulations flooded in from other, less happy parts of the world, Callaghan was able to record in his autobiography: 'all had kind things to say about Britain's way of handling the affair, and contrasted it with their own experience.' (1987:260) Such complacency has not been possible since then. What, subsequently, has gone wrong? Or is it that the workings of the law were never as portrayed by the romantics but rather that in the past miscarriages of justice were less overt or more easily covered up? Whenever the subject of immigration (a touchstone of liberal and illiberal attitudes) comes up, those who advocate more or stricter controls first, almost invariably, advance the claim that Britain is the epitome of liberty and tolerance! Many uneasy or more awkward queries about British justice and its workings have been raised during the 1980s and 1990s, ranging from the almost daily breaches of civil liberties we have come to associate with Ulster, to more remote but none the less vital questions such as that relating to Russian and Yugoslav prisoners being forcibly handed back at the end of the war to face almost certain death, an issue which was raised in the spectacular court case associated with Count Tolstoy. Peter Clarke says of this latter issue: 'The notion that the protection of enemy combatants should have been given a higher priority than the safety of British soldiers, or allowed to compromise cordial relations with Britain's most effective allies in the fight against the Nazis, seems fanciful.' (1991:217) Probably most British people would agree with that judgement, yet the doubts raised by Tolstoy are not entirely dispelled and wherever one question mark is raised there follows the nagging, awkward fear that perhaps other problems have also been handled with less than absolute attention to justice.

An *Independent* editorial of 30 November 1989 began with the sentence: 'A police informer is a figure associated with totalitarian societies.' Well, yes but . . . we have had police informers in Britain ever since the Cato Street conspiracy of 1820 and many of the Ulster atrocities have been against informers. None the less, the idea is abhorrent to us, or at least, we like to think it is. This particular article went on to examine a new trend in Britain which the paper denounced: the police encouraging people to inform on those who drink and drive. Quite rightly, the paper deplored the idea of friends and relations being encouraged, anonymously if they wish, to inform on those they thought were breaking the law, and the editorial continued: 'It should not become normal procedure, the action of first resort. Democracies must trust the people. Only totalitarian states want the fear of spies to become pervasive.' Those three sentences are worth examining: with regard to the first, clearly in this instance the police do want the practice of informing to become the first resort. With regard to the second sentence, the evidence has been dwindling in recent years that the governments of this country 'trust' the people. And with regard to the third, while one would like to believe it to be true Ulster arguably has changed the parameters of British attitudes over civil liberties for good. The final sentence in this editorial reads as follows: 'The authorities' intrusion into the liberties of the people causes resentment, and citizens grow less law-abiding, not more.' That is undoubtedly true but intrusions into the liberties of citizens have been on the increase for years.

A. V. Dicey, whose principal work, *Lectures Introductory to the Study of the Law of the Constitution*, has itself come to be considered part of the Constitution, said:

> The basis of the rule of law is threefold: first, all are equal before the law; secondly, the law is supreme over arbitrary power (which includes wide-ranging government discretion); and thirdly, our constitutional law is derived from judicial decision – that is, citizens' rights are enshrined in the common law and based on the principles of natural justice.

Unfortunately, over recent years, each of these three precepts has come under increasing strain, to put it no higher: equality before the law in our class-ridden society is a myth; the arbitrary use of government power to override the law has become an all too frequent feature of our society; and citizens' rights are increasingly at risk, not always by intent, but as a result of the ever-growing and pervasive use of new techniques whose principal end result is to register more and more information about the individual and then to leave its use available to the discretion of the authorities. The more totalitarian a society becomes – and the trend in modern, complex societies appears to be inexorable – so the more 'special' reasons that are advanced to justify bypassing the laws, always of course, to deal with some particular or exceptional circumstances. As Robert Bolt has Sir Thomas More say in *A Man for All Seasons*: 'This country's planted thick with laws from coast to coast – man's laws, not God's – and if you cut them down . . . do you really think you could stand upright in the winds that would blow then? Yes, I'd give the Devil benefit of law, for my own safety's sake.'

It has long been an accepted British myth that judges are independent and incorruptible. They have security of tenure for life and cannot be removed, even if they pass judgements that are against the wishes and intention of the ruling party at any given time, but there are other factors that govern true independence and the most important of these concerns the background from which judges are drawn. D. N. Pritt was undoubtedly one of the most able lawyers of his generation. He began life with all the advantages to be derived from the right background of class and education and then moved steadily from right to left. He specialised in defending colonial dissidents against British rule and achieved his greatest fame as the defence lawyer for Jomo Kenyatta in the famous Mau Mau trial of 1953 held in Kenya. He might reasonably be described as an enemy of the British class system and he has this to say of the idea that judges are independent: 'The myth that they are "independent" has to rank with such myths as that all women are virtuous, all governments peace-loving, all armaments purely defensive, all soldiers gallant, all lawyers learned, and all newspapers indifferent to the demands of large advertisers.' (1966a:284) Such a stricture may be dismissed as no more than a generalisation but Pritt also makes a far more important point about the undemocratic nature of the judicial system:

In a country whose leaders boast of its democracy, the very idea of the *demos*, the people, having any say in the selection of the judges who may have to deal with their grievances and their misdeeds and send them to prison, fills the establishment with horror – an unconscious revelation of our leaders' deep conviction that only a select, indeed a self-selected, few are fit to exercise any important function. (1971a:46)

The sanctity of juries has also come under increasing strain, and rising crime and inability to control things adequately 'culminated in the Home Office's admission of inability to safeguard juries from being tampered with by criminal influences, and the proposal to counter this by abandoning the immemorial rule of unanimity for verdicts'. (Nicholson, 1967:360) At the same time that the Home Office was complaining of its inability to safeguard juries from tampering by criminals it began some tampering of its own, and in the 1970s the practice of jury vetting came into the open in the course of a trial concerning the Official Secrets Act, when anyone 'known to be disloyal' would be disqualified. (Hewitt, 1982:54) In 1974 the 'liberal' Home Secretary, Roy Jenkins, and the Attorney-General, Sam Silkin, issued secret instructions to the police to vet juries in serious criminal cases or cases with 'strong political motives'. Growing violence has meant that juries have been increasingly tampered with and so have become discredited and, according to some judges, juries are no longer to be trusted. But as is so often the case in Britain the assumption is always that juries – the ordinary people of Pritt's *demos* – are not to be trusted rather than whether judges can be trusted to give impartial hearings. By 1988 senior officials in the Lord Chancellor's Department were drawing up proposals to restrict the right of defendants to choose trial by jury for a number of minor offences and this went into the 1988 Criminal Justice Bill. The reason advanced for the change was to reduce the workload on Crown Courts. At the same time the government abolished the right of defendants in criminal trials to challenge up to three jury members without giving reasons. As the Lord Chancellor, Lord Sankey, said in 1935:

> Juries are always told that, if conviction there is to be, the prosecution must prove the case beyond reasonable doubt . . . No matter what the charge or where the trial, the principle that the prosecution must prove this guilt of the prisoner is part of the Common Law of England and no attempt to whittle it down can be entertained.

Too often the language of the law, which is automatically validated by the courts and the police, is in support of obedience to authority and what Raymond Williams calls the right to manage, to keep society subservient. (1989:25) As Lord Parker told a journalist in the Vassal case, it is one's duty 'in the ordinary way as a citizen to put the interests of the State above everything'. (Blackburn, 1964:4) Class and government interest constantly rear their heads where British law is concerned. Old attitudes to the police as agents of *them* persist among the lower classes and, as Pritt argued,

> The judges, who are the product of their environment – generally a rather narrow 'establishmentarian' one – always tend, often unconsciously, to find ways of so deciding cases as to support government policy and decisions, and to save governments embarrassment. Most laymen take this as a matter of course; many lawyers feel a duty to deny it; and most lawyers know in their hearts that it is true. (1966a:284)

Two contradictory views of criminal trials are as follows. The official view is that: 'Criminal trials in the United Kingdom take the form of a contest between the prosecution and the defence. Since the law presumes the innocence of an accused person until guilt has been proved, the prosecution is not granted any advantage, apparent or real, over the defence.' (COI, 1988:118) A very different view is advanced by Patricia Hewitt: 'The notion that all those charged with criminal offences are guilty and that the purpose of the trial is to confirm the police officer's decision continues to dominate much discussion in police circles and much of the evidence given by police bodies to the Royal Commission.' (1982:7) Certainly until very recently in Britain – if not still, despite scandals of police misbehaviour which emerged during the 1980s – courts have generally preferred to believe the evidence of the police, and accusations against the police for misconduct have not often been successful. Bias in favour of the police was clearly demonstrated in 1988 by the Home Secretary Douglas Hurd when commenting upon the decision of the Director of Public Prosecutions to charge twelve police officers for assault over demonstrations outside the News International plant at Wapping. He was speaking to an audience of Metropolitan Police officers and having said, quite properly, 'The law must take its course', he went on to say: 'I think it right for everyone to be reminded of the stresses and strains to which the Metropolitan Police were exposed by the length and nature of the Wapping dispute.' He then cited statistics for the number and size of the demonstrations which the police had had to control as though he were making a plea in mitigation. There can never be mitigation for incorrect police conduct but too often that now appears to be the government attitude in our 'law and order' society. (*Independent*, 16.12.88)

Class and wealth should make no difference to the way the law operates but of course they do. If a man can afford to pay for counsel he can always get a hearing; if he cannot pay he is in greater difficulty. According to Wayland Young (on the Profumo affair) some brutal activities went on unreported while the law was twisted in the Profumo case to ensure a cover-up. (1963:80) Most special pleading is almost always on behalf of upper-class or rich criminals. Thus, in an article which appeared in the *Standard* on 26 June 1991 Jonathan Guinness made a special plea for the early release from prison of Saunders (the principal accused in the Guinness affair), yet when do writers make comparable pleas on behalf of poor, unknown criminals? In a long article which appeared in the *Independent*, what amounted to a plea on behalf of the defendants in the Guinness affair was put forward on the curious grounds that for business deal-makers cheating some-how came naturally and therefore should not be treated too harshly. Thus the piece began: 'It is not altogether surprising that Mr Justice Henry, a Balliol man, should not have understood the mentality of the men he sentenced yesterday. Why, he wondered, should men so rich have been tempted into deals which they must have suspected were illegal?' (29.8.90) Thereafter the tenor of the article was to suggest that because all entrepreneurs love a deal there was something irresistible about one deal too many, even though they must have known they were entering upon dishonest ventures. And the implica-tion of the piece, which suggests that Gerald Ronson was close to being a figure of tragedy, was to suggest that their crime was not one that merited harsh treatment. In fact the men involved were cheats. It is difficult to imagine such an article 'in mitigation' being written about a factory foreman who did a bit of embezzling on the side; he would be far more likely to get a stern homily from the judge about betraying his position of trust. This and other similar articles typify the way British society so readily goes to the defence of the upper classes or the rich, passing over or at least excusing in their case what in real terms would be far more excusable in the poor. As China's Chairman Deng once said: 'I don't care whether a cat is black or white; the question is – can it catch mice.' British justice ought to be equally class and wealth blind but it is not, and for the extent of the offence the punishments handed down in the Guinness case were derisory if, for example, compared with those handed down for the Great Train Robbery. In November 1991 it was reported that the Marquess of Blandford, serving a three-month sentence for driving while disqualified, was not punished for a prison fight and was released a few days later after serving only six weeks of his sentence. According to another prisoner Blandford was allowed 'after-hours visits from his wife well after other prisoners'. (*Standard*, 15.11.91)

After years of campaigning and one appeal in 1977 which was dismissed, the government finally admitted in 1989 that a miscarriage of justice had taken place over the conviction of the Guildford Four (for a bomb outrage in 1975). Evidence was produced by Roy Amlot QC for the Crown 'that a total of five officers seriously misled the court in relation to two of the four appellants' and concluded that this 'contaminated the case for the prosecution as a whole'. The Director of Public Prosecutions set up a full criminal investigation into the conduct of the five police officers and the Home Secretary announced a judicial inquiry into the case. As the *Observer* commented: 'The story of the Guildford Four is not just a personal tragedy: it is a scandal. How else to describe the wrongful imprisonment of four innocent people for 15 years, not because someone, somewhere made an understandable, if regrettable mistake, but because of a deliberate, organised attempt to pervert the course of justice.' (22.10.89) Following the upsetting of the Guildford Four case came that of the Birmingham Six, accused and convicted of a similar pub bombing in 1974 in which 21 people died. A six-month appeal in 1987 had been presided over by Lord Lane, the Lord Chief Justice, and despite new evidence, which included police beatings of the accused while in custody, and new scientific evidence which cast doubt on the findings relating to the explosives in the case, Lord Lane said that the longer the appeal went on the more convinced he had become that the men were rightly convicted in 1974, and he poured scorn on the credibility of new witnesses. His attitude then led to an unprecedented demand by over one hundred MPs in March 1991 for Lord Lane to resign. In the Birmingham Six case the police had again fabricated evidence. But, as one of the Six, Richard McIlkenny, claimed: 'But I have always said it was not a judicial decision, it was a political one. He [Lord Lane] was chosen to give it.'

The freeing of the Birmingham Six in 1991 was the second spectacular case connected with Ulster and the conclusion is inescapable that this political problem has acted as a corrupting cancer affecting the administration of the law, the behaviour of the police and the curtailing of civil liberties in a way that nothing else has done, not even the emergencies of World War II when miscarriages of justice or curtailment of civil liberties could at least be excused if not justified on grounds of major national emergency. The Stalker affair, the case (which collapsed) against his friend Kevin Taylor that had all the appearance of a put-up job to discredit Stalker, the Blakelock case in which the judge had submitted a report to the Home Office stating that the verdict against Braithwaite, one of the men accused of killing PC Blakelock, was unsafe although nothing was done for four years: each demonstrated comparable attitudes by the state suggesting that it was more concerned to obtain convictions, especially in cases where IRA violence or violence against the police was involved, than it was to see that justice was done. In the Blakelock case Daniel Simpson, the solicitor for Mark Braithwaite, said of the fact that the judge's report had been in the hands of the Home Office for four years before action was taken: 'I find it astonishing that the Home Office has had this report since the end of the trial in March 1987, and yet as recently as last November [1990] it rejected a petition from my client to refer his case to the Court of Appeal. This is secret justice at its worst.' (*Observer*, 29.9.91)

Disquiet with the state of British justice was greater at the beginning of the 1990s than at any time in living memory. It was seen as politically directed, as undermined by police corruption and defended by a legal establishment that had lost touch with the people. Thus, a report by the lobby group Justice, *Freedom of Expression and the Law*, which was published in April 1990, pinpointed areas where government convenience constantly overruled freedom of speech. The chairman of the committee responsible for the report, Lord Deedes, said: 'What has troubled us has been the impression that the Government and judiciary have grown progressively more careless about the principles which should govern all limitations on free expression. Instances of this abound.' The report said of judges granting injunctions:

Faced with an application for an interlocutory injunction or even a permanent injunction ... although reference is often made to the tradition of freedom of speech and even to Article

10 [of the European Convention on Human Rights], these are rarely considered by British judges to outweigh the immediate specific interest to be served by an injunction. (*Independent*, 9.4.90)

In the 1940s and 1950s the general public as well as foreigners used to say that the British police were wonderful; during the 1980s, however, so many instances of police corruption became public knowledge as to create a growing public distrust of the police. Writing in 1964, Raymond Blackburn tells the story of a group of people including himself standing on the pavement opposite the Old Bailey. A policeman told them to 'Move on', to which the author replied: 'We are not obstructing the pavement or doing anyone any harm. Why should we move on?' The policeman only said: 'If you do not move on immediately, I will have you arrested for obstructing an officer in the execution of his duty.' (18) Such arrogance of power has grown since then, yet it took the British long enough to realise it. Writing of a well-publicised case of torture by the CID in Sheffield in 1963 Peter Deeley said: 'If precedent were needed, the Sheffield case established that English policemen are not always gentlemen; the gravity with which that case was viewed by the government shows just how much abhorrence there is towards men who take the law into their own hands.' (1971:43) Another commentator of that time, Ben Whitaker, said: 'In the future, the training of policemen should recognise that, because much of their work is concerned with all those people who, for various reasons, are not integrated into society, the police are in many ways the most important social service of all.' (1964:37) These views from the 1960s seem almost naïve when compared with public perceptions of the police in the 1980s. Thus in *The Abuse of Power*, written in 1982, Patricia Hewitt says: 'The massive development of the police surveillance capability over the last decade has taken place with no legal restraint, no public supervision whatsoever, and the police have denied to the public the information about their activities which could make such supervision effective.' (xii) At the end of the same decade, in an analysis of the growing power and attitudes of the police, the lawyer Peter Thornton quotes the former Chief Constable of Devon and Cornwall, John Alderson, saying in 1987: 'Eventually, all the top people who have held back the tide of paramilitaryism for the last ten to fifteen years will have gone. The whole nature of policing will have changed by the beginning of the next century if the trend continues.' As Thornton points out: 'The police are now controlled and armed by central government and autonomous chief constables. The Special Branch's responsibility is largely undefined. The security services are accountable to no one.' (1989:47, 1)

Public faith in procedures which involve disciplining the police were not improved in 1989 when the Crown Prosecution had come up with 32 separate charges against 26 police officers involved in the Wapping print dispute and picketing, and those of conspiracy to pervert the course of justice which were brought against the first six policemen were dismissed by the magistrates at Bow Street on the grounds of delay in bringing the charges. If such a ludicrous excuse could be made in the case of the police, then half the cases brought in the country ought to be dismissed on similar grounds. It is the perception that different laws apply to policemen who do wrong than to ordinary citizens that does so much damage to the image of the police. The end of the 1980s saw one case after another bringing the police into disrepute or at any rate deeper distrust as far as the general public was concerned. Thus, no action was taken against the police for falsely imprisoning and maliciously prosecuting a 73-year-old woman, Kathleen Gibbons, for selling miners' newspapers outside a London bookshop on the grounds of insufficient evidence. There was the report of the Hillsborough disaster which laid heavy blame on the police; the alleged malpractices of the West Midlands Serious Crimes Squad; the scandal about falsifying criminal statistics; the agreement by South Yorkshire police to settle all claims for the violence on miners' picket lines at Orgreave during the 1984 miners' strike (£500,000 in costs and damages); the Wiltshire police ordered to pay £25,000 damages to members of a hippie convoy that clashed with the police in 1985. These, and other cases against the police, did lasting damage to their reputation and their relations with the public. By 1990 the old myth that the 'British police are wonderful' had faded into a past which in any case would not bear too close a scrutiny.

'One begins by wanting justice and one ends by organising a police force.' (O'Brien, 1970:58) The police ought to be the guardians of our civil liberties; increasingly, however, they appear in the role of agents for an ever more centralised and authoritarian state. In recent years the state has increased its power markedly at the expense of the individual, including state censorship in the form of bans on radio and television programmes, interfering with the right of the press to publish, extending the laws of secrecy so as to deny the public the right to be informed. A genuine democracy accepts a real responsibility to the weak rather than giving rein to the strongest. As Lord Acton put it, 'Laws should be adapted to those who have the heaviest stake in the country, for whom mis-government means not mortified pride or stinted luxury, but want and pain and degradation and risk to their own lives and to their children's souls.' (Foot, 1964:126) Unfortunately, we find it much easier to pay lip-service to civil liberties than actually to insist that they are always observed, while politicians constantly use 'doublespeak' as they defend the notion of civil liberties while undermining them. Thus in 1971 the Franks Committee recommended that information about individuals obtained lawfully by Crown servants while carrying out their duties should subsequently be protected from being put to any other use, but the Home Secretary, Robert Carr, said that such information should remain available to the government. And so, in an age when more and more information is recorded, governments in fact ensure that they have access to it. The police are said to be happy that youngsters in their teens should be given provisional driving licences, for then details about them are placed on record. Generally, civil liberties appear most consistently at risk over issues which embarrass the government – Northern Ireland, immigration control, left-wing protest. In Ulster a new assault on civil liberties was the attack upon the ancient right to silence which presumes innocence. The notorious Clause 28 of the Local Government Act of 1988 (now section 28) bans the intentional promotion of homosexuality by local authorities but it was seen by this particular minority group (and others) as government licence for greater intolerance.

New issues arise constantly and the 1990 Broadcasting Bill proposed to give the police powers to look at programmes prior to broadcasting, a form of censorship by threat, if nothing worse, that we would normally say was natural only to a police state. Such a right granted to the police imperils the principle of no prior restraint. The increasing number of demands for some form of Bill of Rights for Britain that grew through the 1980s reflected growing unease at developing government powers. British insistence upon the absolute paramountcy of Parliament might sound democratic to untutored ears but most major democracies now have some form of Bill of Rights and, given the working of the two-party system as well as the power of the executive in Britain, the refusal to implement a Bill of Rights which would enshrine laws that cannot be automatically changed by every Parliament, appears more and more as a defence of the absolute power of the executive rather than a defence of democracy. In opposition, at least, the Labour Party announced at the beginning of 1991 a package of proposed legislation to include a Freedom of Information Act, tougher oversight of the security services, the right of individuals to know that they have been under surveillance, new rights to privacy and laws to ensure that employers use their best endeavours to have a workforce which represents the local ethnic pattern. Assuming a Labour victory at the polls some time in the 1990s it remains to be seen whether in office the party will actually implement such freedoms.

There has been a steady reduction of liberties since the end of World War II. In 1947 the Attlee government passed into law in a few days the Supplies and Services (Emergency Powers) Act which gave government immense powers to requisition property and direct labour as though in wartime, and on the occasion of that Act becoming law Richard Crossman said: 'It is not a question of dictatorship . . . that is inevitable in the modern state.' A good many people in authority since then have subscribed to that view, usually along the lines of saying that 'the modern state is so complex', 'people cannot understand all the issues', 'if everything were to be subjected to democratic scrutiny we would never accomplish anything' and so on. In other words, leave it to Big Brother. From the passing of the Commonwealth Immigrants Act of 1962 immigrants have been less equal before the law than others, most obviously because they can be deported and, as the *Sunday Telegraph* of 22 July 1962 said: 'Equality before the law is a cardinal principle of British justice. The Courts should hesitate to regard immigrants as less equal than others.' The 1981 British Nationality Act withdrew the right of Commonwealth citizens settled in Britain automatically to register as citizens, obliging them to apply for naturalisation and so putting them at the mercy of the Special Branch. The Home Office has the power to arrest without warrant an immigrant settled in this country, to imprison him on suspicion of being an illegal entrant, the power to deny him bail, to detain him indefinitely and deport him without charging or bringing him before a court. (Hewitt, 1982:vi) As Raymond Blackburn said in the 1960s – and things have not improved since then – 'The best way of testing whether a country is really free is to see how it treats its minorities. A good number of these are in prison.' (1964:192)

The British citizen has no legal right to privacy and much of what he enjoys by custom now seems under threat. One of the most insidious of recent developments has been the interception of communications (telephone tapping) and the use of listening devices (bugs). In 1968 the National Council for Civil Liberties (NCCL) published *Privacy Under Attack*, in which it said: 'What we are faced with is not so much a small coterie of evil men seeking to enslave our minds as a large body of opinion which would whittle away our privacy (and thus the very heart of our liberty) in the service of such vague concepts as state security and the national interest.' (Smith, 1972:85) In 1981 backbench MPs tried to regulate telephone tapping but were defeated by the government, while the Lords ruled that the offence of bugging did not exist. There was an increase in telephone tapping through the 1980s without the knowledge or consent of Parliament (an estimated 10,000 taps a year at a cost of £10 million). As Defence Secretary, Michael Heseltine had the telephones of CND members tapped and in 1985 Cathy Massiter and another MI5 agent revealed that the NCCL, the trade unions and the peace movement were considered subversive and were subjected to routine surveillance. And when (before she resigned) Massiter complained that such surveillance was against internal guidelines, she was told to see a psychiatrist. (Thornton, 1989:24)

The increasing practice of storing information about individuals – the plastic-card revolution – has not been paralleled by safeguards as to the use of that information, while the Police National Computer (PNC) includes information derived from driving licences, criminal records, other local sources, activities as squatters, political activities of jurors. In 1989 the NCCL said that laws should be passed to control the increasing use of video 'spy' cameras in public places. The catalogue of areas in which surveillance of one sort or another is either done automatically – every person who works on the North Sea oil rigs is regularly monitored by the police (Benn, 1990:3) – or can be done without difficulty because of stored information, is growing all the time.

The right to protest should be absolute but in fact demonstrations are at the discretion of the police. The women of Greenham Common protesting at the presence of nuclear weapons showed just how successful determined civil protest can be; and just how determined to put pressure upon such protesters the government can be as well. The journalist Janey Hulme recorded 12,000 arrests during non-violent protests at Greenham Common between 1981 and 1986. The Royal Prerogative is a device to avoid having to legislate or obtain parliamentary approval for actions. It is profoundly anti-democratic and against the principle of the rule of law. In January 1988 Prime Minister Thatcher admitted that officers of the security forces had been told by their MI5 superiors that they could enter, search, burgle and bug private premises under the protection of the Royal Prerogative. In 1991 Amnesty International produced a report, *United Kingdom Human Rights Concerns*, which charged that Britain's human rights record had become so bad as seriously to undermine confidence in the United Kingdom's legal safeguards. It cited the detention of Iraqis and Palestinians during the Gulf War, the treatment of those seeking political asylum and the investigation of killings by the security forces in Northern Ireland. (*Independent*, 8.9.91)

There was always as much pretence as substance in British claims to be the fountainhead of liberties, but the record of the years since 1945 has been one of steady decline in liberties and growth of state powers even as successive politicians and others had laid claim to a record in defence of freedom that, if once justified, no longer relates, even remotely, to present British performance.

16 Secrecy

At every stage in social development freedom has
to be reconquered.

SIR LEWIS NAMIER

'THE MOST POWERFUL REGIME is that which succeeds in excluding
from people's minds the issues most dangerous for the regime.'
(Mackenzie, 1967:231) If exclusion helps regimes maintain
their position then secrecy is clearly a weapon of great
importance. The government of the day will always go as far as it is
able in controlling information. It may not necessarily lie but, for
example, will decide within parameters of its own making when to
release information, and whenever it is able to do so it will ignore or
play down adverse news. Most information, in fact, is available for
those who know where to look for it (95 per cent of all state activities,
it is reckoned, can be uncovered from perfectly legal sources) while
secrecy really has two distinct roles. The first of these is to safeguard
genuinely sensitive information (for example, Britain's nuclear capacity in the years after World War II when the Russians were desperate
to find out what we had developed and were helped by ideological
spies like Klaus Fuchs); and the second is to prevent the disclosure of
information that will embarrass the government of the day. A
majority of the information that governments classify almost certainly
falls into this second category. But secrecy is a self-generating disease
which the British appear to have caught a long time ago; it is so
much easier to classify information, especially if it is liable to
produce controversy, than to publish it and then have to explain
why a particular course of action is being pursued. Emergencies
encourage secrecy and two world wars have made it easy for
successive generations of politicians and civil servants to argue that
it is in the national interest not to reveal information; subsequently,
they have fallen into the habit of secrecy. Those outside the system
are not, as a rule, in possession of enough information to challenge
claims that a subject must remain secret in the national interest; and
those inside the system who could make such a challenge – civil

servants, for example – are bound by the all-embracing Official Secrets Act.

The writer Hilaire Belloc, who worked as a propagandist during World War I, argued, 'It is . . . wise to keep the mass of people in ignorance of disasters that may be immediately repaired, or of follies or even vices in government which may be repressed before they become dangerous.' (Buitenhuis, 1987:39) There may be a justification for such a line in wartime but there is none in peacetime; unfortunately, however, it is such a convenient, as well as outrageously élitist, line that politicians have been only too ready to maintain in relation to the mass of the people in peacetime as well as in war. Leaping from World War I to the 1980s, John Stalker wrote of the special assignment he was given to investigate a 'shoot to kill' policy in Northern Ireland (a job from which he was removed when his inquiries became too embarrassing to those in power), 'I merely wanted the truth, and in searching for it I undoubtedly caused grave offence to a number of people.' (1988:12)

All too often, when governments insist upon national security as a reason for secrecy, what they really want is to retain control over a situation which affects their ability to hold on to power. Typical of this attitude was a reply to an MP's request for information about the Special Branch made to James Callaghan as Home Secretary in March 1970. He said: 'The security of the state necessarily requires that I should be in possession of certain information about political affiliations, which it would not be in the public interest to disclose.' (Bunyan, 1976:131) Why it would not be in the public interest to disclose his reasons we are never told and in recent years in Britain successive governments have been too ready to advance 'reasons of state' as an argument for not answering questions and depriving people of liberties and rights. D. N. Pritt, who always had a sharp eye for government hypocrisy, tells how on one occasion in connection with a legal case he had to ask to see a government file on a particular person – and they showed it to him. He said of this: 'For a government department to show the file of a case to anyone is a great rarity for it implies that the government *has nothing* to conceal.' (1970:84 fn.) Attlee believed in secrecy and closed government and consequently that ministers' discussions were no concern of either Parliament or the public. He allowed phone tapping without any apparent qualms. (Hennessy and Seldon, 1987:52) On the other hand, Richard Crossman, who was something of an intellectual iconoclast to find in government, was fundamentally opposed to secrecy: 'He never wavered in his conviction that the basic flaw in the British political system was its allegiance to secrecy. He particularly resented the feelings of those in charge that the workings of Government were too sacred a mystery even to be explained to the uninitiated.' (Howard, 1990:2) It is little wonder that there was such a furore in the Wilson Cabinet over Crossman's diaries, and an attempt by the Attorney-General in 1975 to prevent publication even though the diaries referred to events that had taken place ten years earlier. As Peter Clarke argues in *A Question of Leadership*, 'Increasingly, what survives in the archives is what was meant to survive. Hence the indispensability of private diaries in reconstructing developments at certain levels of recent political history.' (1991:235)

Symptomatic of the importance that secrecy has in British thinking are the workings of the Public Records Office. At the end of the 1950s, for example, the Macmillan government ordered a comprehensive assessment of Britain's likely world role during the 1960s – it was only a policy study – and yet it had been removed from the files that were made public at the beginning of 1991 when the present thirty-year rule should have made it available to the public. Since the censors are not obliged to say why any papers are not released there is no means of knowing for what reason this particular paper has been held back, although it seems likely that what it says in relation to Britain and Europe is the reason for this decision at a time when Britain is, yet again, negotiating with her European partners. Given the 1991 arguments about future British commitments to Europe, the paper ought to have been released, since any revelations would be likely to have a precise bearing upon decisions for the 1990s. (In any case it is to insult the British public to argue that it ought not to be made aware of a policy study that is thirty years old.) That, however, is not untypical of the way Britain operates. Anything sensitive, keep it secret.

Although the Public Records Acts of 1958 and 1967 suggest that all Cabinet papers should be made public after thirty years (unless they damage national security or embarrass a living member of the royal family) this clearly does not always happen. Departmental records officers say what material should be suppressed, and there is no mechanism for either knowing what they have ordered suppressed or for challenging their decisions, and although a committee which reports to the Lord Chancellor has ultimate responsibility, even its members do not know what the censors have suppressed unless they ask the right questions. (*Independent*, 2.1.91) It is a Byzantine system worthy of the British at their most secretive.

At the height of the Cold War a different angle on secrecy was revealed by the spy scandals surrounding Burgess and Maclean, and later Philby. It was in part a question of class and in part one of saving face. The Foreign Office assumed that the upper class 'chaps' it recruited to the service would not betray their country, but when it found that they were doing so it was deeply embarrassed. Burgess, for example, was a flagrant homosexual (at a time when it was not only against the law but regarded very differently by society than a generation later) and an alcoholic, and yet he was trusted with sensitive information by the Foreign Office: 'one suspects that the official British attitude owes much to the fact that Burgess was such a grotesquely obvious security risk that an admission that he could have been important would be too humiliating. He should have been easy to catch.' (Page *et al.*, 1969:202) It was Burgess who tipped off Maclean on Friday 25 May 1951 that he was to be interrogated the following Monday, and the two men then fled the country together for 'Through an extraordinary oversight, entirely characteristic of both MI5 and the Foreign Office, everyone blithely assumed that a delay of forty-eight hours was unimportant *because* it straddled the English *weekend*, a sacrosanct period during which, it was thought, all normal life was in suspension.' As a result (for it is likely that Maclean would have broken under interrogation) Philby was enabled to continue spying for another fourteen years. (265) MI5, which was responsible for security and had its own suspicions about characters like Burgess and Maclean, was told that its job was to watch typists and clerks, for such lower-class personnel were the stuff spies came from, and when MI5 detectives did have to follow Maclean they were embarrassed (the lower orders spying on the upper classes). Indeed, the whole Burgess, Maclean, Philby story reeks of the class atmosphere of the time: Eton, house-parties, belonging to the right set, social acceptance and the assumption that upper-class people would not betray their country. (Page *et al.*, 1969) It is both ironic and yet to be expected that some of the worst traitors and spies were drawn from this upper-class milieu: ironic because of the assumption that such people would not betray their country; to be expected because only such people were at that time given the sensitive posts that enabled them to obtain the information the Russians wanted. The fourth man in this, Britain's biggest spy scandal since 1945, was of course Anthony Blunt, who had first been named as a Soviet agent in 1951, though a cover-up meant that he continued to operate until further evidence was discovered and he confessed under interrogation in 1964. He was not exposed publicly for another fifteen years, serving meanwhile first as Surveyor of Pictures to George VI (before he was first suspected of being a spy) and then to the Queen, from whom he received a knighthood. He was only finally exposed in 1979 when he was stripped of his knighthood. As Hugo Young says of Blunt: 'his treacheries, his denials, his interrogations, his non-prosecution and his maintenance *en poste* in high society certainly revealed a lot about the methods and the psychology of British security.' (1989:460) Macmillan tended to regard spies and their doings as not very important and, given the relevations of Wright in *Spycatcher*, his attitude seems a sensible one, but part of the problem in a secretive society is the self-generating nature of secrecy and the security services so that in the end hardly anyone knows what is being done by anyone else.

'D Notices' are served on the press, supposedly as a warning against revelations to do with defence matters. They have no legal force but are 'backed' by the Official Secrets Act which if necessary can always be brought into play. D Notices have been used to prohibit articles on non-defence as well as defence questions, and can be used to conceal information which, if it were made public, would show up government incompetence. There was a famous D Notice affair in 1967. Chapman Pincher of the *Express* wrote a story to the effect that out-going British commercial cables were vetted by the government. Although the information was not, in fact, secret, Harold Wilson said the story should not be published but it was. The Foreign Office then denied that cables were vetted by the government on the grounds that Pincher's article said the cables went to the Ministry of Defence (for vetting) when in fact they were vetted by GCHQ (the Foreign Office was being economical with the truth). Subsequently a committee of Privy Councillors under Lord Radcliffe sat on the matter and took the Prime Minister to task for unnecessary secrecy. (Ponting, 1989:179–81) It was, however, an incident that need never have arisen had it not been for constant government paranoia about secrecy.

The Information Research Department (IRD) was established by the Foreign Office after World War II in order to distribute anti-Communist propaganda abroad but also to plant such material in Britain. This included anti-Stalinist material infiltrated into trade-union literature, while money from IRD went into books published under well-known imprints. The IRD was created in 1948 by Christopher Mayhew, who was then a junior minister at the Foreign Office, and within a year it was paying hidden subsidies to the anti-Communist magazine *Freedom First*, which circulated among trade unions. IRD used the publishing company Ampersand Ltd which bought thousands of books for distribution by IRD and published (and paid the authors for) material that was IRD-inspired. When asked about his creation in 1979 Christopher Mayhew said: 'It's difficult to make out that there's anything sinister about this. We were ahead of our time in fighting Stalinism. In the post-war years there were many illusions about Stalinism, not least inside the Labour Party. We were certainly taking great political risks, and quite right too.' (*Observer*, 20.1.79) The IRD also arranged for articles to be distributed cheaply in Third World countries to counter articles originating in Communist countries which were cheaper than anything to be obtained from the West. Before his defection to the USSR Guy Burgess was on the staff of IRD for several months (so its activities were relayed to the Russians) before he was sacked by Mayhew for being 'dirty, drunk and idle'. The IRD was closed down in 1978 by Foreign Secretary David Owen.

In 1981 it was disclosed that four men prominent in the British media had links with the Secret Service network of 'front' news agencies which were funded by government 'secret vote' money as part of its anti-Communist propaganda campaign. The four men were Alan Hare, chairman of the *Financial Times*, Lord Gibson, chairman of the Pearson Group, Maurice Macmillan MP, chairman of Macmillan Publishers, and Gerald Long, managing director of Times Newspapers. The agencies to which they had links were expanded under the 1966 Wilson government but most of them collapsed during an economy drive in 1969. Mr Hare, for example, had worked for the Special Operations Executive (SOE) in the war and subsequently worked on the boards of Britanova, the Arab News Agency and a feature service called Near and Far East News (NAFEN), but despite working for the Foreign Office in jobs that were characteristic of intelligence 'cover' he denied knowing that the news agencies in which he was involved had Foreign Office backing. Maurice Macmillan admitted, 'I was fully aware that what we were doing was consonant with government policy. I didn't expect to make money.' Lord Gibson had also served with SOE during the war. Gerald Long, as managing director of Reuters in the 1960s, discovered that an arrangement existed whereby the Arab News Agency (a Secret Service-controlled front operation) had exclusive rights to distribute Reuters in the Middle East; the Secret Service then paid £28,000 a year to buy the Reuters service. However, Long said bluntly of these activities:

> I do not think those projects were worthwhile. I think that most secret activities are for the birds . . . the trouble with secret services and all parallel activities is that they put a certain amount of money, influence and authority into the hands of clever, silly people. I think these activities are extremely dangerous, although I don't say that of these particular people. I think that everything that government does it should do openly. (*Observer*, 20.12.81)

In 1982, after persistent inquiries, the *Observer* found that the Foreign Office had destroyed nearly all the material which it had secretly distributed through the IRD. Moreover, the IRD files were all suppressed when, under the thirty-year rule, they should have become available to the public. The Lord Chancellor's department blandly commented upon these disappearances that, apart from a handful of papers on general themes, 'The items . . . distributed by IRD to other FO departments and journalists were in the main ephemeral and not considered to be of sufficient historical importance to be selected for permanent preservation.' What this means in fact is that it will no longer be possible to determine how the IRD infiltrated its propaganda into the world's media. At this time, Mr Anthony Fagin, in the section of the Lord Chancellor's office which supervises public records, said that neither the Lord Chancellor 'nor his officials are in a position to scrutinise every record which departments propose to withhold from the PRO on security or intelligence grounds.' (*Observer*, 8.2.82)

'Secrecy is at the heart of the way Whitehall works' (Ponting, 1986:133) and changes in the secrecy laws that would subject decisions to greater public scrutiny are opposed by the Civil Service, since any opening up of government is likely to reduce Civil Service influence and power. Secrecy means lying and, for example, the Civil Service concocted explanations to cover the fact that oil from BP and Shell was reaching Smith's illegal regime in Rhodesia (during the UDI years) via South Africa despite government denials. Tam Dalyell relentlessly pursued Margaret Thatcher over what she said in relation to the sinking of the *Belgrano* and, as he reports:

On the *Belgrano*, I am told by lobby correspondent upon lobby correspondent that 'we don't doubt you're right . . . but nobody's interested now . . . things have moved on . . . it's five years ago . . . it's difficult because the Navy is involved, and no one wants to read about criticism of the Navy'. (1987:133)

Now that passage from Dalyell's book *Misrule* tells us a great deal about how government lying can succeed: first, if you can outlast the critics for a sufficient period new problems come along and the public loses interest; second, if one of the more sanctified 'estates of the realm' are involved (in this case the navy) it is easier to brush aside criticisms and ignore awkward facts. And Whitehall is adept at such tactics.

Arguably the Official Secrets Act is one of the most misused acts on the statute books since, all too often, it is used less to serve the real security of the country, which is its purpose, than to silence criticism of government failings. There are three Official Secrets Acts (1911, 1920 and 1939) and together these three acts 'provide governments with a formidable and all embracing net with which to catch spies, civil servants, the press and the citizen in the field of official secrecy'. As Tony Bunyan, who makes this assertion, also claims, 'In fact the 1911 Act became not just a means of tackling spies but, more importantly, a method of preserving government secrecy.' The acts are invaluable in silencing criticism of government ineptitude and are used to hide the inner workings of government from public view. As Sir Martin Furnival-Jones (of MI5) told the Franks Committee, 'It is an official secret if it is in an official file.' (1976:11, 16) Politicians in opposition do occasionally denounce secrecy as, for example, Leon Brittan in 1978 when he described Section 2 of the Official Secrets Act as 'barely consistent with any proper concept of the rule of law', yet later, when the Tories were in power, they were unwilling to repeal the act which they strengthened despite claims to making it more liberal. (Ponting, 1986:8) The reason, quite simply, is that the Act is too valuable to governments and civil servants, enabling them to cover up mistakes and incompetence. As Lord Scarman has said: 'I would like to see the Official Secrets Act repealed lock, stock and barrel and replaced by a much more narrowly defined protective measure and by a Freedom of Information Act.' (Thornton, 1989:16) Every government since 1945 has resisted any major changes to the secrecy laws that would lay them open to greater scrutiny, and Margaret Thatcher, who constantly emphasised the individual and freedom, was not at all in favour of the right to know.

In 1988 the government published a White Paper on the reform of official secrets legislation; it included proposals whose effect is to make our society more rather than less secretive, including a proposal which protects all foreign communications so that (if a journalist is charged with breaching the act) a prosecutor needs to prove only that the information the journalist made public prejudices dealings between Britain and a foreign state. Further, the White Paper proposed to exclude any public-interest defence for disclosing information. Douglas Hurd, the Home Secretary at the time, who was responsible for the proposed legislation, wanted the new Official Secrets Act to place a lifetime obligation of confidentiality on all MI5 officers so that any revelation about work, even if it is in the public interest, would make the person concerned liable to prosecution. There are about fourteen committees in Whitehall to which the secret world reports and is responsible, and every indication that the number will grow. The Bill published in November 1988 proposed to give new legal authority to the security service to burgle and bug private property, although the Home Secretary Douglas Hurd did say that an independent judicial Commissioner would be appointed to check on burglary and bugging warrants. But the most important area, where the government would not budge, concerned its refusal to allow journalists or others accused of breaching the Official Secrets Act to plead in mitigation that their defiance of the law was in the national interest. Worst still, the Bill makes it an offence to reveal such things as the widespread blacklisting of BBC employees on false MI5 information or attempts to recruit journalists or MPs to spy on their colleagues. (*Observer*, 11.12.88) The Hurd Bill was designed as much to protect secrets of the government as secrets of state and that indeed has long been the complaint of those opposed to existing secrecy measures. In a speech to the Campaign for Freedom of Information in January 1989, the former editor of the *Sunday Times*, Harold Evans, contrasted the British and the American view on public rights:

Here, he argued, Governments start from the premise that rights are granted by the Crown or by the Government. These secrets, say Ministers, are *our* secrets, not yours. They are Crown or Government property. To steal them is theft. The Americans see it differently. Public information, they say, belongs to the public, and the public has a right to know it, except in certain tightly-defined circumstances. In one year alone, the US Defense Department received more than 72,500 requests under the Freedom of Information Act. It granted 92 per cent of them without any demur or deletions. (*Observer*, 5.2.89)

The differences in the approach of the two governments is striking. Although the 1988 Bill placed MI5 on a statutory basis for the first time, it failed to provide any adequate control and perpetuated supervision by ministers. 'Far from being "an essay in openness" as Douglas Hurd, the Home Secretary, has claimed, the combined effect of the Security Service Bill and the Official Secrets Bill is to give the Government greater powers to withhold and conceal information.' (Thornton, 1989:20)

Spycatcher, the memoirs of the former MI5 agent Peter Wright, in which he detailed some of the methods and activities of Britain's secret services, turned into a *cause célèbre* because of the extraordinary lengths to which the government went to prevent what was already widely known from being *legally* widely known. 'What haunted the Prime Minister [Thatcher] had little to do with the security of Britain, and everything to do with Mr Wright's description of bugging and burgling his way through London in the 1970s during the time of Harold Wilson's Government.' (Dalyell, 1987:112) During 1986 the government took legal action in both London and Australia to block the appearance of further revelations about MI5, with an unprecedented ban on British newspapers publishing Australian court reports. High Court injunctions were obtained against the *Observer* and the *Guardian*, and a judge refused permission to the *Observer* to report proceedings taken in open court in Australia. In Australia Peter Wright argued that his memoirs ought to be published because they disclosed serious wrongdoing by MI5. At one point in the Australian court hearings, which were front-line news in that country, the judge, a former Australian army officer, said that

although he had been cleared for security, he himself had still not been shown the controversial manuscript. Mr William Caldwell, for MI5, said the complaints of delay were unjust. All material in the case had to go to and from London 'via secure channels'. Mr Justice Powell said, with more than a touch of sarcasm, that he presumed this meant 'a little man with a chain round his wrist' had constantly to board British Airways jets with documents. Mr Caldwell replied: 'Something like that.' (*Observer*, 29.6.86)

The affair, in fact, became a matter of high farce in which the British government succeeded in making an international fool of itself in its efforts to suppress what became a bestseller.

In his book Peter Wright claimed that the security services acted above the law, committing routine illegal acts (burgling, bugging, telephone tapping, mail interceptions) designed to destabilise the Wilson government. British newspapers argued that the secret services must act within the law. The kernel of the British government case against Wright and its justification for its endless pursuit of him and his book was that he owed 'a lifelong and absolute duty of confidentiality to the Crown'. In the *Spycatcher* trial in Britain Mr Justice Scott argued against the government: 'The importance to the public of this country of the allegation that members of MI5 endeavoured to undermine and destroy public confidence in a democratically elected government makes the public the proper recipient of the information.' But the government persisted in its attempts to prevent publication in Britain and on the final appeal Lord Keith said: 'A government is not in a position to win the assistance of the court in restraining the publication of information imparted in confidence by it or its predecessors unless it can show that publication would be harmful to the public interest.' (Thornton, 1989:6–7)

The obsessive determination of the government to insist upon lifelong confidentiality by Crown servants poses for such servants questions about loyalty that have echoes of the trial of Adolf Eichmann in Israel for his role in exterminating Jews under Hitler. His defence rested upon the premise that as a civil servant he merely carried out orders (to exterminate Jews). The Israeli prosecution argued that higher loyalties – in that case to the human race – must transcend loyalties to the state. The *Spycatcher* revelations were important because they purported to show, first, that there appeared little or no control over secret-service activities and, second, that MI5 determined on its own initiative to destabilise or attempt to destabilise the democratically elected government because the service, which was politically right wing, disapproved of a government which it saw as left wing. The first priority of the Thatcher government at the time *Spycatcher* was published ought to have been to investigate whether or not the allegations were true and, if they proved to be so, to take action to ensure that nothing of the kind ever occurred again. Instead, its first priority was simply to prevent the information from being widely known – that is, to cover up the dubious activities of the secret service. The fact that it failed in this object is beside the point.

By 1988 it became known that GCHQ (the Government eaves-dropping organisation at Cheltenham) was financing a growing number of university research contracts to improve the art of telephone tapping. (*Observer*, 24.7.88) Student campaigners identi-fied 24 publicly financed research projects at eight British universities and, according to the Campaign Against Military Research on Campus (Camroc), such funding poses a threat to the free and open exchange of information between academics. NUS telephones were tapped during the 1960s, leading Wilson to claim that the NUS was dominated by Communists or near Communists – 'this tightly knit group of politically motivated men'. (Ponting, 1989:188) Telephone tapping is now a recognised government activity and although it is a criminal offence to do so unless under a warrant issued by the Home Secretary, the Secretary of State for Scotland or the Secretary of State for Northern Ireland, it is difficult to believe in the wake of the *Spycatcher* revelations that all tapping is so authorised. Perhaps that was the reason for the government's relentless determination to prevent the publication of the book.

In January 1989 Mr Paddy Ashdown, the newly elected leader of the Democrats, attacked Thatcher's appointment of Lord Chalfont to the post of deputy chairman of the Independent Television Authority. He did so on the grounds that Lord Chalfont (apart from having illiberal views on broadcasting) had secret security and intelligence links and that, for example, the private security firm Zeus (of which he had been a director) had been hired to spy on objectors at the Sizewell nuclear power plant inquiry of 1983–5. (*Observer*, 29.1.89) What was disturbing about the appointment was the fact that someone with Lord Chalfont's background should be put in such a sensitive position. It told volumes about government attitudes.

Another secrecy storm of the Thatcher years concerned the banning of the television programme about the Zircon spy satellite (part of the *Secret Society* series) in January 1987. Following the ban legal moves were initiated against Duncan Campbell, the reporter responsible for the programme, and the *New Statesman*, which published Campbell's story. The government even tried to stop MPs from seeing the film in the House of Commons, while the Special Branch who searched Campbell's house were themselves not allowed to see the film. The Special Branch also raided the Glasgow offices of the BBC in what was described by Tam Dalyell as a classic case of intimidation and led Roy Jenkins in the House of Commons to accuse the government of 'running a second-rate police state, infused equally with illiberalism and incompetence'. At the end of 1987 the Attorney-General obtained an injunction to stop the broadcast of the first of three programmes in a radio series, *My Country Right or Wrong*, which included interviews with three former MI5, three MI6 and two ex-GCHQ employees. (Thornton, 1989:9)

According to the NCCL (now Liberty), about one million jobs in the state and private industry are subject to security-service vetting and in 1990 Liberty called upon the government to follow the example of Canada, Australia and Sweden and guarantee that no one can lose his job without the evidence against him being heard or the right to a fair appeal. The General Secretary of Liberty, Andrew Puddephat, said: 'As the Eastern European countries are so clearly demonstrating, true democracy can only exist when the security services are made account-able.' (*Independent*, 29.1.90) Those who *find out* that they have been vetted can appeal to the new Security Service Tribunal but will not be told either why they have been vetted or what information has been used against them. The tribunal is concerned only to determine whether MI5 has 'reasonable grounds' for believing its information is true. While an individual can be vetted and found to be a security risk, a group can be labelled subversive solely by ministerial decision.

But secrecy is not solely a government preserve; it crops up in business, the political parties and a good many other unlikely or unexpected places. Tony Benn describes his attempt to get the Labour Party National Executive Committee (NEC) to record its motions and votes as a minute and publish these in the party's annual report, but he was opposed by Michael Foot, whom he describes as an élitist Parliamentarian, on the grounds that publication would put pressure on members of NEC! Well, of course it would. (1989:40)

In 1989 it was reported that Britain's biggest supermarket chains would not reveal to their customers information about pesticides in the food they sell, while at the same time the government was resisting an EC proposal that would force retailers to tell customers what pesticides have been used on the fruit and vegetables on their shelves. This secrecy was in direct contradiction to campaigns by the chainstores to demonstrate that they were champions of the 'green consumer', and it came just after disclosures that British apples were sprayed with a chemical believed to cause cancer. The *Observer*, which uncovered this story (16.4.89), also published some of the replies from the chainstores. Thus Sainsburys said, 'We consider that this information is confidential to ourselves and our suppliers', while Budgen was even more contemptuous of the pubic which it feeds: 'We see little reason to publicise data which would not be understandable by the majority of the people.'

In a publication of November 1991, *The Great Railway Conspiracy*, the author reveals that the closure of nearly a third of Britain's railway network in the early 1960s was justified by government on the basis of bogus figures and a report that has been suppressed for thirty years – Mrs Thatcher told the House of Commons in 1988 that all copies of the report had been lost. (*Independent*, 18.11.91) For anyone who searches hard enough cover-up appears to be a major occupation of governments – cover-up and a contempt for the electorate which can be described in terms of 'we will decide and in any case you are too stupid to understand – so leave it to us'.

A secret government investigation carried out at the end of the war identified dozens of Nazi war criminals living in Britain but no action to bring them to justice was taken and the records of the inquiry have never been placed in the Public Records Office: instead they are held in a secret Home Office archive that is shared with MI5. The object of this operation, which was known as Operation Post Report, was mainly in order to hunt down possible Communist sympathisers. (*Observer*, 5.5.91) This may have been a perfectly valid government objective at the height of the Cold War but the cover-up of Nazi war criminals was not; nor is there any reason why the information should not be made public forty years after the event.

Again and again, secrecy is shown to be the dominant rule in government activities. As a nation we appear to be obsessed by secrecy, especially over defence matters. Raymond Blackburn tells how a Professor Keaton asked at a police station to see a copy of the Defence of the Realm Regulations but was informed that 'it was not in the public interest that they should be revealed'. (1964:102) As Tony Benn argues, 'Nothing buttresses the established order so effectively as secrecy. The searchlight of publicity shone on the decision-making process of government would be the best thing that could possibly happen.' (1988:71) But, in fact, over many years, ministers in both parties have resisted providing detailed information about the workings of the police, the military, the Special Branch or MI5. 'Many military officers accept that too much is classified and some with experience of NATO felt that Britain generally was too secretive. "We are without doubt the most secretive of all sixteen NATO nations", said one of Britain's most senior military commanders.' (Mercer *et al.*, 1987:27) The general tactic of governments is to say, 'yes, we will inform the public and be less secretive', while ensuring that no more information is made available: that certainly appeared to be the approach in 1988 during the parliamentary discussions of the Security Service Bill and Official Secrets Bill. As Clive Ponting, an ex-civil servant whose career was terminated because he passed on information about the sinking of the *Belgrano* to the Labour MP Tam Dalyell, argues,

> The first course of action is to get rid of the carefully cultivated myth that the small group of about 1,000 Ministers and civil servants at the top of Whitehall are uniquely qualified to govern Britain, free from outside 'interference'. Why should the rest of the country accept this condescending view that they are only entitled to learn about decisions taken in their name long after it is possible to influence those decisions? (1986:228)

Part Three
Modern Case Studies

17 The Thatcher phenomenon

Do you know there are still people in my party who
believe in consensus politics.
                                    MARGARET THATCHER

SOMETIMES THE SYSTEM DEFEATS ITSELF as it did by permitting
Thatcher to become leader of the Tory party. 'The fact that
she was an outsider had caused her to be elected, because it
permitted her alone to run when all the insiders held back.'
(Young, 1989:100) Extraordinary in her single-minded pursuit of
power and her personal convictions that she alone knew what was
right for the country, in the end Margaret Thatcher believed her own
myth. By 1988, when she told *The Times* that she intended to serve a
fourth term as Prime Minister, hubris had set in. She told her
interviewer, Robert Oakley: 'Some time there will come along a person
who can do it better than I can. And I'm always on the lookout. But
I expect myself to do it for the fourth term.' The arrogance of the
remark was part of the woman and, leaving aside the insult to all her
senior colleagues conveyed by her words, it is probable that she had
come to believe what she said literally: she was not consciously being
arrogant or indeed insulting (although she was and is capable of both
qualities) but was simply telling the nation what to expect. It is
doubtful whether she had ever heard Clemenceau's *bon mot* just after
World War I that 'the graves of Europe are full of indispensable men',
but she would not have appreciated it had she done so.

Beginning her long premiership as the 'iron lady' who is 'not for
turning' and winning three elections in a row, she and some of her
more fanatical supporters had come to believe that she was indestruc-
tible. The myths which surrounded her and the longevity of her tenure
of Number 10 Downing Street persuaded her of an invincibility that
was to be cruelly destroyed two years later. As Robert Harris wrote
of her at that time: 'Mrs Thatcher now talks about the premiership
not as an elected office but as something which is hers, to be given up
at her leisure. The fact that she can behave in such a fashion is a
measure of the dominance she now enjoys over her colleagues.' (1988)

It was that dominance which she had worked relentlessly to achieve that allowed the myths to flourish so that people actually believed many of the claims made on her behalf – that she was not for turning, that she was a champion of freedom – without any scrutiny of what was actually being done under her stewardship. According to one Thatcher observer, Professor Anthony King, 'In her relations with her fellow ministers, civil servants and Conservative MPs her distinctive weapon – far more than in the cases of men like Churchill, Macmillan or Wilson – is fear.' (R. Harris, 1988) Fear is an excellent weapon for a ruler to use and Thatcher employed it brutally: between 1979 and 1988 she got rid of 26 Cabinet Ministers with only three surviving from her original Cabinet. Those who did survive tended, inevitably in such a climate, to say 'Yes Prime Minister' rather than anything else, and that habit also contributed to the myths of her invincibility. And it was largely the myths which allowed her – and her principal supporters and myth-makers – to ensure that a particular picture of Thatcher and her achievements was constantly projected at the public. And although she was seen as 'personally unappealing', she also came to be seen as 'an unstoppable force of nature who demands respect'. (R. Harris, 1988) As long as people regarded her in such a light they were prepared to accept the myths about her achievements.

Thatcher's charismatic qualities meant she attracted devotion from the faithful even as she ignored or destroyed much of the old machinery of government and the Establishment, and because she did this successfully she was seen to have a magic that in its turn allowed her to get away with claims which would not have stood up for a moment had she lacked this quality of charisma. Thus, she referred to Churchill as 'Winston' (who in fact was the 'wettest' prime minister since 1945 in his search for the consensus she scorned) and as her hero even as she insisted that a colleague should be 'one of us' – and people swallowed the line. As one MP said of the party conference during the Thatcher years, 'They painted the podium to match her eyes and bussed in the faithful to make up the numbers of passionate devotees.' Such an approach was part of the party technique to which the charismatic leader responded but, unfortunately for her, in the end the leader gets cut off from reality and begins to believe in the fantasy. As another young party worker said: 'You have to understand that the emotions created at party gatherings depend heavily on faith in the leadership. Ordinary party members only have the confidence to stand up and say things when they know what the leadership thinks.' (*Independent*,

11.5.91) Party conferences, indeed, are an object lesson in how to brainwash the faithful. Equally, however, once the faithful lose their faith – and in Thatcher's case some of them had come to see her as a liability who would not win another election – then she was ruthlessly pushed aside by colleagues, most of whom disliked or feared her. As the Conservative party then began to reorganise itself under the banner of John Major, it also embarked upon the awkward yet necessary task of demythologising the fallen idol.

The myth that the 'lady is not for turning' was belied by the performance. Her first U-turn, indeed, came within four months of her May 1979 election victory when at the Lusaka Commonwealth Heads of Government meeting she agreed to the formula which led to an independent Zimbabwe under Robert Mugabe. That was certainly contrary to what everyone expected and a typical example of her political pragmatism. Earlier in her career, as Secretary of State for Education under Heath, 'Margaret Thatcher approved more schemes for comprehensive schools, and the abolition of more grammar schools than any other secretary of state before or since.' (Young, 1989:68) But, as Denis Healey said, 'her U-turns often go unnoticed; once she realises she has made a mistake she is capable of reversing her position in a flash, without explanation or apology.' (1989:489) Moreover, she had an ability to brazen out a situation when she had reversed a policy and was so successful in this that to the end of her premiership many of her admirers – and her foes – were still convinced that she was not for turning. 'I do not believe in retaliatory strikes that are against international law,' she said, but three months later she agreed to the US strike (from British bases) against Libya in 1986. (Young, 1989:475)

Her famous remark that 'As Prime Minister I couldn't waste time having any internal arguments' ought to have told her colleagues all they needed to know about her, but it didn't. (K. Harris, 1988:79) She ruled by fear and her constant query as to whether a person was 'one of us' was the technique of a dictator and had little of democracy about it. As a very senior Conservative backbencher said after John Major came to power: 'Since she went the atmosphere has been transformed. People are speaking to one another again.' Under her leadership attacks were launched upon any institutions which appeared as alternative sources of authority. At the same time Thatcher was the most centralising, authoritarian prime minister of the century who presided over major assaults upon liberty as she elevated the secret world, removed the right of trade-union membership from GCHQ, used dubious tactics in her battle with the National Union of Mineworkers, and threatened the media whenever it refused to be partial to her cause. Like a religious zealot Margaret Thatcher behaved as though she enjoyed a monopoly of the truth: 'When that conviction is entertained, there is no point in discussion and no reason for democracy.' (Barker, 1958:70)

What is most interesting about Thatcher is that while her supporters used techniques of brainwashing to persuade the public at large of her invincibility, she herself became the ruthless – and much loathed – enemy of the Establishment, whose survival has always been closely linked to its capacity to brainwash the public as to its right to rule. 'She showed herself no respecter of persons – or at least, not of the persons whose names figured on the establishment lists of the great and the good. She appointed no royal commissions because that was the last sort of advice she needed.' (Clarke, 1991:314) Or, as Hugo Young put it: 'She took away the children's toys.' At one level Thatcher's prime ministerial career illustrates perfectly the problems which attend any attempt to eliminate brainwashing, no matter what form it takes. Had her assaults upon the Establishment been motivated solely by a desire to cleanse the body politic of Britain they might have had a lasting impact; instead, they were more concerned with destroying a system from which she did not come so as to replace it with those who merited the description 'one of us'. Sir John Hoskyns, head of the Thatcher Policy Unit in Downing Street, said of her attitude to the Civil Service: 'I think first her temperament and background made her impatient with the whole sort of establishment culture and way of thinking, even of talking. And that, I think, is extremely healthy because I happen to think the Establishment . . . is absolutely at the heart of the British disease.' (K. Harris, 1988:95) It is possible to agree with Sir John Hoskyns without welcoming the alternative 'one of us' culture whose end result must be some form of centralising dictatorship.

Thatcher had an instinctive nose for power and her techniques of management were innate rather than learnt, although she was ready enough to learn when she saw the need. Thus she divided the world into 'wets' and 'dries', she took on all who did not qualify as 'one of us' and she appealed to gut reactions about Europe, South Africa, immigration, hooliganism – the list is a long one. She ruthlessly pursued and bullied institutions like the Church or the BBC, insisting that her government stood for greater freedoms even as these were whittled away. 'Her moral populism revealed Gladstone echoes; her raging, tearing propaganda, consciously opting for the frontal assault, stood in the Chamberlainite tradition.' (Clarke, 1991:319) Expressions of disapproval from Thatcher were designed to intimidate as, for example, when she was reported to be 'fizzing with rage' because the High Street banks decided not to participate in the student loan schemes. The issue was no more important than many others but the way she attempted to force people into line was part of a technique that she perfected during her years in Downing Street. She was never able to come to terms with those who did not share her views, so that her Cabinet was always divided into a minority she trusted and the majority whom she regarded as 'wets' or worse. And to control them she employed techniques of smear that were brutally successful: thus, 'Norman St John Stevas was dismissed as "a leaker"; John Biffen was said to be "semi-detached"; Francis Pym a "Mrs Mona-Lot" ' while minister after minister learnt of his impending dismissal through the newspapers. (*Observer*, 25.11.90)

Free enterprise, market forces, people taking responsibility were phrases that came readily to Thatcher and Thatcherites, and as Andrew Thomson, one of her biographers, said: 'But the sheer rushing, gushing spirit of free enterprise in the United States will always reinforce her own vision for Britain.' (1989:157) Much of her reputation rests upon her approach to the economy and yet an analysis of the economic achievements must make uneasy reading for those who accept the myth. When she came to power the rate of inflation was just over 8 per cent and although it went up and then came right down it had just topped the 8 per cent level again when she left Downing Street. When she came to power – and to its peak in October 1980 – the pound was worth as much as $2.40, but when she left Downing Street it was down to about $1.60. Unemployment rose to more than 3 million during her premiership and was at the 2 million mark when she went, and to achieve this latter figure the basis upon which unemployment was calculated had been changed a number of times, always to the advantage of government statistics. Base rates were raised early in her stewardship – 17 per cent in November 1979 – and were consistently high, forcing more small businesses into bankruptcy than at any time since the Chancellorship of Anthony Barber under Heath, and although income tax was reduced and privatisation, a policy stumbled upon by accident, was markedly popular it would be difficult at the end of 1990 to argue that the Thatcher years represented an economic turn-round for Britain although they were persistently represented in such a light. Her assault upon union power undoubtedly had wide appeal but as Tam Dalyell described it, breaking the unions was about domestic politics, not the national interest, and while Mrs Thatcher described the Argentinians as the 'enemy without' she described the National Union of Mineworkers as 'the enemy within', hardly the kind of language the Prime Minister should apply to a major segment of the workforce. (1987:89) She attracted the support, indeed the devotion, of certain business tycoons such as Rupert Murdoch, one of her most persistent backers, or Lord Hanson, whose expertise lay in take-overs, and while 'in the Seventies captains of industry had boasted of the numbers of their employees, like generals of their armies; in the Eighties they boasted of the number they had fired.' (*Independent*, 13.8.91) Interestingly, over these years, there was a turn-round in the values attached to words about management and industry so that 'ruthless' became a word of high praise, a large workforce became 'surplus fat' while companies wanted to be 'lean and mean'. But if business tycoons relished making their companies 'lean and mean' by 'ruthlessly' cutting down the 'surplus fat', they excused the free enterprise which awarded to the top management huge salary increases on the grounds that they were becoming efficient like the Americans. When John Major made known his displeasure at the way the top tycoons consistently awarded themselves high – sometimes outrageously high – salaries, he did much to demystify the Thatcher economic myth which then began to look more like an era that favoured those who favoured Thatcher than a period of rejuvenation for British industry or the economy.

The extreme anger of Thatcherites was directed against Michael Heseltine in 1990 because he was the man who finally took on the myth and brought about its destruction, even though he did not obtain for himself the leadership of the party in the process. And it was Heseltine who very nearly destroyed the Thatcher myth in 1986 over the Westland affair. His dramatic walkout from the Cabinet was not over a helicopter company but in protest at a style of domineering, arrogant behaviour that – at least for him – had gone on long enough. He charged that Cabinet government was being subverted and he very nearly brought her down then. He certainly caused her to demonstrate qualities of behaviour that were far removed from the popular image of an all-powerful, unstoppable force, and, as Denis Healey said of this incident: 'During the Westland affair panic at the prospect of being driven out of office drove her into a ruthless conspiracy for self-preservation worthy of Macmillan or Harold Wilson at their worst.' (1989:505)

The old party claim that the Church of England was 'the Conservative Party at prayer' was effectively destroyed by Thatcher, not least because it provided an enduring alternative of considerable appeal to the faithful. Indeed, her reactions to the Church hierarchy and most especially to its Archbishop, Dr Runcie, came close to paranoia, not so much because the Church in its 'caring' pastoral capacity said things that went against the Thatcher line but even more because it dared to do so at all. As William Keegan wrote in the *Observer* (4.2.90): 'You can always tell when Thatcherites are embarrassed. They lash out at the perpetrators of critical reports before they have read them (if, indeed, they ever do), often before the documents are published.' When the Church of England's report 'Faith in the City' was published . . . Norman Tebbit described it as 'Marxist'. Later, when the Church produced another report – 'Living Faith in the City' – the Conservative MP Ann Widdecombe said: 'If it [the Church] had as much strength of feeling on moral and ethical issues, its congregations might stop declining.' The fact is that the Church commenting upon the plight of the inner cities was touching upon one of the most neglected areas of government policy (or non-policy) so that it was indeed acting as a potential alternative centre of political thought, if not power, which was not to be tolerated. 'Faith in the City' was seen as the final evidence of Runcie's 'wetness', if not treason, for he had already earned opprobrium from Thatcher and her supporters for his markedly untriumphal sermon at what had been meant to be a celebration of victory after the Falklands War. And yet, despite her attitude towards the Church (and, her opponents would add, her attitude towards the poor at large), Thomson, one of her hagiographers, could write of her: 'Margaret Thatcher has been described as the first fully committed Christian Prime Minister since Lord Salisbury, who died in 1903, and she is a more frequent attender at the small church at Chequers than her predecessors.' (1989:64)

Thatcher's attempts to control the press were blatant and smacked of a 'second-class police state', to quote Roy Jenkins. Injunctions, prohibitions and, above all, threats were part of her stock in trade; they were aided and abetted by the periodic threatening speeches against the BBC, for example, by Norman Tebbit, who became her principal 'fear' instrument in relation to the BBC in particular. She used her fear tactics regularly and in relation to the Thames Television programme *Death on the Rock* responded with her accusation of 'trial by television'. In other respects her use of the media was old-fashioned and crude as, for example, her 1986 appearance on the beach described by the *Telegraph*: 'Her run up a Cornwall beach being pulled along by a borrowed dog delighted her Party managers.' But it has to be said that, although Thatcher earned opprobrium by her constant attempts to muzzle or pressurise the media – especially the BBC – she was only the last in a long line of prime ministers to use such tactics, although she was considerably more blatant about it than her predecessors.

Like any good propagandist Thatcher did not know the meaning of impartiality; thus, in the education debate she was above all concerned that history teaching should be about British history and she liked to talk about putting the Great back into Britain. The worst criticism that can be levelled against Thatcher is the fact that she was anti-democratic in the fullest sense of that word, a natural dictator by instinct who, again and again, used her commanding power to cut corners, to evade and avoid the law and, despite paying endless lip-service to freedom, presided over a greater diminution of real freedom during her term of office than any prime minister since World War II. Over the issue of terrorism in Ulster one of her aides said: 'You must understand Mrs Thatcher believes you have to be for or against terrorism. A journalist is a member of the human race, some of them forget that, and a citizen first. You should have nothing to do with terrorists *at all*.' (Bolton, 1990:76) Too often she carried this view into fields far removed from terrorism. As Ponting quotes her on reform of the Official Secrets Act: 'It should be reformed, but only to make some of its provisions against the unauthorised disclosure of official information stronger, not weaker.' (1986:206) Part of her success stemmed from the way she spoke *ex cathedra* as it were so that no one dared question what she said. Thus, the author Kenneth Harris recounts how she told him in 1987, '[by 1979] we were very near to having what I would call a permanent socialist society where freedom was constantly being diminished.' The pity is that Harris did not ask her about the diminutions of freedom that had taken place under her premiership. (1988:91) And though freedom was a word she liked to use, her sustained opposition to sanctions against South Africa, for example, arose out of right-wing gut reactions in support of a racial (and anti-democratic) minority and not because she really believed that persuasion rather than sanctions was the way to deal with the apartheid question.

Perhaps nothing signalled her sense of apartness more – the myth elevated – than the decision in 1989 to erect gates across the entrance to Downing Street. Although these could be excused on the grounds that they were to control terrorists (and in her defence she had good reason to fear terrorist attacks – the deaths by bomb of her close associates Airey Neave and Ian Gow, and the bomb attack on the Grand Hotel at Brighton) there remained the powerful suspicion that they were really a sign of delusions of grandeur, for by then she had taken to referring to herself with the royal 'we'.

A leader in the *Independent* of 22 October 1990 argued that:

The real vision that people cherish is, more prosaically, of living in a country where things work – or work better than they do in Britain. They want a country where the trains run on time, hospital beds are available, public transport is good enough to leave the car at home, schooling is effective, reliable and safe; where yobbishness, public litter and crime are not all seemingly on the rise, where taxation is fair and inflation and high interest rates are not eroding earnings, savings and the entrepreneurial spirit.

Few, if any of those conditions could be said to have existed at the end of the Thatcher reign despite all the claims made on her behalf, yet persistent propaganda in the years following the 'winter of discontent' suggested that Mrs Thatcher had put right all the things which had so manifestly gone wrong in 1979. In fact she had not done so at all.

When first she became Prime Minister Margaret Thatcher quoted from St Francis of Assissi: 'Where there is discord, may we bring harmony. Where there is error, may we bring truth. Where there is doubt, may we bring faith. Where there is despair, may we bring hope.' In retrospect that quotation suggests everything she did not do: she left a country more divided than at any time since 1945 – harmony was never a Thatcher bequest – and in addition left her own party in squabbling disarray. Truth has long been in short supply in Whitehall; under her it fared worse than in many years. Perhaps her best claim would be in the matter of faith or, at least, of conviction politics; she never wavered in her belief that she was right. When finally she left office there was plenty of despair around and not a great deal of evidence that the long years of Thatcherite policies had brought hope to many people. Now it would be unfair to hold this too much against her for, as Enoch Powell has claimed, all politics ends in tears, yet it would be difficult to find a quotation that was more obviously unsuited to the Thatcher approach to solving the nation's problems than that by St Francis. It is almost as though, taking a leaf from Goebbels' book – if you tell a big lie often enough it will be believed – she decided to suggest that she would adopt a course of action that was the opposite to her real intentions. As a MORI poll of May 1989 showed, most people found their fellow-countrymen to be more violent, more selfish and less happy than they had been a decade earlier, when Margaret Thatcher took office, while many of her policies were unpopular and a number of her crucial values were not shared by the mass of the electorate. (*Independent*, 2.5.89) And though a constant Thatcher refrain was that Britain was over-governed, a view she summed up with her phrase 'dependency culture', she left it even more centralised in terms of the operation of power than when she came to office. To a large extent her performance was a compelling exercise in propaganda that was not substantiated by lasting achievements; rarely has any British politician been so much acclaimed for strength and providing the country with a new direction and yet left behind so little of lasting value.

Perhaps, in summary, it is worth turning to Andrew Thomson again, who begins one chapter of his book *The Woman Within* as follows: 'To Margaret Thatcher, the people of her North London constituency are a second family.' Elsewhere in this extravagant encomium of praise he says, 'Something close to bliss for her must be an hour or two spent reading Kipling in the rose garden [at Chequers].' And to round off a wholly unrealistic picture of this extraordinary power-seeker, Mr Thomson describes one of her annual appearances: 'She enjoys a good sing-song at the old people's Christmas party where, with a strong voice, she will join in the renditions of "Daisy" and other old favourites, often calling loudly for more.' (1989:87, 200, 204) When finally she had been forced from office the organisers of the annual Conservative Party Conference of September 1991, true to form, did their best to render her a 'non-person', although they were to find considerable life still remaining in her which she deployed at the end of the year in an attempt to perpetuate divisions over Europe.

18 War and peace

The issue is not whether we will die for our beliefs,
but whether we will kill for them.
THE CHURCH AND THE BOMB

THE FALKLANDS WAR OF 1982 could have been avoided and was less excusable than most; it provided an impetus for the Thatcher government which it sorely needed at the time and was the progenitor of myths and behaviour that Britain would have done better to eschew. As Raymond Williams said of the Falklands War: 'It is because the real national self-identification and self-confidence that once existed have gone, that a certain artificial, frenetic, from-the-top, imagery of a nation can be injected.' (1989:164) As more than one commentator asked at the time, what sort of mood would have emerged had the war been against Germany?

That scourge of Thatcher, Tam Dalyell, had no doubts about the reasons for the war: 'A little war, deemed to be righteous by public opinion, might restore the domestic political fortunes of a Prime Minister who sat lower in the opinion polls than any Prime Minister has done since political polling began.' As he went on to argue, an acceptance of the peace proposals from Peru which were backed by the US was not in Thatcher's interest, for 'had the Prime Minister accepted them, she knew that she would be deprived of the "military victory" which is what the Falklands War was all about from an early stage.' (1987:6) And, Dalyell believed, the sinking of the *Belgrano* was deliberate – to ensure that there would be a war.

As a senior Foreign Office official had said of the Falklands in 1936: 'The difficulty of our position is that our seizure of the Falkland Islands in 1833 was so arbitrary a procedure as judged by the ideology of the present day that it [would not be] easy to explain our position without showing ourselves up as international bandits.' (Ponting, 1990:189) Clive Ponting wrecked his career as a civil servant because he chose to reveal the government cover-up of lies connected with the sinking of the *Belgrano*. In the court case against him Justice McCowan advanced the doctrine that the interests of the state were indistinguishable from the interests of the government: in essence, that 'Ponting could claim no higher duty than to do what ministers told him'. (Young, 1989:287) Echoes of Eichmann once more! Dalyell was given the diary of Lieutenant Sethia of the *Conqueror*, who had had his own doubts about the war 'because some people in the Service had come to believe that they had been used. Some of their friends had returned maimed, others had failed to return at all: not for the national interests of our country, but for the political interests of the Prime Minister.' (Dalyell, 1987:15)

Once the war was over Lord Franks, one of the greatest of the 'great and the good', was appointed to head a committee of privy councillors to produce a report, the *Falkland Islands Review*, whose studied phrases and apparent monumental impartiality are worth examining. After reviewing the history of the preceding twenty years, the report comes to the question of the immediate events prior to the war and asks whether or not it could have been avoided and who, if anyone, was to blame. In answer to the question 'Could the invasion of 2 April have been foreseen?' the report says: 'We believe that our account demonstrates conclusively that the Government had no reason to believe before March 31 that an invasion of the Falkland Islands would take place at the beginning of April.' That statement may be described as strictly accurate but given all that had gone before it does not exonerate the government of blame for what happened (as it appears to do) but only demonstrates that it was taken by surprise at that particular time. As the report says later: 'We conclude . . . that it was inadvisable for the Government to announce a decision to withdraw HMS *Endurance* and that, in the light of the developing situation in the second half of 1981, they should have rescinded their decision to pay off HMS *Endurance* at the end of her 1981/82 tour.'

The report examines the fading chances of reaching a lease-back agreement with Argentina during 1981, and after quoting Lord Carrington, the Foreign Secretary, as saying that he saw no chance at that time of 'selling' the lease-back idea to the Falkland Islanders, the House of Commons or his ministerial colleagues, it concluded that the 'Government were in a position of weakness' so that the initiative passed to the Argentine Government. This really does seem to be a most extraordinary judgement in relation to the government that was in possession, that had universally recognised legal claim to the territory, and that was by far the more powerful and influential of the two contending states. Why did it not keep the initiative by examining some other option? The Foreign and Commonwealth Office then misjudged how the dispute would develop: 'In the event it proved to be a misjudgement, but not one in our view for which blame should be attached to any individual.' At the beginning of March 1982 it would have been possible to dispatch naval vessels to the Islands in time to act as a deterrent, but although officials mentioned to Lord Carrington the fact that the previous government had done that in 1977, no similar decision was taken to do so this time round. Mild blame is suggested in paragraph 302 of the report: 'We believe that Foreign and Commonwealth Office officials did not attach sufficient weight at this time to the changing Argentine attitude . . . We conclude that they should have drawn Ministers' attention more effectively to the changed situation.' Later (paragraph 315), another mild reproof is handed down, this time to the Joint Intelligence Organisation: 'We were surprised that events in the first three months of 1982 . . . did not prompt the Joint Intelligence Organisation to assess the situation afresh.' And in the next paragraph the report continues: 'First, we are not sure that at all important times the assessments staff were fully aware of the weight of the Argentine press campaign in 1982. As a result it seems to us that they may have attached greater significance to the secret intelligence, which at that time was reassuring about the prospects of an early move to confrontation.' Further on in the same paragraph (316) the report continues: 'Our second doubt is whether the Joint Intelligence Organisation attached sufficient weight to the possible effects on Argentine thinking of the various actions of the British Government.' Yet, after this comparatively strong paragraph, the report hastens to add (the opening sentence of paragraph 317) 'We do not seek to attach any blame to the individuals involved.' Why ever not, one is tempted to ask at this point. Margaret Thatcher, according to Sir John Hoskyns (see page 214), objected not only to the 'great and good' of the Establishment but even to the very language they used, and the Franks report uses this 'objectionable' Establishment language throughout. The general tenor of the Thatcher years was to endorse the cut-throat values of the market-place, but in this instance the Prime Minister does not appear to have taken anybody to task for the failure to stop the war although, perhaps, that is because it gave rise to the 'Falklands factor' from which she was to reap such political advantage. At the very end of the report the government is exonerated of all blame: 'Taking account of these considerations, and of all the evidence we have received, we conclude that we would not be justified in attaching any criticism or blame to the present Government for the Argentine Junta's decision to commit its act of unprovoked aggression in the invasion of the Falkland Islands on 2 April 1982.' (Franks, 1983) As Hugo Young says of it: 'Thus the report finds defective machinery but no defective men or women. It soothes and reassures, by performing the ultimate trick of appearing to be so candid. It offers the grace of exoneration without the stain of cover-up.' (1989:284) In fact, it is a masterly example of whitewash whose prime purpose is to get the government of the day 'off the hook' where its own incompetence had brought it.

In his memoirs Lord Carrington says of his resignation: 'It was not a sense of culpability that led me to resign – a subjective judgement of course, but one which was later to find confirmation in the Franks Report.' He resigns, he tells us, first because the 'whole country felt angry and humiliated' (at the Argentine invasion which British policy had failed to prevent) and second, as he candidly avers 'was my awareness that the Government was in for a hard time and that my presence would make it not easier but harder.' (1988:370) It is difficult to understand how, if his presence in the government would make things harder rather than easier he was, none the less, not to blame. The Franks Report and Lord Carrington resigning, although not from a sense of culpability, remind one irresistibly of *Little Dorrit* and the Circumlocution Office and the fact that no one is to blame.

The unique geographic circumstances of the Falklands War meant that the navy had complete control of the media and as David Kimche, Director-General of Israel's Foreign Ministry, said: 'My attitude towards Britain's handling of media coverage of the Falklands campaign was one of envy that they could get away with it.' He was speaking in the aftermath of the Israeli invasion of southern Lebanon which also occurred in 1982 where, in his own words, TV coverage of the invasion did 'irreparable damage to the country'. As an anonymous naval commander with the Falklands task force told Michael Nicholson of ITN: 'If I had my way, we would tell people nothing until the war is over. After that, we would tell them who won.' (*The Times*, 10.5.83) Governments, even those laying claim to full democratic practices, do not like the media except when they can feed them success stories and 'In Israel, there is unstinted official admiration for the way in which the Thatcher government severely limited access to the fighting, yet won a generally favourable world press for its efforts on the battlefield.' Management of the media was, indeed, a Thatcher forte. But unlike Britain in relation to the Falklands War, Israel was not able to control media access to Lebanon in the same way. Since Britain was defending its territory (self-defence) and United Nations Resolution 502 demanded Argentina's withdrawal, there were good reasons for Britain not declaring war. (Mercer *et al.*, 1987:18) As a result the government could not invoke the wartime Emergency Powers to control the media but it did as well, simply because the navy actually controlled both access to the war zone and all the channels of communication from the Falklands to the outside world, allowing it to censor as it chose.

Hypocrisy was a part of the Falklands War, as of all wars. Thus 17 per cent of the Exocets which the Argentinians fired at the British consisted of parts made by the British, and supplies of equipment from Britain to Argentina went on until the last moment, but as Mr Tony Killick of Williams and Glyn's Bank said, it would be 'very wrong for the Government to interfere with a commercial contract'. (*The Times*, 8.3.83) Given the emphasis placed upon market forces by the Thatcher government one can only suppose that whatever it believed about impending trouble with Argentina, Whitehall also regarded commercial contracts in this sacrosanct light. The Prime Minister, indeed, was imbued with a spirit of triumphalism as she showed with her 'Rejoice!' comment when South Georgia was recaptured, to be echoed by the *Sun* headline of 'Gotcha!' for the sinking of the *Belgrano*. When it was all over (July 1982) Thatcher could say: 'We have ceased to be a nation in retreat.' Then, when the service of thanksgiving was held in St Paul's, 'Thatcher was infuriated by the Queen's approval of the St Paul's Cathedral Falklands' Service where prayers were offered for all: both the British *and* the Argentinian combatants who had died.' (Abse, 1989:65) Perhaps a greater understanding of the Falklands War became apparent in November 1991 when the government set in motion the search for oil round the Falkland Islands, and the Governor issued a proclamation asserting the Crown's jurisdiction over the sea-bed and continental shelf 'to the full limits allowed under international law'. (*Independent*, 23.11.91)

The British peace movement has sometimes been seen as sufficient of a threat to the government of the day (and other vested interests) to call forth enormous efforts to discredit it. The importance of the peace movement has resided less in its chances of changing government policy, which have been so slight as to be virtually non-existent, than in its ability at least to force governments to think about how they justify their case. Over the years since Britain produced her own 'bomb' and joined the nuclear club, the peace movement has attracted to its ranks some distinguished thinkers and writers, including Britain's most eminent philosopher, Bertrand Russell. The lengths to which the government was prepared to go were illustrated in what may be termed the Hyde Park incident. 'By the use of a fourteenth-century statute, passed to restrain armed vagrant soldiers returning destitute from the French wars, and not free from suspicion of subsequent amendment by forgery, one of the greatest living Englishmen, Bertrand Russell, was sent to prison at the age of ninety.' (Nicholson, 1967:354) His offence was to use a loudspeaker to address a CND crowd in Hyde Park. At the same time his American secretary was sentenced to a nine-month prison sentence after being told by the magistrate that 'You are a nuisance to the police.'

In 1982 the Church of England published *The Church and the Bomb*, which was its contribution to the debate about Britain's possession of nuclear weapons and arguments as to when and in what circumstances she should use such weapons. Fortuitously, this book was published just after the Falklands War and is another exercise of the (clerical) 'great and good' agonising over where the Church should stand on the bomb. It has been a constant feature of all debates which involve Church and State and the possibility of war that the Christian commandment 'Thou shalt not kill' becomes of only relative rather than absolute importance in such circumstances. As Tony Benn has remarked of such issues, when the government is in doubt it calls to its aid the bishops.

The analysis of the nuclear dilemma – the technological, strategic and political considerations surrounding the subject – is excellent. The difficulties (for the authors of this Church report) arise when they have to consider where the Church should stand on the issues: not just of the bomb but of killing in wartime. As it says of attitudes in World War II: 'The Churches were characterised everywhere by patriotism in the form of uncritical loyalty.' (Salisbury *et al.*, 1982:75) After examining the criteria of a 'just war' and arguing that coercion is sometimes necessary to protect the common good, the report says, 'The Just War doctrine implies that war cannot be abolished yet, while it seeks to keep the actual conduct of the war within bounds which are proportionate to the reasonable goals of the war, namely, the pursuit of peace, order and justice.' (83) There is more reasoning along similar lines whose actual message is that the Church supports just wars. But, of course, on such a topic the writers of the report become increasingly confused as they lay down criteria in support of a just war. Thus, they argue that 'Those engaging in war must have a reasonable hope of success.' Now it is true, at least of those who start wars, that they probably begin with a reasonable hope of success but that would seem to have little to do with justice. And when Poland was attacked in 1939 by both Nazi Germany and Stalinist Russia, she had no hope whatever of winning, but did the just-war criteria really demand that she surrendered at once without any resistance? As the report continues, war should be acceptable to a person of upright conscience, which it then defines splendidly yet hopelessly: 'An upright conscience is one formed by a lifelong habit of love, generosity, mercy, justice, courage, patience and all other virtues.' (86)

Having first argued that the concept of a just war is not out of date, despite the potential scale of modern war in general, the report turns to those critics who suggest that any Christian participation in war is a mistake. It says of this stand: 'That is more properly a pacifist or quasi-pacifist argument. It implies that Just War thinking has always had defects; the nuclear age has simply shown up its inherent weakness. Those however who accept the validity of Just War thinking are obliged to apply its criteria to nuclear war as they do to conventional war.' (93) Having made the point that just wars can be acceptable – in the sense that they right wrongs and restore peace, justice and order – the report passes on to the subject of nuclear war and concludes, quite correctly, that nuclear weapons are inherently unsuitable for the waging of a 'just war' since they would leave behind a wasteland. According to St Matthew's Gospel, Jesus is portrayed as advocating the love of enemies by non-resistance, but as the report continues: 'Such pacifism is not to be confused with *passivity* since it is infused with the positive command to love which does not rule out the use of force, providing, that is, such force is compatible with loving those against whom it is used.' These remarkable sophists go on to suggest that pacifism can be regarded as a 'vocation' that some Christians are called upon to follow while, presumably, others may kill for the state. Later, having quoted a statement first made in 1930 and endorsed by successive Lambeth conferences in 1948, 1968 and 1978 that 'War as a method of settling international disputes is incompatible with the teaching and example of our Lord Jesus Christ', it continues to equivocate by saying that this statement 'offers no practical guidance to a person trying to decide whether a specific war is legitimate'. (125) As the report says, 'nuclear weapons in particular, are only part of the problem, the root of which is war itself.' After a good deal more soul-searching the report comes to the conclusion that the 'just war' theory rules out the use of nuclear weapons. It then proceeds to give a series of recommendations (nos. 1–17) that sound reasonable but in fact leave things as they are: 'Existing disarmament negotiations should be vigorously prosecuted', 'There should be discriminating support for the UN', 'Renewed and determined efforts should be made to secure a Comprehensive Test Ban Treaty', 'Pressure should be brought to bear on the government to make the debate on defence and disarmament a real one', and so on. But then it goes further and its recommendation number 18 says, 'The United Kingdom should renounce its independent nuclear deterrent', cancel the order for the Trident missile and phase out first British and then US nuclear weapons on its soil while remaining a member of NATO. It is a brave report in its way but while it equivocates over the just war and pacifism and clearly denies the commandment 'Thou shalt not kill', it does endorse the popular demand of the time that Britain should renounce nuclear weapons. *The Church and the Bomb* was, no doubt, one of the 'wishy-washy' pronouncements of the Church during the 1980s which ensured the widening gap between the Church and the Thatcherite state.

It was during this debate in the early 1980s that the Duke of Edinburgh came out (carefully) in defence of the bomb (although not too many bombs, his sop to the peace lobby) while the Roman Catholic Archbishop Basil Hume began to doubt publicly the role of Monsignor Bruce Kent, the leader of CND. These cautious, 'balanced' attitudes by two leading Establishment figures showed just how disturbed the anti-bomb campaign had rendered the Establishment of the day. This was hardly surprising, for had the campaign to ban the bomb succeeded during the days of the Cold War it would have entailed a substantial curtailment (in the Atlantic Alliance) of Britain's power and influence and also, therefore, of the Establishment's power.

Anti-nuclear sentiments increased markedly in 1983 with the impending arrival in Britain of Cruise and Pershing missiles. Following the sitting of the International Synod of Bishops at Rome during October 1983, the Catholic Church became more involved in the argument in Britain; its orthodox line was that set out by Pope John Paul II at the United Nations on 11 June 1982:

In current conditions 'deterrence' based on balance, certainly not as an end in itself, but as a stage on the way towards a progressive disarmament, can still be judged morally acceptable. None the less, in order to preserve peace, it is indispensable not to be satisfied with this minimum which is always susceptible to the real danger of explosion. (*The Times*, 17.11.83)

Enoch Powell entered the debate about nuclear weapons during 1983 and began with a typically Powellian assertion when he attacked the misconception that forty years of peace in Europe was due to the availability of nuclear weapons. As Powell argued, 'War is implicit in the human condition', and he then recalled what he had said in Parliament in March 1967:

The crucial question is whether there is any stage of a European war at which any nation would choose self-annihilation in preference to prolonging the struggle. The Secretary of State says, 'Yes, the loser or likely loser would almost instantly choose self-annihilation.' I say, 'No. The probability, though not the certainty, but surely at least the possibility, is that no such point would come, whatever the course of the conflict'.

In an analysis of the deterrence theory Powell then demonstrated the unlikelihood that either side would use nuclear weapons and suggested that the real reason why both sides insisted upon the deterrence approach was that 'the nuclear hypothesis provides governments with an excuse for not doing what they have no intention of doing anyhow, but for reasons which they find it inconvenient to specify.' He suggested that it was not right to take the doctrine of the nuclear deterrent on trust 'without serious debate or examination on the pretext that those who dare to discuss or examine it must be evilly or unpatriotically disposed.' (*The Times*, 1.6.83)

In April 1983 Cardinal Basil Hume, the Roman Catholic Archbishop of Westminster, warned Monsignor Bruce Kent, General Secretary of the Campaign for Nuclear Disarmament, that he might have to stand down if the movement became more 'political'. He suggested that it might become inappropriate for a priest to be so closely associated with the CND. It is difficult to understand how the leader of Britain's Roman Catholics could put such pressure upon a priest for wanting to bring an end to the evil of nuclear weapons, except that the Cardinal himself had been subjected to pressures from leading lay Roman Catholics and especially Conservative politicians. Later that same year another row centred upon the fact that Monsignor Kent had addressed the British Communist Party and had declared that the Communist Party and the CND were 'partners in the cause of peace' while also praising the *Morning Star* (Britain's Communist newspaper) for its 'steady, honest and generous coverage of the whole disarmament case'. He was attacked principally for treating the Communists as allies in the campaign to ban the bomb. (*The Times*, 15.11.83) But as one correspondent (John V. Bettison) wrote to *The Times*:

> Bruce Kent is to be commended for engaging in dialogue with the Communist Party. As a Catholic priest he is not bound to the maintenance of any political ideology. So while the Catholic hierarchy agonizes over whether or not we should eat meat on Fridays we are fortunate to be reminded of the major threat facing our society.

And as another reader (Alec Kassman) reminded *The Times*, had Monsignor Kent, instead of praising the Communist Party, praised the SDP or the Leader of the Opposition or the Prime Minister, no fuss would have been made and no suggestions that he leave the priesthood. A third letter writer (Bill Agnew) pointed out that Monsignor Kent had also praised the Quakers (ideologically committed peace-makers) but that, apparently, did not matter. (17.11.83) However, by 18 November 1983 *The Times* was able to report:

> It will be reassuring to Government, and reassuring to public opinion generally, that Cardinal Hume has arrived by his own route at a qualified endorsement of the defence strategy of nuclear deterrence, as it was similarly reassuring last February when the General Synod of the Church of England reached similar conclusions.

How satisfying for the government of the day – and what a free society it made Britain appear – that both the Church of England and Roman Catholic hierarchies could first indulge in public soul-searching and then come down on the side of the bomb and government policy.

In December 1983 the showing on British ITV of an American television film, *The Day After*, which depicted the effects of a nuclear attack, led the Defence Secretary, Michael Heseltine, to ask for exclusive television time to comment at the end of the film. It was the first time a politician had requested time to reply to a presentation of fiction and he did so because of the apparent impact the film had made in the United States and because he did not wish the unilateralists to gain the initiative in the defence debate. *The Times* argued against the minister having such a right of reply on several grounds: that it would make the film out to be more important than it was; that it would trivialise ministerial statements and express lack of trust in the judgement of both the broadcasting authorities and the public; and that it would bypass the conventions by in effect giving the minister a ministerial broadcast without right of reply. (8.12.83) (These arguments represented an older media attitude towards government that preceded the more frenetic anti-media pressures which surfaced in the latter half of the 1980s.) In the event the Minister's request was refused; instead, he was invited to take part in a discussion of the film on TV-AM chaired by David Frost. The TV film, although dramatic, did not have the effect which the government feared. A MORI opinion poll showed that support for CND was not altered by the film but remained exactly the same before and after: 30 per cent among those who saw the film, 26 among the wider public. The discussion on television in which Mr Heseltine was joined by the former US Defence Secretary Robert McNamara ranged over the whole subject of nuclear deterrence and the need for conventional arms. The to-do about the film was part of the very real public argument (and paranoia) that existed at that time and demonstrated the sensitivity of government to the apparent power of television to alter the public's view of the government case.

The nuclear debate brought out, as perhaps nothing else could, the divergences between the determination of governments to maintain a British nuclear deterrent, despite logical arguments that suggested it could be dispensed with and the equivocation of the Churches, whose instinct based upon their theology was to say 'ban the bomb' but whose political worldliness made them compromise. The peace camps against the bomb, of which the most highly publicised was the women's camp at Greenham Common where Cruise missiles were deployed, created a dilemma for the Conservative government whose only response appeared to be constant arrests of the women involved. As usual, Establishment assumptions played their part and, for example, the Junior Minister of Defence, Peter Blaker, approached a

BBC producer about a programme and assumed that *we* can defeat this (Greenham Common, unilateralism), that the BBC must be on the *right side*, which in this context meant the government side. (Bolton, 1990:115)

During 1991, in the aftermath of the end of the Cold War, the leader of the Labour Party, Neil Kinnock, announced that he had allowed his membership of CND to lapse. It was a sign of the times or, perhaps more accurately, a sign of Neil Kinnock's times as the Labour Party came within measurable distance of power for the first time in a decade. His decision demonstrated, if any demonstration was needed, how persistently power or the prospect of power alters perceptions of ethical issues.

19 Ulster

Here I am . . . dealing with the much more tenable
and dangerous proposition that freedom is
undesirable and that intellectual honesty is a form
of anti-social selfishness.

GEORGE ORWELL

N O OTHER SUBJECT in the period since 1969 has offered so many
examples of government censorship and attacks upon press
or media freedoms, general bullying, downright lying and
erosions of the liberties about which the British are so ready
to boast than Northern Ireland. Tony Benn has often been vilified (or
at any rate treated as though he is politically impracticable and naïve,
if no worse) for suggesting that the real and only long-term solution
to the Ulster question is a united Ireland and yet, in 1940, 'Nearer
home, the Churchill government was to make even more fundamental
concessions, which went as far as offering the Dublin government a
united Ireland, and they brought themselves to the point of forcing
Ulster to accept the deal made behind their backs' – Britain wanted
naval bases in return. (Ponting, 1990:189) Under Thatcher it became
clear that the Six Counties had failed as an entity and that any solution
to the troubles had to embrace the wishes of Dublin as well as London,
while the fact that talks about Northern Ireland are now held between
the two countries destroys the myth that Ulster is an integral part only
of Britain. (Arnold, 1984:403) Why Britain holds on so obstinately to
Northern Ireland can be explained only by a mixture of stubbornness,
political (or party) expediency, security considerations and residual
imperial pride, for Ireland remains the last imperial problem as it
became the first eight hundred years ago. Like a cancer Ulster has
eroded freedoms and constantly revealed the hollowness of British
claims to be a champion of democracy and free speech or, indeed, to
run an open society.

Now it may be true that Ulster represents a special problem and,
as Attlee said, 'It has never been possible to apply logical rules to
Ireland' (1961:18), but that has not excused what has happened for
in essence British governments have come to accept that a different set
of rules applies to the Irish problem than elsewhere in the United

Kingdom. (There is nothing new in this; throughout the nineteenth century and through to the excesses of the Black and Tans after World War I Britain treated the whole of Ireland as a colony; since 1922 successive governments have been prepared, when necessary, to treat Ulster in the same way.) For more than twenty years now, Ulster has been treated increasingly by every British government as though it is a colony under a state of emergency (like Kenya during Mau Mau) and many practices such as 'exclusion' have not only denied to people of Northern Ireland their fundamental rights but, by their application, have brought the British, who are applying these practices, to the point of acting as though such behaviour is both justified and normal. 'Exclusion has in fact created a system of internal exile by executive order, a system which the Government itself condemns when applied in the Soviet Union but which the majority of British MPs and most of the British press condone in this country.' (Hewitt, 1982:168) Indeed, it has long been a British practice to condemn most loudly in other countries what we are prepared to do at home, as though in our own case alone there are always special qualifying circumstances which make such behaviour both necessary and acceptable. This is the kind of argument familiar to dictatorships the world over.

Ulster has always been about bigotry and British imperial interests. 'Left to its own devices the Stormont government, which had been expressly set up to maintain the Protestant ascendancy, rapidly developed into a sectarian, oppressive and discriminatory regime. Westminster politicians preferred to avert their eyes from this un-edifying spectacle as long as Ulster was reasonably quiet.' (Ponting, 1989:336) But from 1967 or 1968 this became increasingly difficult and finally impossible to do. Attempts to achieve reconciliation have always been subordinated to efforts at repression and, as Enoch Powell told James Prior when the latter was responsible for Northern Ireland, he should never use the word 'reconciliation', 'because in Northern Ireland it means reconciliation between the two parts of the island as well as between the Irish and Unionist traditions on the island, and it is therefore totally unacceptable to the Unionists.' (Prior, 1986:183)

The erosion of civil liberties has been steady since the introduction of troops into the province in 1969. In 1970, army searches of Roman Catholic areas for arms were instituted; in 1971 came the practice of internment or detention without trial and a variety of unedifying and brutal accompaniments to interrogation including hooding, electronic noise, spreadeagling against walls, beatings and deprivation of sleep, each of which was contrary to accepted practices in relation to human rights. The introduction of internment in August 1971 effectively brought an end to any hope of a peaceful resolution of the developing conflict. And although internment was ended in 1975, by which time everyone had admitted its failure (for violence had risen on both sides, political talks had become impossible, American assistance for the IRA had increased and Britain found herself heavily criticised internationally for violating human rights), it established a pattern that did not disappear with the end of internment: that is, a pattern of British reaction to unrest that always leant more towards repression than discussion. The fact of IRA violence has, for example, allowed successive British governments to argue that they will not give way to blackmail, thus effectively ruling out of court any discussion of a united Ireland. The security forces rapidly came to be regarded as biased on the side of the Unionists, and the myth that the army stood between the two sides was just that – a myth; it stood against the Catholics. And although, in theory, Roman Catholics can become members of the Royal Ulster Constabulary, in practice its membership is overwhelmingly Protestant.

As the crisis continued, so the impartiality of the courts was brought into question with the introduction of the 'Diplock' courts, without juries, 'with special rules of evidence designed to obtain convictions which might not be obtainable otherwise.' (Hewitt, 1982:161) The result, predictably, was a demand by the Provisional IRA for special 'prisoner' status. Juries were abolished on the grounds that their members allowed themselves to be swayed by sectarian bias, a proposition that was not substantiated, but in fact they were set aside so that the courts could obtain the results they wanted. The former Lord Chancellor, Lord Gardiner, described the methods used in Ulster as 'illegal, not morally justifiable and alien to the traditions of what I still believe to be the greatest democracy in the world', but no action was ever taken against those responsible for such methods. (158) The clamp-down on Ulster continued through the 1970s and, for example, in 1976 the Prevention of Terrorism Act allowed a British citizen born in Northern Ireland to be arrested, detained, deported to Belfast and banned from ever re-entering mainland Britain. The restrictions continued and by 1988 the *Independent* could record that under the new bans introduced by the government it could make 'criminals of television and radio journalists who interview members of certain Irish republican and loyalist movements, including those elected to Westminster. This, according to an unnamed Whitehall source, "is to prevent propaganda" '. Indeed, it was Ulster that produced the situation in which journalists are compelled to surrender film and source material to the police, regardless of the public interest. (20.10.88) Under the provisions of an Act of 1973 the government can introduce legislation for the criminal law by order and it did this on 20 October 1988 to reduce the right to silence, a change with far-reaching implications for British justice, a measure which was debated for three hours on 8 November and then passed. Such a procedure does not allow time for public debate. British actions in relation to Ulster, ever since 1970, have been contrary to all the claims so frequently advanced by Britain about its belief in liberty before the law, justice being seen to be done, impartiality of treatment for everyone and so on.

In 1977, when he was opposition spokesman on Northern Ireland, Airey Neave said:

> We are losing the propaganda war in Northern Ireland ... A review of present attitudes to media freedom is needed therefore, to take account of a desperate emergency. Some of the media deny that we are really at war with terrorism. Some of their actions actually stimulate the hard core terrorist mentality. The BBC, in particular, pronounce on the security situation with studied grandiloquence and ignore the true dangers. (Bolton, 1990:25)

He went on to suggest that 'the BBC have given the impression that they are not really on the side of the civil power in Northern Ireland.' Whether or not Neave's accusations were correct the Thatcher government which came to power in 1979 certainly demonstrated that it has few reservations about forcing the media into line with its policies. In fact, the erosion of freedoms in Ulster has been carried out systematically over many years by successive governments with the connivance, if not active support, of the majority of the British people. Government propaganda, bullying and forceful, as well as being supported by an increasing paraphernalia of censorship, has persuaded a majority of people that what happens in Ulster – 'over there' – is somehow divorced from considerations of justice and liberty on the mainland. It is not. The diminution of freedoms anywhere in Britain is a diminution that affects everyone.

Government censorship has been used to prevent people critical of government policy, such as Ken Livingstone, from broadcasting, and between 1971 and 1984 more than thirty programmes on Northern Ireland were banned. The readiness of both government and media sympathetic to it to twist the truth became glaringly apparent in 1988 over the Gibraltar shootings and the furious public recriminations and accusations launched at Thames Television for its programme *Death on the Rock*. This affair demonstrated just how little the government was interested in liberty if it showed the government up in a bad light.

The story of *Death on the Rock* illustrates everything unpleasant about British officialdom and sycophantic right-wing media. It was a story of deceit, cover-up and smear tactics designed to prevent a full public understanding of just how dubious were the practices to which the government had descended in its fight against terrorism in Ulster. As the *Independent* claimed, 'The assault on the Thames Television programme, *Death on the Rock*, is central to these (newly introduced) controls. The campaign to discredit the programme, and to suppress the issues it raised and the facts it disclosed, shall linger as one of the more shameful propaganda exercises of any country's press.' (20.10.88) What the programme revealed *prima facie* was a 'shoot to kill' policy on Ulster. Moreover, this demonstrated that British policy was failing, since terrorism aims to brutalise the society under attack, and it was clearly succeeding. (Bolton, 1990:194) The tabloids ran a smear campaign against Carmen Proetta, the chief Gibraltar witness of the shootings, in order to discredit her since they could not make her budge over her story. Thus the *Sun* produced a headline, 'For God's sake go, Thomson', attacking the then head of the Independent Broadcasting Authority (IBA) for its refusal to ban the programme, and Thatcher's press officer, Bernard Ingham, speaking on the record, said the standards of the media had declined 'to the point of institutionalized hysteria'.

A subsequent inquiry into the whole affair under Lord Windlesham, a former Conservative minister, and Richard Rampton QC, found no trace of any attempt by Carmen Proetta to exaggerate or embellish her evidence, or any attempt by the interviewer to get her to do so. The Windlesham report of 1989 did not determine what happened in Gibraltar in 1988, but it largely endorsed Thames's right to make the programme and vindicated the way it obtained and presented its evidence. But as the *Independent* commented: 'For just as the Government set out to discredit the programme at the time, Sir Geoffrey

[Howe] is now leading the pack in abusing the Windlesham report. . . . When truth and power conflict, truth can win some individual battles – but in the end . . . power wields the bigger guns.' (30.1.89) And that, in a nutshell, is the story of the British Government and Ulster – power winning over truth.

Roger Bolton, who produced *Death on the Rock* and subsequently wrote a book of the same name, tells how the BBC (in 1972) planned three one-hour programmes on Ulster, looking at the different sides of the problem; the Home Secretary at the time, Reginald Maudling, who had a spurious reputation for liberalism, summoned the Chairman and Director-General of the BBC and 'blew his top'. The process of ministerial bluster and bullying of the media had got under way. 'Throughout the seventies television programmes on Ireland were banned, altered or postponed.' Roy Mason, the Northern Ireland Secretary in 1976, said (*Daily Mail*) 'the BBC was disloyal, supported the rebels, purveyed their propaganda and refused to accept the advice of the Northern Ireland office on what news to carry.' The idea that any broadcasting authority should 'accept the advice of the Northern Ireland office on what news to carry' is illustrative of a totalitarian bent that seems to have affected most Northern Ireland secretaries for years, and such a statement from a minister shows just how little British politicians understand, let alone stand for, the freedoms they so readily endorse from the hustings. At the same time the Lord Chief Justice, Sir Robert Lowery, told the BBC governors to remember 'what is good for the country'. In August 1977 Peter Taylor made a film which he described as 'an alternative diary' of the Queen's Jubilee visit to Northern Ireland. 'He pointed his camera away from the cheering, flag-waving Protestant crowds to silent, angry Catholic streets.' The IBA took exception to this, one presumes on the grounds that royalty must not be upset. Later in this ongoing saga, in 1985, the Home Secretary, Leon Brittan, used pressure to persuade the BBC governors to cancel the programme *Real Lives: At the Edge of the Union*. (Bolton, 1990:21, 24, 35, 37, 162) In March 1988 the Prime Minister attacked both the BBC and ITN for not handing over untransmitted film of the murder of two soldiers at the IRA funeral in Belfast. The broadcasters argued that to do so would be to jeopardise their crews in the future, but the RUC under the Prevention of Terrorism Act seized all the material anyway.

At another level – that concerning the activities of the security services – there is massive evidence of repeated government cover-up for military and RUC abuses of the law as well as brutality. The Stalker affair led to the most obvious government attempts at cover-up when he appeared to have come close to revealing that a 'shoot to kill' policy by the RUC existed in Ulster. He was removed from the investigation which he had been appointed to carry out and subsequently attempts were made to smear his reputation. As Stalker says in his book: 'The way in which my removal was handled has left the firm conviction in many people's minds that I was getting too close to the truth about the activities of policemen operating under cover and without proper control in Northern Ireland.'

In May 1984 John Stalker, the Deputy Chief Constable of the Greater Manchester Police Force, had been asked to undertake an investigation in Northern Ireland

> that soon pointed towards possible offences of murder and conspiracy to pervert the course of justice, these offences committed by members of the proud Royal Ulster Constabulary. I devoted two years of my life to this task, and I failed. In May 1986, three days before I was due to complete the last and very important part of my investigation, I was removed from it. (1988:9)

Stalker was told that he would never be permitted to finish his inquiry if it became a threat to the RUC or the British Government. 'Whatever you say will make no difference over here – the lid has to be kept on. Only the RUC can do it – you won't be allowed to lift it off.' (46) Nor was he. The fact is, as Stalker admitted in his book, that he expected people to be horrified at the possibility of state murder but they were not. As he was to discover, when the security services are involved truth disappears. And when Stalker's investigation was taken over from him 'a clampdown was imposed on all information and a wall of secrecy thrown up around the activities of the new investigators.' (132) He believed that the decision to remove him from the investigation was political and that once his report got to the politicians he and it were doomed. His experiences illustrate the hypocrisy of government-inspired investigations. Government, as a rule, asks for an investigation only if it believes this will demonstrate its concern and whitewash the problem; if such an investigation appears to be achieving more it is liable to be scotched.

In 1990 Stalker threatened to produce a document which, he

claimed, showed that he was removed from the RUC shoot-to-kill investigation on the orders of senior Cabinet and Home Office officials. However, the Home Secretary, David Waddington, refused pressures for an inquiry into the Stalker affair and claimed he was satisfied with the action of Mr Anderton, the Chief Constable of Manchester, in suspending Stalker. He added: 'People are too prone these days to come up with conspiracy theories without looking at what, in fact, happened.' (*Independent*, 20.1.90) One Stalker inquiry was clearly more than enough for the government.

Two years after Stalker had been stood down from his investigation it was announced that twenty Northern Ireland police officers were to face disciplinary action; the recommendation that they should face disciplinary action came from Charles Kelly, the Staffordshire Chief Constable who had been brought in to investigate police handling of shoot-to-kill allegations. But the Northern Ireland Police Authority decided that no charges would be made against Sir John Hermon, the Chief Constable, or his deputy Michael McAtamney and an assistant, Trevor Forbes. The Revd Ian Paisley said of the decision: 'Hermon will go down in history as the buck-passer. This is a typical Hermon move, in keeping with the Chief Constable's character.' (*Independent*, 5.7.88) It was a question of scapegoats since too much had been made public for nothing to be done as a result of four years of investigations, although both sides in Northern Ireland's sectarian divide believed that the twenty officers were being made scapegoats while the bigger fish were allowed to escape. The twenty police officers were accused of attempting to frustrate inquiries into the killing of the six men by undercover security forces in 1982, yet as the Attorney-General, Sir Patrick Mayhew, told the House of Commons, he had decided 'with the deepest anxiety' that it was not in the public interest to prosecute the officers because it might endanger lives. As an *Independent* editorial of 8 July 1988 claimed, 'There can now be little doubt that the members of the RUC were participants in an informal shoot-to-kill policy in parts of Northern Ireland in the early 1980s.' (However, even as the *Independent* was speaking in the past tense of such a policy, the Ministry of Defence was demanding that the Gibraltar coroner (in the 'Death on the Rock' shooting case) should ensure that the SAS soldiers who had shot the three IRA members and were called upon to give evidence should be given absolute anonymity in the court.

During the 1980s major efforts were made to discourage journalists from interviewing 'terrorists'. 'In Britain elaborate efforts have been made by the Thatcher government to stop or discourage journalists interviewing the so-called Northern Ireland "terrorists". Margaret Thatcher has argued that publicity is the oxygen of terrorism.' (Mazrui, 1990:89) Finally, in October 1988, the Home Secretary, Douglas Hurd, went beyond discouragement. He banned a number of organisations such as Sinn Fein or their supporters from being interviewed on television or radio. But no matter how the Home Secretary or the government attempts to justify such bans, these go contrary to the concept not only of a free media but of freedom generally: people have to be allowed to make up their own minds as to the justice or otherwise of a cause, and they cannot do so if those advocating what the government condemns are not to be seen or heard.

Before Douglas Hurd introduced his bans on 19 October 1988 when he said, 'This is not a restriction on reporting', Sinn Fein's appearances on British network television had already been severely restricted, and although Mr Hurd argued when he introduced the ban that television had provided an 'easy platform' on which 'to propagate terrorism' the opposite would appear to be the case. Thus, in the year before the ban there were only 17 interviews with Sinn Fein on BBC News out of 633 on Northern Ireland, including 121 of Conservative MPs and ministers. Moreover, in the period before the ban, when Sinn Fein did appear, journalists' questions were routinely hostile: 'How does it feel to be branded one of the guilty men?' and so on. In terms of the way such interviews were conducted it would be difficult to uphold the Thatcher contention that television provided Sinn Fein with an easy platform from which to propagate terrorism, but her contention was widely accepted, none the less, and represented part of the powerful bullying propaganda line at which she and her government had become adept. Another government contention was that republican appearances caused offence, yet the BBC Deputy-Director, John Birt, said, 'There is no evidence the BBC can uncover that our audiences are offended by responsible and relevant journalism.' Moreover, the IBA also said they had received no complaints. The allegations, in fact, look far more like propaganda excuses to justify what the government had determined to do anyway: ban the republicans and damn the BBC for not clearly and absolutely adopting the government line. As the Glasgow University Media Group (1982a) argued:

What is at stake in the battle over the ban is the official view of the 'Troubles' which seeks to portray its enemies in Ireland as terrorists lacking any political motivation, and as simply criminals and gangsters. Successive governments have tried to limit, and preferably eliminate, any hearing for this opposition in Ireland. The broadcasting ban marked a new attempt to do this directly by legislative action.

Contrary to government claims most interviewers have been hostile to the republicans and in their interviews attempted to discredit them rather than allow an impartial presentation of the anti-government case. One would not suspect this from the way government ministers have attacked the media but such tactics have been in the classic mould of any propaganda campaign designed to stifle an opposition view.

After a decade of bruising confrontations with the Thatcher government it is not surprising, perhaps, that the BBC had become only too anxious to show that it was 'on the government's side' over issues such as Northern Ireland. Thus, following the Deal bombing in which ten Marine bandsmen died, the BBC

> closed their main evening news bulletin with the Marines band playing over slow motion footage of a young boy in uniform laying a wreath to the dead. When a contributor to 'Right to Reply' complained that this was not news but 'pure emotionalism', the BBC responded: 'The day before this item was broadcast 10 Marine bandsmen had been murdered and around 20 injured. We are satisfied that the item properly reflected the feeling of many people in the aftermath of such an event.' That the BBC is in the business of reflecting the perceived feelings of the nation, rather than that of reporting events is simply assumed. (GUMG, 1989b)

That 'assumption' by the BBC in fact takes us back to an earlier period in the BBC's history when it still was regarded as an estate of the realm.

Many of the government's claims about Northern Ireland – as an integral part of Britain – make no sense in the light of continuing talks with Dublin. The Anglo-Irish Agreement, which was signed in 1985, affirmed that Northern Ireland would remain part of the United Kingdom for the foreseeable future and yet also acknowledged that the Republic of Ireland had a legitimate interest in its affairs and a role to play. The long-term aim of the nationalists is a united Ireland.

The aim of the Unionists is integration with Britain or majority rule in Ulster which means a perpetuation of Unionist control as opposed to any power-sharing. Given such opposed aims the Anglo-Irish Agreement would seem, at most, to be a device whereby the British Government seeks Dublin's acquiescence in its continuing control of Northern Ireland while Dublin sees it as a means of gaining increased legitimacy with regard to decisions upon the future of the province.

The continuing troubles in Northern Ireland have meant, among other things, that the province has become something of a laboratory for trying out new techniques or perfecting older ones. This was illustrated by the Colin Wallace affair which made headline news in 1990. Colin Wallace, a civil servant attached to the army in Northern Ireland, had been responsible for a 'dirty tricks' or disinformation campaign, 'Operation Clockwork Orange', during the period 1968–75. Later he disclosed that his operation was extended to cover Protestant organisations or individuals who were blocking government attempts to break the province's political deadlocks, as well as IRA activities. He was dismissed from the Civil Service in 1975 for threatening to reveal the extent of the dirty tricks activities in which he was involved because, he alleged, they were extended far wider than Ulster and included smear tactics against Heath and Wilson, part of the MI5 activities to which Peter Wright refers in *Spycatcher*. The details of the Colin Wallace affair are not that important as far as the Ulster story is concerned except for the fact that he was clearly involved in 'black propaganda' or disinformation and that such activities have long been the norm in the province. By 1975, when Wallace left the province, lying and cover-ups had become a way of life in Northern Ireland. And the continuing troubles have provided the security services with a perfect training ground for trying out new techniques of counter-subversion and civilian control at a time when many of those responsible for long-term planning believe that such activities are likely to be the most important ones in the future for any security services or standing armies.

A revealing response to the subject of brainwashing came from a member of the Foreign Office who, in a private conversation with the author, responded to a question that had not made any reference to Northern Ireland with the reply: 'I suppose you want to talk about what they are supposed to have done in Ulster prisons.'

20 The special relationship

A wise prince must rely on what is in his power
and not on what is in the power of others.
MACHIAVELLI

URING THE YEARS 1945 TO 1960 Britain behaved as a global power, maintaining a world-wide system of military bases to defend global commitments that were beyond her capacity and reflected an imperial age which had passed. In the main her posture was a sham but the carefully fostered 'special relationship' with the United States enabled her to continue acting like a great power when the reality was otherwise. After 1960, as Britain's power declined even more sharply, both absolutely and relative to other nations, she worked all the harder to maintain the special relationship long after this had become little more than a polite fiction in Washington, because it helped her ruling class evade facing the harsh reality about Britain's true global standing.

The special relationship was born during World War II although British policy over a much longer period had been tailored to place good relations with the United States at the top of her international priorities as she had seen the slow diminution of her own power alongside a steady growth of American power. None the less, '1940 marked the final and decisive shift of power in the world from Britain to the United States.' (Ponting, 1990:215) American support for Britain in 1940 was a question of calculation in Washington as to US interests but, with one or two exceptions (most notably Ernest Bevin as Foreign Secretary), the British Establishment (largely to keep itself in power) constantly bowed to US pressures and repeatedly surrendered British viewpoints to those of the United States whether or not to do so was the best way to safeguard long-term British interests. The absolute weakness of the British position in the early days of World War II was brought out clearly on 7 December 1941 when the Japanese bombed Pearl Harbor, prompting Churchill to write – with relief – 'So we had won after all' (Gelber, 1961:47), for the attack had brought the Americans into the war and a British (or Allied) victory was now assured. When this victory came in 1945, however, it left an exhausted Britain which had sold off 28 per cent of its national assets to pay for the war. From that time onwards Britain clung to power – or delusions of power – which her leaders believed could best be propped up by maintaining the special relationship long after its wartime justification had passed. In this connection the Cold War was a godsend to Britain's power brokers, for without it the special relationship would have died a natural death and Britain would have been revealed, far sooner, as the European middle-rank power to which, in reality, she had already been reduced by 1945. Instead, successive prime ministers put relations with the United States before every other consideration, often to Britain's embarrassment or loss, and they did so, moreover, while telling the British people that the special relationship was essential to their survival when they meant it was essential to the survival of the Establishment.

In one crucial area the relationship really did begin as something special and that was in the development of the atomic bomb: 'From the start the adaptation of atomic energy to military use was Anglo-American in origin.' (Gelber, 1961:47) Perhaps nothing in the long run was more important to the special relationship or, in the end, more damaging to Britain's capacity to work as an independent power. When the Americans tried to prevent the British from sharing the secrets of the A-bomb (they were uninterested in a special relationship) Britain went ahead to develop her own in order to demonstrate that she could do it. Subsequently, neither Britain nor the United States wished to help France develop her bomb. (King-Hall, 1962:148) The great irony of the immediate post-war years was the fact that a special relationship was not at once envisaged on either side and when the British acted as equal allies with the Americans they were rebuffed, so that on 8 January 1947, at the beginning of what turned out to be the most difficult year for Britain's post-war Attlee government, the Cabinet decided to make its own atomic bomb because the Americans would not continue to share wartime secrets. As the Foreign Secretary, Ernest Bevin, said: 'We could not afford to acquiesce in an American monopoly of this new development.' And in the same connection he went on to say: 'I don't want any other Foreign Secretary of this country to be talked to or at by a Secretary of State in the United States as I have just had in my discussions with Mr Byrnes. We have got to have this thing over here whatever it costs . . . We've got to have the bloody Union Jack on top of it.' (Hennessy and Seldon, 1987:38)

There spoke the Foreign Secretary of what was still a great power determined that it should remain independent. No one who followed ever displayed the same verve or determination in relation to the United States; instead, Bevin's successors at the Foreign Office – as well as successive prime ministers – became increasingly sycophantic towards Washington as they were obliged to work ever harder to share secrets with the reluctant greater half of the so-called special relationship. Their task was made easier once the Cold War had become a set confrontation, as it had by the end of the 1940s following the Berlin Airlift and the formation of NATO, which was Bevin's greatest achievement. As that Anglophile American, Lionel Gelber, wrote flatteringly of the alliance at the end of the 1950s: 'But it is the strength of the West that has ruled out military conquest, and at the heart of that strength, as the Russians appreciate, is Anglo-American solidarity.' (1961:21)

In July 1939 the Tory, Rab Butler, wrote: 'In my political life I have always been convinced that we can no more count on America than Brazil.' (Ponting, 1990:35) Now, since that attitude was widely shared, why did the Establishment, which was basically Tory anyway, pursue the special relationship with such assiduity? There is really only one answer: that in a new world-power structure which made Washington and Moscow the only effective centres of decision-making, thus threatening to marginalise Britain, the special relationship appeared the only way that would allow the ruling Establishment to retain its position and maximise its influence. In the immediate post-war period the determination to remain at 'the top table' led Britain to pursue policies which she would have been unlikely to adopt had she been a major power, equal to the United States and the USSR. As Denis Healey tells us: 'The period of Bevin's main achievement was pre-eminently the period of the Big Three, a trinity to which Britain belonged more by prestige and diplomatic skill than by right of power.' (1990:12) But once Bevin had gone and during the Korean War, in which the United States shouldered the main burden of fighting the 'Communist menace', even the pretences began to wear thin.

In any case, British appeasement of Germany prior to 1939 had already signalled a declining will to power, and although she had made a magnificent recovery during World War II, subsequently she faced an even more rapid decline than that which she had been experiencing before the war. Churchill, who in any case was half American, early recognised the extent to which Britain's survival depended upon

American involvement in the war, yet the habits of power die hard. 'Psychologically, the British could not relinquish the leadership of the West without a pang; historically, the manner in which the primacy was transferred from Britain to the United States reveals how unique the Anglo-American factor has been.' (Gelber, 1961:9) The point is debatable, yet the fact that both countries spoke the same language and that there had been a close if often fraught historical relationship undoubtedly helped in the process of transferring leadership, just as the pressures of the Cold War, by making Britain far more important to the United States as it faced up to the Soviet threat than otherwise would have been the case, helped prolong British illusions. Thus, as late as 1957 (the year after Suez) William Clark, who had been Eden's press officer, could write of the special relationship that 'It is an association between equal or at least comparable partners.' (1957:4) Right up to the Suez fiasco of 1956 the idea persisted among at least some members of the British Establishment that the Alliance was led by British initiatives even if in name it was led by the United States; this was an idea which was to be given a new lease of life by Harold Macmillan when he succeeded Eden and, in the wake of the Suez rupture, made his first priority the mending of the Anglo-American Alliance. He compared the relationship of Britain to the United States with that of the Greeks to the Romans, a comparison that was unflattering to Washington as far as he was concerned: 'the British had the brains and subtlety, the Americans had the brawn'. But, as Britain discovered at the time of the Cuban crisis, there was no effective British veto over American military actions: 'Just before he died, Dean Acheson spoke admiringly of Attlee's attempt to achieve the promise of consultation, but added "we had to unachieve that".' (Dalyell, 1987:76) By 1968 the US Secretary for Defence, Clark Clifford, could say: 'The British do not have the resources, the backup, or the hardware to deal with any big world problem . . . they are no longer a powerful ally of ours because they cannot afford the cost of an adequate defence effort.' (Ponting, 1989:59) Clifford said that, moreover, at a time when the British contribution to NATO was far greater than that of any other power apart from the United States.

Britain certainly tried hard to be Washington's most important ally; she might have done better to direct her efforts into other channels. It is now forgotten that there were calls from influential people for Britain to create and lead a Third Force (between the two superpowers), and although the idea was never really put to the test, this was less because it was impossible than because it was generally derided by the political Establishment. But, as Stephen King-Hall argued, we had forgotten a precept which was regarded as fundamental by an earlier generation: 'Our Victorian ancestors were conscious of the fact that it was beyond a nation's capacity to create power based on resources it did not possess.' (1962:28) Part of the story of the special relationship concerns the way in which British politicians too readily treated American power as a British resource. Eden was the most obvious exponent of this view: ' "Our aim", wrote Eden, "should be to persuade the United States to assume the real burdens in such organisations [for defence] while retaining for ourselves as much political control – and hence prestige and world influence – as we can." ' (Kyle, 1991:44) In terms of hard political reality – which British leaders understood only too well – a reversal had taken place and, as Gelber argued, 'Until recent years American regional interests were reinsured by general British power. Today it is British regional interests which may be reinsured by general American power.' (1961:8) By allying themselves with the USA and becoming dependent upon it the British either forgot everything they had ever learnt about the exercise of power (a proposition that seems inherently unlikely) or, knowing the conse-quences of such dependence they yet went ahead, forging an unequal alliance which they euphemistically called the 'special relationship' because the Establishment saw that as the best means of prolonging its own dominant position.

Naturally, at one level, it suited the United States to play up to the concept of a special relationship if as a result they obtained such a willing and useful lieutenant. And, although in the immediate after-math of World War II the United States had been opposed to the continuation of the European-based empires, Washington changed its tune once the Cold War became its principal preoccupation, and was happy for Britain to slow down the pace of decolonisation, at least in those sensitive areas where the Communist threat seemed most likely to undermine Western interests. The result was a willingness in Washington to play up to the British and treat them as more important, in power terms, than was the case: 'But examination (of the UN, NATO, SEATO, etc.) shows that all these rest on the basic union of American and British interests. If that goes, everything goes.' (Middle-ton, 1957:161) The title of Lionel Gelber's book, *America in Britain's Place* (coming from the pen of an Anglophile American), is designed to make the British feel good, with its implication that the great power which had led the world for so long was now gracefully handing on the baton of leadership to the new – and friendly – giant. Such an attitude must have acted as a salve to wounded pride, making it that much easier for Britain to decline in power. But such an attitude also had a soporific effect, and while it may have been welcomed by the Establishment it did little to help the British face up to new realities.

By the beginning of the 1960s, however, as Western Europe appeared to be getting its act together, Washington began to lose patience with British reluctance to join the EC and exerted increasing pressures upon her to do so.

> When, in 1962, Acheson said that Britain 'has lost an empire and has not yet found a role', Macmillan's immediate private reaction was that Acheson was 'always a conceited ass'. The notion that the emperor had no clothes, as seemed devastatingly obvious to these foreigners, was somehow regarded as capable of refutation by shutting one's eyes and thinking of Winston Churchill. (Clarke, 1991:229)

At that time, moreover, the old wartime allies (Eisenhower, Churchill and Macmillan) were passing from the political scene as a younger generation came to the forefront (most notably John Kennedy as President in the United States) so that Drew Middleton could write in the early 1960s: 'Henceforth, whether or not the United Kingdom enters Europe, the United States will have to deal with British leaders less involved emotionally in strengthening and perpetuating the American link and less likely to be guided by the Churchillian precept that the alliance with Washington comes first.' (1963:217) Middleton's assessment, which by any reasonable criteria of political judgement ought to have been correct, in fact proved false, for he reckoned without the determination of the British to perpetuate a relationship that gave them so much more comfort and standing than any obvious alternative: Wilson, Callaghan and, above all, Thatcher were to cling to the Churchillian precept long after the *raison d'être* for it had disappeared.

The years 1956 to 1963 established the parameters of the special relationship for another twenty years: up to Suez it was at least just possible for Britain to claim certain equalities of partnership with the United States but after Suez such claims could no longer be sustained and Britain had to accept the junior role without any of the pretences that had been practised prior to 1956. Macmillan worked very hard to restore the special relationship and was able to do so while his old wartime colleague Eisenhower remained US President, but once the young Kennedy succeeded to that office it became much harder to have British pretensions accepted in Washington. In January 1963 President de Gaulle cast his veto on the British application to join the European Community so that, even had Britain genuinely wanted to give Europe priority over the special relationship, that avenue had been blocked, at least for the time being. Thus from the early 1960s, in part from choice and in part because the alternative of Europe had been closed to her, Britain continued to play the role of lieutenant to the United States. In his own inimitable way Macmillan became the principal exponent of the school of thought which saw Britain acting as the trusted counsellor of the United States, but no longer holding the sceptre of power. As Tony Benn was to record in his diary later in the 1960s, 'the general attitude is that if the Americans want to do something, the British ought not to differ from them. This is the plain truth about our position in the world, we are just number two to the United States on everything.' (1988:219) Anthony Nutting, who parted company with Eden over Suez and was an ardent pro-European, wrote accurately of his former colleagues in government: 'there existed also among the top echelons of the Government and their advisers an obsessive determination to preserve the Anglo-American Alliance as something exclusive. This school of thought feared that the closer we got to Europe, the more we should have to share America with Europe.' (1960:5) The 'dog-in-the-manger' attitude outlined here by Nutting goes to the heart of the British Establishment fears of their diminishing power; they were quite right to fear sharing the special relationship with Europe, for then it would cease to be special and Britain at the same time would simply become one of the European powers in the eyes of Washington. Had this happened at that time the special relationship would have fallen away and Britain might have faced up to some of the power realities which her leaders then and later were so determined to ignore. The 'American disease' at the heart of the British Establishment dated back to the turn of the century, when a confrontation between Britain and the USA occurred over British intervention in Venezuela: 'Ever since the Venezuelan crisis of 1902 it had been a dogma of British foreign policy that nothing should be done to offend the USA, and from there to basing policy on an Anglo-American alliance, with Britain as the junior partner, was only a step.' (Hartley, 1963:60) The term 'interdependence', which was coined by Macmillan, was a portmanteau word that emphasised British independence while acknowledging her junior status with regard to the United States in the alliance or special relationship.

In 1959, at the time of President Eisenhower's visit to Britain, it was still possible to argue that 'the principal English-speaking countries stood closer to each other than either stood to other major allies' (Gelber, 1961:327), but such a claim, in so far as it was true, was carefully reinforced by those whose policy it was to place the special relationship at the top of the political agenda. 'Frenchmen are foreigners; Americans are not. It is irrational that Englishmen feel this way, but they do.' (Mander, 1963:31) Whether or not Englishmen felt like this, there was a powerful school of thought which insisted that they did, if only to ensure that the special relationship would continue and could be shown to be the paramount foreign-policy option. Thus, the Cuban missile crisis of 1962 came as a great shock to Britain, since it demonstrated clearly that when it came to a real power showdown between the two superpowers the special relationship was all but meaningless. Britain's ambassador in Washington, Lord Harlech, a personal friend of John Kennedy, might have been the first of the allies to receive confidences but that did not mean that Britain was able to influence what the President and his advisers decided to do. And if Britain could not use the special relationship to influence decisions in the all-important matter of a possible nuclear war, what on earth was the value of the relationship? The fact that for many years after this event London continued to act as though the special relationship did give her such influence is a measure of its hollowness as a policy.

The Cold War made the special relationship possible. Constant British loyalty to the United States, especially when the other European powers were behaving more independently, as well as aggressive toughness about the Communist enemy, an attitude which was to be given a new lease of life by Margaret Thatcher, gave an appearance of a partnership which in fact was nothing of the sort. Much of the special relationship was no more than a carefully fostered British mirage which had its origins in the myth that Churchill's wartime speeches had had a major impact upon Americans during the dark days of the war. The Churchill–Roosevelt relationship was nothing like as cosy as Churchill made out or as the British myth-maker extraordinary, Sir Arthur Bryant, suggested when he gilded the American decision to supply Britain with desperately needed arms in 1940: 'Franklin Roosevelt responded to a faith and courage that matched his own.' (1990:275) Roosevelt backed Britain in 1940 because he saw it as in the American interest to do so. But from that time onwards the British (although not the American) myth-makers worked very hard and with considerable success to turn myths into a policy. 'The myth of the "special relationship" with the United States was sedulously cultivated, in part to help support the dreams of strategic strength but also to disguise Britain's real role as a client state of the Americans.' (Ponting, 1990:235) But although there were acute British observers who saw the special relationship for what it was, they were relatively few and far between. In 1967 Max Nicholson wrote: 'Its [the special relationship's] perpetuation is one of the least rewarding and most objectionable of the fruits of the British System, and it should be publicly recognised as having long since served its purpose.' (398) Yet almost a quarter of a century later in the aftermath of the Gulf War – a bonus to the Thatcher/Major Conservative governments – the British were able to give the special relationship a new lease of life.

Every British prime minister since Attlee – with the sole exception of Edward Heath who determinedly put Europe first – saw the special relationship as the cornerstone of Britain's foreign policy. Attlee and Bevin at least tried to maintain a British policy distinct from that of the United States. Attlee's visit to President Truman at the time of the Korean War, when the Chinese crossed the Yalu River and the possibility of using nuclear weapons against China had been discussed in Washington, was the action of an independent if deeply worried partner rather than a dependent one. In his second term of office (1951–5), Churchill was constantly making the journey back and forth across the Atlantic (his fares on the luxury 'Queens' being paid for by rich American admirers) and behaved as though British and American policies were inseparable. Eden foolishly and arrogantly took the Americans for granted at the time of Suez; he very nearly succeeded in wrecking the special relationship entirely in the process (although not from choice) and it took all Macmillan's considerable skills in the succeeding four years to rebuild it again. Macmillan managed one of his masterful set-pieces when he used the occasion of President Eisenhower's visit to London in 1959 to have the two of them appearing on television together, enabling him both to boost his own image and that of the so-called special relationship. Sir Alec Douglas-Home spoke wistfully of Britain regaining its place at 'the top table' (meaning alongside the Americans as one of the world's principal power brokers). Wilson actually helped the United States extend its world-wide system of bases and in 1965 created a new colony in the Indian Ocean (Diego Garcia) to give away as a base to the United States. (Ponting, 1989:47–59) Yet despite Wilson's efforts Dean Rusk told the US National Security Council in 1968: 'Operationally the US and UK are working on fewer real problems. The concept of Atlantic co-operation (Europe as well as Britain) could reduce the special relationship.' Wilson did manage to avoid sending British troops to Vietnam despite intense pressure from President Johnson to do so but this was a victory for internal Labour Party politics rather than an objective decision about policy. In other respects he was the ultra-loyal lieutenant and his subservience to Washington was followed by his Labour successor, James Callaghan. Heath alone of post-war prime ministers was prepared to subordinate the special relationship to his determination to take Britain into the European Community.

And then we come to Margaret Thatcher, the 'iron lady', who worked as hard as Churchill and Wilson to subordinate British interests to American hegemony. At least at the time of the Falklands War she got her reward in major American assistance, yet it is hard to understand why she was so determined to be a loyal American lieutenant and Cold War hardliner except in the same context as that of her predecessors: that the special relationship was seen as the easiest if most transparent means of boosting Britain's influence and her image, if not her power. And, for all the tough talk that came to be associated with the 'iron lady', the realities had not changed. Thus, when Rear-Admiral Eugene Carroll Jr of the Center for Defence Information in Washington was questioned about the 1986 US bombing raid on Libya to which Mrs Thatcher so readily agreed and was asked if F-111s based in Britain would have been used anyway (with Britain being asked for permission afterwards) he replied: 'That was the basis on which the plan was prepared.' (Dalyell, 1987:65) So much for Washington's view of the special relationship, and that was over a minor quarrel with an insignificant power as opposed to any major Cold War crisis such as that in Cuba a quarter of a century earlier.

The extraordinary personal chemistry that worked between President Reagan and Prime Minister Thatcher was an unexpected bonus for the British leader, and the fact that they saw eye to eye on so many issues helped to cloud, yet again, the realities of power and the real degree of British dependence upon the United States. If the Falklands War became an unexpected triumph for Thatcher this was not a little because of American back-up and a quiescently sympathetic president in the White House. Even so, the United States behaved as it wished, with scant reference to London, on two subsequent occasions which in real terms were sufficiently unimportant that Washington could have indulged Britain by much fuller prior consultation had the thought occurred to American policy-makers – but it didn't. The first such occasion was the invasion of Grenada in 1983 following the coup by General Hudson Austin that led to the overthrow and death of Prime Minister Maurice Bishop; rightly or wrongly, Washington saw the presence of Cubans in Grenada as a threat and its intervention, although generally welcomed in the Caribbean, was a deep embarrassment to the British Government which saw Grenada, a small Commonwealth country, as in its sphere of influence. The second occasion, already referred to, was the bombing of Libya in 1986. The fact is that by the 1980s the special relationship was an irrelevance to American policy-makers and, if it was remembered at all, it would be in the context of not offending Britain rather than of needing her support.

Such a scenario, at any rate, had emerged by early 1990 when President Bush had replaced President Reagan and showed little indication that he thought the special relationship mattered. Thus Mrs Thatcher was informed of Bush's defence cuts after President Mitterrand of France. Ironically, the members of the American Establishment surrounding Bush were far more akin to the British Establishment than those who surrounded Reagan (the poor boy from the Midwest), and like their British counterparts put their own interests before all else. A very senior US State Department official summed the situation up as follows: 'Look, I certainly don't consider myself pro-Germany, pro-UK, pro-Japan, pro-anybody except the United States,' he said. 'That's my job.' (*Independent*, 4.2.90) That is, of course, as it should be but even as late as 1990 the lesson had yet to be learnt in London. By this time Britain had less to offer than Germany or Japan or the USSR, so what could possibly justify a special relationship in Washington?

And then came the Gulf crisis. The speed with which Thatcher ranged herself alongside the United States as an ally in Gulf intervention had far less to do with British perceptions of how to tackle Saddam Hussein – despite Thatcher's natural instinct for warlike confrontation – than it did with her need to demonstrate to a new and markedly sceptical American president that Britain really was a valuable ally, ready at once to support an American war policy no matter how the rest of Europe behaved. Margaret Thatcher got her Gulf War, with a larger British military commitment to it than from any other European power, even if by the time it was fought she had been replaced by John Major. In the euphoria of Anglo-American relations that followed the Gulf War the Queen was dispatched to Washington in May 1991 on a state visit – to cement a renewal of the special relationship – and, from the British point of view, a suddenly transformed Bush could say graciously at the banquet he hosted for the Queen that: 'The relationship between America and Britain has never been more special.' (*Standard*, 15.5.91) The result was a spate of press articles in Britain lauding the special relationship, mainly because it appeared to make Britain seem more important again. The Queen then awarded General Norman Schwarzkopf an honorary knighthood for his outstanding performance as allied military commander in the Gulf. (An honorary knighthood was also awarded to Lieutenant-General Prince Khalid bin Sultan bin Abdul-Aziz, the Saudi joint commander, but that award was hardly noticed in the British press.) In June 1991 British contingents took part in a gigantic ticker-tape parade in New York.

Over the years since 1945 the Americans, usually politely, have tried to rid themselves of the encumbrance of the special relationship, but such attempts have only led the British to cling to it all the more fervently, like children about to lose a toy. Dean Acheson's famous though ill-received aphorism that Britain had lost an empire and not yet found a role, which he made in 1962, seemed as apt in 1991 when Britain still fought against any further involvement in the European Community while insisting upon her special American connection. It never seems to have occurred to the British that American reluctance to continue treating Britain as special was no more than a recognition of political realities and that, as Machiavelli said, 'a wise prince must rely on what is in his power and not on what is in the power of others'. In relation to the United States, Britain fails Machiavelli's test absolutely and she does so, mainly, because a determined Establishment has insisted upon pursuing a policy which reflects its own interests rather than those of the nation. De Gaulle understood such matters better.

21 The Salman Rushdie affair

As for those that recant and die unbelievers, no ransom shall be accepted from them: although it be as much gold as would fill the entire earth. They shall be sternly punished and none shall help them.

THE KORAN

THE RUSHDIE AFFAIR has provided the British with a unique mix of concerns – free speech, religion and racism – overlaid with hypocrisy. Bigotry is no less bigotry because it is adhered to in the name of religion. On the one side are those who argue that free speech is everything. On the other those who manage to inject some poisonous racism into the argument by suggesting that since many Muslims are simple, ignorant people words that offend them should be censored and that we should pander to their ignorance by banning *The Satanic Verses*. With the furore still continuing three years after the *fatwa* (death sentence) was pronounced on Rushdie for his 'blasphemy' by the late Ayatollah Khomeini of Iran, one has to ask: why such a to-do? Is it because an individual who is a British subject has been threatened with death in this violent age? Or is it because the threat comes from the Iranians who are seen by the British as Muslim, fanatical and Third World? The row certainly possesses all those ingredients most calculated to appeal to the freedom-loving British liberal Establishment and also most calculated to irritate a Foreign and Commonwealth Office that has long ceased to be concerned with anything except trade.

It is simply not possible to be both a believer in the open society and at the same time accept the dogmas of a fanatical and closed religious system that demands the death penalty (and can call upon its members to carry it out) for what it describes as blasphemy. A choice has to be made and Rushdie (although he subsequently wavered, perhaps understandably, under the strain) chose the open society. In medieval Europe offenders against the Church often faced death for their heresies. We have moved on from such barbarism. Now, if it was barbarous to put people to death for heresy or blasphemy or dissent against the orthodoxies of the Christian Church (as most people in Britain would accept) then it is equally barbarous to demand the death of a 'blasphemer' against Islam today, and no amount of special pleading can alter that fact. Either such behaviour has to be condemned without reservation, or the very basis of our claims to believe in an open society which includes freedom of speech is a sham. It is necessary to state this clearly because there has been a great deal of wavering over this issue by those who ought to know better, including the Archbishop of Canterbury, Dr Carey.

Reactions to an article (or rather essay) which Salman Rushdie had published by the *Independent on Sunday* on 5 February 1990, defending *The Satanic Verses*, provided the occasion for a debate by members of the literary establishment. Arnold Wesker made the point that 'The fury directed against Salman Rushdie's novel is the fury of a kind of dark human stupidity which is incapable of perceiving itself. That is a human flaw not a Muslim one, and it's there for ever.' Wesker was certainly correct although he might have added that since it was dark human stupidity at work there was absolutely no reason to pander to it in any sense whatever. At this stage in the controversy Rushdie was pushing for the paperback edition of his novel to be published, a fact which caused an awkward split in the ranks of those who defend free speech. Some were unequivocally for the paperback to be published and saw any move to stop this – in the name of preventing further violence or bloodshed – as a backdoor means of censorship. In this, of course, they were correct. Others, however, wanted to be liberal but also wished to pander to restrictive religious practices. Thus Roald Dahl said of Rushdie's insistence upon a paperback edition: 'I think that is a rotten thing to do. If it is published it is going to create a great deal of trouble and possibly bloodshed; no book is worth publishing in those circumstances.' And Bhikhu Parekh, the deputy Chairman of the Commission for Racial Equality, first praised the article, which he described as deeply moving and conciliatory, but then went on to say of any proposed paperback edition: 'I disagree that not bringing out the paperback would be a backdoor means of suppressing the book. It is a way of diffusing the crisis and acknowledging that the book has caused great pain.' Now these and similar statements suggesting that the book was the cause of bloodshed and violence should not be allowed to pass as if they were true. The book did not cause violence or bloodshed. Fanatical men (religious fundamentalists, if one wishes to use such a term) used the book as a weapon to stir up violence for their own purposes. And certainly, many of those shouting the loudest about *The Satanic Verses* will not have read it. No *book* causes violence or bloodshed and to argue thus is to suggest that the book burners through the ages, from China's first emperor Shih Huang-ti to Hitler, were doing their bit to avoid violence as they burnt the books which they felt endangered their power. And that surely goes to the root of the problem and the Muslim outbursts of rage. Yes, the book may have caused pain and, yes, many Muslims take the Koran literally but the issue at stake is essentially one of fear on the part of fundamentalists (and not just Muslims) at a book which is likely to cause doubts about the religion in question. People, not books, are responsible for violence and, to repeat Wesker's phrase, such people are possessed 'of a kind of dark human stupidity'. It is that dark human stupidity which is at the root of the Salman Rushdie affair, and it is notable that few people wish to speak in such terms; rather, they gloss over the dark human stupidity because other considerations need to be attended to: renewed diplomatic relations with Iran, freeing the Beirut hostages, trade with the Islamic world, political constituencies in Britain with large Muslim communities, or distaste on the part of the British political right that such a furore should be centred upon a book by an Indian apostate Muslim who writes intellectually baffling novels but, none the less, is a British citizen and can therefore claim the protection of the state. All this is very confusing for those who like their problems to be straightforward.

After spending twelve months in hiding following the Islamic sentence of death upon him, Salman Rushdie wrote an essay in the *Independent on Sunday* in which he said that he recognised 'the shock and pain' which *The Satanic Verses* had caused Muslims and suggested that there might be 'a way forward through the mutual recognition of mutual pain'. He went on to say that all should accept that the other parties had acted in good faith. Now with due respect to Mr Rushdie, who has come to realise that he may have to spend the rest of his life in hiding, such a claim is a nonsense and he must know that it is a nonsense. In his novel he effectively questions the entire 'sacrosanct' basis of Islam and he knew what he was doing, although he may not have gauged the strength and fury of the reaction to come. On the other side, those who call for his death and offer rewards for his killing know just as surely what they are doing. It is not a question of mutual pain: it is a matter, on the one hand, of intellectual amusement if not contempt at the absurdities of religion; and on the other of bigoted defence of a system, if necessary to the death. In such circumstances, to speak of mutual pain is disingenuous. None the less, Mr Rushdie did at least provide an opportunity for some Muslim leaders to suggest a compromise and move away from the idea of a religious execution. Thus, Shabbir Akhtar, a member of the Bradford Council of Mosques, described the essay as thoughtful and said there was scope for reconciliation; but he then destroyed his moderate approach by adding that such reconciliation would be possible only if Mr Rushdie abandoned plans for a paperback edition. And this, essentially, goes to the nub of the problem: the determination of Muslims to censor *The Satanic Verses*. Muslims in Britain, however, do have an important argument on their side. The law of blasphemy applies only to Christianity and had *The Satanic Verses* been a critique of Christianity instead of Islam its critics would have been able to take Mr Rushdie and his book to court in an effort to suppress it. The logical solution to this situation should be either an amendment of the blasphemy law to include all religions, or its abolition, for, in a plural society, it is clearly wrong that 'blasphemy' against one religion may be subject to court action while 'blasphemy' against another is not. At this point in the argument Mr Rushdie said he had no objection to the book being published in paperback by a consortium of publishers to protect Penguin and that he would accept a 'health warning' to say that the author did not consider himself to be a Muslim and that his purpose had not been to abuse or cause hurt. In fact what he was doing amounted to much more than abuse; he was saying that the whole religion was a nonsense.

The British outcry about freedom of expression in relation to Rushdie was a *de rigueur* temporary reaction to be followed by largely irritated silence on the part of the Foreign Office, because Rushdie's continued existence as a problem threatened its efforts to achieve a *rapprochement* with Iran which in its turn would lead to the release of the Beirut hostages. Throughout the Rushdie affair the British authorities have been awkwardly squirming on the horns of a dilemma: of course they believe in freedom of speech, and the rights of an individual to write what he pleases how he pleases, and of course they abhor the call by foreigners for the murder of a British subject; at the same time there are a large number of Muslims in parts of the world where Britain does lucrative business and she would prefer that they are not unnecessarily antagonised. Efforts to steer a course between these two extremes have left a good many people looking foolish if no worse. Thus, the British Board of Film Classification banned the

Brainwash

Pakistani film *International Guerrillas*, which showed Salman Rushdie being killed by a bolt of lightning after he had tortured some Muslims by playing them tapes of his novel, on the grounds that the film contravened the law of criminal libel and would expose Mr Rushdie to public hatred. This was done in mid-1990 at a time when the Law Commission had recommended the law's abolition as obsolete and a Law Lord had pointed out that its provisions conflict with the European Convention on Human Rights. Now while this archaic law was being used to 'protect' Mr Rushdie, although only by banning a Pakistani film (Mr Rushdie argued that the grounds for the ban should be tested in court), not a single prosecution was brought by the authorities against any Muslim in Britain who had called for Mr Rushdie's murder. (*Independent*, 23.7.90)

Meanwhile, the debate as to whether or not to publish a paperback edition of the novel continued. Mr Rushdie had said: 'My main reason for wanting the paperback is to prevent this book from being banned by the back door,' (*Independent on Sunday*, 4.2.90) and, understandably, publishers had to think in terms of publicity and profits on the one hand and the expense of turning their headquarters into fortresses against attack by fanatics on the other. Thus at Penguin's headquarters in London all staff members have to show passes, and despite high sales world-wide of the hardback edition of the novel during its first year, the £1.8 million in profits was cancelled out by £2 million spent in world-wide security costs. (*Independent*, 5.2.90)

The Labour Party got itself into an embarrassing tangle, since on the one hand it wished to defend freedom of speech but on the other did not wish to offend the significant numbers of Muslims in a number of Labour constituencies. Mark Fisher, the Party's spokesman on arts and media, said:

> If you believe in something then you have to stand up for what you believe. For Penguin not to publish now would be a huge victory for those who have threatened Salman and driven him into hiding. The only way to reassert the primacy of freedom of speech and the excellence of the book itself is to publish the paperback edition. (*Independent*, 6.2.90)

That was forthright enough but, as Mr Rushdie pointed out in his piece in the *Independent on Sunday*, other members of the Labour Party had been vocal in their attacks upon him. At this stage the book becomes mixed up in the politics of race rather than the question of free speech. One Labour MP whom Mr Rushdie attacked was Keith Vaz, who sits for Leicester East, is of Asian origin and represents a constituency with one of the largest numbers of Muslims in the country. Mr Rushdie also attacked Labour equivocation over the matter of Muslim education and whether or not there should be separate Muslim schools. He wrote: 'Muslim religious leaders may wish female children of Muslim households to be educated in segregated schools, but the girls, as they say every time anybody asks them, do not wish to go. The Labour Party doesn't ask them and plans to deliver them into the hands of the mullahs.' The deputy leader of the Labour Party, Roy Hattersley, managed at the same time to be forthright in support of the book and freedom of speech and equivocal about any paperback edition:

> I stand firmly by the absolute right of Salman Rushdie to publish *The Satanic Verses*, and utterly condemn all threats of violence against him . . . There are a variety of opinions on whether or not the paperback should be published. On balance I believe it better were it not to be published.

Lambeth Palace issued a statement saying: 'We believe the time has come to balance the principle of free speech against that of self-restraint, which is also necessary in any civilised society.' That last statement hardly bears examination. How is it possible to balance free speech against self-restraint in such a case? Is Rushdie, who is already in hiding and likely to be forced to remain in hiding for the rest of his life, also being asked by the Church of England to abandon his right to free speech (and publication)?

Ali Mazrui, whose capacity for intellectual gymnastics matches Salman Rushdie's, fell into the trap of blaming the book for killings: 'Even without being published in India, *The Satanic Verses* has already killed more than a dozen people in Rushdie's country of birth.' (1990:94) To blame a book that has not even appeared in India for violent deaths in the subcontinent is to stretch every point in favour of fanaticism and is not a tenable intellectual proposition, but if someone of Mazrui's intellectual stature can make such a statement it becomes more readily understandable why ordinary Labour MPs can equivocate on an issue that might lose them votes.

At least the Rushdie affair might lead to a revision of the blasphemy law. In December 1989, for example, an 18-minute video, *Visions of Ecstasy*, was refused a certificate by the British Board of Film Classification on the grounds that it ran the risk of being blasphemous (because it included erotic scenes involving Christ). Had the criminal offence of blasphemy also applied to Islam the authorities (and many others) would have been spared a great deal of bother because *The Satanic Verses* could have been banned on the grounds that it was blasphemous and that would have been the end of the matter. Readiness to ban is certainly a familiar aspect of British politics and Lord Hailsham, for example, led protests in the House of Lords against the BBC for showing the film *The Last Temptation of Christ*, resorting in his protest to a familiar kind of threat, suggesting that the BBC was 'endangering its future by acting in this irresponsible way' (since it was disregarding many of its licence-fee payers). But as the Home Office Minister of State, Earl Ferrers, replied tartly: 'They don't have to switch on and can always turn it off.' That advice could also be given to Muslims: no one has to read *The Satanic Verses*. In the same debate Lord Tonypandy said: 'No one would tolerate abuse of the prophet Mohammed and why should we tolerate in our land abuse of our Lord?' (Mazrui, 1990:94) There is no lack of would-be censors in Britain.

Ali Mazrui admitted his own quandary, both as a Muslim and as an author who has had his own works censored, when he mixed the politics of censorship and race in his arguments about the Rushdie affair. He implied that since the British government was quite prepared to censor – he pointed to its pursuit of Wright's book *Spycatcher* halfway round the globe or the banning of interviews with Sinn Fein and other Irish organisations – why should it not also censor Rushdie for the peace of mind of Muslims? He was also making the point that British protestations about Rushdie's freedom of speech had something of a hollow ring to them. (1990:90)

The story took a new twist at the end of 1990 when Salman Rushdie met with liberal Muslim leaders in London and agreed not to publish a paperback version of his book or to allow more translations of it. Further, he said that he did not agree with any of the statements by characters in his book which were considered blasphemous to the Prophet Muhammad although just how he managed to disagree with himself in that respect is not clear. He then 'witnessed' that Allah was the only God and Muhammad his last prophet, an act of *Shahadatine* which is all that is necessary to embrace Islam. In Iran these efforts of

Rushdie to achieve reconciliation by renunciation and personal conversion were ridiculed and the Office of the Supreme Spiritual Leader, Ayatollah Khamenei, insisted that the *fatwa* against Rushdie was irrevocable and would remain unchanged even if Mr Rushdie repented to become 'the most pious man of his time'. Not only was Rushdie's effort at reconciliation rejected in Teheran, but it was also rejected by Mohammed Siddiqui, leader of the Muslim Youth Movement of Great Britain, who said he could never be forgiven. Thus he learnt the lesson that to give way to blackmail does not pay. It was hardly a pleasing outcome for the Foreign Office, since Britain had renewed diplomatic relations with Iran in September 1990, presumably in the hope of renewed trade. But what was most humiliating about the whole affair, not only for Rushdie himself but for any civilised society, was the fact that barbarous threats of death against a man for his opinions and writings had forced him to such a pass while his own country appeared unwilling to insist that the would-be murderers should back down.

By the end of the year Rushdie found himself defending his new position against his friends and supporters; his claim that his acceptance of Islam was part of a personal and spiritual journey did not carry a great deal of conviction and threw the committee of writers and human-rights campaigners formed to support him into disarray. One member of the committee, the author and barrister Francis Bennion, resigned and said:

There are several reasons why Rushdie is not worth defending . . . He has decided not to proceed with the paperback, so surrendering to would-be murderers. He has decided not to proceed with translated editions of the book, another form of surrender. Worst of all, he has now confounded his supporters by embracing the bigoted creed that holds its followers entitled to murder a novelist for what he has written in a novel.

Arnold Wesker described Rushdie's conversion to Islam as a victory for religious terrorists. (*Independent*, 4.1.91)

In May 1991 Rushdie was writing to the *Independent* in response to the statement from the Regent's Park Mosque's two leading Imams, who had apologised for their 'mistake' in meeting Rushdie on Christmas Eve 1990 because he had not completely withdrawn *The Satanic Verses*. According to Rushdie, the two Imams, Sheikh Gamal and Sheikh Hamed, had 'plainly been intimidated by the bully-boy tactics used against them in recent months'. He was right, just as intimidatory tactics seemed to have made him change his own stand. (9.5.91) The reality of the physical threats was borne out by the stabbing of his Italian translator, Ettori Caprioli, on 3 July, and then the stabbing to death of his Japanese translator, Professor Hitoshi Igarashi, on 11 July. Principles, and most especially the principles of governments, are constantly tempered by political expediency and it is notable that the same British government that has always insisted it will have no dealings with the IRA or give way to the blackmail of violence in relation to Ulster was prepared to have dealings with the Teheran government even as comparable violence inspired by that government had forced a British subject into permanent hiding. But, as a number of political commentators pointed out, the Rushdie affair became less and less a question of free speech and increasingly a matter of race and white fears of Asians and Asian demands in Britain for equality, for example in the matter of the blasphemy laws. Muslims who campaigned against *The Satanic Verses* (but not those calling for the death penalty) were instantly condemned as the Ayatollah Khomeini's 'Bradford-based fifth column'. (Green, 1990:7)

The pusillanimity of the British (and American) governments in the face of the Iranian *fatwa* was highlighted by Edmund Keeley, President of PEN American Center, New York, following the two stabbings of the Italian and Japanese translators, when he wrote as follows to the *Independent* (15.7.91):

> Many governments around the world, most notably the British and US governments, have maintained a lamentable silence of late on the Rushdie affair arguing, quite erroneously, that this approach is likely to be most effective. Now that two stabbings have occurred it is imperative that the British and US governments make the lifting of the *fatwa* a firm pre-condition for any renewal of formal diplomatic relations with Iran.

At the same time Frances D'Souza of the Rushdie Defence Committee wrote to the same paper to remind its readers that the countries which reacted strongly in defence of freedom of expression to the February 1989 *fatwa* by Iran were, by July 1991, developing significant trade contacts with Iran. In March 1989 Britain had stated unequivocally: 'a normal relationship with Iran is absolutely out of the question while that country is threatening the life of our citizens', and had also insisted that Iran should demonstrate its willingness 'to renounce the use or threat of violence'. Yet by mid-1991 Britain (along with other freedom-loving Western countries such as France, Germany, Canada and the USA) was refusing publicly to condemn renewed threats against Mr Rushdie's life or the doubling of the reward offered for his murder.

Few issues have brought out so many two-faced responses at all levels as the Rushdie affair. Although blasphemy in Britain is no longer a capital crime it is still a crime, although applicable only to Christianity. It is worth asking just what kind of response there would have been had another writer, a white rather than an Asian-born Briton, produced a comparable book blaspheming Christianity, for example by suggesting that Mary was a whore, or a book attacking Judaism? Would the same literary establishment have risen to the defence of such a writer or did they do so in the Rushdie case, at least in part, to demonstrate their liberalism since the author was of Indian origin and was attacking Islam? The thought is worth pondering. There is, as we have already noted, a case for abolishing the crime of blasphemy and, alternately, there is a case for extending its provisions to cover all religions and not just Christianity. But to adopt that latter course would be to open a Pandora's box with every kind of sect, each one more absurd than its predecessor, claiming rights under the law. Ziauddin Sardar first claimed that a *fatwa* can never be revoked and then said that for Mr Rushdie to seek some kind of pardon from Teheran was plainly daft; then, having detailed some of the literary experience of the Indian subcontinent, he suggested that 'the best course for Mr Rushdie and his suppporters is to shut up'. (*Independent*, 11.11.91) This is the line adopted by all tyrants or supporters of tyranny through the ages, and ignorant mobs or bigoted religious hierarchies are every whit as tyrannical as absolute rulers. In British terms the Rushdie affair has highlighted the dilemma of a government that has long lost interest in real liberty and, although it is quick enough to point to the shortcomings of others, especially when to do so does not harm British interests or is seen as a mark of Britain's belief in freedom, it is also very quick to keep silent when to defend the claims of liberty gets in the way of other, more profitable interests. That, indeed, has been the British record in relation to the Rushdie affair, South Africa and Kenya, to name only three instances.

Iran has been as two-faced over the issue as everyone else. Thus, in September 1991, its foreign minister assured Britain's Douglas Hurd that since the *fatwa* was a religious decree there was nothing the government could do about it. But since Iran is an Islamic state this is clearly nonsense. In any case, while taking a reasonable line with the West, with which it wants renewed links, Iran poses as the 'sword of Islam' to the Muslim world. As a result, 'Rushdie, thus far, has been the victim of the semi-religious axiom of European foreign policy: at all costs guarantee stable oil supplies.' (Ignatieff, 1991) And, although it is possible and right to condemn Iran for its double standards, the worst instances of these come from Europe and Britain. For example, only an outcry from German publishers and writers prevented the German government inviting Iranian publishers to take part in the annual Frankfurt Book Fair, while in November 1991 the British Foreign Office persuaded Rushdie's supporters to call off a demonstration in his support for fear of antagonising the Iranians when negotiations for Terry Waite's release were coming to a climax, even though Iran has never linked the Rushdie affair to the question of Terry Waite. The Foreign Office, it was clear, was prepared to use any excuse to damp down the Rushdie affair in the hope of not offending those who had called for the murder of a British citizen. Later in November 1991 the Iranian Foreign Minister, Ali Akbar Velayati (a secular rather than a religious appointee), none the less said: 'Our position toward this question [Rushdie] is the same as it was previously.' Yet, despite this, British officials said that relations with Iran would be reviewed on the release of Terry Waite. (*Independent*, 23.11.91)

The postponement of the vigil planned by Rushdie's supporters to mark the 1,000th day of his being in hiding was agreed at Foreign Office request because it might jeopardise the release of Waite and other Western hostages. As Rushdie said of this linking of his case with that of Terry Waite: 'The bad faith lies in the Foreign Office's abandonment of the position that it ought never to trade in human rights. It now appears to have taken the position that the rights of those named in the *fatwa* are to be sacrificed.' (*Independent*, 7.11.91) Apart from the shortsightedness of the Foreign Office in demonstrating its susceptibility to Iranian blackmail, its decision to link the Rushdie question to that of Waite merely demonstrated its unwillingness to stand firm on an issue where there was little enthusiasm, moral or otherwise. By resuming relations with Teheran in September 1990 the Foreign Office had accepted for all practical purposes Iran's claim that it could not overturn a religious decree and, therefore, had also accepted that Rushdie must remain in hiding for the rest of his life. Lord Palmerston would not have put up with such nonsense.

Then the Archbishop of Canterbury, Dr George Carey, added his voice to the anti-Rushdie or pro-Iranian lobby by referring to the 'pain' devout Muslims felt at the publication of *The Satanic Verses*. Like all churchmen he had a position to defend, yet the fact is the leader of the Church of England seemed more concerned to support the Muslim position than he did to condemn calls for murder.

How, then, can the Rushdie question be summarised in relation to British attitudes? Rushdie himself probably does not appear as an especially sympathetic character: abrasive, prickly, intellectually complex and 'born in India' are not, perhaps, the qualities which appeal most readily to those Britons seeking a symbol. If the British have got to go out on an awkward limb, as it were, in order to protect the rights of the individual they would undoubtedly prefer to do so on behalf of some other figure possessed of a different combination of characteristics. But we are rarely able to pick and choose our martyrs or symbols. Rushdie, whatever the eventual outcome of his 'affair', has already served a secondary purpose in demonstrating the deep tensions that currently exist between Western conscience and Islamic temper. He has been taken up by the liberal Establishment as a cause and has been regarded as an irritant, if nothing worse, by the Foreign Office, which prefers that such awkward symbols of principle should not stand in the way of practical considerations such as trade. The political right cannot actually condone Islamic calls to murder a British subject but finds Rushdie not to its taste as a person or cause to champion, so that many of those ready to speak out most in his favour have been foreign intellectuals. Nadine Gordimer (the winner of the 1991 Nobel Prize for Literature) claims that Rushdie is a victim of religious terrorism (which is to call the *fatwa* by its proper name) and suggests his case be taken to the United Nations (not that such a move would do any good). She says: 'There is no asylum for him anywhere. Every morning when this writer sits down to write, he does not know if he will live through the day.' (*Irish Independent*, 8.12.91) And so, perhaps in recognition of the hopelessness of his case, Rushdie surfaced from hiding during December 1991 to make a speech in New York where he said: 'Free speech is the whole thing, the whole ball game. Free speech is life itself.' He went on to say that he had no regrets for writing his book and that it must be freely available for people to read. (*Standard*, 12.12.91) By then he had faced the reality of his position:

that he was not going to obtain any religious reconciliation and he abandoned his earlier conversion to Islam, claiming instead to be a 'secular Muslim'. At the same time he said that he had been wrong to 'give way' on the paperback edition of his book. A leading Muslim 'moderate' reacted to his speech by saying that Salman Rushdie had put his life in even greater danger. Dr Hesham El-Essawy, chairman of the Islamic Society for the Promotion of Religious Tolerance, said Rushdie was now in danger from Muslims who had previously supported his conversion because he had reneged on it. He said:

> His remarks are a slap in the face for the Muslim community. Mr Rushdie is now in far more danger of being harmed by Muslims – not because of the Ayatollah's *fatwa*, but because he has reneged on his conversion last year. If the paperback comes out, it will be a continuous reminder to Muslims, and he will be in danger from generations to come. (*Independent*, 16.12.91)

So much for tolerance! Had Mr Rushdie attacked not Islam but a political creed – capitalism, Marxism or one-party rule in Africa, for example – and had the aggressive supporters of such a creed called for his murder, we should not have been treated to so many equivocating arguments. The equivocation over the Rushdie affair arises, quite simply, from our attitudes to religion and the fact that brainwashing through the generations has persuaded us to accept levels of cruelty and stupidity and nonsense in the name of religion which we would not accept in the name of anything else.

22 The Iraq War

This is no time to go wobbly.

MARGARET THATCHER

THE INVASION OF KUWAIT by Saddam Hussein of Iraq on 2 August 1990 sparked off a world crisis; it also created a political opportunity which Margaret Thatcher seized with both hands. She happened to be on a visit to the United States at the time and so was at hand to stiffen the President's resolve: 'This is no time to go wobbly,' she told a less than warlike President Bush. The 'iron lady' was herself again. She certainly needed a 'war' opportunity, for by then the political tide in Britain was clearly turning against her while she had found that under the newly elected President Bush the special relationship which she had enjoyed with President Reagan had faded away. A limited war in which Britain could act as principal lieutenant to the United States might transform her political standing and show her, as she liked to view herself, as the 'iron lady', not just of Britain but of the whole Western world. By the end of the year Margaret Thatcher had been forced out of Downing Street but there was little to suggest such a fate awaited her at the time that Kuwait was annexed by Iraq and the world waited to see what would happen next.

The Iraq War went through well-defined stages. First, the invasion and occupation of Kuwait which was all over in a few days. Second, the near universal condemnation of Saddam Hussein and the discovery that the crisis would not automatically produce a confrontation between the USA and the USSR. Third, the patient creation of an alliance nominally under the auspices of the United Nations but in fact under the leadership of the United States. Fourth, the aerial bombardment of Iraq which began on 16 January 1991, after the United Nations deadline for Iraq to quit Kuwait had expired, and continued for more than a month. Fifth, the land war which was launched on 23 February and lasted a mere 100 hours before Iraq had conceded the demands of the United Nations and Kuwait was declared liberated on 28 February. Then came the messy part. Although firm figures were never possible, an estimated 100,000 Iraqis were killed, mainly as a result of the aerial bombardment; something like $50bn worth of damage was done to Kuwait whose oil had been set alight and pumped into the Gulf; while damage to Iraq had set that country's development back by at least a decade. Moreover, although civil war followed between the supporters of Saddam Hussein and the Shiahs (mainly those based upon Basra) as well as between the central government and the Kurds of the north, Saddam Hussein remained in control and was able to deploy his renowned ruthlessness to crush the opposition, creating an estimated two million Kurdish refugees in the process, while the victors sat round the edges of his country doing nothing. What, then, had the West and particularly Britain gained from this war?

Britain, as so often turns out to be the case in Third World affairs, had played a part in laying the groundwork for what was to come. Confidential Whitehall policy papers for 1960, which were released under the thirty-year rule at the beginning of 1991, showed that protection of Kuwaiti oil was seen as Britain's 'irreducible interest' in the Gulf, an interest which was to be defended by arms if necessary. The following year (1961), Britain annulled her agreement of 1899 with Kuwait under which she had managed that country's foreign affairs. As the Foreign Office head of the Arabian Department, Dick Beaumont, had written to the British political resident in the Persian Gulf, Sir John Middleton, in January 1960: 'The irreducible interest of the United Kingdom in Kuwait is that Kuwait shall remain an independent state having an oil policy conducted by government independent of other Middle East producers.' And he went on to say that other governments in the Gulf must be made to understand Britain's willingness to defend Kuwait. Subsequently, after Britain formally ended her protectorate over Kuwait, Iraq, which was then led by General Abdul Karim Quasim, declared that Kuwait was a 'long lost, but integral part of Iraq', prompting Macmillan to send a fire-fighting force of brigade strength to Kuwait. (*Independent*, 2.1.91) Thus, any British intervention in the Gulf would be in accordance with the past imperial traditions in the region, whether or not it was under the auspices of the United Nations.

Saddam Hussein's seizure of Kuwait at the beginning of August 1991 was seen as a major threat by all his Gulf neighbours and, in the wake of the international outcry which followed, it became plain that the United States and its allies – most notably Britain at that stage – were determined not to let Hussein get away with his aggression. But although the intention of the allies was clear enough, the principles upon which that intention was based were nothing like so obvious. Thus, it could hardly be argued that, as a matter of principle, Britain and the United States had ever followed a policy of carrying out United Nations resolutions since, blatantly and repeatedly over the years, they had failed to act on UN resolutions on Israel or South Africa when their interests dictated otherwise. Nor could they claim to be acting on principle to prevent annexation as such, for they had done nothing, for example, about China's annexation of Tibet in 1950, the Israeli annexation of the Golan Heights or its *de facto* incorporation of the West Bank and Gaza Strip into its territory, or Turkey's annexation of the northern third of Cyprus in 1974. And although it might be argued that the confrontations of the Cold War prevented action in those earlier cases, in fact there was no evidence to suggest that they would have taken action had no Cold War been in existence. Nor, despite denunciations of Saddam Hussein's brutal regime and the fact that he possessed a range of dangerous weapons including missiles, germ warheads and possibly nuclear warheads, did there appear to exist any principle in relation to checking dangerous dictatorships. Both powers, after all, had been prepared to do business with the equally unpleasant Iranian regime of the Shah as well as many others round the world. Moreover, Western opposition to the Islamic fundamentalism of Khomeini's Iran had led it to supply arms to Saddam Hussein right up to the point of the Iraq War, for he had been seen as a useful counterweight to Teheran. Nor was any liberating or democratic principle at stake, for once the war was over the West stood by while Hussein crushed the Kurds and the Shiahs, and did little in Kuwait to encourage the returning al-Sabah family to become more democratic, watching instead as they allowed an apparent policy of revenge killings to be carried out against the Palestinians.

There was, in fact, only one principle of overriding importance which led the USA and the West to intervene: oil. As almost every observer, of no matter what political persuasion, has agreed, had there been no oil in Kuwait there might have been outraged denunciations of a bullying regime but there would not have been a war. It was the threat to Western economic interests and the fear that Saddam Hussein would end up controlling the largest world oil reserves outside Saudi Arabia that ensured Western intervention, since the addition of Kuwait to Iraq would mean that Baghdad controlled 25 per cent of the world's known oil reserves. Here, then, was the reason for the Western determination to put Hussein in his place or at least to push him out of Kuwait; yet a Martian observer of the war would have been hard put to understand this had he come to earth for the nine-month period August 1990 to May 1991 and listened to all the justifications for intervention that were to be advanced, although he might have worked it out from the fact that once Hussein was out of Kuwait again the allies were basicallly uninterested in doing much else in the region.

The war provided Britain with a number of what might be described as national 'photo-opportunities' to show herself at her most smug or sanctimonious. The Americans, we were told, were tremendously pleased to have the British with them in the Gulf, 'shoulder to shoulder' as President Bush obligingly put it, a reminder that the special relationship was working once more. But, of course, the British soldiers in the desert did not have the problems which faced the Americans. Thus: 'It used to be axiomatic that soldiers living in the harsh conditions of desert foxholes and camps were bound to fall victim to morale-sapping despondency. But then the British arrived and confused everyone by being generally cheerful and bewilderingly serene.' (*Standard*, 6.12.90) Comparisons were made between the apparent self-sufficiency of the British troops on the ground and the elaborate programme, costing £35m, under which American forces were flown to Bahrain for three-day breaks. Compensating for the fact that 90 per cent of the fire power and military might was American, the British felt obliged to emphasise their superiority. Perhaps this is a characteristic of behaviour that few can ever resist; it is certainly a line that the British pushed relentlessly through the period of the war.

Saddam Hussein acted as a catalyst to bring a good many interesting worms out of the British woodwork. In an article in which he attacked the 'liberal conscience', John Casey suggested that the real reason why we opposed Saddam Hussein was not because he was a monster or an aggressor but

> because we would oppose anyone who might set about uniting a large part of the Arab world. We would prefer the Arabs to revert to being clients of the West (in which we shall increasingly have to include the Soviet Union). In other words, we now have the opportunity to reverse the political tide which began to flow when Nasser came to power in the early 1950s. (*Standard*, 29.1.91)

As Casey also argued, liberal deference to the nationalisms of the Third World had not been about principle but about wooing allies against the Soviet threat; the disappearance of the threat meant it would be possible to revert to more naked old-fashioned power politics with less pretence. At least that would be a change for the better if some of the sanctimoniousness could be ditched along the way.

A long article which appeared in the *Observer* on 20 January 1991 examined the concept of a 'just war' to suggest that such a description could be applied to the war against Saddam Hussein. Admitting that civilians suffer in war – 'This is inevitable' – the author, Richard Harries, said: 'Nevertheless, to kill civilians *qua* civilians is murder. We can be grateful for the assurances of John Major [the British Prime Minister] that it is missile sites, airports, command and control centres, etc. that are being targeted. Even more, we can be grateful for the high precision modern electronics which makes accurate targeting in principle possible.' None of this was exceptionable in the circumstances, nor should it cause surprise. The author also said, 'A just war must also be prosecuted with a right intention. This means with an eye on a just order and a lasting peace. . . . Once Saddam Hussein has been rendered harmless.' In war there is never any lack of people to argue along such lines. In the same article, for example, Harries tells us that in relation to the morality of going to war, 'There have been some distinguished contributions by the Archbishop of Canterbury and a very measured, proper pastoral letter from the Roman Catholic bishops, which was read out in every church.' As Tony Benn has remarked in a different context, when governments are in trouble they call in the bishops to their aid. Once the 'just war' had concluded, Saddam Hussein was left to deal with the Shiahs and Kurds whose uprising had been sparked off by this just war and encouraged, at least in part, by the allies.

On the home front, just before the commencement of the aerial bombardment in January the BBC came in for the usual accusations that it was not sufficiently 'gung-ho'. Viewers complained about the 'peacenik' tone of a *Panorama* programme in which David Dimbleby asked whether war was inevitable and questioned whether there had been sufficient debate on the subject: despite the fact that such non-'peacenik' characters as Edward Heath, Denis Healey and the American defence secretary Richard Cheney were interviewed, the BBC was obliged to defend such a programme against the usual war hysteria, and a BBC spokesman said: 'Our coverage of the Gulf crisis is balanced and it is not a question of putting a stopwatch to every programme to measure how much time was given to each point of view.' (*Standard*, 15.1.91) It is a remarkable fact of British public life that the great majority of complaints about 'balance' come from the political right and usually in situations where it both expects and demands that *imbalance* towards its own viewpoint should take place. The BBC decided to refer to 'British troops' rather than 'our troops' if a war broke out.

Although media reports from Baghdad where, remarkably, Western reporters were permitted to operate after the war began, stated that they were subject to Iraqi censorship, in general the media did not admit to any censorship from Western governments. In a little bit of self-censorship in which it contrived to make itself look ridiculous, the BBC (in terms of taste and sensibility) withdrew certain programmes, including *Carry On Up the Khyber* which was replaced by *Carry On Cowboy*. Censorship by the allies was well planned and efficient: 'So thorough has been the preparation for this war, so dependent have journalists become upon information dispensed by the Western military authorities in Saudi Arabia, so enamoured of their technology, that Press and television reporters have found themselves trapped.' (*Independent*, 6.2.91) And this, no doubt, was the intention. Hyperbole and nonsense arise only too quickly in situations such as that presented by the Iraq War so that a British reporter could tell her television audience, speaking of RAF fighter-pilots taking off from a Gulf airstrip, that 'their bravery knows no bounds'. Assisted by a good deal of nonsense about a just war, there was a real danger of the enterprise developing into a crusade – Western Christianity versus militant and evil Islam – except for the awkward fact that half the alliance consisted of Islamic countries. All too quickly there was a readiness on the part of the media to accept unquestioningly their own side's version of events.

One of the least acceptable aspects of British behaviour concerned the treatment of Iraqi and other detainees during the war. MI5, acting on flimsy and out-dated evidence, had a number of Iraqis and other Arabs living in Britain arrested and interned as potential terrorists. The government acted on the MI5 information without question and the suspects were interned for the duration of the hostilities. It is significant that no other member of the alliance against Hussein felt it necessary to act so arbitrarily against foreign residents; only the freedom-loving British did so, allowing their usual distaste for foreigners in general and

Arabs in particular to surface, even though half-a-dozen Arab states were their allies. As an editorial of the *Independent* said:

The recent detentions have provided evidence enough of the corrupting effects that these unchecked powers [of the Home Secretary] have had on the authorities. Spared the need to present evidence or submit to proper scrutiny, their procedures were sloppy, their behaviour lazy, and their initial response to criticism smug, reflecting the comfortable inertia of the too-well-protected. (9.3.91)

The fuss and 'hype' that went with the Queen conferring an honorary knighthood upon General Norman Schwarzkopf after the war was over had everything to do with the 'special relationship' and not much to do with his conduct of the war. Just as soon as the West had achieved its objective – freeing oil-rich Kuwait of Iraqi control – it stopped the war, leaving Saddam Hussein in place and able to turn much of his still largely intact war machine to the easier proposition of eliminating internal opposition to his regime. The public outcry in Britain at the treatment meted out to the Kurds forced the Major government to do something and made the winning of a so-called 'just war' look sour indeed. It was in April 1991, at the height of the Kurdish insurrection, that Britain's new Prime Minister, John Major, said what he thought before thinking: 'I don't recall asking them [the Kurds] to mount this particular insurrection.' This remark, from the nice Mr Major, whose non-abrasive style had won many plaudits during the war in contrast to what the public would have got had Mrs Thatcher still been in Downing Street, is imbued with the worst kind of British arrogance and indifference towards any members of the Third World who cause us embarrassment. The British, in fact, have a long history of involvement in the affairs of the Kurds. Largely due to British pressure the Kurds had been promised a state of their own under the terms of the Treaty of Sèvres in 1920 but in face of renascent Turkish power we reversed this promise at the 1923 Treaty of Lausanne. Iraq was made a British Mandate in 1919 and the first recorded bombing of civilian targets by the RAF was against Kurdish villages in northern Iraq during Kurdish uprisings in 1922–3 and 1931–2. True to form, the US and other permanent members of the UN Security Council determined in March 1991 that once Iraq had accepted the Security Council's terms for a ceasefire, Baghdad would be permitted to use its fighter and ground-attack aircraft to quell internal dissent (the Kurds) – not because to do so was a natural corollary of the 'just war' that had been fought so recently but because they did not wish to see the break-up of Iraq or the further destabilisation of the oil-rich Gulf region. And, although during the course of the war, the allies were happy enough to see insurrections that put pressure upon Baghdad, they were only too anxious afterwards to see the Kurds' bid for independence defeated. Thus:

> The five powers [permanent members of the Security Council] all implicitly agreed that Baghdad should be allowed to put down the Kurdish rebellion with its fighter aircraft, if that can prevent the disintegration of the country. The one accommodation to the Kurds is that Iraq must promise not to use its chemical weapons – as it has done in the past – and that it must eventually destroy all its stocks of such weapons. Neither Britain, France nor the US has insisted that Iraq comply with basic human rights law in dealing with internal dissent. (*Independent*, 28.3.91)

It is true that Mr Major, perhaps conscious of the effect that his throwaway remark about the Kurds had made, subsequently came up with the suggestion of an 'enclave' for the Kurds – neither a separate state nor just a province of Iraq but a sort of classic British fudge – but, as events showed, once the furore and television pictures of miserable Kurdish refugees had lessened, the Iraqis continued without hindrance to tighten the screws upon their Kurdish people. As the *Independent* editorial of 16 April 1991 commenced: 'Why should nations that can fly thousands of sorties a day against Iraq and launch "smart" bombs with great accuracy find it so difficult to distribute a few planeloads of food and blankets to destitute Kurds?' Why indeed! So much for the just war.

John Major was at least a good deal more reserved about a victory celebration than ever his predecessor at Number 10 had been at the time of the Falklands War, although he confirmed that one would take place; in this respect, at least, he showed a better appreciation of the national mood. There was the usual public discussion with the Bishop of Durham, the Right Revd David Jenkins, designating such a celebration as 'obscene', while a spokesman for Neil Kinnock (determined as ever to be in the centrist mainstream of British politics) said that the Labour Party did not oppose the idea in principle although 'it would have to be something appropriate'. Air Commodore Alastair Mackie, a vice-president of CND (and presumably a turncoat to his traditional military caste) said: 'The victory parade is another piece of great British bombast. What we should be celebrating is the fact that war is over.' (*Independent*, 4.3.91) It is, perhaps, something of a plus for the British 'thinking classes' that after both the Falklands and the Iraq wars there were substantial public rows and protests at the very idea of victory services or parades.

Right up to the outbreak of the war Britain was not just dealing with Iraq but doing her best to become one of its major suppliers: 'In a playground full of bullies Saddam Hussein was the biggest of all. But he held the keys to the tuck shop, so we had to stay on his side.' Thus speaks a British diplomat who had responsibility for British policy towards Baghdad prior to the war, incongruously using the language of a schoolboy. He went on to explain that had Saddam not been so greedy but had taken only the Rumailah oil field and occupied the two islands at the mouth of the Shatt al-Arab, then perhaps there would not have been a war at all. He went on, engagingly, to say: 'Nobody in the West or the Middle East had any time for the rulers of Kuwait and we might have just let Saddam keep certain bits. What the Gulf War boiled down to was major misjudgement, on both sides.' Only six months before the war began, Foreign Office officials had drawn up an advisory paper: 'Britain and Iraq – THE BIG PRIZE'. The big prize, of course, was trade with the holder of the largest oil resources outside Saudi Arabia. This former Iraq desk officer of the Foreign Office, Mark Higson, gave away a good deal more. Thus, of the Big Gun whose components were constructed in Britain and sent to Iraq, despite an embargo on arms exports, he had this to say:

> We knew all about the Iraqi 'Big Gun' a long time before the story broke last April. We knew about a lot of things, but who is to say, for sure, that this particular factory component is going to help construct an arms plant, or this bit of mechanics will be used in gun mounting. Getting into that lucrative market meant ignoring a lot of things they were up to. (*Observer*, 28.7.91)

And ignore them the British certainly did until the last possible moment. Such engaging cynicism is the British norm rather than concern with justice although, of course, when it comes to the point it sounds good to speak of fighting a 'just war'.

23 Political doublespeak

Families, when a child is born
Want it to be intelligent.
I, through intelligence,
Having wrecked my whole life,
Only hope the baby will prove
Ignorant and stupid.
Then he will crown a tranquil life
By becoming a Cabinet Minister.

SU TUNG-P'O (1036–1101),
translated by ARTHUR WALEY

POLITICIANS ALWAYS ARGUE that what they do is in the national interest and that they are there – as politicians – for the good of the public. They are there in pursuit of their own ambitions.
Moreover, it is a misrepresentation to suggest that government (and its representatives such as the Civil Service or the police) are there to look after the interests of society as a whole. They are not. There are two classes, exploiters and the exploited, and governments represent the exploiters. (Weldon, 1953:133) Class is a constant of British life and endlessly rears its head in the political field, and, as one commentator, Douglas Sutherland, suggests, has dominated politics for most of the century: 'Every general election in this country since the end of the First World War has been basically fought on the issue of class.' (1988:143) The political ideal, of course, is something quite different, not only from what we have got but from what our politicians aim to give us. 'The form of government we have to find is one which elicits and enlists – or at any rate is calculated to elicit and enlist, so far as is humanly possible – the thought, the will, and the general capacity of every member.' (Barker, 1958:36) That ideal is so far removed from what we have as to make a nonsense of most claims advanced by politicians. There have been periods in our history when those in power have been motivated by at least a measure of idealism; they do not occur frequently and, arguably, the last such period was that of the post-war Attlee government. But although some of its leading members genuinely wished to implement policies on behalf of the people, they also suffered from delusions of grandeur about Britain and her capacities so that they failed to come to terms

with the realities of British power. 'In stark terms, Britain in 1945 no longer had the economic sinews to sustain a world and imperial role abroad while constructing a welfare state at home. This was not a prospect either of the main political parties addressed in 1945.' (Hennessy and Seldon, 1987:34) That failure lies at the root of many subsequent British attempts to persuade herself that she had a place in the world out of proportion to her capacities and power, and those efforts at self-deception have been a principal explanation for so much brainwashing at both national and élite levels about Britain's world role. As Sir Henry Tizard, Chief Scientific Adviser to the Ministry of Defence, said in 1949: 'We persist in regarding ourselves as a Great Power, capable of everything and only temporarily handicapped by economic difficulties. We are not a great power and never will be again. We are a great nation, but if we continue to behave like a Great Power we shall soon cease to be a great nation.' Tizard's dictum, of course, was ignored as is usual with anyone who tells the truth so bluntly, with the result, as some at least would argue, that the British have now also ceased to be a great nation.

Lloyd George put his finger on the party process accurately enough when he said, 'What Conservatives want is for the good of the nation; what anyone else wants is party politics.' (Thornton, 1959:94) We often hear demands for strong government – from the electorate as well as the politicians – but in fact strong government as a rule means a government that diminishes rather than enhances freedoms. The 'first-past-the-post' system which the British set such store by allows governments with massive majorities which subsequently override all opposition, especially if such majorities are also accompanied by strong leaders. Such a system does not often enhance the democratic process. But the electorate, as much as the politicians, is to blame. 'It is the electorate, rather than the party machines, which has destroyed the back-bench MP's independence. It appears that the voter resents independence in his MP, and prefers one who is tied by the two-party system to what he, perhaps optimistically, regards as predictable policies and stable leaders.' (Nicholson, 1967:125) In his *Portrait of a Decade*, published in 1988, Douglas Sutherland gives the following, perhaps already dated, view of the two main political parties: 'The Labour Party traditionally relies on the well-tried dogmas like "You have nothing to lose but your chains"; "Only Labour can talk to Labour"; "Be loyal to your class"; "Down with the rich".' But even if such an approach is now out-dated by events, the attitude is fundamental to British party and class politics. Sutherland continues: 'To which the Tories blandly reply: "Wouldn't you like to be like us?"; "Join the property-owning democracy"; "Life is better under the Conservatives"; "God Save the Queen"; a simply infuriating attitude for the "haves" to adopt against the "have-nots".' (143–4)

In the early 1950s the Tories used the election slogan 'set the people free', which was later described by a Conservative minister as 'little more than an electoral flourish'. The Conservatives in office are generally authoritarian, although Labour is not much less so. An interesting reflection upon the party's perceptions of itself, however, may be seen in its treatment (posthumously) of Iain Macleod. The young Macleod first drew attention to himself with a brilliant speech in which he attacked Nye Bevan, then at the height of his power and influence as the architect of the National Health Service, with the result that Churchill gave him office in his 1951 government at the Ministry of Health. He really came to prominence under Macmillan, who made him Colonial Secretary in 1960 in succession to Lennox-Boyd, with a brief to implement the 'wind of change' in Africa. This Macleod did with sufficient success as to infuriate much of his own party and call forth from the ageing Lord Salisbury the sneering comment that he was 'too clever by half', since he was not only dismantling the Empire to which the party was still greatly attached but endangering the position of the white settlers in Kenya and the Rhodesias as well. His judgement was not always good and his refusal in 1963 to serve under Alec Douglas-Home made him still more enemies in his own party. When Edward Heath won the election of 1970 he appointed Macleod Chancellor of the Exchequer, but within weeks he died. Subsequently, and this is the point, the Tories have raised Macleod into a kind of icon figure, the 'great leader they never got', the man who could have made all the difference during the disastrous Heath years, and so on. Now this exercise in posthumous elevation to lost greatness has much less to do with Macleod himself than it has to do with the way the Conservative Party would like to be regarded by the electorate at large. Macleod 'the radical', who was disliked and feared by considerable numbers of his own party when alive, became, when dead, a useful pseudo-image of caring, 'radical' Conservatism when, of course, no one would be obliged to implement any of his possibly radical policies.

By 1987, seventeen years after Macleod's death, the Conservative Party under Margaret Thatcher had changed out of recognition from the party in which he had operated. Michael Heseltine, who had resigned in spectacular fashion from the Cabinet over the Westland affair, spent some of his suddenly acquired extra time writing a book – *Where There's a Will* – in which he delights his readers with the following description of Tory capitalism: 'Tory capitalism is a caring capitalism, energetic but never rapacious, and ensures that the citizen who uses his economic freedom to enrich himself will also enrich society at large.' (1987:6) The reader is bound to wonder whether, at the height of the Thatcher era of ruthless yuppie rising, Mr Heseltine was being ironic, although irony is not among his obvious talents.

Talk of socialism as applied to British politics is usually a sham. Members of the political 'left' have long used the rhetoric of socialism without intending the reality, while members of the political right play up to the prejudices of a generally conservative electorate by suggesting the Labour Party is socialist when it is nothing of the kind. Harold Wilson, in the days when he spoke of a white-hot technological revolution, gave to the Labour Party a certain middle-of-the-road appeal, and his first speech to the Labour Party Conference as leader in October 1963 drew from Macmillan the comment: 'It was excellently done, if fundamentally dishonest.' (Horne, 1989:535) Wilson *par excellence* had the ability to sound outraged on behalf of the people or to speak like a principled statesman until action was required. Thus, over the Profumo affair, he used such phrases as 'odious record', 'the sickness of an unrepresentative section of our society', 'the moral challenge with which the whole nation is faced', wallowing in moral outrage over something that was fundamentally unimportant but also something that British politicians found hard to leave alone. On more important issues such as the question of South Africa the moral outrage takes on more statesmanlike tones: 'There is no standing aside, no comforting refuge in abstentions or vetoes, we are either against oppression, or we condone it. In these issues, there can be no neutrals, no escape.' (Wilson, 1964:83) In power Wilson condoned it.

In the early 1970s Tony Benn was seen as a likely future leader of the Labour Party and was feared as such not least by members of his own party. In his diaries he recounts how in June 1973 the Labour MP Brian Walden came to see him to tell him that he was not getting across to Labour MPs but frightening them! As Benn records: 'They had their constituencies, a good job in the House of Commons and I disturbed them, disrupted life and made them feel they might lose. What they wanted was reassurance.' (1989:45) That comment, which could be applied equally to the ranks of the Tory Party if similarly disturbed, tells nearly all we need to know about our politicians. Two comments upon the party system are worth recording. Clive Ponting (1986) draws attention to the constant way in which those in opposition say one thing and then reverse it, discovering that it is not, after all, in the public interest, when they come to power, and suggests that those in power are also in a conspiracy, a conclusion that the British people generally seemed to have begun to accept by the last decade of the century. Possibly a more telling point was made a quarter of a century earlier by Max Nicholson who simply asked: 'Is it possible to have a good system of government which consistently gives bad results?' (1967:73)

Politics has always included a large measure of hypocrisy and the British are renowned world-wide for this quality. After Yalta, Churchill and other Western leaders lied about their belief in the integrity of Stalin when they shared no such beliefs. As Churchill said at the time: 'The impression I brought back from the Crimea, and from all my other contacts, is that Marshal Stalin and the Soviet leaders wish to live in honorable friendship and equality with the Western democracies. I also feel that their word is their bond.' (Deacon, 1986:20) Now pragmatists will no doubt claim that under the strained circumstances of wartime such lies can be excused as a necessary part of politics; the difficulty about such a claim is that lies of this kind are a permanent part of politics and not simply used in emergency situations. Politicians somehow always manage to find justifications for not telling the truth.

At least it is possible, occasionally, to claim that our politicians make us laugh. The following description of the Conservatives comes from that extraordinary post-war icon of the party, Lord Hailsham: 'For Conservatives do not believe that political struggle is the most important thing in life. In this they differ from Communists, Socialists, Nazis, Fascists, Social Creditors, and most members of the British Labour Party. The simplest among them prefer fox-hunting – the wisest, religion.' It is difficult, but not impossible, to believe that he is serious; his real target is the British Labour Party. Lord Hailsham goes on to claim that 'The man who puts politics first is not fit to be called a civilized being, let alone a Christian.' (1959:13) Admittedly, this was written in 1959, yet the mixture of total rejection of any view except his own and cant about Christianity is symptomatic of those deeply ingrained attitudes that the two-party system has helped perpetuate in British political life. By the 1990s almost no one believed politicians any more, although they alone were not to blame for this state of affairs. Macmillan was a first-class intellectual, whatever his political or other failings might have been, and he showed it, yet such is British mistrust of brains that Deryk Winterton could write of him in the *Daily Herald*: 'An intellectual without the grace to pretend that he is not.' (Horne, 1988:457) Few other people regard intellectuals with such general scorn as do the British and so they cannot complain if a great deal of hypocrisy surrounds the subject of brains in high places.

From time to time great issues – or issues that have been spuriously elevated – have dominated the political scene for a spell and given rise to some of the hypocrisies for which the British are justly renowned. Since World War II such issues have included Suez, the Profumo affair, aid to the Third World, the European Community, and sanctions (and their application or non-application). Over the Suez adventure Hugh Gaitskell demanded an answer to the accusation of collusion between Britain and Israel, to be told by the Foreign Secretary, Selwyn Lloyd: 'It is quite wrong to state that Israel was incited to this action by HMG. There was no prior agreement between us about it.' A few years later, for a lie to the House of Commons about his mistress, Profumo was ruined, but for a lie about collusion with Israel Lloyd was to be honoured by all parties when he was elected Speaker. As Keith Kyle says of this: 'It still remains astonishing that the man who spoke these words was subsequently elected Speaker of the House of Commons.' (1991:379) During Suez the *Voice of Britain* broadcasts beamed from Cyprus were brutally anti-Nasser, and calculated to cause insurrection against him; they did not employ the language of a 'peace-keeper', which was the pose the Eden government had adopted; Nye Bevan asked that the government should stop lying to the House of Commons.

The Profumo affair set off one of those calculated wallows in hypocrisy which the British love, although foreigners, the French for example, must be bemused by them. Harold Wilson, on great form, told the House of Commons: 'This is a debate without precedent in the annals of this House', arising from 'disclosures which have shocked the moral conscience of the nation'. (Horne, 1989:480) Wayland Young, whose book *The Profumo Affair* became an instant bestseller, waxed eloquent in his pursuit of rectitude: 'It was the natural fruit of a period of government when convenience was set above justice, loyalty above truth and appearance above reality.' When, one might enquire, was it ever not so? He quotes with obvious relish from the court records the charges against Stephen Ward: 'attempted to procure Miss

X, a girl then under the age of twenty-one, to have unlawful sexual intercourse with a third person, against the peace of our sovereign lady the Queen, her crown, and dignity.' (1963:112, 76) Ward, the scapegoat for higher people, could hardly have been charged with anything more beastly! While he was about it, the author also lambasted the upper classes (in the name of our children): 'For the sake of our children and all that we hold in regard we can no longer uphold the polluted mentality of those who claim "we are born to lead" – in other words the doubtful spawn of Eton and Harrow, who too often have exercised power in our land.' One would like to think Wayland Young had a sense of humour but this seems doubtful.

On the issue of aid, the Tories at least have always been more hard-headed and demonstrably self-interested than Labour, recognising that aid is an instrument of foreign policy to be used to the advantage of the donor. The Labour Party has been far readier to make special claims on its behalf, as did Harold Wilson when he said that aid 'is a welcome proof that the Socialist principles of the Welfare State; from each according to his capacity, to each according to his need; is beginning to come into its own in international affairs,' (1964:86) although Reg Prentice gave the game away at a public meeting (he was then in the Labour Party and responsible for aid) when he replied to a questioner 'that for every pound Britain provided through multilateral organisations such as the World Bank she received one pound fifty pence back in purchases of British goods'.

Over the question of whether or not Britain should join the European Community or remain part of it, an argument that has lasted for thirty years, there has been a great deal of both hypocrisy and deception. Thus, the Conservative government of 1959–63 consulted certain interest groups, decided to join the EEC, announced its intention when the crucial decision-taking was over, and then the public was allowed to take part in the debate. (Windlesham, 1966:28–9) Thirty years later it was possible for *The Sunday Times* to editorialise as follows:

It is extraordinary that in a country that prides itself on freedom of speech there has been almost no public debate on what could be the most exciting – or the most disastrous – reform of the British constitution since the Norman Conquest. But what is the Conservative party's position on Europe? Now that Mrs Thatcher is no longer the leader, we do not know.

It went on:

> What is the Labour party's position? Most of the Shadow
> Cabinet have, at one time or another, outspokenly opposed the
> very idea of Britain's membership of the EC. (11.6.91)

The British people would be justified in rejecting membership of the
European Community on the simple grounds that they have never been
fully informed of the key issues before decisions on these have been
taken, and have never been allowed to participate in a full-scale debate
of an issue which, arguably, is the most important to their future to
be taken this century.

On the issue of sanctions and their use, perhaps only one comment
needs to be made: 'that Britain's expectation that her allies should
apply sanctions to Argentina over the Falklands goes ill with her
determined opposition to any sanctions against South Africa.' (Freedman and Gamba-Stonehouse, 1990:347)

Open public discussion of issues is the essence of democracy but
how often, in real terms, are the British people consulted about what
the politicians do in their name? Debate under the two-party system is
largely meaningless since in the end everyone votes along party lines
anyway. And even when individuals abstain or vote against the party
line they do so only when there is no danger of forcing the government
to alter the policy. One of the latest anti-democratic developments to
emerge in Britain is the new practice of hiving-off parts of the Civil
Service into Next Steps agencies which operate at 'arm's length' from
ministers. What this means in practice is that questions by MPs to
ministers which are deemed to cover 'operational' questions about the
running of departments are referred to the agency's chief executive, who
in due course writes to the MP; the answer is then placed in the House
of Commons Library, to which the general public has no access, rather
than appearing in the daily *Hansard*, which has been the practice up
to the present time. The practice was described by Tony Banks, MP for
Newham North West, as 'another attempt to make the business of
government less accountable and more secretive'. (*Independent*,
20.6.91) A classic example of an old attitude which these new
procedures will encourage appeared when the Labour MP for Coventry
South East, David Nellist (since expelled from a newly 'orthodox'
party), asked on 1 May 1991 what operational guidance is used by
social-security benefit officers in deciding when to pursue overpayments.

His question was referred to the Benefits Agency which at first refused to answer, saying the information was too technical to be easily understood, to which Mr Nellist replied that as an MP he was actually responsible for framing the legislation the agency operated. The chief executive of the agency, Michael Bichard, then agreed to put a copy of the answer in the House of Commons Library, although he told the MP that he believed the answer 'should not become a public document'. (*Independent*, 20.6.91) Now if an MP has to face that kind of difficulty and arrogance before a public servant can be made to provide the information he requests, there is not much chance for most of the ordinary public. It is, of course, a way to delay providing information on subjects that are politically sensitive, and delay in such circumstances is often crucial in defeating the impact of a story about government intentions or incompetence.

Some aspects of policy have always been controlled with minimum reference to Parliament, let alone the public at large, but the practice is undoubtedly growing. Back in the 1940s the money for a British atomic bomb was obtained from Parliament without its members knowing what the money was for, despite the fact that in theory the House of Commons controls all financial decisions. 'Yet in the light of these fundamental principles, the Government of the day were able to embark on the manufacture of the bomb, in full confidence that the House would allow them the money without knowing what it was to be used for.' In those days the sum of £100 million was necessary for this clandestine operation, but it was set aside without difficulty. 'This one example illustrates the ease with which a determined Government can achieve their ends, whether or not the House approves them. It spells out, with brutal clarity, the ineffectiveness of the House's procedure for controlling expenditure.' (Hill and Whichelow, 1964:19–20)

The Royal Commission has long been regarded as a means of evading action: show concern when an issue is at boiling point by appointing a Royal Commission and with luck, by the time it reports, the public will have other things on its mind and little or no action need be taken. It is also, of course, a means of whitewashing government deficiencies, as was the Franks Commission to inquire into the causes of the Falklands War. That particular exercise was a masterpiece of cover-up, for an analysis of the evidence which the Commission considers demonstrates repeatedly that the government had all the evidence of impending war yet still failed to take appropriate action. It is time for a reforming government to abolish the system of the 'great and the good', the approved names of Establishment figures deemed worthy of sitting on Royal Commissions. A far more healthy way to use the device and one that would restore confidence in Royal Commission recommendations would be to select members of the public at random, as jurors are selected, and give them the right to call upon experts to sit with them if and when necessary. One of the greatest points in Margaret Thatcher's favour was that she did not employ the device of Royal Commissions, thus putting a lot of the 'great and the good' out to grass, as it were, another reason why they so disliked her. As the *Standard* tells us of the 1989 inquiry into school violence:

> Lord Elton's inquiry into violence in schools follows a long-established tradition. Its committee of seven of the great and the good spent a year sampling, monitoring and cogitating, and have come up with a report which tells us with reassuring authority nothing that the average parent didn't know already. (14.3.89)

Devices, dishonesty and self-delusion make up the armoury of governments. When politicians argue – for example in Brussels – that the British people won't stand for something, they mean they have manufactured a particular concern in order to give their arguments more weight. One astonishing defence of the use of the guillotine in a House of Commons debate runs as follows: 'It is not generally realised that a Government could not have recourse to a guillotine in the Commons if it were not confident that the measure would be examined in detail, and if necessary improved, in the Lords.' (Hill and Whichelow, 1964:13) The simple answer to this extraordinary piece of doublethink is not to use the guillotine but to allow detailed examination of the measure in the Commons before it goes to the Lords. This kind of argument is especially dangerous because it gives the impression that the safeguard is there – the Lords – while the House of Commons is actually being denied its right to examine something in depth. Many people can be persuaded to accept the bypassing of a right provided they are also told that the right still exists – to be used on other occasions! The people, in fact, have great powers at their disposal if only they were aware of them and knew how to use them.

In political terms the problem is to conceal from the masses the fact that the material preconditions for social liberation already exist. On the one hand the best energies of modern capitalist societies are devoted to the profitable waste of resources (arms expenditure, advertising, built-in obsolescence, etc.) and on the other, to the distraction of the masses from awareness of the repression of man's historic possibilities which it practices on so vast a scale. (Cockburn and Blackburn, 1969:8)

The readiness of politicians in power to deceive the people sometimes appears to be their principal concern, as though honesty is the commodity most likely to endanger the body politic. Always, there appears to be some good (or bad) reason for making less than the whole truth available. Thus, of the Chernobyl nuclear disaster in the USSR Tony Benn says: 'Of course the reason it hasn't been widely publicised is simple: they are happy to criticise the Russians over their technical incompetence but not when it damages the case for nuclear power – that is when the technical loyalty of scientists overrides political one-upmanship.' (1990:248)

Once they had come to terms with it (Churchill never did), television offered enormous opportunities to politicians; as William Deedes said: 'No field of communications offers greater possibilities in the time at our disposal before an election to improve the public mood towards Government than that of broadcasting television. Their impact on the public mind is immense.' (Cockerell, 1988:82) And, of course, politicians quickly sought to have special television rights. Thus, Macmillan found it inconceivable that anyone should question the right of the Prime Minister to use television to address the nation at moments of national significance, although whether his contrived appearance on television with the visiting President Kennedy could be described in such a way is another matter altogether. Since both Wilson and Thatcher accused television, and especially the BBC, of bias against them it is conceivable that television was doing a reasonably impartial job. But impartiality is something politicians abhor. Both Eden at the time of Suez and Thatcher at the time of the Falklands War 'considered the country to be at war with our servicemen at risk: therefore the duty of broadcasters was to support Britain and maintain morale.' (Bolton, 1990:127)

Under Thatcher the New Right condemned permissiveness: that is, those activities especially associated with the decade of the 1960s which had released many of the inhibitions of an earlier age and had in consequence allowed a far greater questioning of the established order of things, a questioning which, by its very nature, was a danger to politicians. Yet, at the same time, under Thatcher a greater degree of permissiveness than ever before was permitted to business, with little government restraint or intervention of any kind. In other words, and as usual, permissiveness was acceptable for those who were seen as allies of the government, but not for others. 'What really distinguishes the modern Tories from the old, or Mrs Thatcher from Mr Heath, is that they want above all to win. Winning has become an obsession. For the Prime Minister, and all those budding Ministers to whom she sets an example, scruples and integrity of behaviour simply clutter the path to victory.' Now despite the fact that this judgement comes from a political opponent (Tam Dalyell) it does seem to reflect the atmosphere of the 1980s. He goes on to say: 'This Government [Thatcher's] has changed the ground rules, for the worse. It reflects a society in which the electorate in general expects the politicians to gull them.' (1987:43, 135)

Accountability, too often, is represented by ritual charades that have an appearance of public probing into the workings of government and the decision-making process, but little substance. The high point of this sort of deception comes with the twice-weekly fifteen-minute Prime Minister's question-time sessions in the House of Commons, which any well-briefed Prime Minister can handle without giving anything away, and which John Biffen has described as 'high circus'.

Denis Healey tells the story of how Richard Crossman, one of the most brilliant intellectuals in politics, made a mistake which caused immense Labour Party anger against him. 'Crossman was genuinely surprised when his announcement of an increase in charges on teeth and spectacles three days before the local elections in 1969 produced an explosion of anger in the Party.' (1989:330) What Healey does not go on to say is that manipulation is what a great deal of politics is about. All too often it is not the issue that matters to politicians, for in that they often have little choice anyway; it is the presentation. It just appeared possible at the beginning of the 1990s that the cynicism of politicians – 'What businessmen do not understand is that exactly as they are dealing in oil so I am dealing in votes' (Bottomore, 1966:114) – had become sufficiently resented by the British public at large as to set off a backlash that at least had a chance of producing some changes in both attitudes and methods. The growing public demand for political and constitutional reform that developed at the end of the 1980s demonstrated both a distrust of the existing system and a weariness with its current manipulators. A major poll conducted by MORI for the Joseph Rowntree Reform Trust in April 1991 showed that 63 per cent of voters thought the system needed 'quite a lot, or a great deal of improvement'. A majority thought that government power was too centralised, that rights were too easily changed, and that Parliament did not have enough control over government. There was general disillusionment with two-party politics and a clear majority for both proportional representation and a Bill of Rights, reforms which are not favoured by either of the main parties. (*Independent*, 25.4.91) For the first time in decades it appeared that reform just might be forced upon reluctant politicians from below, and principally because they are seen as divorced from any grass-roots contact with the people they supposedly represent. Mr Tony Benn's proposed Commonwealth of Britain Bill, with its constitutional reforms, the Charter 88 group of reformers, the Prime Minister John Major's idea of a citizen's charter, each in their different ways indicated that the 1990s might face the politicians with demands for reform that they could find irresistible. This is no more than an over-delayed reaction to a long period in which politicians who readily pay lip-service to British freedoms have in fact, by design or inertia, allowed them to be whittled away. Writing of his proposed reforms Tony Benn said:

It hardly ever occurs to . . . opinion formers that a contributory factor to our frustration might be the fact that at the very top of our society there is a great deal of flaunted privilege and power with very little accountability to anyone. We have been given a lopsided view of reality, and the reporting of our affairs has been confined primarily to the conduct of the principal actors on the political stage as they engage in the elaborate parliamentary shadow-boxing that often conceals an unspoken agreement about the main issues of the day. (*Independent*, 11.7.91)

Mr Benn, who has so often been deliberately marginalised by the combined efforts of the Conservative Party as well as his own, found for once that he was in the company of an increasing number of people tired with a system that is so manifestly manipulated by the minority on behalf of the few, rather than organised for the benefit of the many. Whether any real changes are achieved remains to be seen but at least there is growing and increasingly articulate public awareness of both the flawed nature of the existing system and the need for changes that will increase the accountability of the rulers to the ruled and enhance truly democratic processes.

Part Four
Conclusions

24 Truth and freedom

They have vanquished freedom and done so to make men happy – for nothing has ever been more insupportable for a man or a human society than freedom.

FYODOR DOSTOEVSKY

A s THE HISTORIAN, Lewis Namier, said; 'At every stage in social development freedom has to be reconquered.' Perhaps that has never been more true than in our present age, for the pressures to surrender freedom, always of course in the name of better government, greater security, the convenience of the community or any of the other arguments that are so readily advanced to justify the concentration of decision-making in the smallest number of hands, have never been greater. In the eighteenth century Thomas Paine set a precedent of appealing to the intelligence of the common man and he was not forgiven for this by the Establishment of his day. As Paine claimed, attacking a central shibboleth of his and later times, 'it is nevertheless true that the age of ignorance commenced with the Christian system. There was more knowledge in the world before that period than for many centuries afterwards.' Paine was concerned with truth and believed that organised religion – and many other aspects besides of the society in which he then lived – were antithetical to the truth. As he said: 'Truth never envelops *itself* in mystery; and the mystery in which it is at any time enveloped is the work of its antagonist, and never of itself.' (1937:33) That is as true today as it was in the eighteenth century. A belief in truth must assume a readiness to disbelieve passed-on truths: the 'revealed' truths so beloved of the doctrinaire, whether religious or political. 'The Catholic and the Communist', said Orwell, 'are alike in assuming that an opponent cannot be both honest and intelligent', since both claim truth has been revealed to them (1957:162), and although the Communist age has suddenly collapsed there is no lack of dogmatists to take the place of the Communists, with militant Islam at present in the vanguard. John Sparrow, with one of the sharpest minds of the present age, said people got angry when truth was thrust at them, for they do not want precision of truth but only generalities. (1966:65) Generalities encompass people broadly and give them comfort; precise truths disturb their lives and force them to face what they would prefer to ignore. When a segment of the established order is faced by a dangerous defection from its ranks, for example, it resorts to a variety of techniques in order to stifle or render innocuous the defector, as Charles Davis records of the Roman Catholic Church when he fell foul of it: censorship, disciplinary action, refusal of permissions, off-the-record telephone calls to newspapers, each used to prevent the emergence of new ideas or inconvenient questioning. (1967:73)

As Charles Davis said of truth: 'Man's relation to truth – at least in this world – is that of unwearying pursuit, not of final possession. This pursuit demands complete openness.' (26) Purists, of course, will argue that truth is to be pursued for its own sake, to which the pragmatist replies that the possession and, still more, the proclamation of the truth more often than not lead to harm rather than good, although this pragmatic argument, as a rule, comes from those who would defend the system and so fear change. Writers who refuse to sell their opinions, as Orwell claimed, are branded egoists or accused of shutting themselves in ivory towers, a phrase that has been used and over-used whenever a society has no answer to its critics: when there is no answer then damn the critics by suggesting they live in ivory towers and are out of touch with reality. Pursuit of the truth leads on naturally to a demand for freedom. Dostoevsky's Grand Inquisitor in *The Brothers Karamazov* spoke for all organised societies when he said he had vanquished freedom to make men happy, and although in Britain we have endless arguments about freedom, 'the controversy over freedom of speech and of the Press is at bottom a controversy over the desirability, or otherwise, of telling lies'. (Orwell, 1957:161) The endless pursuit of the book *Spycatcher* round the world by the British government drew from the Master of the Rolls, Lord Donaldson, the statement: 'The existence of a free press ... is an essential element in maintaining Parliamentary democracy and the British way of life as we know it.' Such a statement, even from so eminent a source, is unexceptionable, and given the constant way British politicians like to emphasise how free the country is (in comparison with other less fortunate lands) ought not to have needed saying at all. But it did need saying very badly indeed, for in almost inverse proportion as the Thatcher government spoke of British freedoms it clamped down upon those individuals, organisations or groups whose activities queried the growing power at the centre.

Organised societies and the élites or establishments which control them feel threatened by truth and truth-tellers, and all too often truth is subordinated to power and authority as, for example, when Clive Ponting described how a discussion in the Ministry of Defence about whether or not to cover up over the sinking of the *Belgrano* produced the decision (which he claims led to his own resignation) to cover up. Perhaps some individuals have a special role to expose falsehoods: there will, of course, always be more falsehoods than can ever be uncovered but if a sufficient number are uncovered often enough then at least the power brokers will be kept on their toes. Back in 1920 Walter Lippmann said, 'There can be no liberty for a community which lacks the means by which to detect lies', and the detection of lies is half the battle for the truth. Fashion has a great deal to do with both brainwashing and truth for 'Truth does not, and never has, come unadorned.' (Postman, 1985:23) Bertrand Russell spoke of 'immunity to eloquence', for he wished to distinguish between pleasure in language and the logic of the argument and that is sometimes far from easy to do. Often the greatest immediate enemies of truth and freedom of thought 'are the Press lords, the film magnates, and the bureaucrats, but that on a long view the weakening of the desire for liberty among the intellectuals themselves is the most serious symptom of all'. (Orwell, 1957:165) The essence of brainwashing is to manipulate people into accepting, if only passively, norms of behaviour which conveniently ignore or bypass awkward truths. Brainwashing makes evasion possible: evasion of truth and evasion of thought. When people succumb to this temptation they diminish both themselves and their society. One of the greatest casualties of the near half-century of the Cold War has been truth, but there are not many indications that in the process of the sorting out of a new world order which is now under way truth will fare any better. C. P. Snow had a high regard for scientists and once said of them: 'The remarkable thing is not the handful of scientists who deviate from the search for truth but the overwhelming numbers who keep to it. That is a demonstration, absolutely clear for anyone to see, of moral behaviour on a very large scale.' (1971:192) Now if we accept Snow's judgement on scientists without debating whether they are more or less moral than other groups because they tell the truth, the question to ask is why, if they can tell the truth, others cannot be persuaded to do so at least as often? It is an intriguing question and Snow is being somewhat disingenuous here, for he spent a good deal of his life in the 'corridors of power' among civil servants and must have seen that in career terms, for example, a scientist has to tell the truth if he is to advance while a civil servant is often trained to do the opposite and may rise to the top if he knows how and when to be 'economical with the truth'. And having said that, are scientists as a group any better men and women than civil servants as a group?

Diplomats lie abroad for their countries, and truth generally is the first casualty in war. Early in World War I (29 September 1914) a short story by Arther Machen appeared in the *Evening News*: called 'The Bowmen', it was a fantasy in which the author called upon the bowmen of Agincourt to come to England's aid. But a credulous public turned his mythical bowmen into the Angels at Mons and when the author disclaimed anything to do with angels and said, in effect, that he had written a fantasy, he was dismissed with further counter-claims, anger, and lies. Now, if people can be as foolish and credulous as that, brainwashing will have the field pretty much to itself as indeed it did during the course of that war. And, far more dangerous than the insistence that fantasies were real was the fact that disasters like Cambrai, which was due to bad staff work, continued to occur because the propagandists such as Belloc spent the war lying and covering up the truth. (Buitenhuis, 1987:103, 39)

Many terrible things were done in World War II but, for example, only very recently have some of them come to light, for the interest in covering up, at many different levels, has been profound. There has been the Tolstoy case, with accusations and counter-accusations about whether the British commanders were to blame in handing over Cossack and Chetnik prisoners to the Russians and Yugoslavs, since these prisoners were subsequently executed. There are the revelations, at long last, about the Katyn massacre of Polish officers by the Russians, a massacre that was long put down to the Nazis; despite the evidence to the contrary, this version was persisted in by the Foreign Office as late as 1988, although it had known the truth since 1943 when Owen O'Malley, the British ambassador to the Polish Government-in-exile, collected the evidence that placed a strong presumption of guilt upon the NKVD. But for political reasons of convenience and the desire to maintain a solid front with its wartime Russian allies, Britain suppressed the evidence and endorsed the Soviet Government's lies about the massacre and continued to do so for forty-five years. While it may be seen as excusable to lie over the issue during the war, to continue to do so afterwards – as much as anything to cover up for the Foreign Office – was not only morally inexcusable but a distortion of history as well. Nearer home, revelations about collaboration with the Germans in the Channel Islands, including assisting in applying the 'final solution' to Channel Island Jews, came to light only in 1991. Unfortunately, and not just in relation to national emergencies such as wars, the cover-up has long been an accepted way of behaviour.

Freedom might be described as truth's twin, but how much freedom do the citizens of Britain have as opposed to the regular pronouncements about British liberties which are indulged so often by politicians? Not many people talk of freedom as possessively as do the British and a foreigner might be pardoned for thinking Britain had invented the concept. Frequent references to the 'Mother of Parliaments', Magna Carta, habeas corpus, freedom of the press and other liberties imply that these are natural for Britons but not for many others. Writing in 1964, at the height of the Cold War, Raymond Blackburn said: 'In the West, with one or two happy exceptions, there is far less freedom for the individual than there was. Britain is typical of this erosion of freedom, and it has the least right to excuse itself for it.' (1964:9) At the 1989 Tory Party Conference in Blackpool, Mrs Thatcher claimed that her government were pioneers of world freedom, sweeping socialism from Britain and then inspiring the people of Eastern Europe to throw off their chains. That was to indulge in fantasy even by Thatcher's standards yet plenty of Britons would prefer to accept such a version of events than believe that Britain, whether by action or example, had in fact had very little to do with the ending of Communism in Eastern Europe.

Freedom of dissent has always been relative in Britain and the safest dissent has been orthodox in nature, launched from the ranks of the official or expected opposition to mainline policies. Unusual or logical dissent has thrown the Establishment into confusion because it has not known how to stifle it. D. N. Pritt, a brilliant lawyer from an upper-class English background, who was able by argument to reduce Lord Hailsham to silence; Raymond Blackburn, a Labour MP who turned his first-class mind to the way in which the government of the day permitted the erosion of freedom; Bertrand Russell, the scion of an old aristocratic family championing the lost causes of pacifism and the CND; Enoch Powell, a high Tory whose 'logic' once led him to advise members of his own party to vote Labour; Tony Benn, whose calls for socialist measures have infuriated the party that should be carrying them out: the list is an intriguing one and such individuals have an especially important role to play in a society which goes to great lengths to extol the trappings of freedom while it often smothers the reality.

Enoch Powell's appeal is derived from a curious mixture: his interest in apparently lost causes that few understand; and his championing, no matter in how unorthodox a fashion, of popular fears about issues such as immigration or Europe. A man of paradox, Powell caused his own party to disown him, not least because he articulated what many of them wished to hear but were restrained from saying, since to do so went against the orthodoxy of the time. But, as is usual in such a case, the contradictions are hard to reconcile. It is, despite the myth of Powell the man of logic, very difficult to argue that his logic and his opposition to immigrants can be matched: 'I will always set my face like flint against making any difference between one citizen of this country and another on grounds of his origin', he said (Foot, 1969:104), but such a statement is not to be reconciled with the thrust of his notorious speech of 20 April 1968 in which, for example, he gave an unsubstantiated story of an old lady in Wolver-hampton who had excreta pushed through her letter-box. That speech got for Powell major publicity and dismissal from the Shadow Cabinet, and although he subsequently denied that he was a racialist, claiming indeed the reverse ('What I take a racialist to mean is a person who believes in the inherent inferiority of one race of mankind to another, and who acts and speaks in that belief. So the answer to the question of whether I am a racialist is no – unless, perhaps, it is to be a racialist in reverse.' [Cosgrave, 1989:9]) Such a speech is almost impossible to accept in any context except that of racialism. *The Sunday Times* said of his Birmingham speech: 'His latest speech no doubt accurately represents Wolverhampton's fears of being swamped by immigrants. But its unreliable statistical projections and its tones of lurid menace are irresponsible.' (Cosgrave, 1989:243) The myth of Powell, the man of logic, is part of his attraction yet in that same speech he tells of a constituent's fears of blacks in Britain and says: 'Here is a decent, ordinary fellow Englishman, who in broad daylight in my own constituency says to me, his Member of Parliament, that this country will not be worth living in for his children. I simply do not have the right to shrug my shoulders and think about something else.' That passage is worth analysing for the techniques it employs: the use of the words 'decent' and 'ordinary' to describe a 'fellow Englishman' who approaches his Member of Parliament 'in broad daylight' (nothing underhand about this chap) to tell him that the country will not be worth living in for his children. That, of course, is a matter of opinion but the entire passage is designed to create an emotive atmosphere far removed from anything to do with either logic or, indeed, accuracy. The fact that a constituent tells Enoch Powell in broad daylight that the country will not be worth living in for his children (because of the presence of Blacks in the community) is neither more nor less than a single individual's reaction to the presence of an ethnic minority in the country and carries no more and no less weight than any other comparable view. From that time onwards Powell had excluded himself from the possibility of high office; thereafter, he sought other causes to champion and ended, most notably, championing the right of Ulster to remain part of the Union. Over Ulster at least his logic was impeccable: Ulster is part of the United Kingdom and, therefore, should be treated as such. The consequence of that belief is that there should be no discussions about its future and no form of liaison with the Dublin government. Powell, whom his contemporary Iain Macleod said suffered from an excess of logic, was at least precisely logical in this particular regard. His belief in the unique nature of Britain has made him a champion of the Constitution:

> From the common root of the feudal court there grew and flourished in the special conditions of Britain alone, by a kind of ecological exception, the institution of Parliament. The British are a parliamentary nation: internally and externally they are conditioned and defined by that institution and that historical experience. (*Hansard*, 19.12.74)

The mixture of brainwashing (the Birmingham speech), logic (Ulster) or exaggerated reverence for the British parliamentary system which is now demonstrably creaking at the joints (brainwashing again) make Powell an especially interesting object of study. In India during the war, when travelling in Bihar, Powell records: 'It struck me almost as a blinding revelation that I was the only Englishman within thirty, forty, maybe fifty or sixty miles, and *that this was a part of the natural order of things*.' (Cosgrave, 1989:87) It would be hard to find a better instance of self-brainwashing than that, yet this is the man the British so often portray as 'too logical'. The reactions to Powell are certainly paradoxical.

Public lying to achieve a particular end is an art form in Britain.

Tito, who in his way was as ruthless a dictator as they come, was painted very differently in Britain through most of the Cold War because he had stood up successfully to Stalin and it suited Britain's policy to make him out to be something that he was not. When the life of the Central African Federation (the Rhodesias and Nyasaland) was coming under increasing strain from the opposition Black majority, the government invented a 'massacre plot' in Nyasaland to justify arresting the nationalist dissidents although, for once, outrage in Britain over a colonial issue forced the government to hold a commission of inquiry which found there was no plot. Cover-up may be achieved by the simple expedient of not asking the right questions, an expedient which was used in the Denning Report on the Profumo scandal. (Young, 1963:110–11) Over the Skybolt missile which Britain urgently needed for its nuclear delivery system, the Macmillan government repeatedly told Parliament there was no reason to suppose that the United States was going to cancel its manufacture. Yet a senior British officer involved in the negotiations between Britain and the United States later revealed that there was no occasion when the Americans had not warned that it might be cancelled and government clearly lied to the House of Commons. (Young, 1963:108)

When Emperor Hirohito of Japan finally died in January 1991, controversy erupted in Britain over the decision to send Prince Philip to his funeral, leading Sir Geoffrey Howe (Deputy Prime Minister) to insist that this did not mean Japanese war crimes had been 'forgotten or forgiven'. If the war crimes had not been forgotten or forgiven, and clearly the intention was that they should continue not to be overlooked, then it would have been best to send no one at all. Hirohito was as guilty of war crimes, in his approving role as Emperor of Japan, as those who actually ordered and implemented the policies but it suited the West after the war to use Hirohito as a symbol to unite the new Japan, so his past record was ignored.

Lies and half-truths and evasions have become so much a part of the Ulster story that howls of rage greeted the new Secretary of State for Northern Ireland, Peter Brooke, when he said in 1989 that it was 'difficult to envisage' a military defeat for the IRA and drew a parallel with EOKA in Cyprus during the 1950s. When he went on to say that the government should be prepared to talk with Sinn Fein if it renounced violence he made matters worse. It is one of the ironies of our age that when a politician actually tells the truth (at least as he sees it) he is howled down, for we no longer assume that politics are related to the truth and the public is bemused when it is treated to a bit of this rare commodity.

During the 1980s both truth and freedom were hard pressed in Britain and the list of subjects affected – Ulster, freedom of speech, the sinking of the *Belgrano*, the Westland affair, *Spycatcher*, the Wallace affair – grew longer as the Thatcher prime ministership continued, so that 'being economical with the truth' appeared to have become second nature in government circles with Downing Street giving the lead. In few areas was the British record for upholding freedoms so tarnished as in that pertaining to refugees and asylum-seekers: whether it was the manner in which Britain denied the right of abode to Hong Kong Chinese who as 'citizens of the United Kingdom and colonies' were entitled to British passports, the forced return of the boat people to Vietnam (a country Britain was only too ready to castigate for its poor human-rights record) despite any claims about human rights to the contrary, or the increasingly restrictive regulations applied to anyone seeking residence in Britain, the attitude was always the same, that freedoms and rights cease to be enforceable or indeed to matter much when they pertain to people other than our white British selves. Perhaps Britain's behaviour over these questions, more than anything else, signalled the final 'end of empire' and retreat into a rather nasty and dishonest 'little England'.

Possibly the greatest 'untruth' that will be converted into a myth during the 1990s will be that the end of the Cold War and collapse of Communism was a Western achievement, the result of the kind of steadfastness on behalf of liberty that the 'iron lady' liked to believe was her hallmark, while we hastily forget how we gave honours to such representatives of oppression as Romania's Ceausescu. The auguries are not good. Authoritarian governments tend to use their powers more openly and nakedly than do democracies, with the result that their peoples expect little except repression from them. In Britain, on the other hand, talk of freedom is too often matched by manipulation, and the denial of rights (in relation to trade-union membership at the Cheltenham GCHQ, for example, or the broadcasting ban on IRA apologists, or the change in the 'right to silence' in court) is explained away by endless references to national security or terrorism. Real freedom is always painful, principally because it demands standards of behaviour that are difficult to apply and much easier to ignore or bypass. And sadly, it is not just the government or the politicians who are to blame for the steady erosion of liberties that has taken place in Britain since 1945. It is also the British people themselves, for too often and too readily have they accepted or at least condoned anti-libertarian actions by their governments. Moreover, they have failed to insist as they should upon freedom of information: 'Above all, however, there is no great demand for freedom of information in this country. The British seem strangely indifferent, confusing it with freedom of speech.' (Bolton, 1990:304) Surrender is usually easier and more tempting than resistance, and this is especially the case when an immediate assault upon freedom is not upon us all but only upon an individual or group which, for whatever reason, is seen by the majority to be an outsider or a potential threat. Thus do repressive governments always work. Freedom and truth demand perpetual vigilance and *thought*, for only the application of thought to these matters can demonstrate just what and how much is at stake. And here the last word can be given to Bertrand Russell: 'Men fear thought as they fear nothing else on earth – more than ruin, more even than death.'

Conclusion

To have contemplated human life for forty years is
the same as to have contemplated it for ten
thousand years. For what more wilt thou see?

MARCUS AURELIUS

I N THE COUNTRY OF THE BLIND the one-eyed man is not king but is taken
to be 'an hallucinated lunatic'. The problems of brainwashing are
twofold: those who are in a position to do so will brainwash or
manipulate those they see as their natural targets; and those who
are brainwashed are often happy to remain in such a state since the
alternative of facing difficult and sometimes awful truths is too painful.
One inescapable fact emerges from any study of Britain in recent times:
that ideals about tolerance or freedom or liberty operate best *in
absentia*, as abstract goals that are approved in theory, although the
moment they have to be applied in practice they are rejected or, if not
rejected outright, so distorted and controlled as to be deprived of their
essential value. Thus, we have long persuaded ourselves that we believe
in ideals which in practice we rarely apply or at any rate rarely apply
to their full extent and value. As psychologists like to point out,
torturers and the tortured need each other; similarly, brainwashers of
all kinds would not get far without willing subjects and, perhaps, the
most depressing question which an inquiry such as this raises is what
would happen if brainwashing were to be eliminated? What would
we put in its place? How would people behave who were washed clean
of past brainwashing and really did have to think out problems for
themselves? Perhaps, like the civilised people in Huxley's *Island*, they
would find the outside world of the brainwashing manipulators
forcibly returning in order to make them like everyone else. And if, in
fact, that is what would most likely happen, it represents a sorry
judgement upon humanity.

It is the invasion of the privacy of the mind which is the real offence
of brainwashing, yet if people are willing to be brainwashed maybe
that is because there is nothing else there, so that it becomes a form
of intellectual arrogance, itself a kind of brainwashing, to imagine that
people could get by without such manipulation of their lives. Richard

Deacon suggests as follows: 'In most democracies it is realised that once the people learn that they have been deceived by their leaders, their faith in them is permanently destroyed, often even if the reason for the deception was a good one.' (1986:15) That seems a facile judgement and the evidence points the other way: that those who are deceived none the less come back again and again for more. Now if people keep returning to the same political leaders – as they do – how much more do they also keep returning to the same ideologies or religions. There is little evidence that people learn from past mistakes, and a great deal to suggest that they keep turning to the same expedients despite their proven inability to solve problems.

'Outside human desires', said Bertrand Russell, 'there is no morality' and few people are interested in principle any more, at least to the extent of pushing it beyond their personal comfort. What people want, in an increasingly overcrowded and brutal world, is as much comfort as they can find, and it is in such circumstances that brainwashing in its many manifestations comes into its own. More and more, it seems, we live in an age of organised 'norms' or bites. People do not watch television so much as 'graze, zapping back and forth between channels'; we take in three or four products during advertising breaks; politicians don't any more make speeches but fill in television opportunities; everything in fact is geared to television, the quick appearance, the ready fix, the appreciation of how short the attention span has become. (*Independent*, 7.1.89) Marketing, advertising, cleverness, the quick bite which assumes the short attention span, these characteristics of the age in which we live are antithetical to intellect, contemplation, individuality. They are the stuff of brainwashing if only because they assume that everyone is hooked on such an approach to information of all kinds. Surrender to brainwashing is easy and even those who pride themselves on their capacity to resist the blandishments of the media age fall victims to subtler assaults on the mind. The greatest hope might appear to be that people will become bored with the activities of the Establishment, but that possibility was foreseen long ago by our élites, who are masters of the technique of 'buying in': never be exclusive despite endless talk of exclusivity; the most intelligent or aggressive enemies of the system have to be beguiled and brought into its upper ranks, then they can use their intelligence to devise new methods of brainwashing the outsiders.

In his book *Battle for the Mind*, William Sargant admits defeat right at the beginning when he says in his opening paragraph: 'It must be emphasised as strongly as possible that this book is *not* concerned with the truth or falsity of any particular religions or political belief.' Now by excepting those two classes of belief before he begins Sargant in essence is admitting that he accepts manipulation in those areas, no matter how mistaken or false it may be. He continues to claim that he is concerned only to examine the mechanisms used to fix or destroy such beliefs. 'My concern here is *not* with the immortal soul, which is the province of the theologian, nor even with the mind in the broadest sense of the word which is the province of the philosopher, but with the brain and nervous system, which man shares with the dog and other animals.' (1957:9) Since the brain, which does concern Sargant, is the receptor of all brainwashing it is difficult to see how he can make his enormous exceptions, since the 'truth' and 'falsity' of the systems he does not wish to comment upon are arrived at by the very processes he examines. It is as though Sargant is terrified of upsetting the religious and political prejudices of his readers: 'you may keep those dearly held prejudices, many of which are the obvious result of brainwashing, for I am only going to examine techniques in the abstract, then no one need be offended.' Too often, indeed, those who write about the process of brainwashing either make exceptions – *we* are not brainwashed about our religion or philosophy of life but *other* creeds are the result of brainwashing manipulation; or, they suggest that it happens 'out there' – to *them* (whoever they might be) but not to us. British intellectuals, in their superior way, seem more prone to this kind of assumption than do their American counterparts, for example, and repeatedly, over a wide range of activities, the British convince themselves that others are wrong, dishonest or brainwashed – but never themselves.

Contrary to the images of brainwashing we have inherited from the Cold War, the really insidious kind is more likely to be the manipulations of Dostoevsky's Grand Inquisitor 'to make us happy'. As William Whyte wrote in the mid-1950s, when Cold War hysteria was at its height: 'But in the other kind of 1984 one would be disarmed for not knowing who the enemy was, and when the day of reckoning came the people on the other side of the table wouldn't be Big Brother's bad henchmen; they would be a mild-looking group of therapists who, like the Grand Inquisitor, would be doing what they did to help you.' (1956:34)

Knowledge is power, and if people know what is going on and understand the techniques of manipulation that are employed then they can say no. Whether they will say no is another matter. Tolerance ought to mean the protection of dissent and opposed views, but too often it means no more than an acceptance of a damaging status quo that needs to be overthrown. The stoic Roman Emperor, Marcus Aurelius, who laid claim to being a philosopher, argued that forty years was enough to understand what drives our world: 'He who is forty years old, if he has any understanding at all, has seen by virtue of the uniformity that prevails all things which have been and all that will be.' (1956:140) The Emperor, of course, appeals to the intellect, and inherent in such thinking must be a rejection of manipulation, for it is the power of reasoning which distinguishes man above all other living creatures, and if he allows outside forces to usurp his powers of reasoning then he surrenders the quality which makes him unique. The Venerable Bede, writing his *Ecclesiastical History of the English Nation* early in the eighth century, makes a similar point to Marcus Aurelius, although from a very different standpoint. In a charming, almost lyrical, passage he likens our journey through the world to the flight of a sparrow:

> The present life of man, O King, seems to me, in comparison of that time which is unknown to us, like to the swift flight of a sparrow through the room wherein you sit at supper in winter, with your commanders and ministers, and a good fire in the midst, whilst the storms of rain and snow prevail abroad; the sparrow, I say, flying in at one door, and immediately out at another, whilst he is within, is safe from the wintry storm; but after a short space of fair weather, he immediately vanishes out of your sight, into the dark winter from which he had emerged. So this life of man appears for a short space, but of what went before, or what is to follow, we are utterly ignorant.

It would seem a pity that man should be subjected to brainwashing on his brief flight through the lighted hall.

In the end, of course, we are left with a number of open questions: can we escape brainwashing? Do we want to escape it or is it the essential fix that makes life bearable? Which in the end do we prefer: the manipulations of the Grand Inquisitor to make us happy, or, by accepting brainwashing, do we despise 'the choicest gift of God to men – The GIFT OF REASON'? (Paine, 1937:20)

Bibliography

Abse, Leo (1989) *Margaret, Daughter of Beatrice* Jonathan Cape.
Allen, Charles (1977) *Raj. A Scrapbook of British India 1877–1947* André Deutsch.
Anderson, Bruce (1991) *John Major* Fourth Estate.
Andrews, Kay and Jacobs, John (1990) *Punishing the Poor* Macmillan.
Arnold, Bruce (1984) *Margaret Thatcher, A Study in Power* Hamish Hamilton.
Arnold, Guy (1989) *Britain Since 1945* Cassell.
—— (1991) *Wars in the Third World Since 1945* Cassell.
Article 19 (1989) 'No Comment: Censorship, Secrecy and the Irish Troubles'.
—— (1991) 'Freedom of Expression and Information in the United Kingdom'.
Attlee, Clement (Earl) KG PC OM CH (1961) *Empire into Commonwealth* OUP.
Aurelius, Marcus (1956) *Meditations* Gateway.
Barker, Ernest (1958) *Reflections on Government* Galaxy (first published in 1942).
Bede, The Venerable (c. 731) *The Ecclesiastical History of the English Nation* Dutton (Everyman Library 1910).
Benn, Tony (1987) *Out of the Wilderness (Diaries Vol. 1, 1963–67)* Hutchinson.
—— (1988) *Office Without Power (Diaries Vol. 2, 1968–72)* Hutchinson.
—— (1989) *Against the Tide (Diaries Vol. 3, 1973–76)* Hutchinson.
—— (1990) *Conflicts of Interest (Diaries Vol. 4, 1977–80)* Hutchinson.
Berkeley, Humphry (1968) *The Power of the Prime Minister* George Allen & Unwin.
Blackburn, Raymond (1964) *The Erosion of Freedom* Times Press.

Bolton, Roger (1990) *Death on the Rock and Other Stories* W. H. Allen.

Bonheur, Gaston (1963) *Qui a cassé le vase de Soissons?* Robert Laffont.

Bottomore, T. B. (1966) *Elites and Society* Penguin.

Brooke, Richard (1990) in the *Observer* 29.10.90.

Brown, J. A. C. (1961) *Freud and the Post-Freudians* Penguin.

—— (1963) *Techniques of Persuasion* Penguin.

Bryant, Arthur (Sir) (1990) *The Search for Justice* Collins.

Buckman, Peter (1970) *The Limits of Protest* Panther.

Buitenhuis, Peter (1987) *The Great War of Words* University of British Columbia Press.

Bunyan, Tony (1976) *The Political Police in Britain* Julian Friedmann.

Burgess, Anthony (1962) *A Clockwork Orange* Heinemann.

Calder, Angus and Sheridan, Dorothy (1984) *Speak for Yourself* Jonathan Cape.

Callaghan, James (1987) *Time and Chance* Collins.

Callander, Thomas (1961) *The Athenian Empire and the British* Weidenfeld & Nicolson.

Carmichael, Stokeley and Hamilton, Charles V. (1968) *Black Power* Jonathan Cape.

Carrington, C. E. (1961) *The Liquidation of the British Empire* Clarke, Irwin & Co.

Carrington, Peter (Lord) (1988) *Reflect on Things Past* (Memoirs) Collins.

Carvel, John (1984) *Citizen Ken* Chatto & Windus.

Cattell, Raymond B. (1965) *The Scientific Analysis of Personality* Penguin.

Chardin, Pierre Teilhard de (1964) *The Future of Man* Translated from the French by Norman Denny. Collins (France: 1959).

Clark, William (1957) *Less than Kin* Boston: Houghton Mifflin.

Clarke, Peter (1991) *A Question of Leadership* Hamish Hamilton.

Cockburn, Alexander and Blackburn, Robin (1969) editors *Student Power* Penguin.

Cockerell, Michael (1988) *Live from Number 10* Faber & Faber.

COI (1988) *Britain 1988: An Official Handbook* HMSO.

Coleman, Terry (1987) *Thatcher's Britain* Bantam Press.

—— (1990a) in the *Independent* 26 May.

—— (1990b) in the *Independent* 29 May.

—— (1990c) in the *Independent* 4 June.

Coleman, Terry (1990d) in the *Independent* 1 September.

Condon, Richard (1960) *The Manchurian Candidate* Pan Books.

Cosgrave, Patrick (1989) *The Lives of Enoch Powell* The Bodley Head.

Crawshay-Williams, Rupert (1970) *Russell Remembered* OUP.

Critchley, Julian (1987) *Heseltine: The Unauthorised Biography* André Deutsch.

Cross, Colin (1968) *The Fall of the British Empire* Hodder & Stoughton.

Cruickshank, Charles (1977) *The Fourth Arm Psychological Warfare* Davis-Poynter.

Dalyell, Tam (1987) *Misrule* Hamish Hamilton.

—— (1986) '10 Downing St, Chief Information Officer' *Hansard* 28 April.

Daniel, W. W. (1968) *Racial Discrimination in England* Penguin.

Davis, Charles (1967) *A Question of Conscience* Hodder & Stoughton.

Deacon, Richard (1986) *The Truth Twisters* Macdonald.

Deeley, Peter (1971) *Beyond Breaking Point* Arthur Barker Limited.

Dorril, Stephen and Ramsay, Robin (1991) *Smear: Wilson and the Secret State* Fourth Estate.

Eden, Anthony (Sir) (1960) *Full Circle* Cassell.

Eldridge, John (1987) *Mass Media, Public Opinion and Democracy* British Association for the Advancement of Science.

Eysenck, H. J. (1953) *Uses and Abuses of Psychology* Penguin.

—— (1957) *Sense and Nonsense in Psychology* Penguin.

—— (1965) *Facts and Fiction in Psychology* Penguin.

Fabian Society (1991) *Labour and Whitehall*.

Fairlie, Henry (1962) 'The BBC', in Thomas (1962).

Fisher, Nigel (1973) *Iain Macleod* André Deutsch.

Fleming, Gerald (1985) *Hitler and the Final Solution* Hamish Hamilton.

Foot, Hugh (Lord Caradon) (1964) *A Start in Freedom* Hodder & Stoughton.

Foot, Paul (1965) *Immigration and Race in British Politics* Penguin.

—— (1969) *The Rise of Enoch Powell* Penguin.

Forster, E. M. (1947) 'The Machine Stops' in *Collected Short Stories* Penguin.

Franks, The Rt Hon. Lord OM GCMG KCB CBE (1983) *Falkland Islands Review* HMSO.

Freedman, Lawrence and Gamba-Stonehouse, Virginia (1990) *Signals of War* Faber & Faber.

Gelber, Lionel (1961) *America in Britain's Place* Frederick A. Praeger.

Gelber, Lionel (1966) *The Alliance of Necessity* Robert Hale.

Glasgow University Media Group (GUMG) (1989a) 'Speak No Evil: The Broadcasting Ban, the Media and the Conflict in Ireland', extract published in the *Guardian* 15 October 1989.

—— (1989b) David Miller in the *Irish Times* 18 October 1989.

Green, Jonathan (1990) *Them* Secker & Warburg.

Gunn, John (1962) *The Immortals* Bantam Books.

Hailsham, Quinton (Viscount) (1959) *The Conservative Case* (revised) Penguin.

Hamilton, Willie (1975) *My Queen and I* Quartet.

Harris, Kenneth (1988) *Thatcher* Weidenfeld & Nicolson.

Harris, Robert (1988) in the *Observer* 30 October.

Harrisson, Tom (1976) *Living Through the Blitz* Collins.

Harrisson, Tom and Madge, Charles (1939) *Britain by Mass Observation* Penguin.

Hartley, Anthony (1963) *A State of England* Hutchinson.

Hayter, William (Sir) (1960) *The Diplomacy of the Great Powers* Hamish Hamilton.

Healey, Denis (1989) *The Time of My Life* Michael Joseph.

—— (1990) *When Shrimps Learn to Whistle* Michael Joseph.

Hennessy, Peter (1991) *Whitehall* Secker & Warburg.

Hennessy, Peter and Seldon, Anthony (1987) editors *Ruling Performance* Basil Blackwell.

Heseltine, Michael (1987) *Where There's a Will* Hutchinson.

—— (1989) *The Challenge of Europe: Can Britain Wait?* Weidenfeld & Nicolson.

Hewitt, Patricia (1982) *The Abuse of Power* Martin Robertson.

Hill, Andrew and Wichelow, Anthony (1964) *What's Wrong with Parliament* Penguin.

Himmelweit, Hilde T., Oppenheim A. M. and Vince, Pamela (1958) *Television and the Child* OUP.

Hitler, Adolf (1943) *Mein Kampf* (first published 1925) Houghton Mifflin.

Hobson, J. A. (1902) *Imperialism: A Study* George Allen & Unwin.

Hoggart, Richard (1957) *The Uses of Literacy* Penguin.

Holmes, Colin (1988) *John Bull's Island* Macmillan.

Horne, Alistair (1988) *Macmillan 1894–1956* (Vol. I official biography) Macmillan.

—— (1989) *Macmillan 1957–1988* (Vol. II official biography) Macmillan.

Howard, Anthony (1990) *Crossman: The Pursuit of Power* Jonathan Cape.

Hutchinson, Michael and Young, Christopher (1962) *Educating the Intelligent* Penguin.

Huxley, Aldous (1948) *Ape and Essence* Harper & Bros.

—— (1955) *Brave New World* Penguin (1932).

—— (1958) *Brave New World Revisited* Harper & Bros.

—— (1961) *The Devils of Loudun* Chatto & Windus.

—— (1964) *Island* Penguin.

Ignatieff, Michael (1991) in the *Observer* 10 November.

Inglis, Brian (1965) *Private Conscience Public Morality* Four Square.

Innes, Michael (1956) *Appleby Plays Chicken* Penguin.

Jackson, Brian and Marsden, Dennis (1962) *Educating the Working Class* Penguin.

Jackson, George (1971) *Soledad Brother* Jonathan Cape.

Jennings, Anthony (1988) in the *Independent* 20 October.

Kelly, Richard H. (1989) *Conservative Party Conferences (The Hidden System)* Manchester University Press.

Keynes, J. M. (1949) *Two Memoirs: Dr Melchior: A Defeated Enemy and My Early Beliefs* Rupert Hart-Davis.

King-Hall, Stephen (Commander Sir) (1962) *Power Politics in the Nuclear Age* Victor Gollancz.

Koestler, Arthur (1963) editor *Suicide of a Nation* Hutchinson.

Kyle, Keith (1991) *Suez* Weidenfeld & Nicolson.

Lederer, William J. (1961) *A Nation of Sheep* New York: W. W. Norton & Co. Inc.

Letwin, Oliver (1988) *Privatising the World* Cassell.

Lewis, Roy and Foy, Yvonne (1971) *The British in Africa* Weidenfeld & Nicolson.

Linne, Olga (1991) 'Journalistic practices and news coverage of environmental issues' *The Nordicon Review* No. 1.

Macbeath, A. and Westmann, H. (1955) editors *Man in his Relationships* Routledge & Kegan Paul.

Machiavelli, Niccolò (1940) *The Prince* Random House, The Modern Library.

Mackenzie, W. J. M. (1967) *Politics and Social Science* Penguin.

MacLeish, Archibald (1956) *JB* Riverside Press.

McLuhan, Marshall (1951) *The Mechanical Bride: Folklore of Industrial Man* Routledge & Kegan Paul.

—— (1962) *The Gutenberg Galaxy* Routledge & Kegan Paul.

Bibliography

McLuhan, Marshall (1964) *Understanding Media* Routledge & Kegan Paul.
—— (1967) *The Medium is the Massage* Allen Lane, The Penguin Press.
Mander, John (1963) *Great Britain or Little England* Secker & Warburg.
Marcuse, Herbert (1969) *An Essay on Liberation* Beacon Press.
Marquand, David (1988) *The Unprincipled Society* Jonathan Cape.
Marx, Karl and Engels, Friederich (1848) Communist Manifesto.
Mazrui, Ali (1990) *Cultural Forces in World Politics* James Currey/ Heinemann.
Mercer, Derrik, Mungham, Geoff and Williams, Kevin (1987) *The Fog of War* Heinemann.
Middleton, Drew (1957) *The British* Pan Books.
—— (1963) *The Supreme Choice* Secker & Warburg.
Miller, David (1990) 'The history behind a mistake' *British Journalism Review* Vol. 1, No. 2 *Winter.*
Mills, C. Wright (1958) *The Power Elite* New York: OUP.
Morris, Colin (1969) *Unyoung Uncoloured Unpoor* Epworth Press.
Morris, Desmond (1967) *The Naked Ape* Jonathan Cape.
Morris, James (1968) *Pax Britannica* Faber & Faber.
—— (1973) *Heaven's Command* Faber & Faber.
—— (1978) *Farewell the Trumpets* Faber & Faber.
Nicholson, Max (1967) *The System* Hodder & Stoughton.
Nutting, Anthony (PC) (1960) *Europe Will Not Wait* Hollis & Carter.
O'Brien, Conor Cruise (1970) *Camus* Fontana/Collins.
Orwell, George (1945) *Animal Farm* Penguin.
—— (1954) *Nineteen Eighty-Four* Penguin (1949).
—— (1957) *Selected Essays* Penguin.
Packard, Vance (1959) *The Status Seekers* New York: David McKay Company Inc.
—— (1960a) *The Hidden Persuaders* Penguin (1957).
—— (1960b) *The Waste Makers* New York: David McKay Company Inc.
Page, Bruce, Leitch, David and Knightley, Phillip (1969) *Philby: The Spy Who Betrayed a Generation* Penguin.
Paine, Thomas (1973) *The Age of Reason* The Pioneer Press.
Pannikar, K. M. (1953) *Asia and Western Dominance* George Allen & Unwin.
Parsons, Anthony (1984) *The Pride and the Fall* Jonathan Cape.
Part, Antony (1990) *The Making of a Mandarin* André Deutsch.

Pavlov, Ivan (1928) *Lectures on Conditioned Reflexes (Vol. I)* Lawrence & Wishart.

—— (1941) *Lectures on Conditioned Reflexes (Vol. II)* Lawrence & Wishart.

Pearson, Geoffrey (1983) *Hooligan* Macmillan.

Pedley, Robin (1963) *The Comprehensive School* Penguin.

Ponting, Clive (1986) *Whitehall: Tragedy and Farce* Hamish Hamilton.

—— (1989) *Breach of Promise: Labour in Power 1964–1970* Hamish Hamilton.

—— (1990) *1940: Myth and Reality* Hamish Hamilton.

Postman, Neil (1985) *Amusing Ourselves to Death* Methuen.

Prior, James (1986) *A Balance of Power* Hamish Hamilton.

Pritt, D. N. (1965) *From Right to Left* (autobiography) Lawrence & Wishart.

—— (1966a) *Brasshats and Bureaucrats* (autobiography) Lawrence & Wishart.

—— (1966b) *The Defence Accuses* (autobiography) Lawrence & Wishart.

—— (1970) *Law, Class and Society* (Book One *Employers, Workers and Trade Unions*) Lawrence & Wishart.

—— (1971a) *Law, Class and Society* (Book Two *The Apparatus of the Law*) Lawrence & Wishart.

—— (1971b) *Law, Class and Society* (Book Three *Law and Politics and Law in the Colonies*) Lawrence & Wishart.

Quigley, Isabel (1982) *The Heirs of Tom Brown* Chatto & Windus.

Radcliffe, Lord (1952) *The Problem of Power* Secker & Warburg.

Rodney, Walter (1969) *The Groundings with My Brothers* Bogle L'Ouverture Publications.

Russell, Bertrand (1956) *Portraits from Memory* George Allen & Unwin.

—— (1957) *Why I Am Not a Christian* George Allen & Unwin.

Salisbury, Bishop of *et al.* (1982) *The Church and the Bomb* Hodder & Stoughton.

Sampson, Anthony (1962) *Anatomy of Britain* Hodder & Stoughton.

—— (1971) *The New Anatomy of Britain* Hodder & Stoughton.

Sargant, William (1957) *Battle for the Mind* Pan Books.

Segal, Ronald (1966) *The Race War* Jonathan Cape.

Shanks, Michael (1961) *The Stagnant Society* Penguin.

Smith, Trevor (assisted by Alison Thomson) (1972) *Anti-Politics: Consensus, Reform and Protest in Britain* Charles Knight.

Snow, C. P. (1960) *Science and Government* Harvard University Press.

—— (1961) *The Two Cultures and the Scientific Revolution* New York: Cambridge University Press.

—— (1971) *Public Affairs* (collection) Macmillan.

Sparrow, John (1966) *Controversial Essays* Faber & Faber.

—— (1981) *Words on the Air* Collins.

Speer, Albert (1976) *Spandau: The Secret Diaries* Collins.

Spinola, Baruch (1955) *Ethics* Everyman (J. M. Dent).

Stalker, John (1988) *Stalker* Harrap.

Steel, David (1969) *No Entry* C. Hurst.

Sunday Times Insight Team (1982) *The Falklands War* Sphere Books.

Sutherland, Douglas (1988) *Portrait of a Decade* Harrap.

Tawney, R. H. (1961) *The Acquisitive Society* Fontana (G. Bell, 1921).

Taylor, G. Rattray (1968) *The Biological Time Bomb* Thames & Hudson.

—— (1979) *The Natural History of the Mind* Secker & Warburg.

Tebbit, Norman (1988) *Upwardly Mobile* Weidenfeld & Nicolson.

Temple, William (Archbishop of York) (1942) *Christianity and Social Order* Penguin.

Thomas, Donald (1969) *A Long Time Burning* Routledge & Kegan Paul.

Thomas, Hugh (1962) editor *The Establishment* The New English Library/ACE (Anthony Blond, 1959).

Thomson, Andrew (1989) *Margaret Thatcher, The Woman Within* W. H. Allen.

Thornton, A. P. (1959) *The Imperial Idea and its Enemies* Macmillan.

Thornton, Peter (1989) 'Decade of Decline' Liberty (NCCL).

Thorpe, D. R. (1989) *Selwyn Lloyd* Jonathan Cape.

Trevor-Roper, Hugh (1978) *The Goebbels Diaries* Secker & Warburg.

Veblen, Thorstein (1899) *The Theory of the Leisure Class* Mentor.

Waley, Arthur (1962) translator *170 Chinese Poems* Constable & Co. (1918).

Ward, Barbara (1957) *The Interplay of East and West* George Allen & Unwin.

—— (1959) *Five Ideas that Change the World* W. W. Norton.

—— (1961) *The Rich Nations and the Poor Nations* CBC.

Watson, Peter (1978) *War on the Mind* Hutchinson.

Weldon, T. D. (1953) *The Vocabulary of Politics* Penguin.

Whitaker, Ben (1964) *The Police* Penguin.

Whyte, William H. Jr (1956) *The Organization Man* Doubleday Anchor.

Williams, Raymond (1962) *Communications* Penguin.

—— (1989) *Resources of Hope* Verso.

Wilson, A. N. (1991) article in the *Standard* 24 May.

Wilson, Harold (1964) *The Relevance of British Socialism* Weidenfeld & Nicolson.

Windlesham, Lord (1966) *Communications and Political Power* Jonathan Cape.

Wolff, Robert Paul, Moore, Barrington Jr, and Marcus, Herbert (1969) *A Critique of Pure Tolerance* Beacon Press (1965).

Young, Hugo (1989) *One of Us* Macmillan.

Young, Wayland (1963) *The Profumo Affair: Aspects of Conservatism* Penguin.

Yutang, Lin (1938) *The Wisdom of Confucius* Modern Library.

Zweig, Ferdynand (1952) *The British Worker* Penguin.

Index

accents 59, 121
accountability, political 287
advertising
  aim 132
  appeal 131–2
  cigarette 139
  deceitful 131, 136
  dependence of media 132
  depth 139–40
  repetitive 130
  target groups: children 134;
    teenagers 134; women 135
  television 137–9
  tools 133
Anglo-American Alliance *see* special
  relationship
Anglo-Irish Agreement 242–3
anti-Semitism, British 117
army
  cuts 78, 79–81
  instrument of brainwashing 59
  regimental tradition 80
  tourist attraction 81

Battle of Britain myth 91
BBC (British Broadcasting
  Corporation) 59, 61, 68, 93,
  148, 202, 236, 238, 241, 262
  and advertising 138–9
  and Thatcher 147, 153
  believed 29
  bias 141, 144, 154, 157, 167
  controlled by government 149,
    231–2
  doubtful future 150
  fears non-conformity 39
  'impartial' 43–4, 149, 273–4

  importance and power 146–7
  'independent' 147–8
  monopoly 145
  pressured by Thatcher
    government 27, 147, 148,
    149–50, 165, 167, 214,
    217–18, 242
  right to criticise government 148–9
Belgrano sinking 63, 160, 200–1,
  208, 221–2, 297, 303
beliefs 5, 14, 17, 21, 83
  sanctity 35
Benn, Tony (formerly Anthony
  Wedgwood) ix, 37, 64, 233,
  281, 290–1, 299
  (cited) 44, 46–7, 61, 63, 66–7,
    75, 85, 90, 126, 144, 146–7,
    148, 157, 192, 206, 207, 226,
    288, 290
Birmingham Six case 179, 187
Blakelock case 187
Blitz myth 94
Blunt, Anthony 67, 126–7, 197–8
bomb (atomic) 245 *see also* nuclear
  debate
brainwashing *see also*
  indoctrination; manipulation
  acceptability viii–ix, 3, 4, 5, 39,
    59, 305
  Catholic 83
  Chinese techniques 10, 17: success
    12
  CIA experiments 22–3, 30
  Communist techniques 17
  definition 3–4, 5, 7, 41
  essential to racism 109
  Establishment beneficiary ix, 5, 12

Index

'D' Notices 198
Dalyell, Tam 63, 201, 206, 208, 216, 221, 222, 253
Davis, Charles 6–7, 33, 34–5, 81, 296
Day After, The (film) 230–1
Death of a Princess (TV programme) 158
Death on the Rock case 29, 70, 145, 154, 159, 218, 237–8, 240
'decision-makers' 4 *see also* Establishment
decolonisation 106–8
disinformation 243
dissent 299
dissidents, controlling 31
Dunkirk myth 91, 92

education 121–3
  encourages conformity 124–5
  failure of British 125
  for élite 128
  imperialist 105
  indoctrination 17, 122, 129
  Marxist 6
  mass 119–20
  poor quality 122–3, 127–8
  public school 123–4
  television 151–2
élites 36 *see also* Establishment
  concept of 5–6
  reinforcement 36
  training 123
emotions, basis for persuasion 4–5
Empire 99–100, 105–6 *see also* decolonisation; Rhodesia
  extent 100
  mythology 101–3
  racist 103–4, 111–12
'Englishness' 93, 96, 116
Establishment 66–8
  benefits from brainwashing ix, 5, 12
  controls institutions 61–2
euphemisms 177
  imperial 101–2
Eysenck, H. J. (cited) 4, 18, 24, 30, 37, 44–5

'face' 105
Falklands War 46, 47, 79, 85, 96, 149, 217, 221–5, 226, 253–4, 276, 286, 288 *see also* Franks report
  censorship 164–5
Forster, E. M. 168
Franks report (Falklands War) 222–4, 286
freedom 299–303
  of information 162
  of speech 163–4, 259, 261, 267, 303: Rushdie affair 256–7
  Thatcher assault 214

genetic engineering 51–5
Goebbels, Joseph 8–9, 30, 43, 174, 220
group system, control by 35–6
Guildford Four case 179, 186
Guinness case 185, 186
Gulf War 50–1, 73, 79, 193, 252, 254–5, 269–77
  and Mrs Thatcher 275, 276
  cause: oil 271
  censorship 274
  internment 274–5
  Western gains 270

Hamilton, Willie 72, 73, 76
Heseltine, Michael 192, 216–17, 231, 280–1
history teaching
  debate 218
  indoctrination 128
Hitler, Adolf 7–8, 9, 34, 53, 155, 156
honours system 68–71, 75, 76
Hoskyns, Sir John 223
Hume, Cardinal Basil 228, 229–30
Hussein, Saddam *see* Gulf War
Huxley, Aldous 21, 29, 30, 33–4, 49, 51, 119–20, 154, 169–70, 305 *see also Brave New World*

IBA (Independent Broadcasting Authority) 241
immigration 109–11, 112–14, 118, 180